CAMBRIDGE STUDIES IN EIGHTEENTH-CENTURY
ENGLISH LITERATURE AND THOUGHT 1

The Transformation of
The Decline and Fall of the Roman Empire

Opening our new series, Cambridge Studies in Eighteenth-Century English Literature and Thought, David Womersley's book is the first fully to investigate Edward Gibbon's *The Decline and Fall of the Roman Empire* as both a work of literature and a work of history, examining its style and irony, tracing its classical and French sources, and highlighting the importance of its composition in three instalments over a period of twenty years. Dr Womersley discusses each of these instalments in detail, plotting the work's transformation from conception to completion, and relating this to the achievements and limitations of the philosophic historiography which Gibbon inherited from Montesquieu and Hume, but finally discarded.

The Decline and Fall of the Roman Empire emerges from this study as a work more flexible in its sympathies and surprising in its judgements than has hitherto been granted, while the magnitude of Gibbon's achievement as a stylist, historian and thinker is brought into sharper focus.

CAMBRIDGE STUDIES IN EIGHTEENTH-CENTURY ENGLISH LITERATURE AND THOUGHT

General Editors: Dr HOWARD ERSKINE-HILL, FBA, *Pembroke College, Cambridge*
and Professor JOHN RICHETTI, *University of Pennsylvania*

Editorial Board: Morris Brownell, *University of Nevada*
Leopold Damrosch, *University of Maryland*
J. Paul Hunter, *University of Chicago*
Isobel Grundy, *Queen Mary College, London*
Lawrence Lipking, *Northwestern University*
Harold Love, *Monash University*
Claude Rawson, *Yale University*
Pat Rogers, *University of South Florida*
James Sambrook, *University of Southampton*

The growth in recent years of eighteenth-century literary studies has prompted the establishment of this new series of books devoted to the period. The series will accommodate monographs and critical studies on authors, works, genres and other aspects of literary culture from the latter part of the seventeenth century to the end of the eighteenth.

Since academic engagement with this field has become an increasingly interdisciplinary enterprise, books will be especially encouraged which in some way stress the cultural context of the literature, or examine it in relation to contemporary art, music, philosophy, historiography, religion, politics, social affairs, and so on. New approaches to the established canon are being tested with increasing frequency, and the series will hope to provide a home for the best of these. The books we choose to publish will be thorough in their methods of literary, historical, or biographical investigation, and will open interesting perspectives on previously closed, or underexplored, or misrepresented areas of eighteenth-century writing and thought. They will reflect the work of both younger and established scholars on either side of the Atlantic and elsewhere.

Published
The Transformation of The Decline and Fall of the Roman Empire,
by David Womersley

Other titles in preparation
*Plots and Counterplots: Politics and Literary Representation
1660–1730,* by Richard Braverman
Warrior Women and Popular Balladry 1650–1850, by Dianne Dugaw
Women's Place in Pope's World, by Valerie Rumbold

£35.00

Martial Rose Library
Tel: 01962 827306

To be returned on or before the day marked above, subject to recall.

£35.00

T

The Transformation of
The Decline and Fall of
the Roman Empire

DAVID WOMERSLEY

Official Fellow and Tutor in English Literature
Jesus College, Oxford

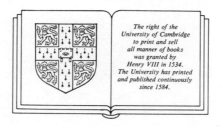

The right of the
University of Cambridge
to print and sell
all manner of books
was granted by
Henry VIII in 1534.
The University has printed
and published continuously
since 1584.

CAMBRIDGE UNIVERSITY PRESS

Cambridge

New York   New Rochelle   Melbourne   Sydney

Published by the Press Syndicate of the University of Cambridge
The Pitt Building, Trumpington Street, Cambridge CB2 1RP
32 East 57th Street, New York, NY 10022, USA
10 Stamford Road, Oakleigh, Melbourne 3166, Australia

© Cambridge University Press 1988

First published 1988

Printed in Great Britain at the University Press, Cambridge

British Library cataloguing in publication data
Womersley, David
The transformation of The decline and fall
of the Roman Empire – (Cambridge studies
in eighteenth-century English literature
and thought; 1).
1. Ancient Rome. Historiography. Gibbon,
Edward, 1737–1794. Decline and fall of the
Roman Empire. Critical studies
I. Title
937'.06

Library of Congress cataloguing in publication data
Womersley, David.
The transformation of The decline and fall of the
Roman Empire.
(Cambridge studies in eighteenth-century English
literature and thought)
Bibliography.
Includes index.
1. Gibbon, Edward, 1737–1794. History of the
decline and fall of the Roman Empire. 2. Rome –
History – Empire, 30 B.C.–476 A.D. 3. Byzantine
Empire – History. I. Title. II. Series.
DG311.W65 1988 937'.06'0924 88–4352

ISBN 0 521 35036 0

GG

For Caro

Contents

Acknowledgements

I have been more than fortunate in the academic bowers which have sheltered myself and my work. This study was begun at Trinity College, Cambridge; advanced through the great generosity of Pembroke College, Cambridge; and completed at Jesus College, Oxford. My experience of 'our English Universities' has been exactly the reverse of Gibbon's. I cheerfully acknowledge my obligations, and hope not to be renounced as a son.

Many individuals have helped me write this book. At Cambridge Ian Jack and Elsie Duncan-Jones gave me valuable suggestions for improvement. More recently I have benefited from the advice and kindness of Peter Burke, John Burrow and Isabel Rivers. But my greatest debt is to Howard Erskine-Hill, who as supervisor, colleague and friend has from the first criticised, supported and encouraged.

Jesus College, Oxford.

A note on references and quotations

All quotations are intended to be unregularised transcriptions of the quoted edition. Wherever appropriate and possible I have used either editions listed in Keynes' catalogue of Gibbon's library, or editions to which Gibbon could have had access. Quotations from and references to *The Decline and Fall* are keyed to the first edition. It is by no means a perfect text (Gibbon's carelessness in correcting proofs was notorious). But all subsequent editions extend the corruption by introducing errors of their own. This is true even of Bury, who proclaims the freedoms he has taken.[1] References to the first volume of *The Decline and Fall* are in the first instance to the first edition in state 'a' of 1776, and secondly to the third, corrected, edition of 1777 (for example, I.394–5:I.469 refers to pages 394–5 in the first edition of Volume I and to page 469 in the third edition of Volume I).[2] If quoted, the text is that of the third edition. Where there are discrepancies between that edition and the first, I give the unrevised text in a footnote.[3] References in the footnotes are given in a shortened but unambiguous form. Full details of the works cited will be found in the bibliography.

[1] See, in Bury's edition, I.xliii n. 4.
[2] On this subject, see J. E. Norton's *Bibliography*, pp. 36–47.
[3] On the subject of Gibbon's revisions of the first volume, see P. B. Craddock, 'Gibbon's Revision of The Decline and Fall'.

A note on references and quotations

Introduction

In 1936 Friedrich Meinecke scanned the features of eighteenth-century historiography in his *Die Entstehung des Historismus* – a study which remains the most recent attempt to take in the historical endeavour of that period in a single draught.[1] Reviewing the origins of the intellectual movement of which he was himself a late product, Meinecke made large claims for its significance:

. . . [historism is] one of the deepest and most incisive revolutions in the history of Western thought in general, whereby the Western genius worked out its own individuality in distinction from that of the ancient world without, however, losing the thread of continuity that bound them together.[2]

For Meinecke, then, the achievement of historism stemmed from the fullness with which its practitioners understood that we can properly comprehend the relation of what has been to what is only when we have recognised the independence of the past from the present, and acknowledged that they may be divided, even sundered, from each other.

This mental flexibility – the capacity to seek out both division and continuity in history without sacrificing the legitimate claims of either to the other – typifies Meinecke's formulation of the historist's characteristic strategy when contemplating the past. The historist's ambition is to free the past from the condescension of the present, and thereby to free the present from its own, more insidious, bondage. To do so requires that he should disembarrass himself of all the impediments the present can interpose between an historian and the past by embracing 'the great methodological principle that one must banish from the mind the customary conceptions of one's own period before one can rightly understand the past'.[3] At first sight, this seems to beg the question. To assume such a principle from the outset appears to entail an assumption of the disjunction between past and present, the possibility of which it is the business of historiography to investigate, and which consequently cannot be one of its axioms. But this is not so. The historist's freeing of himself from the conceptions of his own time is a step towards his attaining

---

[1] All references are to, and quotations from, the translation by J. E. Anderson.
[2] *Historism*, p. 491.
[3] *Historism*, p. 121.

the poise of pure impartiality, able to recognise continuity as promptly as discontinuity. The historist's desire to step outside the assumptions of his own period stems from his wish to see the past as it truly was, and from his acknowledgement that the present has no sovereign place in the sequence of time.

Meinecke draws a clear contrast between this new historiography and that which it replaced. He styles that superseded historiography 'pragmatic' and sees it exemplified most fully in the work of Voltaire and the other Enlightenment historians. Pragmatic historiography is determined by a cardinal article of faith, heavy with consequences for its intentions and character:

. . . since it [pragmatic historiography] was based upon an assumption of an invariable human nature, it treated history as a useful collection of examples for pedagogical purposes, and explained historical changes in terms of superficial causes, either of a personal or a material kind.[4]

Its aim is the acquisition of policy, its characteristic method is the emphatic analysis of causality. But the apparent rigour of pragmatic historiography is spurious, because it is involved in just the circularity which historism seems to embrace, but in fact eludes. The pedagogical intentions of pragmatic historiography required that it should ascertain, as Hume pointed out, the constant and universal principles of human nature; yet its critical method, on the basis of which a pragmatic historian would winnow truth from falsehood in the testimony before him, demanded that the historian also begin with a knowledge of such principles, for without that criterion he would not be able to pick out and reject the prodigies the unscrupulous would foist on him. Thus the pragmatic historian cannot avoid projecting his own ideas into the past, thereby putting history in thrall to the present. As a consequence, pragmatic historiography can be recognised as much by its vision of the past, in which a factitious homogeneity holds sway, as by its stress on causality and search for example:

For the Enlightenment had already, in its own way, established a sense of unity between the past and the present. Admittedly, this had only come about through mechanistic lines of thought. The life of history had appeared in principle to be similar in all periods, ruled by the same constant forces of human reason and unreason. The only variation between past and present was the variation in the proportions between these two.[5]

Pragmatic historiography accords a sovereign position to the present. But in so doing it subtly impoverishes the present, despite seeming to serve its ends. The belief of the pragmatic historian that the discrepancies between one period and another betray not genuine discontinuities, but mere fluctuations in the mix of the small number of constant elements which always and

[4] *Historism*, p. lviii.   [5] *Historism*, p. 419.

everywhere combine in human affairs, deprives the present of the possibility of invigorating contact with the completely foreign. In pragmatic historiography time contains no radical revolutions or innovations. The appearance of historical change is a mirage.

It is a measure of Meinecke's achievement that, having followed his exposition, one does not discount as hyperbole the claims he has made for the magnitude of the intellectual shift he has undertaken to map. Yet, as is inevitable in a book of such vast scope, and with an author whose perspective contrives to be at once long and wide, one notices distortions. For example, Meinecke's discussion of those moments in the work of Voltaire and Montesquieu which suggest a frame of mind close to historism, and which he highlights as an incipient loosening of the bind of pragmatic historiography, is beside the mark in its suggestion that such moments are evidence that these writers were moving towards historism. The unwavering fundamental commitment of the *philosophes* to social amelioration (which Montesquieu expressed so nobly) required historiography to be functional in that struggle.[6] That requirement in its turn demanded that philosophic historical writing embrace the procedures of pragmatism in order to reap its pedagogic reward.[7] Before Montesquieu and Voltaire could have entertained a form of historical thinking akin to historism, they would have had to abandon the heart of the *philosophe* programme – and there is no suggestion that either of them did so.

Moreover, Meinecke's subject, which focuses on the phenomenon of historical change and our strategies for understanding it, is not always reflected in his own practice. His tendency to depict an individual's thought as an instantaneous and complex entity, instead of throwing light on its development through time, is out of kilter with the finest aspects of the historism he celebrates.[8] In addition, to scrutinise the emphasis historism places on particularity, as Meinecke invites us to do ('The essence of historism is the substitution of a process of *individualising* observation for a *generalising* view of human forces in history'), may lead us to question his strongly purposive account of the intellectual adjustments he documents.[9] I cannot com-

---

[6] Consider 'Pour leur assurer à tous le pain, le bon sens, et les vertus qui leur sont nécessaires, il n'y a qu'un moyen: il faut beaucoup éclairer les peuples et les gouvernements: c'est là l'œuvre des philosophes; c'est la vôtre', quoted in R. Shackleton, *Montesquieu, a Critical Biography*, p. 392.

[7] Throughout this study I shall use the phrase 'philosophic historiography' to denote the historical writing of figures such as Montesquieu, Voltaire and the other *encyclopédists*, and Hume. I am aware that in some respects the works of these figures diverge very sharply. But I nevertheless believe that it is possible to discern a number of ideas about the purposes and methods of historiography which would on the whole have drawn a large measure of support from them all, even if perhaps none of them would have given such a synthesis their entire approval.

[8] To use J. G. A. Pocock's words, Meinecke approaches the thought of a writer as 'a problem in conceptual resolution', not 'a problem in the reconstruction of performance' (*Virtue, Commerce and History*, p. 24).

[9] *Historism*, p. lv.

ment on his conviction that 'historism is nothing else but the application to the historical world of the new life-governing principles achieved by the great German movement extending from Leibniz to the death of Goethe'.[10] But to assess (for example) eighteenth-century British historiography in terms of whether or not it anticipates the position of the German writers whom Meinecke knew so well, and in whom he insists the culmination of historism is to be found, is as blatant a refusal of autonomy to an area of the past as any in the *Essai sur les Mœurs*. It also obscures the genuinely 'historist' developments to which Meinecke is inattentive because of his conviction that the heart of historism is German. His final adverse judgement on the triumvirate of eighteenth-century British historians (Gibbon, Hume and Robertson) catches one's attention because he unwittingly reveals the faltering of the imagination which impairs his understanding of these men:

The three great Englishmen of the Enlightenment, Hume, Gibbon and Robertson, who had gone furthest in presenting political history in scrupulously factual terms, leave us nevertheless with a feeling of coldness and emptiness.[11]

Might it not be that the coldness and emptiness Meinecke felt stemmed not from the writers he was studying but from his approaching them with Goethe so powerfully in mind? Meinecke's treatment of Hume, Robertson, and especially Gibbon, constitutes a failure of just the individualising vision he so admires.

In this study I intend to examine the same intellectual moment as that to which Meinecke devoted his *Historism*: namely, the point of transition from pragmatic historiography to a less instrumental attitude towards the past. But I intend to concentrate on the work of one man, Edward Gibbon, and not to undertake any general account. I shall attempt to redraw this small section of Meinecke's large map and to replot the contours of *The Decline and Fall*.

My methods, as well as my scope, are different from Meinecke's. Whereas he took an author's whole intellectual disposition for his province, thereby extending historism far beyond the writing of history, I shall concentrate overwhelmingly on historiographic practice. My reading of *The Decline and Fall* aims to show that the three instalments of its serial publication mark substantive, and not just accidental, divisions of the narrative; and that careful attention to these divisions can awaken us to the magnitude of the revolutions of historiography and sensibility contained in this reputed triumph of successful, single design.[12] It is my contention that, when he begins *The Decline and Fall*,

---

[10] *Historism*, p. lv.

[11] *Historism*, p. 366.

[12] The boundaries between instalments have been obscured in later reprintings of *The Decline and Fall*, such as Bury's, and this has clearly not aided contemplation of the significance of the instalments. Moreover, some critics have been content to base their judgements almost exclusively on the first instalment, thus neglecting five-sixths of the work; for an egregious example of this, see R. N. Parkinson, *Edward Gibbon*.

Gibbon embraces the pragmatic, philosophic historiography of his predecessors; that he is gradually forced to revise and supplement that historiography when he moves into a region of the past hostile to its central tenet of the uniformity of human nature; and that the dislodgement of this keystone of philosophic historiography entails far-reaching changes, akin to historism but not identical with it, in the most diverse areas of the history. I shall be searching for the turbulence when writing slides away from its previous intentions and processes, and when the past diverts the historian's sensibility and intelligence from the fulfilling of his design or from his customary ideas, by obliging him to contemplate objects and assume positions which unsettle his general notions. I shall therefore be much preoccupied by the ways in which apparently individual histories or historians are fractured. I hope, by treating *The Decline and Fall* as itself an extremely complex and layered historical event, to make an approach to precision in describing the mediations whereby it moves from being a philosophic history and becomes a much less decided, more hybrid and nuanced work.

My first section, entitled 'The historiographic milieu', paints the background for *The Decline and Fall* in broad strokes by describing the work of two of its important predecessors. I do not offer this section as by any means an exhaustive account of the historical writing to which Gibbon was exposed. Such an account, as well as ranging more widely across the work of the *philosophes*, would have to look at the work of the *érudits*, and I have not done so in any systematic way. My intention is simply to describe first a style of pragmatic, philosophic historiography and secondly a response to a predicament posed by that historiography, both of which are pertinent to what I shall go on to say about *The Decline and Fall*. I begin by examining Montesquieu's *Considérations sur les Causes de la Grandeur des Romains, et de leur Décadence* in order to trace the features of philosophic historiography in a single text. I do this not because I believe Montesquieu to be a perfect embodiment of the *philosophe* disposition, but because his *Considérations* is a book to which Gibbon was demonstrably indebted and which looks in a philosophic spirit at much of the material later assayed in *The Decline and Fall*.[13] Moreover, it seemed to me that certain aspects of philosophic historiography on which I wanted to lay particular emphasis would appear more clearly in a sustained account of a single work than in one which tried to synthesise many. I then move on to the work of David Hume and assess the fortunes of philosophic historiography in his *History of England*. My intention here is to show how

---

[13] References to the *Considérations* litter *The Decline and Fall*, as a glance at any index will show. Giuseppe Giarrizzo has stressed the importance of Montesquieu to Gibbon: 'Gibbon procede . . . dietro le orme di Montesquieu'; 'decisamente le *Considérations* sono l'ossatura della prima parte della *History*' (*Edward Gibbon e la Cultura Europea del Settecento*, pp. 133 and 270). On the centrality of Montesquieu to the *philosophes*, see d'Alembert's 'Éloge de Montesquieu' which prefaces Volume VI of the *Encyclopédie* and Louis de Beaufort, *La Republique Romaine*, I.ii.

guarded and defensive is Hume's reaction to the questioning of his axioms by
the past. Hume's comparative incorrigibility forms a sharp contrast with
Gibbon's more creative response to much the same experience.[14] Turning to
The Decline and Fall and looking successively at each of the three instalments,
I attempt to trace in detail how the initial philosophic historiography of 1776
is checked and disrupted and how Gibbon then forges a new historiography
which is both more ample in its sympathy and hesitant in its judgement.
Gibbon is normally praised on the grounds of intellectual clarity and the extraordinary singleness of his mind. However, 'no one qualification is so likely
to make a good writer, as the power of rejecting his own thoughts'.[15]
Gibbon's greatness as an historian is displayed in his willingness to rethink
and reform.

[14] Once again, the comparison is given pertinence by the evident importance of Hume to Gibbon. Giarrizzo maintains that Hume and Montesquieu form a creative polarity in Gibbon's
thought: 'E il successivo travaglio di Gibbon, che si riassumerà poi nella grande *History*, sarà
tutto impegnato alla scoperta di una formula storiografica che accordi Hume e Montesquieu'
(*Edward Gibbon e la Cultura Europea del Settecento*, pp. 145–6). Naturally, I no more imagine that
Hume is typical of eighteenth-century British historiography than I imagine that Montesquieu
can be made to 'stand for' its French counterpart; and a thorough account of the domestic
elements in Gibbon's historiographic milieu would need to pay attention to the work of
Robertson, Bolingbroke and historians of Rome such as Hooke, Ferguson and Goldsmith.

[15] Pope, 'Preface', *Works* (1717); *Works*, I.vi. Pope is perhaps recalling Dryden's *A Defence of an
Essay of Dramatic Poesy* (1668): 'A great wit's great work is to refuse.'

PART I

The historiographic milieu

1

Montesquieu's *Considérations*

Is he not too universal? Can any writer be *exact*, who is so comprehensive?

Lyttelton

In 1721 Montesquieu published his *Lettres Persanes*, a philosophic satire in which Usbek and Rhédi, two Persian noblemen, visit Europe and comment on its culture. Rhédi, the younger and less experienced of the two travellers, is particularly struck by European history:

Pendant le séjour que je fais en Europe, je lis les historiens anciens & modernes: je compare tous les temps; j'ai du plaisir à les voir passer, pour ainsi dire, devant moi; & j'arrête sur-tout mon esprit à ces grands changemens qui ont rendu les âges si differens des âges . . . J'ai resté plus d'un an en Italie, où je n'ai vu que le débris de cette ancienne Italie, si fameuse autrefois. Quoique tout le monde habite les villes, elles sont entièrement désertes & dépeuplées: il semble qu'elles ne subsistent encore que pour marquer le lieu où étoient ces cités puissantes dont l'histoire a tant parlé . . . Voila, mon cher Usbek, la plus terrible catastrophe qui soit jamais arrivée dans le monde. Mais à peine s'en est-on apperçu, parce qu'elle est arrivée insensiblement, & dans le cours d'un grand nombre de siècles: ce qui marque un vice intérieur, un venin secret et caché, une maladie de langueur, qui afflige la nature humaine.[1]

Rhédi experiences history as a spectacle in which great revolutions are the most noteworthy events. Historical knowledge is a vision dominated by ruins, those arresting tokens of catastrophe, and sensitive above all to the variety in the past, the differences between age and age. It gazes in awed fascination at the wonderful, disjunctive surface of history and resists the temptation to penetrate to a deeper level of understanding by keeping its notions of causality imprecise and obscure: 'un venin secret et caché'. It would rather be thrilled, dazzled and diverted than informed.

The more philosophic Usbek replies to Rhédi in a long series of letters proposing an alternative way of contemplating the past.[2] He accepts the fact of depopulation which so transfixes his younger companion, but instead of standing agog at its awfulness, he reconciles it with the general principles to which civil society is naturally and permanently subject:

---

[1] *Lettres Persanes*, letter cxii, *Œuvres*, III.221–4.   [2] *Lettres Persanes*, letters cxiii to cxxii.

Tu cherches la raison pourquoi la Terre est moins peuplée qu'elle ne l'étoit autrefois: &, si tu y fais bien attention, tu verras que la grande différence vient de celle qui est arrivée dans les mœurs.[3]

The phrase 'bien attention' suggests that what Usbek offers here, both as an answer and as a rejoinder to Rhédi, is a more searching reading of the past which penetrates behind the spectacle of mutability to perceive the constant principles shaping the course of events. As Usbek sets out the consequences of changing usages in matters of divorce and slavery, we find answers to the problems Rhédi had raised, and also a more dignified level of discussion. Wonder is replaced by a patient knowingness which smooths out the vicissitudes of history to unveil the underlying homogeneity of all time.

The emphases in Rhédi's rhapsody on European history should be kept in mind during the ensuing discussion, since they embody a naive response to the past – the historical sense in a state of nature – which the philosophic historian undertakes to educate into maturity. The polarity Montesquieu sets up between Rhédi's perspective on history and that of the wiser Usbek is an early eighteenth-century mapping of the terrain of historiography and a characterisation of adequate and inadequate idioms. An acquaintance with its firm distinctions, and the powerful clarity of its preferences, is essential before the heterogeneity of *The Decline and Fall* can be fully appreciated.

In Usbek's response to Rhédi's letter Montesquieu gives us the sketch of an historiography which dissolves man's naturally glassy, uncomprehending and wondering stare at history in order to draw practical benefit from the past. The *Considérations sur les Causes de la Grandeur des Romains et de leur Décadence* (1734) shows Montesquieu applying this mature historiography to the subject which Voltaire, in the *Encyclopédie*, would acknowledge as the most important to be found in the annals of humanity.[4]

---

[3] *Lettres Persanes*, letter cxiv, *Œuvres*, III.226.

[4] 'L'*histoire* de l'empire romain est ce qui mérite le plus notre attention, parce que les Romains ont été nos maîtres & nos législateurs' (*Encyclopédie*, VIII.223). This was a commonplace and can be traced back to Polybius (I.i.5); see also Louis de Beaufort's *La Republique Romaine*, I.i, F. E. Manuel also points out the centrality of Rome for philosophical historians (*Shapes of Philosophical History*, pp. 51–2). Basil Kennett opened his *Romae Antiquae Notitia* with confidence in his subject and his audience's acknowledgement of it (sig. a5r). Chesterfield, influenced probably by his occasional political ally Bolingbroke, adduces a similar reason when urging his bastard, Philip Stanhope, to pay particular attention to this segment of the past (*Letters*, I.122–3). Yet the very pre-eminence of Rome was also wearisome. Voltaire stigmatised it as 'matière usée' in his *Catalogue des Écrivains du Siècle de Louis XIV*. Goldsmith's *Roman History* begins ominously by commenting that 'the facts which it [Roman history] relates, have been an hundred times repeated, and every occurrence has been so variously considered, that learning can scarce find a new anecdote, or genius give novelty to the old' (I.i); and Johnson, reviewing Blackwell's *Memoirs of the Court of Augustus*, brands the Romans 'a people, who, above all others, have furnished employment to the studious, and amusements to the idle; who have scarcely left behind them a coin or a stone, which has not been examined and explained a thousand times' (*The Literary Magazine* (1756): reprinted in *Works*, VI.9–16; this quotation occurs on p. 9).

Montesquieu gives his work no epigraph, but the Virgilian tag 'felix qui potuit rerum cognoscere causas' has strong claims were one ever to be sought.[5] As his title makes clear, Montesquieu aspires to weigh and ponder the causes which moulded Roman history; to peel away the fascinating heroic surface and reveal the informing, efficient structure of constant principles which operated in the past and (so he maintains) which still operates. This quest for a knowledge of causation depends on a conviction about the constancy of human nature, for only if history is fundamentally uniform will the historian's conjectures about causality be accurate; moreover, only if history is uniform will the investigation of causality have any point, for only then will its results be applicable to the present. That conviction is revealed quite candidly at the beginning of the *Considérations*, when Montesquieu compares the constitutional reforms of Servius Tullius with the policy of Henry VII:

L'histoire moderne nous fournit un exemple de ce qui arriva pour lors à Rome, & ceci est bien remarquable; car, comme les hommes ont eu dans tous les temps les mêmes passions, les occasions qui produisent les grands changemens sont différentes, mais les causes sont toujours les mêmes.[6]

The distinction between 'occasion' and 'cause' indicates Montesquieu's delving beneath the various surface of history to reach an underlying region of constancy and uniformity. Towards the end of the *Considérations* he restates the distinction (this time in terms of 'accidens' or 'causes particulières' against 'causes' or 'causes générales'):

Ce n'est pas la fortune qui domine le monde: on peut le demander aux Romains, qui eurent une suite continuelle de prospérités quand ils se gouvernèrent sur un certain plan, & une suite non interrompue de revers, lorsqu'ils se conduisirent sur un autre. Il y a des causes générales, soit morales, soit physiques, qui agissent dans chaque monarchie, l'élèvent, la maintiennent, ou la précipitent; tous les accidens sont soumis à ces causes; &, si le hasard d'une bataille, c'est-à-dire une cause particulière, a ruiné un état, il y avait une cause générale qui faisait que cet état devoit périr par une seule bataille: en un mot, l'allure principale entraîne, avec elle, tous les accidens particuliers.[7]

Some of the detail here is intriguing: to specify 'chaque monarchie' implies that different 'causes générales' will operate in different kinds of state, while offering a Machiavellian hint that there may be constitutional forms not subject to the trajectory of political rise and fall which overtook even Rome; and one might want to pause over the phrase 'allure principale'. But, for our pur-

---

[5] This tag (*Georgics*, II.490) actually was the epigraph of Mably's *Observations on the Greeks*.

[6] *Œuvres*, III.354.

[7] *Œuvres*, III.482. Montesquieu's insistence on the causal regularity to be found even in what seems history's greatest example of calamitous reverse had been anticipated by Walter Moyle (*Works*, I.98). The English roots of much of Montesquieu's thinking have been long uncovered; see J. Dedieu, *Montesquieu et la Tradition Politique Anglaise en France*.

poses, we need note only that for Montesquieu to repeat his initial axioms
with such vigour at this late stage in the *Considérations* announces that, at least
to his own satisfaction, his historiographic principles have come through the
test of practical application unscathed. Usbek's philosophic historiography
has proved its competence on the greatest subject history affords.

This central contention of a regular causality operating in the past, together
with its inevitable presupposition of a constant human nature, draw in
their wake other prominent 'features of the *Considérations*; for instance,
Montesquieu's flaunting of the 'presentness' of his perspective on the past.
Frequently the discussion of an issue in Roman history is illustrated (and
apparently clinched) by the dramatic citation of examples from much later
times – even from the 1730s:

Les Romains, accoutumés à se jouer de la nature humaine, dans la personne de leurs
enfans & de leurs esclaves, ne pouvaient guère connoître cette vertu que nous appelons
humanité. D'où peut venir cette férocité que nous trouvons dans les habitans de nos
colonies, que de cet usage continuel des châtimens sur une malheureuse partie du
genre humain? Lorsque l'on est cruel dans l'état civil, que peut-on attendre de la
douceur & de la justice naturelle?[8]

The essential homogeneity of all time, of a fragment of which the concluding
generalisation is the expression, legitimises this virtuoso orchestration of past
and present into a synthetic and static present within the mind of the
philosophe, who thus becomes Plato's spectator of the eternal. Viewed from the
correct point of vantage, properly *considéré*, all the apparently irreducible facts
of history align themselves into serried ranks, and each of these ranks offers
the philosophic observer an insight, however small, into the nature of things.
This reduction of raw multiplicity to its basic simplicity is doubtless part of
the ambition of the *philosophes* to do for the study of mankind what Newton
had done for natural science. Just as he had reconciled the movement of the
planets and the fall of an apple, so they aspired to 'remonter aux idées
simples; à saisir et à combiner les premiers principes'.[9] They would apply
his experimental method to history:

Le plus grand philosophe est celui qui rend raison du plus grand nombre de choses
. . . mais être philosophe, ce n'est pas simplement avoir beaucoup vû et beaucoup lû

---

[8] *Œuvres*, III.451. Such moments abound. Compare also III.426–7, where Montesquieu's
perspective of congruent examples running down the length of history is particularly full and
well developed. This viewing of the past through the present also occurred in English
historiography. Thomas Blackwell commented that 'if I have indeed comprehended the Power
and explained the Policy of the *Roman* Government, it is chiefly owing to the long Attention
I have given to the *British Constitution*' (*Memoirs of the Court of Augustus*, I.9), provoking
Johnson's sour remark that 'He [Blackwell] is a great lover of modern terms' (*Works*, VI.11).
We shall see that Gibbon also illustrates ancient history with modern examples in Volume I
of *The Decline and Fall*.

[9] Gibbon on the *philosophe* in his *Essai sur l'Étude de la Littérature* (1761); reprinted in *Miscellaneous
Works*, IV.1–93. This quotation is to be found on p. 58.

. . . c'est avoir des principes solides, & surtout une bonne méthode pour rendre raison de ces faits, & en tirer de légitimes conséquences.[10]

Taking as an axiom that history is 'liée dans toutes ses parties', the philosophic historian is thus always struggling to accelerate away from the particular and towards the general by dint of hermeneutic energy normally reserved for works of art.[11]

There is consequently a depreciation of historical difference in philosophic historiography. The intention of the *philosophes* to broaden the scope of historical study beyond Europe is suggestive of their attitude to the diverse: they seek it out, but only in order to transcend and assimilate it.[12] The *Considérations* opens with a frank acknowledgement of the variety displayed by the past: 'Il ne faut pas prendre, de la ville de Rome, dans ses commencemens, l'idée que nous donnent les villes que nous voyons aujourd'hui.'[13] But it soon becomes clear that Montesquieu's idea of historical 'différence' is, paradoxically, necessary in order to perceive the underlying unity of all time:

Comme les peuples de l'Europe ont, dans ces temps-ci, à peu pres les mêmes arts, les mêmes armes, la même discipline, & la même manière de faire la guerre, la prodigieuse fortune des Romains nous paroit inconcevable. D'ailleurs, il y a aujourd'hui une telle disproportion dans la puissance, qu'il n'est pas possible qu'un petit état sorte, par ses propres forces, de l'abaissement où la Providence l'a mis.

Ceci demande qu'on y réfléchisse; sans quoi, nous verrions des événemens sans les comprendre; &, ne sentant pas bien la différence des situations, nous croirions, en lisant l'histoire ancienne, voir d'autres hommes que nous.[14]

This was precisely the problem that the naive Rhédi had encountered with Roman history: he would 'voir des événemens sans les comprendre' and thereby experience history as spectacle. No sensitive observer of the past can ignore historical 'différence'; but only the weak-minded, so Montesquieu implies, will be content to repose in the condition of merely registering the thrilling variety of the surface of events. This is why Montesquieu entitles his work 'Considérations'; it involves both observation and judgement, seeing and assessing. The *philosophe* will aspire to a higher reading, vigorously conjecturing on the basis of his supposition that, beneath its opaque particularity, the past is in essence unified and transparent. Rising to the

---

[10] *Encyclopédie*, art. 'Philosophie', XII.514; see also art. 'Philosophe': 'Le *philosophe* forme ses principes sur une infinité d'observations particulieres' (XII.509).

[11] Louis de Beaufort, *La Republique Romaine*, I.iii.

[12] Giuseppe Giarrizzo has written well about the omnivorousness of the *philosophes*: 'L'uomo del Settecento, il lettore della *Universal History*, ha dinanzi a sè un quadro non solo spazialmente più ampio dell'antico umanesimo classicheggiante. La conoscenza di altri popoli, di culture diverse alimenta il relativismo . . . e insieme il comparativismo storico–etnologico' (*Edward Gibbon e la Cultura Europea del Settecento*, p. 15).

[13] *Œuvres*, III.351.

[14] *Œuvres*, III.365–6.

interpretative challenge posed by this essential unity, he will 'sentir *bien* la différence' (my emphasis), and thereby attain a properly adult understanding of the constant principles which everywhere and at all times inform human society.

As one might expect, this desire to see through the past tends to make Montesquieu casual in his use of sources. Any writer is grist to his mill, providing that the testimony gives a helping hand to the generalisation he is currently freeing from its confining integument of historical 'fact'. So Appian (whose *floruit* was A.D. 160) is allowed to put what for Montesquieu are convenient words into the mouth of Tiberius Gracchus, who was cut down in 133 B.C.[15] But to snipe for long at this airy overlooking of scholarly nicety would be to distort the *Considérations* by dwelling on symptoms to the exclusion of causes. Montesquieu's rejection of antiquarian practice is not mere intellectual *hauteur*, but a consequence of his generous determination to make history serviceable in the struggle for social betterment which enlists the energies of all the *philosophes*. For the knowledge in which Montesquieu believes the study of history results is knowledge of the perennial conditions of social and political life. Rome thus has a central place in history for Montesquieu because, in the trajectory of its rise and fall, it offers a complete instance of prosperity and decline and thus holds out the possibility of revealing, as no other historical example could, the essential political and social configurations which lead to both advancement and decay, 'grandeur' and 'décadence'.[16] The aim of historical study is not to make nice discriminations about the past, but to ascertain the principles of political life.[17] We have reached the heart of the *Considérations* when Montesquieu, his tone rising to a pitch of indignation, considers the scandalous calamities which overtake even the greatest state the world has known as a direct result of the Romans' imperfect grasp of the principles which generated their greatness:

C'est ici qu'il faut se donner le spectacle des choses humaines. Qu'on voie, dans l'histoire de Rome, tant de guerres entreprises, tant de sang répandu, tant de peuples détruits, tant de grandes actions, tant de triomphes, tant de politique, de sagesse, de prudence, de constance, de courage; ce projet d'envahir tout, si bien formé, si bien soutenu, si bien fini; à quoi aboutit-il, qu'à assouvir le bonheur de cinq ou six monstres? Quoi! ce sénat n'avait fait évanouir tant de rois, que pour tomber lui-même

[15] *Œuvres*, III.368.
[16] These views are not confined to France. Bolingbroke also insists that the cogency of the causal demonstrations of history depends on the completeness of its examples (*Works*, II.277): see also Chesterfield, *Letters*, I.308 and II.227 and Thomson, *Winter*, 1. 589. The contrast between the decay of modern Italy and the glory of its ancient past is a topos in eighteenth-century literature, supposedly illustrating the decisive effect of principles of government on national prosperity: compare Montesquieu, 'Voyage de Gratz à la Haye'; Thomson, *Liberty*, Part I; and Gray, *Poems and Memoirs*, pp. 61 and 93.
[17] This contempt for minute accuracy is not confined to the Continent: compare Bolingbroke in the *Letters on the Study and Use of History* (1735–8: published 1752) (*Works*, II.263). Such disavowals tend, of course, disingenuously to be written from positions of some learning.

dans le plus bas esclavage de quelques-uns de ses plus indignes citoyens, & s'exterminer par ses propres arrêts? On n'élève donc sa puissance, que pour la voir mieux renversee? Les hommes ne travaillent à augmenter leur pouvoir, que pour le voir tomber contre eux-mêmes dans de plus heureuses mains?[18]

Such horror provides a telling argument for the philosophic study of politics through the medium of history. Only when the principles of political prosperity have been established will men be safe from the threat of decay; and only history provides sufficiently ample and complete evidence from which to abstract such principles. It is for this reason that only those histories which investigate causes and thus help to establish these principles are worthy of the name.[19]

Montesquieu's style is a suitable register for this analytical, applied historiography. Comparing the *Considérations* with the serried quartos and folios of earlier histories of Rome, such as that of Catrou and Rouille, or Tillemont's *Histoire des Empereurs* (from whose labours Montesquieu profits), one immediately notices its defiant and ostentatious brevity. There is a provocative element of bravura in this, but it is more than a pose. Montesquieu's conciseness implies that, for the true and philosophic historian, even the grandest historical subject can be reduced, purified, and in its profitable essence displayed.[20] Another aspect of that conciseness is his wish to free historiography from narrative. His analytical purposiveness demands that the historian be released from the burden of telling the story of the past, just as the past itself must be emancipated from the juvenile historiography which is content to trace events and to marvel at wondrous vicissitudes. Although the *Considérations* discusses Roman history chronologically, Montesquieu everywhere assumes that his reader is perfectly familiar with the mere *circumstances* of the past.[21] Instead of a narrative line, we are given a mosaic of often short paragraphs, each one a thought, couched for the most part in the spare, apophthegmatic idiom of one who wishes to proclaim his devotion to matter above words.

Montesquieu's innovative mind transforms the substance of Roman history, as well as the style in which it is written. In his *Réflexions sur les divers*

---

[18] *Œuvres*, III.453–4.

[19] The widespread conviction that it was the investigation of causality which dignified historiography is evident in the literary preferences of the eighteenth century. Wotton is typical: 'Of all the Ancient Historians before *Polybius*, none seems to have had a right Notion of writing History, except *Thucydides*' (*Reflections upon Ancient and Modern Learning*, p. 40).

[20] The eschewing of particularity was a common *philosophe* decorum: 'The reader I hope will excuse the detail into which I am now going to enter' (Mably, *Observations on the Romans*, pp. 51–2). Montesquieu was perhaps its most devoted observer (see Louis de Beaufort's *La Republique Romaine*, I.ii). Later in the century the 'demi-savans' hit back in the person of Gibbon's friend Chastellux (*De la Félicité Publique*, I.ii–iii). The first edition of this work was published in 1772: Gibbon could thus have been acquainted with it before writing *The Decline and Fall*.

[21] Coleridge complained that Gibbon recounted Roman history as if his reader were already familiar with its substance (*Notebooks*, note 3823).

Génies du Peuple Romain, dans les divers tems de la République (1664), Saint-Evremond accounted as follows for Hannibal's apparent failure to capitalise on his victory at Cannae:

Il est certain que les Esprits trop fins, comme étoit celui d'*Annibal*, se font des Difficultés dans les Entreprises, & s'arrêtent eux-mêmes par des Obstacles, qui viennent plus de leur Imagination, que de la chose.[22]

By contrast, Montesquieu offers an explanation which is at once more intricate and more intimate. In place of Saint-Evremond's limp hypothesis about human nature (which is in effect merely a restatement of the crux), Montesquieu conceives and polishes a subtle insight into the inherent instability of conquest:

On dit encore qu'Annibal fit une grande faute de mener son armée à Capoue, où elle s'amollit: mais l'on ne considère point que l'on ne remonte pas à la vraie cause. Les soldats de cette armée, devenus riches apres tant de victoires, n'auroient-ils pas trouvé par-tout Capoue? . . . Les conquêtes sont aisées à faire, parce qu'on les fait avec toutes ses forces; elles sont difficiles à conserver, parce qu'on ne les défend qu'avec une partie de ses forces.[23]

Montesquieu's shrewd finesse of hypothesis in the discussion of particular events is not matched on the higher level of his discussion of the contour of Roman history as a whole, where we seem to have simply a restatement of the Augustinian account of Roman decline; namely, that Roman power grew, broke under its own weight because of sedition and civil strife, and then degenerated into a monarchy.[24] However, Montesquieu holds this point of view not out of piety, but because of his republican sympathies.[25] Hence his unillusioned handling of the 'achievement' of Augustus; 'Auguste (c'est le nom que la flatterie donna à Octave) établit l'ordre, c'est-à-dire une servitude durable.'[26] Yet his careful adjustment of the vocabulary used of Augustus by the majority of writers of the preceding decades indicates that here, too, there is no automatic conformity to the received notions of history: this re-ordering of the relative merits of republic and empire, together with its cool

---

[22] *Œuvres*, I.227.

[23] *Œuvres*, III.378–9. Montesquieu's revisionist eye is also in his reduction of Roman public spirit to self-interest (III.357); or in his refusal to be impressed by the Gallic sack of Rome (III.359); or in his desire to escape from the concentration on character in history (III.427).

[24] *De Civitate Dei*, XVIII.xlv. That Rome fell through immoderate greatness was thus already a well-used explanation of Roman decline when Gibbon returned to it in his *General Observations on the Fall of the Roman Empire in the West*. It had been restated in the years between *The Decline and Fall* and the *Considérations* by Mably (*Observations on the Romans*, p. 39). Walter Moyle had also adopted it ('An Essay upon the Roman Government', *Works*, I.148).

[25] 'Il n'y a rien de si puissant qu'une république où l'on observe les loix, non pas par crainte, non pas par raison, mais par passion, comme furent Rome & Lacédémone: car, pour lors, il se joint à la sagesse d'un bon gouvernement toute la force que pourrait avoir une faction' (*Œuvres*, III.372).

[26] *Œuvres*, III.439.

estimate of the first *princeps*, marks a sharp break with the assumptions and values of the Roman history written under Louis XIV.[27]

The superiority of republics to monarchies on the grounds of their greater durability is a central tenet of the civic humanism so thoroughly described by J. G. A. Pocock.[28] Montesquieu works within this tradition; as a political commentary on Roman history, the *Considérations* owes a debt to Machiavelli's *Discorsi*. But Montesquieu is not just Machiavellian in his politics; his views on religion are also shaped by Machiavelli. In both the *Dell'arte della guerra* and the *Discorsi*, Machiavelli comments on the debilitating influence that Christianity can exert on political virtue.[29] Montesquieu, as the author of a *Dissertation sur la politique des Romains dans la religion* (1716), might have been expected at least to endorse, and probably to augment, the hostile implications his political position holds for Christianity. As it happens, Christianity is hardly mentioned in the *Considérations*. Yet this in itself is loaded with significance. Bossuet, in his *Discours sur l'Histoire Universelle* (1681), and Tillemont, in his *Histoire des Empereurs* (1700–38), had both treated Roman history as a footnote to Christian history.[30]. The secular Montesquieu takes revenge by reversing this priority. There is clearly a sweetness in this; but he cannot afford to seem straightforwardly dismissive of the role of Christianity in Roman history since, as a counterpart to the aspersions he casts on absolute monarchy under the cover of discussing Augustus, he wishes also, by indicating the role of Christianity in the decline of Rome, to bring out how a Christian Church which meddles in politics undermines civic virtue. Both these issues speak directly to the France of Louis XV, and so Montesquieu has to proceed by means of studied understatement. The disjointed paragraphs, which had earlier been the register of an analytic intelligence too mercurial to explore all the implications of its insights and too teeming with such insights to pause for long on any one of them, now form telling juxtapositions. Between them leap the sparks of an ironic mind which has taken the measure of despotisms both past and present and which sees through the obfuscations of the old just as easily as it can evade the censorship of the new:

---

[27] Howard Weinbrot's *Augustus Caesar in 'Augustan' England* indicates the nature of Augustus' image during the reign of Louis XIV (pp. 218–31).

[28] *The Machiavellian Moment*.

[29] See, e.g., *Tutte le Opere*, II.28–30.

[30] This is a tactic originated by St Augustine in his argument that the *pax Romana* achieved by Augustus had no other purpose than to facilitate the spread of Chrisitianity. It is also repeated in Aquinas' *Summa Theologica* (III.xxxv.8). Tillemont states the doctrine, which reduces the magnates of worldly power to the puppets of a providential God, concisely (*Histoire des Empereurs*, I.2). It is implicit in Milton's *On the Morning of Christ's Nativity* and very common in English literature of the eighteenth century; see, e.g., *A Defence of Natural and Revealed Religion*, I.518. Defoe's repetition of it in his *General History of Discoveries and Improvements* would have disseminated it widely (p. 171): one imagines that Thomas Bever's more elegant statement of it in his *History of the Legal Polity of the Roman State* would have had fit audience, though few (p. 168).

Comme les maladies de l'esprit ne se guérissent guère, l'astrologie judiciaire et l'art
de prédire par les objets vus dans l'eau d'un bassin avoient succédé, chez les chrétiens,
aux divinations par les entrailles des victimes ou le vol des oiseaux, abolies avec le
paganisme. Des promesses vaines furent le motif de la plupart des entreprises
téméraires des particuliers, comme elles devinrent la sagesse du conseil des princes.

   Les malheurs de l'empire croissant tous les jours, on fut naturellement porté à at-
tribuer les mauvais succès dans la guerre, & les traités honteux dans la paix, à la
mauvaise conduite de ceux qui gouvernoient.[31]

Montesquieu makes no explicit connexion between the rise of superstition and
the decline of empire; but it has been such a strong presupposition of the *Considérations* that facts which seem discrete are actually not so, that it is
impossible for such a collocation to remain inert. Moreover, elsewhere
Montesquieu has been so quick to make causal connexions that these
moments, in this respect, stand out as salient abstinences, or instants of
restraint, which lead the reader to supply what is omitted. It was these
eloquent silences which d'Alembert singled out for special praise:

M. de Montesquieu ayant à présenter quelquefois des vérités importantes, dont
l'énoncé absolu & direct auroit pû blesser sans fruit, a eu la prudence loüable de les
envelloper, & par cet innocent artifice, les a voilées à ceux à qui elles seroient nuisibles,
sans qu'elles fussent perdues pour les sages.[32]

   Montesquieu's irony thus seems a canny response to a state of affairs in
which, for reasons both rhetorical and prudential, it is wiser not to speak
out.[33] But, at the very end of the *Considérations*, he suggests another reason
why one might choose to employ irony, with all its various obliquities and
disguises, against the Church:

On doit donner une grande attention aux disputes des théologiens, mais il faut la
cacher autant qu'il est possible; la peine qu'on paroît prendre à les calmer les accrédi-
tant toujours, en faisant voir que leur manière de penser est si importante, qu'elle
décide du repos de l'état et de la sureté du prince.[34]

Like the patricians of ancient Rome, who declined to give their slaves a
uniform lest they realise their numbers, the *philosophes* are trapped in the
accents of veiled and dissimulating utterance by the massive but blind force
of the institutions against which they are struggling. Thus their disingenuousness pretends to an urbanity and dismissiveness it does not really

---

[31] *Œuvres*, III.506–7.
[32] 'Éloge de Montesquieu', *Encyclopédie*, V.xiii. The twenty-fourth book of the *Esprit des Loix*
(1748) comprises Montesquieu's most sustained exploitation of this ironic strategy.
[33] Anthony Collins, in his *Discourse Concerning Ridicule and Irony in Writing*, draws a connexion
between social repression and the appeal of irony (pp. 23–4). This idea of a necessary connexion between political and literary freedom goes back to Tacitus' *Dialogus de Oratoribus*. Collins, however, is more likely to have been influenced by Shaftesbury's essay 'On the Freedom
of Wit and Humour', *Characteristicks*, I.62. The topic has been canvassed by a modern scholar:
see Michael Meehan's *Liberty and Poetics in Eighteenth Century England*.
[34] *Œuvres*, III.518.

possess. The *philosophes* are masters of irony, in that they have a perfect control of its techniques; yet they are also *condemned* to be ironists, not simply by the repressiveness of the *régimes* under which they wrote, but also by their clear understanding of what is in their own polemical interests. They are cheated of the heroically direct idiom which should naturally accompany their Promethean, humane ambitions. What appears the very register of their secular hostility to the Church is also (no matter how indirect) an acknowledgement of the power and continuing influence of their enemies.[35] Setting aside the laughing mask of the ironist and excavating beneath the polished literary surface, we may locate an intent ferocity of emotion, born of fear and hatred, and nursed by resentment at the restriction of literary liberty.

There is, then, a deep ambivalence in philosophic historiography. On the one hand, there is its flamboyant modernity, visible in its political thought, its calmly adult determination to be free of credulity and of a depraved appetite for the marvellous, and its sane desire to enlist historiography in the service of sociology. On the other hand, there is its dissimulation and sly reserve. It pursues the aims of enlightenment in a style characterised, at least in part, by shadow and obscurity. This is a tension which we shall find duplicated in the first volume of *The Decline and Fall*. Furthermore, we have seen that the clarities of philosophic historiography are sometimes achieved at the expense of scholarly exactness. What does the philosophic historian do, however, when the mass of anomaly for which he can find no place is too large to be ignored? The historical writings of David Hume exemplify one response to the awkwardness with which the past is always liable to confront the philosophic historian.

---

[35] As we shall see when we come to review the social pressures on Chapter XV of *The Decline and Fall*, the notion that the forces of religion were weak in the eighteenth century is misfounded. Jonathan Clark's *English Society 1688–1832* argues powerfully for the centrality of Anglicanism to its period.

2

Hume

Wee envy the present, and reverence the past   Jonson

So long as we confine our speculations to trade, or morals, or politics, or criticism, we make appeals, every moment, to common sense and experience . . .   Hume

We have recently been reminded that Hume was for long more famous as an historian than as a philosopher.[1] It seems remarkable that the now largely unread *History of England* should ever have been valued as a more significant achievement than Hume's more narrowly 'philosophical' work. Yet Hume seems to have turned to history in an attempt to find the celebrity which had eluded him as an epistemologist; and his acquaintance with Montesquieu presumably showed him that he could be an historian without sacrificing his intellectual probity.[2]

Reflection on these topics very quickly becomes thought about how and to what extent Hume's philosophical writings, particularly those which touch on historiographic issues, influenced his practice as an historian. Hume published his *History of England* between 1754 and 1761, and one might think, therefore, that it is a straightforward realisation of the theorising on historiography which he had developed in his philosophical and discursive works of the previous two decades.[3] Such a supposition might seem even more probable were one to notice that, for Hume, history and philosophy share the same purpose. Of history, he famously remarks that

Its chief use is only to discover the constant and universal principles of human nature, by shewing men in all varieties of circumstances and situations, and furnishing us with materials, from which we may form our observations, and become acquainted with the regular springs of human action and behaviour.[4]

Of philosophy, he writes in *A Treatise of Human Nature*:

---

[1] See the introduction to Duncan Forbes' Penguin edition of Hume's *History of England*.

[2] For the correspondence between Hume and Montesquieu, see the Masson edition of the *Œuvres Complètes*, III.1230 and 1255, and *The Letters of David Hume*, I.133 and 176.

[3] The *Treatise of Human Nature* was published in 1739 and 1740; the *Essays Moral and Political* in 1741 and 1742; and the *Enquiry concerning Human Understanding* and the *Enquiry concerning the Principles of Morals* in 1748 and 1751 respectively.

[4] *Essays and Treatises on Several Subjects*, III.130. Compare Gilbert Stuart: 'It is in the records of history . . . that human nature is to be studied' (*A View of Society in Europe*, p. v).

Here then is the only expedient, from which we can hope for success in our philosophical researches, to leave the tedious lingring method, which we have hitherto followed, and instead of taking now and then a castle or village on the frontier, to march directly to the capital or center of these sciences, to human nature itself; which being once masters of, we may every where else hope for an easy victory.[5]

This congruence is striking, but possibly deceptive. J. B. Black, for instance, in setting as a problem for the student of Hume 'to investigate the extent to which Hume the philosopher guided the pen of Hume the historian', thereby acknowledged that the relation between Hume's philosophy and his history was problematic.[6] My own belief is that by juxtaposing the *History of England* with the theoretical work which preceded it, we can gain valuable knowledge of how Hume's historiographic position moves, and of the pressures his abstract thought placed on his practice as an historian. The relation between Hume's philosophy and his historiography is thus of extreme interest, but not simple; and just as Hume began his *History* with the most recent past and then dug deeper into history, so I will begin with the *History of England*, rather than with the earlier philosophical work.

In the year before he published the first volume of his *History*, Hume, writing to James Oswald, made no bones about the poor opinion he had of his predecessors: 'The more I advance in my undertaking, the more am I convinced that the History of England has never yet been written, not only for style, which is notorious to all the world, but also for matter; such is the ignorance and partiality of all our historians.'[7] It is interesting that Hume should consider style the most glaring deficiency of British historiography. In a critical remark on Thomson, noted by Boswell, Hume lets us glimpse the qualities he values in style: 'Mr. Hume said that Armstrong's *Art of Preserving Health* was the most classical Poem in the english language, that Thomson's *Seasons* had more luxuriance or splendour, but that it had not order and the transitions were rude.'[8] A good style is ordered. It is articulated. It presents its material in such a way that the parts do not obscure the whole. This smoothing away of saliencies and creation of the sense of seamlessness is a fundamental part of the courtesy of good writing. It is also a strategy the writer must employ if his work is to take effect in the mind of the reader. In his essay 'Of Simplicity and Refinement in Writing', Hume cites wit as a quality in a writer which can disturb the relation of parts to the whole and

---

[5] *A Treatise of Human Nature*, p. xvi. Gibbon possessed no copy of this work.

[6] *The Art of History*, p. 79. Since 1926, other critics have considered the question: see E. C. Mossner, 'Was Hume a Tory historian?' and P. H. Meyer, 'Voltaire and Hume as Historians'.

[7] *Letters*, I.179. See also a letter written to John Clephane, written earlier in the same year and on the same subject (*Letters*, I.170). The poverty of English historiography was almost proverbial in the eighteenth century. See Lyttelton, *Letters from a Persian in England* (1735) (*Works*, p. 219); William Warburton (*A Critical and Philosophical Enquiry into the Causes of Prodigies and Miracles*, pp. 61–2 and 134); and most famously Johnson, in *Rambler* no. 122.

[8] Quoted in E. C. Mossner's *The Life of David Hume*, p. 108.

illustrates his point with an architectural image: 'As the eye, in surveying a GOTHIC building, is distracted by the multiplicity of ornaments, and loses the whole by its minute attention to the parts; so the mind, in perusing a work overstocked with wit, is fatigued and disgusted with the constant endeavour to shine and surprize.'[9] It is clear that style, in the sense of *lucidus ordo*, is a matter to which Hume must pay close attention if his *History* is not to fatigue and disgust in the way that those of his predecessors had done.

In an historical narrative, smoothness of style can be recognised in the absence of digression, which betokens the weight of methodical thought brought to bear on the business of writing. It is this canon of taste which lies behind Hume's tactfully hesitated criticism of the opening chapters of Robertson's *History of Scotland*:

But what will really give you pleasure, I lent my copy to Elliot during the holidays, who thinks it one of the finest performances he ever read; and tho he expected much, he finds more. He remarked, however, (which is also my opinion) that in the beginning, before your pen was sufficiently accustomed to the historical style, you employ too many digressions and reflections.[10]

Hume's idea of 'the historical style' has weight in this letter, because by this time he had already published the 1754 and 1757 instalments of his own *History of England*, and so can speak as a blooded historian. Digression and reflection are historiographic vices in that they make the historian too prominently busy in his work. If we turn to the final 1761 instalment of Hume's history, when his style has ripened into ease and correctness, we can see that an important feature of a smooth, articulated historical style is the way it contrives almost to remove the historian from his history, and to give the impression that the past is somehow telling its own story:

Gregory wrote a letter to Ethelbert, in which, after informing him that the end of the world was approaching, he exhorted him to display his zeal in the conversion of his subjects, to exert rigour against the worship of idols, and to build up the good work of holiness by every expedient of exhortation, terror, blandishment or correction; A doctrine more suitable to that age, and to the usual papal maxims, than the tolerating principles which Augustine had thought it prudent to inculcate.[11]

In that single sentence, the three clauses and the four nouns placed in apposition suggest a prose style which can politely but firmly maintain its own decorous patterns in the face of the past – and yet, in so doing, not falsify the past but bring out its intrinsic, if hidden, proportion. The sentence suggests, not multiplicity damagingly *reduced* to unity, but rather the elision of a merely apparent multiplicity. Note how easily all the various historical 'facts' which lie behind the sentence are brought into the generalisation which concludes it, and how the phrasing of that generalisation itself has a fine delicacy.

[9] *Essays and Treatises*, I.315.   [10] To William Robertson, 25.i.1759 (*Letters*, I.294).
[11] *History of England*, I.37–8.

Do the words 'to that age, and to the usual papal maxims' belong to Gregory, or to Hume? Are we faced with simple reportage of Gregory's letter, or is Hume here infusing the prose with an irony mild in expression but strong in blame? Little wonder that the historical artist who could so deftly make his own thoughts and comment *emerge* from narrative winced at Robertson's bluff way of passing judgement at the top of his voice.

Hume is unobtrusive as a narrator: yet he is also deferentially present. The cultivated blandness of Hume's style and his suave demeanour as an historian can easily be appreciated if one recalls, say, Carlyle's *French Revolution*. But in the very mildness of his style, in the way that it seems so little the product of mere personality, we recognise a distinctive, controlling intelligence. Its operations are most palpable when the subject is atrocity:

Nothing but her death could now give security to Odo and the monks; and her most cruel death was requisite to satiate their vengeance. She was hamstringed; and expired a few days after at Gloucester in the most acute torments.[12]

The chiastic arrangement of the two sentences gives the historical account an urbanity of finish quite foreign to the appalling event itself. This refusal to attempt any duplication of the past's texture bespeaks not indifference (Hume's abstention from the denunciation and dramatisation of monkish barbarity, even though it must have mobilised his contempt, makes the writing gently, reticently elegiac), but the belief that an historian cannot embody the past in his writing; he cannot make his narrative in any sense a model of the past. His province is to recount and, without hectoring, to analyse and judge. Thus Hume would never try to make his writing mimetic or enact the past directly. A comment in a letter of 1739 is apposite here:

There are different ways of examining the Mind, as well as the Body. One may consider it either as an Anatomist or as a Painter: either to discover its most secret Springs & Principles or to describe the Grace & Beauty of its Actions. I imagine it impossible to conjoin these two Views.[13]

Of these two modes of examination, the second, that of celebratory description, is unavailable to the historian. He can never consider the past 'as a painter', because his object is not before him. He is condemned to be an anatomist, to infer the past from its memorials and then to comment on it. His prose must always be an emulsion of narrative and judgement.

The undisturbed manner in which Hume recounts the death of Elgiva stands out because of the disturbing cruelty of the event. But it is worth noting that, for Hume, the past must be approached dispassionately, as he implies in a letter of 1748 to Lord Kames: 'I leave here two works going on, a new

---

[12] *History*, I.125.

[13] *Letters*, I.32. Compare R. G. Collingwood: 'Historical thought is of something which can never be a *this*, because it is never a *here* and *now*. Its objects are events which have finished happening, and conditions no longer in existence. Only when they are no longer perceptible do they become objects for historical thought' (*The Idea of History*, p. 233).

edition of my *Essays*, all of which you have seen, except one, *Of the Protestant Succession*, where I treat that subject as coolly and indifferently, as I would the dispute betwixt Caesar and Pompey.'[14] Hume's assumption of indifference to the past, his assumed feeling of separation from its conflicts, clearly contributes to his unruffledness as a narrator. It is a sign, not of the sluggishness of his historical sympathy, but of his faith in the docility of the past to the historian. The way he handles narrative transitions shows this well. It is in those passages where he transfers his attention from one area of the past to another that we might expect some sense of the way the single focus of historical narrative belies the broad, multifarious front along which events move. But what is remarkable here is the way Hume manages to suggest that the movement of his narrative has been sanctioned by the past:

And thus all Europe seemed to repose herself with security under the wings of that powerful confederacy, which had been so happily formed for her protection. It is now time to give some account of the state of affairs in Scotland and in Ireland.[15]

The image of Europe sheltered within protective wings implies that for the moment the past itself has reached a point of repose, and so there is no wrench as Hume's narrative eye turns away from Europe and back to Britain. The past, it seems, has spontaneously formed itself into patterns which translate into prose. A remark in the *Treatise of Human Nature* reveals Hume's faith in the competence of narrative to transcribe the past: 'An historian may, perhaps, for the more convenient carrying on of his narration, relate an event before another, to which it was in fact posterior; but then he takes notice of this disorder, if he be exact; and by that means replaces the idea in its due position.'[16] Even when narrative departs from the past, it need not be untrue to it.

We may now draw together some of the implications of Hume's theorising and practice of the historical style and historical narrative. The historian occupies an independent point of vantage, apart from the past and untroubled by its turbulence. Consequently his judgement is never seduced by the lurid historical fact, such as the death of Elgiva; but nor is his understanding of history crippled by his remoteness. The historian's vision is not particularising, his tone neither rhapsodic nor dramatising. Cool and dispassionate (though not callous), he scans the past and penetrates beneath its surface to obtain knowledge of its underlying structure. The character of the historian is close to that of the Stoic:

The temple of wisdom is seated on a rock, above the rage of the fighting elements, and inaccessible to all the malice of man. The rolling thunder breaks below; and those more terrible instruments of human fury reach not to so sublime a height. The sage, while he breathes that serene air, looks down with pleasure, mixed with compassion,

[14] *Letters*, I.111.   [15] *History*, VII.468.
[16] *Treatise of Human Nature*, p. 9.

on the errors of mistaken mortals, who blindly seek for the true path of life, and pursue riches, nobility, honour, or power, for genuine felicity.[17]

The essence of Hume's views on historical narrative is that composure, and the perspective conferred by distance, yield insight.

Hume writes as if the past were intrinsically amenable to narrative. But, in order to profit from the propitiousness of events, the historian must himself adopt a particular stance. Hume's ideas about how time can be redeemed and made fertile in literature lie behind his admiration for Alfred, who, because of his 'natural bent and propensity towards letters', is as much a literary figure as a monarch:[18]

He usually divided his time into three equal portions; one was employed in sleep, and the refection of his body by diet and exercise; another in the dispatch of business; a third in study and devotion; And that he might more exactly measure the hours, he made use of burning tapers of equal lengths, which he fixed in lanthorns; an expedient suited to that rude age, when the geometry of dialling and the mechanism of clocks and watches were totally unknown. And by such a regular distribution of his time, tho' he often laboured under great bodily infirmities, this martial hero, who fought in person fifty-six battles by sea and land, was able, during a life of no extraordinary length, to acquire more knowledge, and even to compose more books, than most studious men . . .[19]

To account precisely for time is the duty of the historian as well as of the right-living sovereign; self-discipline is necessary for literary fecundity. A vigilant self-awareness in writing, a careful preservation of narrative independence, a refusal to allow oneself to be immersed in the past; these virtues, for Hume, compose the core of the historian's art.

To what end, however, does the historian so control himself? Hume's idea of the purpose of historiography is bound up with his thinking about the phenomenon of law. In the essay 'That Politics may be Reduced to a Science', we find a Montesquieu-like insistence on the usefulness for the historian of a consideration of social laws: 'So great is the force of laws, and of particular forms of government, and so little dependence have they on the humours and tempers of men, that consequences almost as general and certain may be deduced from them, on most occasions, as any which the mathematical sciences afford us.'[20] To study the laws of lapsed societies aids the historian in his aim of formulating those more general laws about man in which his research terminates. This process is at work in the following passage, where we find the tacit belief that legal conventions stabilise and

[17] *Essays and Treatises*, I.250. In a footnote, Hume says that these four essays – 'The Epicurean', 'The Stoic', 'The Platonist' and 'The Sceptic' – are intended 'not so much, to explain accurately the sentiments of the ancient sects of philosophy, as to deliver the sentiments of sects, that naturally form themselves in the world' (*Essays and Treatises*, I.231).

[18] *History*, I.103.

[19] *History*, I.104.

[20] *Essays and Treatises*, I.27.

define not only the society that produces them, but also subsequent scrutiny of that society:

> But tho' all kinds of government be improved in modern times, yet monarchical government seems to have made the greatest advances towards perfection. It may now be affirmed of civilized monarchies, what was formerly said in praise of republics alone, *that they are a government of Laws, not of men.* They are found susceptible of order, method, and constancy, to a surprizing degree. Property is there secure; industry encouraged; the arts flourish; and the prince lives secure among his subjects, like a father among his children.[21]

The historian studies the laws of a society, not because he has any anti-quarian interest in the legislative procedures of vanished civilisations, but because laws speak eloquently of the society which gave them birth. The knowledge the historian thereby gains, which is free from the distortions of personality that disfigure most historical testimony, allows him to trace, with an otherwise unobtainable fidelity, the 'natural course of improvement' which Hume discerned as the shape of the past.[22] The purpose of history is to instruct: to this extent Hume and his major predecessor as a pragmatic historian in English, Bolingbroke, are agreed.[23] But, instead of Bolingbroke's belief, voiced in the *Letters on the Study and Use of History* (1735–8), that the profit of history is to be found in the numerous and various examples which can be extracted from it, Hume finds that the chief reward of historical study can be reaped only by a larger vision. Like Montesquieu, Hume discards the notion of history as a school of moral virtue; the *History of England* is governed by the conviction that now, in the eighteenth century, men turn to the past in order to hone their ideas of civil policy and govern-ment. Consequently its educative value is to be found not so much in its discussion of particular *exempla*, as in its anatomising of the long span of English political life. Hume may have scorned the Whig tenet that early in their history the English enjoyed, and then lost, an ancient constitution: but he nevertheless believed that men could draw political guidance from the past, and that the study of a nation's laws was likely to yield such guidance generously.[24]

So to favour the study of laws entails that the examination of documents will occupy a cardinal position in the practice of historiography. For Hume, history is ineluctably documentary; not only in the sense that an important

---

[21] 'Of Civil Liberty', *Essays and Treatises*, I.160.

[22] *History*, III.430.

[23] 'Every work of art has also a certain end or purpose, for which it is calculated; and is to be deemed more or less perfect, as it is more or less fitted to attain this end. The object of elo-quence is to persuade, of history to instruct, of poetry to please by means of the passions and the imagination' ('Of the Standard of Taste', *Essays and Treatises*, I.383).

[24] Consider Hume's statement in 'My Own Life': 'In about a hundred alterations, which far-ther study, reading, or reflection engaged me to make in the reigns of the first two Stuarts, I have made all of them invariably to the Tory side. It is ridiculous to consider the English constitution before that period as a regular plan of liberty' (*Essays Moral, Political and Literary*, I.5–6). Gibbon owned no copy of this essay.

focus of the *History* is the way that documents have formed the past (in the shape of laws), but also because he felt that historical facts had their sole life in documents. He makes this clear in the statement of policy which opens the collected volumes of the *History* but which (given the order of composition) is also a definitive statement by a man who has worked his way back through the past as far as he can go:

> Ingenious men, possessed of leisure, are apt to push their researches beyond the period in which literary monuments are framed or preserved, without reflecting, that the history of past events is immediately lost or disfigured when intrusted to memory and oral tradition, and that the adventures of barbarous nations, even if they were recorded, could afford little or no entertainment to those born in a more cultivated age.[25]

This conviction was anticipated in the penultimate instalment of the *History*, when Hume, pondering the new certainty imparted to history by the proliferation and accuracy of documentation in the Tudor period, looks askance at any historiography written without the stabilising influence of ample documentation and is more explicit about exactly what gratifies men 'born in a more cultivated age':

> Here therefore commences the useful, as well as the most agreeable part of modern annals; certainty has place in all the considerable, and even most of the minute parts of historical narration; a great variety of events, preserved by printing, give the author the power of selecting, as well as adorning, the facts which he relates; and as each incident has a reference to our present manners and situation, instructive lessons occur every moment during the course of the narration. Whoever carries his anxious researches into preceding periods is moved by a curiosity, liberal indeed and commendable; not by any necessity for acquiring a knowledge of public affairs, or the arts of civil government.[26]

In thus asserting that documents are not only the most rewarding, but also the most reliable kind of historical evidence, Hume is in fact returning to a position he first held in the *Treatise of Human Nature*, where he drew a distinction between historical knowledge and the impressions we have of the world around us, which indeed do fade as they are handed on:

> 'Tis from the original impression, that the vivacity of all the ideas is deriv'd, by means of the customary transition of the imagination; and 'tis evident this vivacity must gradually decay in proportion to the distance, and must lose somewhat in each transition. . .

[25] *History*, I.1–2.

[26] *History*, III.434. This is a very conservative position, in view of the eighteenth-century vogue for 'historical retrodiction', that is to say, the inference of historical events from principles of human nature. Fontenelle had given the impulse to such study by maintaining that knowledge of human nature should enable one to divine all past and future history simply by reflection (*Œuvres*, II.430). Hume's own *Natural History of Religion* is an example of this 'history without documents'. Its prominence in the Scottish Enlightenment is discussed by P. H. Scott, in his *John Galt*.

But here it may not be amiss to remark a very curious phaenomenon, which the present subject suggests to us. 'Tis evident there is no point of ancient history, of which we can have any assurance, but by passing thro' many millions of causes and effects, and thro' a chain of arguments of almost an immeasurable length . . . But as it seems contrary to common sense to think, that if the republic of letters, and the art of printing continue on the same footing as at present, our posterity, even after a thousand ages, can ever doubt if there has been such a man as JULIUS CAESAR; this may be consider'd an objection to the present system. If belief consisted only in a certain vivacity, convey'd from an original impression, it wou'd decay by the length of the transition, and must at last be utterly extinguish'd: And *vice versa*, if belief on some occasions be not capable of such an extinction; it must be something different from that vivacity.[27]

Documents make historiography not only possible and profitable, but also certain.

However, the example Hume uses in the *Treatise* – the existence of Julius Caesar – is both crude and too flattering to historians.[28] It is a large leap from a conviction of Caesar's mere existence to the elevated, analytic and generalising practice of history as Hume conceives it. The information which an historian will find it worth thinking about and establishing as certain is likely to be more elusive, and likely not to admit of such easy settlement. The example of Caesar's existence may reassure us that in searching out historical knowledge, we are not chasing a chimera: but it does not help us in the awkward, real business of recognising truth and rejecting falsehood.

It is in this area of critical method that Hume's historiography ceases to be urbane, rational and confiding. It clouds over, assumes the divided character of philosophic historiography, and becomes guarded, opaque and reticent. The question of how we can evaluate historical testimony perplexed Hume for the whole of his adult life, from the first draft of the essay 'Of Miracles', which was written by December 1737, to his testy remarks on Ossian in a letter to Gibbon penned just before his death in 1776.[29] Throughout he attempts to ascertain and formulate irrefragable principles which (given that historical knowledge can at best be only extremely probable) would allow the historian always to incline towards the superior probability. Yet Hume finds himself entangled in the logical consequences of such principles, and these embarrassments eventually impart movement to the final volumes of the *History of England*.

Critical method aspires to overcome the credulity of the present and to nullify the mendacity of the past. Hume considered both these hindrances to historical knowledge separately in two essays: the essay 'Of Miracles', composed in the 1730s but first published in the *Enquiry Concerning Human*

---

[27] *Treatise of Human Nature*, pp. 144–5.

[28] Julius Caesar was the example commonly chosen by those who wanted to combat extreme pyrrhonism and assert the possibility of historical knowledge; compare Bayle, *Dictionaire Historique et Critique*, art. 'Beaulieu', remarque 'F', I.490 and Locke, *Essay Concerning Human Understanding*, IV.16.8.

[29] *Letters*, II.309–11.

Understanding of 1748, which reflects, despite its mischievous choice of title, on the issue of how the historian ought to deal with accounts of prodigies and the essay 'Of the Populousness of Ancient Nations', composed early in 1750, which addresses itself to a flagrant example of the human tendency to glamorise the past.[30] The dating is significant. Just before beginning work on the *History of England*, Hume composed and prepared for publication his two most sustained reflections on the practice of history.[31]

The argument of 'Of Miracles' may be summarised as follows. A wise man will proportion his belief to the nature and weight of evidence. In any instance he will bestow or withhold his belief on the basis of a calculation in which the evidence for the contention is compared with that against: and he will be determined by whichever body of evidence preponderates. However, there are some assertions which lie too far outside the normal course of nature for them to be believed on any human authority whatsoever; and given the disposition of men to lie, it becomes clear that only a very moderate degree of improbability is necessary in an assertion for a wise man to suspend his belief. Indeed, because of the prevalence of falsehood, the position Hume adopts in this essay would seem to make him a thorough sceptic, like the fabulous Hardouin. But Hume believes that men lie only when it is in their interest to do so:

The wise lend a very academic faith to every report which favours the passion of the reporter; whether it magnifies his country, his family, or himself, or in any other way strikes in with his natural inclinations and propensities.[32]

Much of history is neutral in this respect, and so one may assume that with no motive to lie, men straightforwardly report the truth.[33]

Yet, as Hume also recognises, there is a subtle self-interest gratified by telling monstrous lies which is quite independent of any narrow profit which might accrue as a result of the lie. In 'Of Miracles', Hume suggests that this failing chiefly serves to make men receptive to untruth: 'The *avidum genus auricularum*, the gazing populace receive greedily, without examination, whatever soothes superstition, and promotes wonder.'[34] But this greed for the marvellous may induce men to connive at, foster, repeat or even invent prodigies, which then gain currency. And in 'Of the Populousness of Ancient Nations', Hume turns to this aspect of critical method.

---

[30] *Letters*, I.140 and 152.

[31] 'In 1752, the Faculty of Advocates chose me their Librarian, an office from which I received little or no emolument, but which gave me the command of a large library. I then formed the plan of writing the History of England' ('My Own Life', *Essays Moral, Political and Literary*, I.4). 'Of the Study of History' is about how history is to be consumed, not composed.

[32] *Essays and Treatises*, III.195. Such formulations are extremely common in eighteenth-century literature on critical method.

[33] See the *Treatise of Human Nature*, pp. 404–5 (Book II, Part III, Section I) on the reliability of human testimony on indifferent matters.

[34] *Essays and Treatises*, III.195.

In 'Of Refinement in the Arts', Hume deplores the astigmatism of our historical vision: 'To declaim against present times, and magnify the virtue of remote ancestors, is a propensity almost inherent in human nature.'[35] In the *Treatise of Human Nature*, Hume had offered an explanation of this distortion: 'But tho' every great distance produces an admiration for the distant object, a distance in time has a more considerable effect than that in space.'[36] And men are not inclined to check or correct this distortion because of their 'usual propensity . . . towards the marvellous'.[37] Hume regards this failing as a vestigial trace of barbarousness which must be purged in any urbane, civil historiography. 'Of the Populousness of Ancient Nations' is his attempt to do so.

However, when in that essay Hume once more restates our weakness for the prodigious, he shows that in the year or so since he had finally published 'Of Miracles', his idea of the problem has changed:

The humour of blaming the present, and admiring the past, is strongly rooted in human nature, and has an influence even on persons endued with the profoundest judgment and most extensive learning.[38]

Previously Hume had implied that this defect in vision attacked only the vulgar and barbarous. It now seems more widespread, and in this essay Hume tries to excise and treat a particularly virulent outbreak in the heartland of academic studies which one might have supposed most proof against it. The opinion that the population of the world had declined disastrously since ancient times was firmly held by many who could not be written off as superstitious illiterates. Indeed, it was an opinion which could be held only by the educated, since only they could take part in the debate. Hume attempts to correct this by marshalling an impressive array of erudition; he wrote to Gilbert Elliot that he had 'read over all the Classics both Greek and Latin' since forming the plan of writing the essay.[39] To this extent 'Of the Populousness of Ancient Nations' is the reverse of 'Of Miracles', where Hume had been very sparing with his examples. Yet, when one considers the way Hume uses the evidence he has gathered, the two essays show their kinship. As Hume collects evidence about, say, the size of ancient cities and then from it makes inferences about the size of population they could sustain, it is clear that 'Of the Populousness of Ancient Nations' is designed to issue not in any proof, but in a strong probability. Now, if such probabilistic reasoning is to be cogent, we must endorse the supposition on which it relies: namely, that despite the irregularities on the surface of history, there is an essential constancy shared by both the past and the present. For Hume's implicit method in 'Of the Populousness of Ancient Nations' is to

---

[35] *Essays and Treatises*, II.38.
[36] *Treatise of Human Nature*, p. 433.
[37] *Essays and Treatises*, III.182.
[38] *Essays and Treatises*, II.285.
[39] *Letters*, I.152.

apply principles of human nature which he has, necessarily, abstracted from his observations of the present, to the fragments of information he has about the past; and in so doing he assumes that those principles are as true for the past as they are for the present. In *The Natural History of Religion* Hume revealed that he took it as an axiom that the world had a regular structure, even though we might not be able to perceive it:

Could men anatomize nature, according to the most probable, at least the most intelligible philosophy, they would find, that these causes are nothing but the particular fabric and structure of the minute parts of their own bodies and of external objects; and that, by a regular and constant machinery, all the events are produced, about which they are so much concerned.[40]

In 'Of the Populousness of Ancient Nations' Hume takes this regularity to extend in time as well as space.

The congruence of these two essays, 'Of Miracles' and 'Of the Populousness of Ancient Nations', lies in the investment they both make in the idea, widespread throughout the eighteenth century but especially crucial for philosophic historiography, of uniform principles of human nature. 'Of Miracles' depends on our willingness to extend our perceptions of present deceitfulness in men to cover the past; 'Of the Populousness of Ancient Nations' on our belief that the ancient and the modern worlds share common principles of human nature. Moreover, in both essays we can see that the discerning of such principles is powerfully reductive. Both essays aim to banish the marvellous, be it prodigies or belief in the extraordinary size of the population of the ancient world. Thus their thinking is not only regularist, but normative. They both stake out, and rely on, 'the normal course of nature', and discount as improbable – and hence unworthy to be believed by a wise man – anything which falls outside that area.

This is not just a theoretical position; Hume carried it over into his historical practice. He states it quite plainly in a late volume of the *History of England*:

It is the business of history to distinguish between the *miraculous* and the *marvellous*: to reject the first in all narrations merely profane and human; to scruple the second; and when obliged by undoubted testimony, as in the present case [the life of Joan of Arc], to admit of something extraordinary, to receive as little of it as is consistent with the known facts and circumstances.[41]

It also governs his attitude to Ossian. In the last months of his life, Hume wrote to Gibbon on this subject and stiffened his resistance to anything which lies outside the normal: 'I see you entertain a great Doubt with regard to the

[40] *Essays and Treatises*, IV.266.
[41] *History*, III.152. Compare Warburton, *A Critical and Philosophical Enquiry into the Causes of Prodigies and Miracles* (p. 2) and Louis de Beaufort on Lars Porsena's siege of Rome (*Dissertation sur l'Incertitude des Cinq Premiers Siecles de l'Histoire Romaine*, II.316). This conviction of the incompatibility of history and romance is very apposite to the final instalment of *The Decline and Fall*, where Gibbon finds that he cannot refuse romance entry into history.

Authenticity of the Poems of Ossian. You are certainly right in so doing . . . Where a Supposition is so contrary to common Sense, any positive Evidence of it ought never to be regarded.'[42] These firm statements of principle suggest that Hume is clear in his own mind about critical method, and unshakeable in his convictions. But beneath his apparently immoveable confidence one can detect traces of slippage and doubt.

Hume was already sure, when he wrote the *Treatise of Human Nature*, that the convictions about normality we use in evaluating testimony can be reduced to our notions of 'the governing principles of human nature' which alone 'can give us any assurance of the veracity of men'.[43] The question of exactly what Hume meant by the phrase 'the governing principles of human nature', and the precise nature of the constancy he believed ran through mankind at all times and in all places, is a critical mare's-nest which Hume's notorious remark that the chief use of history 'is only to discover the constant and universal principles of human nature' in large part created.[44] Initially the careless idea prevailed, upheld by J. B. Black and J. Y. T. Greig amongst others, that Hume believed in a straightforward way that men have always been the same:

But the weakness of the XVIIIth-century historians, taken as a group, is their lack of what we now call historic sense. Bringing the whole culture of their age to bear upon the past had its dangers; for the spirit of their age was self-assured, positive, and rather smug, and they judged the past as if it were the present. They came to history with their minds made up in matters of religion, morals, politics and common life. They possessed their own fixed standards, which were apt, more or less, to the times they lived in; but they took for granted that the same standards must be apt to past centuries as well.[45]

Since then, Duncan Forbes has administered a much-needed corrective and, by paying finer attention to Hume's choice of word and by introducing into the debate the neglected but central *A Dialogue*, has advanced the more plausible idea that Hume was fully aware of the enormous variations history revealed in, say, moral belief; but he held that these striking vicissitudes could all be reconciled in a common denominator.[46] This was Hume's position in the 1730s:

The skin, pores, muscles, and nerves of a day-labourer are different from those of a man of quality: So are his sentiments, actions and manners. The different stations of life influence the whole fabric, external and internal; and these different stations arise necessarily, because uniformly, from the necessary and uniform principles of human nature.[47]

[42] *Letters*, II.310–11.
[44] *Essays and Treatises*, III.130.
[46] See his *Hume's Philosophical Politics*, pp. 102–21.

[43] *Treatise of Human Nature*, p. 113.
[45] *David Hume*, p. 268.
[47] *Treatise of Human Nature*, p. 402.

In *A Dialogue*, he illustrates it with a striking example:

The RHINE flows north, the RHONE south; yet both spring from the *same* mountain, and are also actuated, in their opposite directions, by the *same* principle of gravity.[48]

We may, then, discount the idea that Hume believed mankind to have been always and everywhere eighteenth-century Scotsmen with a weakness for claret and intricate reasoning.[49] Forbes has certainly replaced a caricature of a belief with a position which an intelligent man might adopt, and has revealed more clearly what Hume's convictions probably were. But to describe them more accurately is not to make them less problematic: and one result of Forbes' revision is that we can now appreciate more finely the difficulties created by the central role of the principles of human nature in Hume's critical method.

As we have seen, Hume believed that 'the governing principles of human nature' must possess sovereign authority in any sound critical method: the 'experienced train of events is the great standard' by which we regulate our intellectual life as well as our conduct.[50] But how do we acquire knowledge of these principles? It cannot be, in Hume's scheme of things, a priori: and thus must be the product of our personal experience of life or of our knowledge of history. Yet who would be so arrogant as to assert that his own life formed a sufficient basis for this kind of reasoning? Not Hume surely; for in his 'Of the Study of History', he says that

If we consider the shortness of human life, and our limited knowledge, even of what passes in our own time, we must be sensible that we should be for ever children in understanding, were it not for this invention [history] which extends our experience to all past ages, and to the most distant nations.[51]

We are thus perforce thrown back on history; but it was precisely to discover how to conduct such study that we began our inquiry.[52]

The implications of this contradiction are brought out in a concrete way by the response to 'Of Miracles'. Campbell, before his essay meanders off into irrelevance and piety, accurately spots how Hume has tried to delimit the basis of our reasonings concerning testimony:

All the contrariety then that there is in miracles to experience, doth, by his [Hume's] own concession, consist solely in this, that they have never been observ'd; that is, that

---

[48] *Essays and Treatises*, IV.237. Compare also 'Of some Remarkable Customs', *Essays and Treatises*, II.153). Such a notion seems to have been widely held in the eighteenth century: compare Boulainvilliers (*La Vie de Mahomed*, pp. 172–4) and Lady Mary Wortley Montagu (*Complete Letters*, I.272 and II.392).

[49] Such a notion appears to have been held by R. G. Collingwood (*The Idea of History*, p. 224).

[50] *Essays and Treatises*, III.217.

[51] *Essays and Treatises*, I.67. For Hume's final misgivings about the usefulness of analogy, see *Dialogues Concerning Natural Religion*, pp. 31–2.

[52] Giuseppe Giarrizzo and R. G. Collingwood both touch on this circularity in philosophic historiography (Giarrizzo, *Edward Gibbon e la Cultura Europea del Settecento*, p. 112 and Collingwood, *The Idea of History*, pp. 84–5).

they are not conformable to experience. To his experience personal or deriv'd he must certainly mean; to what he has had access to learn of different ages and countries.[53]

William Adams, in his earlier riposte to Hume, shows that he has thoroughly understood the implications of Hume's rationalist critical stance, which he then proceeds to wield against its originator:

We perceive in ourselves, that a love and reverence for truth is natural to the mind of man: and the same self-experience teaches us, that there are certain other principles in human nature, by which the veracity of men may be tried, and the truth of testimony be often put out of doubt, as will be hereafter seen.[54]

Whether men have an inclination to lie or to tell the truth is, of course, beside the point. What Adams has grasped so well is that Hume has effectively reduced the principles of rational belief to an assertion about human nature. Accordingly, he places his optimistic view of man in the scales, opposite Hume's pessimistic view, confident that Hume can do nothing to tip the balance his way and augment his authority without sacrificing the whole of his argument. In a similar way Tytler, writing eight years later and replying to Hume's assertions about the complicity of Mary Queen of Scots in the murder of Darnley and the genuineness of the Bothwell letters, rests his argument on a view of human nature: 'From the letters themselves, the presumption seems to stand in favour of the Queen; that neither she, nor indeed any woman of common prudence or modesty, could have written them.'[55] The only way Hume can bolster his position against both Adams and Tytler is by appealing to history; but the question of on what grounds we can appeal to history remains.

Thus Hume's historiography rests on a huge begging of the question. It purports to result in knowledge of human nature; yet the historian must already possess such knowledge before he can begin to examine his material.

Forbes' refinement of our ideas about what Hume meant by 'the constancy of human nature' does nothing to remove the tail of Hume's belief from its mouth. Instead, what it reveals is Hume's determination to preserve the circularity of his historiography, by adhering firmly to his conviction that there is a central core of human nature which runs unchanged throughout history. Because, although the model of human nature that Forbes proposes, which we have seen was also adopted by Montesquieu and which it seems certain Hume actually held to – that of constant principles informing the various expressions of humanity – seems at first more accommodating to the multifariousness of historical experience than the crude notion of a constant and universal human nature advanced by J. B. Black and J. Y. T. Greig, on closer inspection it reveals an absolute resolution not to abandon the tenet of a constant and universal human nature. The subtlety of the model is a

[53] *A Dissertation on Miracles*, pp. 41–2.
[54] *An Essay on Mr Hume's Essay on Miracles*, pp. 8–9.
[55] *An Historical and Critical Enquiry*, p. 4.

measure of the absoluteness of the resolve. Hume cannot ignore the weight of evidence history provides of the manifold forms that human life has taken. However, by promulgating his model of unchanging principles being variously realised, he can at least make the variety of history seem a mere superficies by which the vulgar are amused but which cannot, for the wise man, obscure history's underlying uniformity. Hume takes it as an axiom that constant principles of human nature exist. Having assumed their existence, he can then make a show of ascertaining their precise qualities inductively. But the fundamental question of whether or not they really do exist is never posed. And Duncan Forbes maintains that it is in fact impossible not to agree with Hume that human nature is structured in this way.[56]

However, when (as he does in *A Dialogue*) Hume collects such plentiful evidence of the multifariousness of human morality which he then attempts to prestidigitate into unity by asserting that 'the principles upon which men reason in morals are always the same; though the conclusions which they draw are often very different', it is hard to fend off the questions of why he thus privileges the idea of unity and why he invests so heavily in a segregation of history into the categories of 'various but illusory' and 'constant but real'.[57] Hume does not seem even to entertain the possibility that the various might be the real and the constant a comforting story we tell ourselves.

There are moments in the final volumes of the *History of England* which nevertheless suggest that Hume *did* eventually move, at least fractionally, from this fortified, yet weak, position; that at length the insistence with which the past displayed its plurality buckled Hume's faith in its essential unity. The change can perhaps be shown most clearly by recalling the *Treatise of Human Nature*. In the 1730s Hume's idea of human nature was banal:

For nothing is more certain, than that despair has almost the same effect upon us with enjoyment, and that we are no sooner acquainted with the impossibility of satisfying any desire, than the desire itself vanishes.[58]

The conviction that the constitution of human nature is reasonable emerges strongly from this extract; the possibility of contradiction – of desire remaining despite there being no chance of satisfaction – is not admitted. But in the final instalment of the *History of England*, Hume is compelled to acknowledge 'the strange contradictions in human nature'.[59] In a footnote to *The Decline and Fall*, Gibbon points out how differently Hume and Voltaire have narrated the same event, the celebration of divine service by the Crusaders who had just taken Jerusalem and massacred the inhabitants:

This union of the fiercest and most tender passions has been variously considered by two philosophers; by the one, as easy and natural; by the other, as absurd and incredible.[60]

[56] *Hume's Philosophical Politics*, pp. 115–16. [57] *Essays and Treatises*, IV.240.
[58] *Treatise of Human Nature*, p. xviii. [59] *History*, I.332.
[60] *The Decline and Fall*, VI.61.

Hume's account is worth quoting in full:

After a siege of five weeks, they took Jerusalem by assault; and, impelled by a mixture
of military and religious rage, they put the numerous garrison and inhabitants to the
sword without distinction. Neither arms defended the valiant, nor submission the
timorous: No age nor sex was spared: Infants on the breast were pierced by the same
blow with their mothers, who implored for mercy: Even a multitude, to the number
of ten thousand persons, who had surrendered themselves prisoners, and were
promised quarter, were butchered in cool blood by these ferocious conquerors. The
streets of Jerusalem were covered with dead bodies; and the triumphant warriors, after
every enemy was subdued and slaughtered, immediately turned themselves, with the
sentiments of humiliation and contrition, towards the holy sepulchre. They threw aside
their arms, still streaming with blood: They advanced with reclined bodies, and naked
feet and head to that sacred monument: They sung anthems to their Saviour who had
purchased their salvation by his death and agony: And their devotion, enlivened by
the presence of the place where he had suffered, so overcame their fury, that they
dissolved in tears, and bore the appearance of every soft and tender sentiment. So inconsistent is human nature with itself! And so easily does the most effeminate superstition ally both with the most heroic courage, and with the fiercest barbarity?[61]

One sees at once how misleading is Gibbon's comment that Hume's attitude
to this event is to treat it as 'easy and natural', for although Hume indeed
uses the word 'easily', it is precisely the facility with which superstition,
courage and barbarism can combine, the immediacy (here denoting much
more than time) with which savagery can become devotion, and the propinquity of the site of the crucifixion to a scene of unmeaning and promiscuous
slaughter that he finds disturbing. Unlike Voltaire who, employing a critical
method which seems very close to Hume's, finds the whole business too far
outside what he takes to be the normal course of nature to be believed, Hume
finds that he cannot discount facts which are as certain as they are baffling.

The recognition of the unsettling antinomies men have shown in history,
and the implications of those antinomies for belief in the universality of
human nature, change Hume's ideas of the function of historiography and of
how we respond to it. The essay 'Of the Study of History' first appeared in
the 1741 edition of Hume's *Essays*; it thus comfortably predates his decision
to write the *History of England* and his experience of actual research and composition. In that essay, Hume gives the following account of the profit of
history and of the mood in which we experience it:

In reality, what more agreeable entertainment to the mind, than to be transported into
the remotest ages of the world . . . To remark the rise, progress, declension, and final
extinction of the most flourishing empires: The virtues, which contributed to their
greatness, and the vices, which drew on their ruin. In short, to see all [the] human
race, from the beginning of time, pass, as it were, in review before us; appearing in
their true colours, without any of those disguises, which, during their life-time, so

---

[61] *History*, I.341–2. The impact of this account of the taking of Jerusalem can be gauged by its
being reprinted in John Adams' anthology *The Flowers of Modern History*, p. 64.

much perplexed the judgment of the beholders. What spectacle can be imagined, so magnificent, so various, so interesting? What amusement, either of the senses or imagination, can be compared with it?[62]

The separation from the past which makes the spectacle of history a mere entertainment that can amuse, instruct and gratify, but never discompose or unsettle us, breathes through this passage, as does the blithe confidence in the rational regularity of human affairs which contends that virtues lead to greatness and that only vices can bring on ruin. But Hume withdrew this piece after the 1760 edition of his *Essays*; and the probable inference is that, as a result of his historiographic practice, he no longer found that the essay accurately expressed his beliefs. Certainly a parallel passage taken from the 1761 instalment of the *History* marks an important inflection of his ideas:

The view of human manners and actions, in all their variety of appearances, is both profitable and agreeable; and if the aspect in some periods seem horrid and deformed, we may thence learn to cherish with the greater anxiety that science and civility, which has so close a connexion with virtue and humanity, and which, as it is a sovereign antidote against superstition, is also the most effectual remedy against vice and disorders of every kind.[63]

Hume still finds history 'agreeable', but he also acknowledges that because of its deformity, it can throw us back into the present with anxiety, not complacency. To know the dreadful things mankind has done and been must undermine any easy faith in the security of the present disposal of affairs as the stable product of an ameliorating historical process. The anomalies and inconstancies of human nature forbid the historian to ignore the fact that the present is as provisional and volatile as was the past. Taste, science and civility may all disappear: 'We know not to what lengths enthusiasm, or other extraordinary motions of the human mind, may transport men, to the neglect of all order and public good.'[64] Hume reports the evidence history provides to support this fear with trepidation, not relish: and so Hurd and Warburton are quite at sea in their attack on the *History of England*:

TACITUS laments bitterly that his fortune has thrown him in an age, when there was nothing to write of but these horrors, *faction, seditions, public convulsions and Revolutions*. 'Opus aggredior opimum casibus, atrox praeliis, discors seditionibus, ipsa etiam pace saevum: quatuor principes ferro interempti: tria bella civilia, plura externa, ac plerumque permixta.' Our Christian Historian riots in these calamities; and thinks that *what inflames faction, animates sedition, prompts rebellion, and distinguishes itself on the open theatre of the world, is the only thing becoming the dignity of History.*[65]

Hume recounts the excesses and barbarities of the past in a style which is cool and unmoved, but with a very different emotion. He shudders anxiously at

---

[62] *Essays and Treatises*, I.66.
[63] *History*, III.317.
[64] 'The Idea of a Perfect Commonwealth', *Essays and Treatises*, II.378–9.
[65] *Remarks on Mr. David Hume's Essay*, p. 22.

those moments, even though his prose may not register those shudders. But although the enormities of history offend Hume's humanity, he does not allow them to loosen the mortar or abrade the fabric of the edifice of critical thought about history which was in place before he began the *History of England*. When brought up against the strange humanity of the Crusaders, he seems aware of the limits of his understanding, but is not led, in response to this check, to revise his fundamental conception of the historian's principles. The more history showed Hume the frailty of politeness and enlightenment, the less willing he was to surrender the small enclave of those precious qualities he believed he had established in historiography.[66]

To turn to Hume's historical writing after that of Montesquieu is to discover both continuity and divergence. Their respective prose styles, of course, are quite distinct: 'le bon David' aspired to ease, not to the affected brevity of Montesquieu. But beneath that difference of surface, there is a substantial intellectual community between the two men. They share a faith in the uniformity of human nature, a wish to disclose the lineaments of that uniformity through history, and a strong interest in the historical study of law. Yet, one imagines that their inward experience of composing history was very different. Montesquieu's treacherous facility with hypothesis, which so consistently drew Gibbon's criticism in *The Decline and Fall*, his ability to move swiftly from the particular to the general, suggests that the past seems never to have checked his understanding. Hume did encounter such contrarieties in history; but he did not respond positively to those rebuffs. It is as if he could conceive of no alternative to the harsh choice between the tense rationalism displayed in 'Of Miracles' and flaccid credulity. It is in the later volumes of *The Decline and Fall*, after Gibbon has had much the same experience of disorientation as had Hume with the Crusaders, but met it in a different spirit, that we find some egress from the dilemma in which the anomalous places philosophic historiography.

[66] Michael Meehan has recently drawn attention to Hume's anxious cultural conservatism (*Liberty and Poetics in Eighteenth Century England*, p. 96).

PART II

The Decline and Fall of the Roman Empire

1776–1781–1788

. . . the order of time, that infallible
touchstone of truth.   Gibbon

3

Introduction

Those whom the appearance of virtue, or the evidence of genius, have tempted to a nearer knowledge of the writer in whose performances they may be found, have indeed had frequent reason to repent their curiosity; the bubble that sparkled before them has become common water at the touch; the phantom of perfection has vanished when they wished to press it to their bosom.   Johnson

In its original quarto form, *The Decline and Fall* bulks to approximately one and a half cubic feet. The Hanoverians are not renowned for their literary acuity, but no one could deny the accuracy of the Duke of Gloucester's assessment of at least the look of the volumes with which Gibbon presented him in 1781: 'Another damned thick square book!'[1] However, despite its monumental appearance, the production of *The Decline and Fall* was beset by vicissitudes. From the first its publication was subject to postponement. Gibbon treats this as a fact of authorial life: 'In every great work unforeseen labours and difficulties and delays will arise.'[2] But his deferrals are unusually plentiful and repeated. In 1774, he makes plain his hopes to publish Volume I in 1775. In June 1775, he talks of 'next winter'. The first volume of *The Decline and Fall* was eventually published on 17 February 1776. The second instalment of Volumes II and III was published on 1 March 1781: but in the correspondence that precedes it we are again faced with multiple postponements. Four times in 1779 he predicts that he will publish in 1780. In March 1780, he reckons on 'next Winter' as a certain date; and in September, 'about next February' is his revised prediction. The manifold delays which hampered preparation of the third instalment in 1788, and which led Gibbon to move back his estimated time of completion from September 1786 to spring '87 and finally to summer '87, are set out at length in Norton's *Bibliography*.[3]

The Decline and Fall repeatedly overleapt the temporal bounds within which Gibbon tried to confine it. It seems also to have eluded his attempts to say

---

[1] J. E. Norton, *Bibliography*, pp. 50–1.
[2] *The Letters of Edward Gibbon*, III.37. Compare Pope on completing the *Iliad*: 'I find it is in the Finishing a Book, as in concluding a Session of Parliament, one always thinks it will be very soon, and finds it very late. There are many unlook'd for Incidents to retard the clearing *any Publick Account*, and so I see it is in mine' (*The Correspondence of Alexander Pope*, II.43).
[3] *Letters*, II.21–2 and 32; *Letters*, II.75; *Bibliography*, p. 37; *Bibliography*, p. 49; *Letters*, II.205, 211, 215 and 225; *Letters*, II.240; *Letters*, II.250; *Bibliography*, pp. 57–8.

definitely when he began work on it. His account of the conception of his masterpiece is rightly famous, and will bear one more repetition:

> It was at Rome, on the 15th of October 1764, as I sat musing amidst the ruins of the Capitol, while the bare-footed fryars were singing vespers in the Temple of Jupiter, that the idea of writing the decline and fall of the city first started to my mind.[4]

Modern scholarship has poured cold facts on this celebrated sentence.[5] Nevertheless, we will be disappointed if we look for similarly precise information (fictitious or not) concerning when Gibbon actually started work on *The Decline and Fall*. J. E. Norton says firmly that 'he did not, however, set seriously to work on the book until 1768'.[6] Gibbon's own indications are not so unequivocal: 'Though my reading and reflections began to point towards the object, some years elapsed, and several avocations intervened before I was seriously engaged in the execution of that laborious work.'[7] A comment in the *Memoirs* throws both light and shade over the issue: '1773 February &c – No sooner was I settled in my house and library than I undertook the composition of the first Volume of my history. At the outset all was dark and doubtful . . . and I was often tempted to cast away the labour of seven years.'[8] But from which date do we subtract the seven years to arrive at the beginning of the labours that produced *The Decline and Fall*? The remark could mean that Gibbon had been working on his history for the seven years before 1773, and that he had therefore started in 1766. Two other comments in the *Memoirs* support this construction. Recalling the months following his return from the Tour on 25 June 1765, he writes that 'In the first summer after my return . . . we [Gibbon and Deyverdun] freely discussed my studies, my first Essay, and my future projects. The decline and fall of Rome, I still contemplated at an awful distance.'[9] Yet that awful distance may have been overcome by the following year, for he notes that the letter of congratulation on the first volume sent him by Hume in 1776 'over paid the labour of ten years'.[10]

However, when Gibbon speaks of the 'labour of seven years', he may equally mean that by the time Volume I was published, he had been working on it for seven years: that is to say, he had begun it around 1769. Once again, supporting evidence exists. Thinking back to his inconsequential 'prentice

---

[4] This is the account as published by Lord Sheffield (*Miscellaneous Works*, I.198); compare *Memoirs*, p. 136. For a discussion of the possible significance of the revisions of this passage, see below pp. 226–7.

[5] Compare Ducrey et al., *Gibbon et Rome*, p. 103 and *Memoirs*, pp. 304–5. Yet it may be that Gibbon refined and clarified this moment not out of a desire to mislead, but from loyalty to a truth deeper than that of circumstance.

[6] *Bibliography*, p. 36.

[7] *Memoirs*, pp. 136–7. See also Peter Ghosh's 'Gibbon's Dark Ages: some remarks on the genesis of the *Decline and Fall*', which describes Gibbon's 'hesitant shuffle' towards his subject with scholarship and imagination.

[8] *Memoirs*, p. 155.

[9] *Memoirs*, pp. 137 and 140. This must have seemed a long summer to Deyverdun.

[10] *Memoirs*, p. 158.

work, he writes: 'As soon as I was released from the fruitless task of the Swiss revolutions, I more seriously undertook (1768) to methodize the form, and to collect the substance of my Roman decay, of whose limits and extent I had yet a very inadequate notion.'[11] Reviewing his active literary life as a whole, he computes the time occupied by *The Decline and Fall* at twenty years, a calculation which places the first research in 1768: 'Twenty happy years have been animated by the labour of my history.'[12] Clearly, there was no single day when Gibbon sat down and began work; at different moments, he estimated the beginning of his labours at different times.

These indeterminacies which hedged the birth of *The Decline and Fall* go well with the other indeterminacy to which the history is prone, namely the way it expands the further into it the historian progresses. In November 1779, Gibbon writes to Robertson: 'The subject has grown so much under my hands that it will form a Second and third Volume in 4o.'[13] The experience is encountered again in the third instalment. In December 1786, Gibbon knew that his latest labours would demand three volumes, but he thought they might be 'somewhat thinner, perhaps, than their predecessors'.[14] In fact, they are just as thick as the first three volumes. As he tackled the final stages Gibbon called Pope to mind when expressing how what he had taken in hand had swelled: 'But alas when autumn drew near, hills began to rise on hills, Alps on Alps, and I found my journey far more tedious and toilsome than I had imagined.'[15] Consequently we hear the voice of experience when Gibbon writes to Langer in 1790: 'Un objet interessant s'étend et s'aggrandit sous le travail: je pourrois être entrainé au delà de mes bornes.'[16]

Notwithstanding this evidence of the complications which surrounded the delivery of *The Decline and Fall*, the overwhelming majority of Gibbon's critics feel that the work which resulted is perfectly formed: 'une belle histoire où le génie de l'ordre, de la méthode, de la bonne administration, domine'; 'from first to last he is an artist in form'; 'whatever objections other critics have advanced, few of them have questioned the pre-eminence of *The Decline and Fall* as a monument of historical construction. Dr G. M. Trevelyan, who has always insisted upon form as a vital element in the writing of history, has spoken for the present age: "Gibbon's work comes as near perfection as any human achievement"'; 'by its conclusion the *Decline and Fall* has become an enclosed object, to be contemplated as much for its formal and detailed beauty as for its accurate transcription of what was'; 'a masterpiece of . . . perfect form' and 'his whole genius was pre-eminently classical: order, lucidity, balance, precision – the great classical qualities – dominate his

[11] *Memoirs*, p. 146.   [12] *Memoirs*, p. 187.
[13] *Letters*, II.233.   [14] *Letters*, III.54.
[15] *Letters*, III.59.   [16] *Letters*, III.204.

work'; 'the masterpiece of a master craftsman'; 'in the case of the *Decline and Fall* a close study of the narrative design would probably reveal a complex but orderly and balanced pattern similar to that of Gibbon's sentences'; 'une colossale structure symetrique'; 'one of the architectural wonders of historical writing'; 'the final impact is of a perfectly proportioned work, a faithful and wonderful realization of the architect's design'. Against this eulogy we should set Sir Ronald Syme's temperance: 'Gibbon was in trouble from time to time on the large structure.'[17]

I shall argue that *The Decline and Fall* is not architecturally perfect, that Gibbon's conception of his great work undergoes a series of revisions and distensions, that these changes are the effects of pressures generated by researching and composing the history of the declining empire, and that they are part of a larger evolution from one apprehension of the nature and function of historical writing to another. This evolution finds expression not simply in a loosening of the design of *The Decline and Fall*, but also in inflections of Gibbon's prose style, in new ideas about the very structure of the past, about historical causation, and in a greatly enriched awareness of the possibilities contained within human nature, which demands from him fresh ways of understanding and depicting character and a more flexible critical method capable of a greater scrupulousness in its handling of the anomalous and extraordinary.

Even if its author had dropped no hints of it, one might reasonably expect change and development in a work planned and published over two decades. But Gibbon does drop such hints plentifully. When we look closely at his comments about the publication of *The Decline and Fall*, second thoughts and proposals for correction are prominent: 'I print no more than 500 copies of the first Edition, and the second . . . may receive many improvements'; 'I could now wish that a pause, an interval had been allowed for a serious revisal.'[18] It is more than a literary pirouette when Gibbon echoes Tacitus' admission of errant analysis in his own manuscript annotation appended to the opening paragraph of *The Decline and Fall*:

Should I not have given the *history* of that fortunate period which was interposed between two Iron ages? Should I not have deduced the decline of the Empire from the Civil Wars, that ensued after the fall of Nero or even from the tyranny which succeeded the reign of Augustus? Alas! I should: but of what avail is this tardy knowledge? Where error is irretrievable, repentance is useless.[19]

[17] Sainte-Beuve, *Causeries du Lundi*, VIII.435; J. M. Robertson, *Pioneer Humanists*, p. 296; Michael Joyce, *Edward Gibbon*, pp. 126–7; Leo Braudy, *Narrative Form in History and Fiction*, p. 214; Lytton Strachey, *Portraits in Miniature*, pp. 156 and 161; D. Thomson, 'Edward Gibbon the master builder', p. 591; Lionel Gossman, *The Empire Unpossess'd*, p. 106; Michel Baridon in Ducrey et al., eds., *Gibbon et Rome*, p. 87; David Jordan in Bowersock et al., eds., *Edward Gibbon and the Decline and Fall of the Roman Empire*, p. 1; David Jordan, *Gibbon and his Roman Empire*, p. xii; Ducrey et al., eds., *Gibbon et Rome*, p. 53.

[18] *Letters*, II.81; *Memoirs*, p. 179.

[19] *The English Essays of Edward Gibbon*, p. 338. Compare Tacitus: 'sed aliorum exitus, simul cetera illius aetatis memorabo [the age of Augustus] si effectis in quae tetendi plures ad curas vitam produxero' (*Annales*, III.24).

There seems plentiful external evidence to support the view that *The Decline and Fall* is not, when taken as a whole, the perfect exemplification of a single thesis.[20]

It is clear that Gibbon, for one, did not regard *The Decline and Fall* as an achieved work incapable of revision or improvement; he might have smiled with amusement as well as complacency at Trevelyan's extravagant praise of his history. Moreover, his realisation of the provisionality of his writing did not dawn on him as he dropped his pen in the *berceau* of La Grotte that evening in June 1787 when he completed his great work.[21] Even as we read it through, we notice traces of rethinking and rewriting. There are some striking changes in Gibbon's opinions. In the fourth volume (the first of the three that comprise the final instalment of 1788), he discusses the Isaurians, 'those bold savages'. In a footnote, he deplores his earlier treatment of the race:

Turn back to vol. i p. 340, 341. In the course of this history, I have sometimes mentioned, and much oftener slighted, the hasty inroads of the Isaurians, which were not attended with any consequences.[22]

Writing the history of irreversible downfall, Gibbon learns that actions may be inconsequential, yet substantial. The change in temper that *The Decline and Fall* exhibits is in part precisely this realisation that we dupe only ourselves in attacking many of what seem history's broadest targets for scorn. It marks a significant move away from the peremptory, pedagogic idiom of a philosophic historian such as Voltaire, and towards a style where precise knowledge of the past is joined to imaginative sympathy of judgement, and where, in fulfilment of Pope's wish that we should learn 'with reason to admire', to wonder (despite the strictures against admiration of a *philosophe* like Montesquieu) is to take the first step towards knowledge.

This abatement of scorn accompanies Gibbon's corrected view of the past as a setting for the improbable. In Chapter IX Gibbon digresses on the inevitable torpor of those who can neither read nor write:

. . . let us attempt, in an improved society, to calculate the immense distance between the man of learning and the *illiterate* peasant. The former, by reading and reflection, multiplies his own experience, and lives in distant ages and remote countries; whilst the latter, rooted to a single spot, and confined to a few years of existence, surpasses, but very little, his fellow-labourer the ox in the exercise of his mental

---

[20] Patricia Craddock, though, has suggested that the period in which *The Decline and Fall* was composed and published was, for Gibbon, a time of intellectual constancy: 'His values and value judgements, however, show relatively little change in the same period (1771–88)' (*The English Essays of Edward Gibbon*, p. 564). This is a view with which I take strong issue.

[21] *Memoirs*, p. 180.

[22] *The Decline and Fall*, IV.102 and n. 119. Some critics have noted that *The Decline and Fall* lacks the unity of convincing interpretation or successful argument: 'It is worth remembering that the *The Decline and Fall*, written over a period of nearly twenty years, does not represent a coherent vision or provide a single, sustained interpretation' (G. W. Bowersock in Ducrey et al., eds., *Gibbon et Rome*, p. 194).

faculties . . . and we may safely pronounce, that without some species of writing, no
people has ever preserved the faithful annals of their history . . . [23]

Such were Gibbon's thoughts before 1776 – perhaps shaped by a recollection
of Fleury: 'Car la mémoire des faits ne se peut conserver long-tems sans
écrire.'[24] Yet history, and the multiplication of experience he had praised
twelve years before, fractures Gibbon's confident conjecture. Researching on
the Arabs, he learns that he had not taken the true measure of the human
mind:

. . . [Arabia's] speech could diversify the fourscore names of honey, the two hundred
of a serpent, the five hundred of a lion, the thousand of a sword, at a time when this
copious dictionary was entrusted to the memory of an illiterate people.[25]

The criterion of probability, which is the guiding light of the critical method
whereby a philosophic historian secures his pragmatic ends, is a will-o'-the-
wisp in these areas of the past.[26]

A final example of Gibbon's increased susceptibility to the unforeseen and
extraordinary; contemplating the ruins of Baalbec in 1788, the historian is
stupefied:

. . . we are at a loss to conceive how the expence of these magnificent structures could
be supplied by private or municipal liberality.[27]

To be sure, Gibbon's imagination had received a powerful stimulus: 'Every
preceding account is eclipsed by the magnificent description and drawings of
M. M. Dawkins and Wood, who have transported into England the ruins
of Palmyra and Baalbeck.'[28] But this hardly closes the large interval of
sensibility and understanding which yawns when we contrast the dumbfound-
ed admiration the historian expresses in his final instalment with his composure in viewing Roman magnificence in 1776:

But if the emperors were the first, they were not the only architects of their dominions.
Their example was universally imitated by their principal subjects, who were not
afraid of declaring to the world that they had spirit to conceive, and wealth to
accomplish, the noblest undertakings.[29]

[23] *The Decline and Fall*, I.222; I.265.
[24] *Discours sur l'Histoire Ecclésiastique*, I.17. Compare also Hume, *History*, I.1–2.
[25] *The Decline and Fall*, V.187.
[26] It is clear that Fleury influenced Gibbon's thought on critical method: he quotes the
     Frenchman in support of his own practice in adjudicating between conflicting testimony about
     Constantine (*The Decline and Fall*, II.74 n. 1). In Volume III, Gibbon still feels that history can
     be preserved only in script: 'The Saxons, who excelled in the use of the oar, or the battle axe,
     were ignorant of the art which could alone perpetuate the fame of their exploits' (*The Decline
     and Fall*, III.610).
[27] *The Decline and Fall*, V.316.
[28] *The Decline and Fall*, V.315 n. 71.
[29] *The Decline and Fall*, I.44–5; I.53–4. First edition: '. . . who were not afraid of declaring that
     they had spirit to conceive . . .'

As a man of fifty-one, Gibbon finds that he had scorned too much and stood in awe of too little when, as a man of thirty-nine, he had published his first volume in 1776.

Gibbon archly portrays the consequences of this evolution in his opinions as a predicament facing his reader. In the knowledge of imminent death, Mahmud the Gaznevide parades his troops and weeps 'the instability of human greatness':

The following day he reviewed the state of his military force; one hundred thousand foot, fifty-five thousand horse, and thirteen hundred elephants of battle.[30]

To this is appended a note: 'From these Indian stories, the reader may correct a note in my first volume (p. 253, 254.); or from that note he may correct these stories.'[31] The reference is to note 49 of Chapter VIII, in which Gibbon, extrapolating from the present back into the past, follows the example set by Hume's 'Of the Populousness of Ancient Nations' in trying to purge ancient history of its improbable statistics. Had Hume written the note in Volume V, one would have had no doubt that it was ironic, and that he firmly expected his reader to correct these 'stories' by his note. But the choice with which Gibbon presents the reader of *The Decline and Fall* is not a barely concealed, ironic trap for the credulous. At this late stage of the history, it has become clear that the attempt to adjudicate between truth and exaggeration by calculations of probability is vain.[32]

This greater willingness to entertain the wonderful, the awe-inspiring and the improbable has implications for the structure of *The Decline and Fall*. Spectacular events tend to seduce the historian's attention and distend the form of his narrative. It is also symptomatic of the larger change I spoke of earlier, from one view of the business of the historian to another. When, in February 1776, the first volume of *The Decline and Fall* was 'on every table, and almost on every toilette', it seems likely that the world of fashion saw little more than a flourish of literary *politesse* in the first sentence of the 'Preface':

It is not my intention to detain the reader by expatiating on the variety, or the importance of the subject, which I have undertaken to treat: since the merit of the choice would serve to render the weakness of the execution still more apparent, and still less excusable.[33]

[30] *The Decline and Fall*, V.650.

[31] *The Decline and Fall*, V.650 n. 10.

[32] Shifts in Gibbon's opinions during these years are not confined to *The Decline and Fall*. In 1764, the youthful Gibbon would happily sell Lenborough to ease his father's debts, despite the diminution in the estate he would inherit (*Letters*, I.187). In 1789, he prefers to own property in land, rather than in liquid form (*Letters*, III.150). Equally, however, there is constancy as well as change: in his *Memoirs*, written after the completion of *The Decline and Fall*, as well as in the first volume of his history, Gibbon feels that certain noble families are most distinguished in their literary scions (*Memoirs*, pp. 4–5: *The Decline and Fall*, I.325; I.386). I argue not for a total *bouleversement* in Gibbon's opinions on all subjects, but merely for important changes in crucial areas.

[33] *Memoirs*, p. 157; *The Decline and Fall*, I.v: I.iii.

This seems like ordinary authorial modesty. When we turn to the personal writings, this opening sentence ceases to seem a gesture and emerges as an expression of the anxiety which gnawed at Gibbon's mind in the months before publication. Writing to his stepmother in June 1775, the question of the problems which might impede the realisation of his project accompanies its announcement: 'The subject is curious and never yet treated as it deserves . . . during some years it has been in my thoughts, and even under my pen. Should the attempt fail, it must be by the fault of the execution.'[34] Later that year, the same note is struck in a letter to John Whitaker: 'For my own part, about February next, I intend to oppress the Public with a quarto of about five or six hundred pages, and am only concerned that the happy choice of the subject will leave no excuse for the feebleness of the execution. I do not say this from any false modesty, but from a real consciousness that I am below my own ideas of historical merit.'[35] In attempting to rise to the majesty of his subject, Gibbon employs a range of tactics designed to translate the past into language. I shall try to follow these tactics, as new ruses for capturing history with words succeed one another through the length of *The Decline and Fall*; and I shall hope to unfold their implications for Gibbon's volatile ideas about the nature both of the past and of historiography. To trace these tactics, one must follow the advice of J. G. A. Pocock: 'We need to read the work [*The Decline and Fall*] as its author planned and executed it.'[36] And so my discussion falls into three parts, in which I successively discuss the three instalments of *The Decline and Fall*: Volume I (1776), Volumes II and III (1781) and Volumes IV, V and VI (1788).

Before I begin my inquiry in earnest, I ought to acknowledge and if possible dispel a reservation which might trouble even a candid reader. My account of *The Decline and Fall* is much concerned (but not exclusively concerned) with the detail of Gibbon's prose. My belief is that the great virtue of his writing in *The Decline and Fall* is its extraordinary plasticity; that is to say, the fidelity with which it will take and preserve an intimate impression of the process of composition. It may appear that this is a trivialising and myopic approach, calculated to upset the settled image of Gibbon as an historian with paradoxes which are dull because merely fabricated. But if we are serious in our claims for Gibbon as a great historian and writer, it is on the detail of his achievement that we must base and vindicate those claims. The historian's acolytes have heaped incense on the altar of *The Decline and Fall*, and if the rising smoke has intoxicated with its grateful fragrance, it has also obscured both the fine chiselling and even the large shape of the altar it was intended to adorn. The misty views and fond reverence of these enthusiasts require the mild correction of a closer inquiry into the object of our mutual veneration; and my hope

---

[34] *Letters*, II.75.
[35] *Letters*, II.90. Compare *Letters*, II.93 and II.263.
[36] Bowersock, et al., *Edward Gibbon and the Decline and Fall of the Roman Empire*, p. 118.

is that our admiration for *The Decline and Fall* will emerge from this study both amplified and purified. Idolatry we shall not feel; but no genuine achievement can be lessened by a polite and careful inspection. And, to lay aside pastiche, I take it as an elementary courtesy that we should at least begin with the modest belief that a great writer means what he says; for those who recoil from close scrutiny of Gibbon's prose in effect maintain that they know what he meant better than he himself.

Gibbon's comments on the historical style sanction such careful attention. He frequently repeats the substance of a maxim first uttered by Dionysius of Halicarnassus:

. . . Style is the image of character . . .

The style of an author should be the image of his mind . . .

. . . the immortal mind is renewed and multiplied by the copies of the pen . . .[37]

The mind and character of the active historian bent upon his task are marked by the struggle to get the past into words; and they in their turn determine the historian's command of language. The style of *The Decline and Fall* − taking style here to mean not the ornaments of writing but the full resources of language − is moulded by Gibbon's historiographic effort, and is thus a means whereby we can trace Gibbon's evolving ideas about the past and about how it may receive literary expression. This may seem at odds with Sheffield's famous description of Gibbon composing:

. . . before he sat down to write a note or letter, he completely arranged in his mind what he meant to express. He pursued the same method in respect to other composition; and he occasionally would walk several times about his apartment before he had rounded a period to his taste. He has pleasantly remarked to me, that it sometimes cost him many a turn before he could throw a sentiment into a form that gratified his own criticism.[38]

Sheffield's reminiscence carries conviction because it corresponds with Gibbon's own account: 'It has always been my practise to cast a long paragraph in a single mould, to try it by my ear, to deposit it in my memory; but to suspend the action of the pen, till I had given the last polish to my work.'[39] The laboriously obtained patina of art seems to preclude the qualities of immediate responsiveness I have claimed for Gibbon's prose. But in fact this is another example of how far the artistry of the eighteenth century could be from artfulness.[40] The constant aim is to give art a transparency and fidelity which will make pertinent, and satisfy, unusually stringent criteria; Gibbon, like

---

[37] *Roman Antiquities*, I.1.3; *Memoirs*, pp. 1 and 155; *The Decline and Fall*, VI.471.
[38] *Miscellaneous Works*, I.278.
[39] *Memoirs*, p. 159.
[40] Compare Lady Mary Wortley Montagu: 'You will accuse me of Deceit when I am opening my Heart to you, and the Plainesse of expressing it will appear Artificial' (*Complete Letters*, I.181). Plainness is dissimulating, and art confiding.

Pope, 'thought a Lye in verse or prose the same'. Gibbon was fully conscious of the transforming pressures to which *The Decline and Fall* was prone; and, because of the way he eventually built on the insights which at first seemed purely negative and no more than the solvents of his philosophic composure, we can see that he responded positively to the disorientation he underwent in tracing the empire's decline. It was to this experience of the dissolving of certitude, as well as to the imaginatively perceived past, that Gibbon ultimately tried to be true. The forms which eventually gratified his criticism, the mould and polish which satisfied his eye, did not veneer the past, but tried with suppleness to follow its surprising contours.

Volume I – 1776

The human genius knows not a nobler effort than that of collecting the various events of distant times, and placing them in such successive order and arrangement, as to exhibit a perfect delineation of the rise and progress of states, the civilization of mankind, and advances of science.   Hutchinson

4

Style

. . . the choice and command of language is the fruit of exercise . . .   Gibbon

. . . an account of the ancient Romans . . . cannot nearly interest any present reader, and . . . can owe its value only to the language in which it is delivered, and the reflections with which it is accompanied.   Johnson

The true value of Gibbon's personal writings lies not so much in the biographical information they provide as in the flickering light they cast on *The Decline and Fall*.[1] It is, for instance, of great importance to know that Gibbon expended many pains over the opening of his history:

. . . three times did I compose the first chapter, and twice the second and third, before I was tolerably satisfied with their effect.[2]

To be aware that the 'effect' of the first pages of *The Decline and Fall* is the product of conscious and successful intention is to be reassured that, at this point, Gibbon's prose will bear a large pressure of attention, and that the fruit of such attention is likely, given his satisfaction that he had made his design legible, to be what he desired it should be. The unusual care Gibbon took over the first three chapters of *The Decline and Fall* springs from his understanding of the rhetorical importance of the beginning of a work in creating the relationship between writer and reader to be sustained or modified in the pages that follow. By scrutinising the style of these initial chapters, we can study the 'effect' Gibbon produces in his readers, and from that infer the relationship he creates between himself and his public.

The opening of *The Decline and Fall* is justly celebrated:

In the second century of the Christian Aera, the empire of Rome comprehended the fairest part of the earth, and the most civilized portion of mankind. The frontiers of that extensive monarchy were guarded by ancient renown and disciplined valour. The gentle, but powerful influence of laws and manners had gradually cemented the union of the provinces. Their peaceful inhabitants enjoyed and abused the advantages of wealth and luxury. The image of a free constitution was preserved with decent reverence. The Roman senate appeared to possess the sovereign authority, and devolved on the emperors all the executive powers of government. During a

---

[1] The loss of the manuscript of *The Decline and Fall* makes what we can infer about the composition of the history from the *Memoirs* and other personal writings especially precious.

[2] *Memoirs*, pp. 155–6.

happy period of more than fourscore years, the public administration was conducted by the virtue and abilities of Nerva, Trajan, Hadrian, and the two Antonines.[3]

In his final volume, Gibbon proposes this maxim: 'Nor may the artist hope to equal or surpass, till he has learned to imitate, the works of his predecessors.'[4] Here, at least, his practice is consonant with his theory. This first paragraph is a careful imitation of Tacitus. In its parataxis, it echoes the beginning of the *Annales*. In taking for its subject the state of the empire, it shadows the *Historiae*.[5]

Allusion to a past master affords an easeful introduction into narrative.[6] Following a great predecessor – and Gibbon follows Tacitus not only by echoing his manner but also by beginning his narrative where the senator ended the *Historiae* – may lessen the awkwardness of beginning a major work. But Gibbon's opening proclaims his independence as well as his indebtedness. In this initial paragraph, he begins to establish his authority over his readers. He insinuates his right to speak, and we are led to acknowledge our obligation to listen.[7]

The triumph of the passage lies in its ability to suggest that it is supported by an intricacy and profundity of thought too rich to be expressed fully and directly in words, and yet too potent not to leave its impress on language. The writing is unmistakably more paratactic than Gibbon's normal style. In consequence, all the sentences seem in apposition; each addition seems to spread

---

[3] *The Decline and Fall*, I.1: I.1. First edition: '. . . the virtue and abilities of Trajan, Hadrian, and the two Antonines'. Compare *Annales*, I.1. For other discussions of this paragraph, see Peter Gay, *Style in History*, p. 41 and Martin Price, '"The Dark and Implacable Genius of Superstition": an aspect of Gibbon's irony', pp. 241–59.

[4] *The Decline and Fall*, VI.433.

[5] J. F. Gilliam has noted the closeness of the first paragraph to Tacitus (in Ducrey et al., *Gibbon et Rome*, p. 137; but see also E. Badian in *Gibbon et Rome*, p. 109). Tacitus was recognised in the eighteenth century as a consummate, if perhaps too deliberate, stylist: 'Even the eloquence of Tacitus, however nervous and sublime, was not unaffected' (Lyttelton, *Works*, p. 369; for a hostile assessment, see Warburton, *A Critical and Philosophical Enquiry into the Causes of Prodigies and Miracles*, p. 116). Gray considered Tacitus' style 'inimitable' (*Poems and Memoirs*, p. 141). It is interesting to note, given the ultimate tendency of Volume I of *The Decline and Fall*, that Warburton saw an interest in Tacitus as a sign of free-thinking (*The Divine Legation of Moses*, Book II, Sect. 6).

[6] The *Memoirs* begin by citing the precedents for such an endeavour: 'The authority of my masters, of the grave Thuanus, and the philosophic Hume might be sufficient to justify my design' (*Memoirs*, p. 2). The *Essai sur l'Étude de la Littérature* begins with the words 'Mais je ne me suis point dit avec le Corrège; "et moi aussi je suis peintre"' (*Miscellaneous Works*, IV.6). Montesquieu had felt no such diffidence on the brink of the *Esprit des Loix*: 'Quand j'ai vu ce que tant de grands hommes . . . ont écrit avant moi, j'ai été dans l'admiration, mais je n'ai point perdu le courage. *Et moi aussi je suis peintre*, ai-je dit avec le Corrège' ('Preface', *Oeuvres*, I.lxii). Johnson remarks on the awkwardness of making a beginning in the first *Rambler*: 'The difficulty of the first address on any new occasion, is felt by every man in his transactions with the world' (*Works*, II.1).

[7] It was the impossibility of legitimately laying claim to such independent authority which made Gibbon give up the idea of writing about Sir Walter Ralegh: 'What new lights could I reflect on a subject which has exercised the accurate industry of *Birch*, the lively and curious acuteness of *Walpole*, the critical spirit of *Hurd*, the vigorous sense of *Mallet* and *Robertson*, and the impartial philosophy of *Hume*' (*Memoirs*, p.121).

his attention to a new, but adjacent, issue. And this is in fact the case with
the first three sentences, in which Gibbon successively tells us more about the
state of the empire in the second century and advances neither in time nor
in argument.

The fourth sentence seems another exemplary bead on that same descrip-
tive string. But 'enjoyed and abused' introduces a subtlety of judgement
absent from the earlier description, and a hint of blame which darkens the
preceding praise. The simple structure to which the paragraph had so far
tended – a general view in the first sentence, followed by a succession of
restricted perspectives as the historian dwells on the frontiers, the provinces
and then their inhabitants – is enlarged when we see that Gibbon's attention
is not confined to depicting the empire, but is also concerned to evaluate it.
In this synthesis of narrative and judgement, akin to the simultaneity of observation and assessment in Montesquieu, we recognise the voice of a guiding,
critical intelligence, selecting and ordering material, and then choosing,
moulding and commanding the language in which to express it. There is a
firm distance, reminiscent of Hume, between the historian and his subject;
the latter may include perturbation and caducity, but the historian is
imperturbable.

The words 'image' and 'appeared' in the fifth sentence repeat and amplify
these enriching suggestions of the fourth, while in the sixth, the phrase 'public
administration' shimmers between remark and comment by tempting us to
doubt the soundness of the empire's subjects – the private side of the political
body in which all the vices hinted at before must reside if the government is
really the repository of 'virtue and abilities'.

These insinuations make the tone highly nuanced, the thought seem complex and elusive. The experience of reading is one of feeling the writing shift
and slide: in its delicacies of phrase, movement, allusion and structure, the
prose repeatedly provokes fleeting responses which the reader cannot fully
articulate. We are forced to admit that a greater degree of critical judgement
has gone into the composition of this prose than we can bring to bear in our
analysis. In October 1775, William Strahan wrote to Gibbon praising the first
volume of *The Decline and Fall* with a warmth which freshens the cliché of
'mastering a subject': 'The work abounds with the justest maxims of sound
policy, which, while they shew you to be a perfect master of your subject,
discover your intimate knowledge of human nature.'[8] But before we have
assessed the validity of Gibbon's judgements about human nature, his manner has already announced his mastery. Shaftesbury held that 'the Historian
or Relater of Things important to Mankind, must, whoever he be, approve
himself many ways to us; both in respect of his Judgment, Candor, and
Disinterestedness; e'er we are bound to take any thing on his Authority'. Gibbon begins *The Decline and Fall* with a view so to approving himself; and he

8 *Miscellaneous Works*, II.138–9.

does so through the medium of a style which, in Blair's words, 'is a picture of the ideas which rise in his mind, and of the manner in which they rise there'.[9]

In a later volume Gibbon will write of 'the truth and simplicity of historic prose'.[10] But in this first volume the confidingness of his prose is disingenuous.[11] Here the historian is in one sense perpetually ironic, because although he wishes to give the impression of confidentiality, he also makes us feel that we are unworthy recipients of his confidence; just as those who are perfectly at home manage to insinuate to those they welcome that, as newcomers, they are not quite at home. To this end Gibbon delights in creating sentences which invite the reader to give them a meaning which, on closer inspection, they disavow. A whimsical example occurs when he is discussing Ossian: 'The uniform imagery of Ossian's Poems, which, according to every hypothesis, were composed by a native Caledonian.'[12] The word 'Caledonian' tempts us to think this asserts the genuineness of Ossian; but the adroitly judged effect of 'every' punctures the bubble of our surmise. Even Hume and Johnson would allow that Macpherson was a Scot.

A less playful example soon follows:

In the purer ages of the commonwealth, the use of arms was reserved for those ranks of citizens who had a country to love, a property to defend, and some share in enacting those laws, which it was their interest, as well as duty, to maintain.[13]

Does 'the purer ages of the commonwealth' contrast pure commonwealth with base empire? Such is our immediate assumption. Yet we soon remember (and Gibbon surely knew) that Marius enrolled soldiers without property before campaigning against Jugurtha. The contrast is thus not between republic and principate, but between virtuous and vicious republicans; and the importance of this second meaning, from the perspective of Gibbon's overall strategy in Volume I, is that it cancels any notion that the principate destroyed a perfect constitution.

A third instance will suffice. Gibbon cites the full severity of Roman military discipline:

The centurions had a right to punish with blows, the generals with death; and it was an inflexible maxim of Roman discipline, that a good soldier should dread his officers

---

[9] Shaftesbury, *Characteristicks*, I.146; Blair, *Lectures on Rhetoric and Belles Lettres*, I.183.

[10] *The Decline and Fall*, III.115.

[11] In this respect, I think Lionel Gossman confuses the surface of Gibbon's writing with its intentions: 'The maintenance of a relation of compatibility and confidence between himself and the reader is, indeed, an essential concern of the historian throughout the *Decline and Fall*' (*The Empire Unpossess'd*, p. 90).

[12] *The Decline and Fall*, I.i n. 12: I.6 n. 12. First edition: '. . . which, in every hypothesis . . .'

[13] *The Decline and Fall*, I.9: I.11. John Barrell's *English Literature in History 1730–80: An Equal, Wide Survey*, pp. 17–50, provides a vigorous account of the centrality of these Machiavellian, republican ideals in eighteenth-century England. J. G. A. Pocock's *The Machiavellian Moment* remains the classic study of the origin and history of these ideas in Western culture.

far more than the enemy. From such laudable arts did the valour of the Imperial troops receive a degree of firmness and docility, unattainable by the impetuous and irregular passions of barbarians.[14]

The brutality of the punishment has been stressed to the point where 'laudable' seems at first to be straightforwardly ironic: but when Gibbon turns from the methods to the beneficial effects of Roman discipline, the word's literal meaning seems more acceptable. In all three examples, Gibbon lures his reader into a position where he subsequently abandons him. The authority of the figure who can make us realise the error he had avoided, and into which we fell, is increased. In 1710 Steele had deplored an innovation in the prose of his day:

My contemporaries the Novelists have, for the better spinning out Paragraphs, and working down to the end of their columns, a most happy art in saying and unsaying, giving hints of intelligence, and interpretations of indifferent actions, to the great disturbance of the brains of ordinary readers.[15]

By the final quarter of the century, this habit of teasing in prose has spread beyond the realm of journalists (to whom Steele is referring in the word 'Novelists') and has been applied to more serious ends than that of padding.

We might at this point recall Leavis' comment on Gibbon's prose:

Gibbon as a historian of Christianity had, we know, limitations; but the positive standards by reference to which his irony works represent something impressively realized in eighteenth-century civilization; impressively 'there' too in the grandiose, assured and ordered elegance of his history.[16]

This is a judgement with almost every word of which my argument will take silent issue: but for the moment we need only remark that Leavis' notion of an assumption of solidarity with his reader on Gibbon's part, expressed in a ponderous solidity of prose, is not borne out by our examination of the *soigné* paragraphs in which one would most expect such qualities if they were indeed to be found in *The Decline and Fall*. Instead of solidity and the lifeless decoration suggested by 'grandiose', there is mobility of meaning and vitality of verbal resource; and instead of an expansive relaxation induced by confidence in shared values and a relationship of equality between historian and reader, there is an illusory confidingness which, as we shall see, smooths the way for the exertion of authority over the reader.

That authority is amplified by Gibbon's ability to distil large amounts of judgement and information into few words.[17] Often it is an adjective that

---

[14] *The Decline and Fall*, I.10–11: I.13. First edition: '. . . imperial . . .'.
[15] *The Tatler* no. 178 (30.v.1710), III.270.
[16] 'The irony of Swift', *The Common Pursuit*, p. 75.
[17] Eighteenth-century taste was Horatian in deploring obscurity (see Gibbon's adverse judgement on his *Essai: Memoirs*, p. 103); but it admired successful brevity. Gray records that Shaftesbury 'was reckoned a fine writer, and seemed always to mean more than he said' (*Poems and Memoirs*, p. 263).

serves his turn. When we are told that the praetorian camp at Rome was 'fortified with skilful care', it is the word 'skilful' which carries the largest weight of adverse comment and which tells us much about the false, mistrustful caution that the emperors mistook for prudence.[18] When those who conduct the auction of empire between Didius Julianus and Sulpicianus are styled 'faithful emissaries', Gibbon relies on the word 'faithful' to convey both the fact that now fidelity can be awakened only by such unworthy objects and his quiet disapproval.[19]

Gibbon's judgement thus has the air of a concentrated sureness which elicits our admiration by convincing us that it would defeat our emulation. Yet he is concerned that we should not only appreciate his intelligence in its fruits, but understand with what difficulty they were produced. A footnote in Chapter VII uncovers a dilemma facing the historian:

> The election of Gordian by the senate, is fixt, with equal certainty, to the 27th of May; but we are at a loss to discover, whether it was in the same or the preceding year [A.D. 237 or 238]. Tillemont and Muratori, who maintain the two opposite opinions, bring into the field a desultory troop of authorities, conjectures, and probabilities. The one seems to draw out, the other to contract the series of events, between those periods, more than can be well reconciled to reason and history. Yet it is necessary to chuse between them.[20]

Rarely will the alternatives be so equally unappealing. Yet Gibbon leaves the issue unresolved, letting us feel the awkwardness of the historian's simultaneous obligations to suspend judgement and resist the opiate of a hasty persuasion, and still to arrive at a judgement which can be justified. Walpole, taken by the apparent modesty of Gibbon's style, the way it seems shyly to bestow its fruits, expresses this balance well:

> How can you know so much, judge so well, possess your subject and your knowledge, and your power of judicious reflection so thoroughly, and yet command yourself and betray no dictatorial arrogance of decision?[21]

In fact, it is precisely through this Augustan pretence of laying aside authority that Gibbon manages to lay hold on an imperial sway over his readers. The burdens of power revealed to us, as they were to the senators who urged Augustus to reassume all his offices, we hurry to shelter behind Gibbon's competence and learning. In the same moment we admit the magnitude of his achievement, both as a commentator on the past, and as a stylist. We can endorse Virginia Woolf's description of the dawning virtues of Gibbon's style, its richness, life and authority; 'The pompous language becomes delicate and exact.'[22] Yet it is Suard who shows the deepest understanding of the *purpose*

---

[18] *The Decline and Fall*, I.107: I.128.   [19] *The Decline and Fall*, I.109: I.131.
[20] *The Decline and Fall*, I.xxvii n. 31: I.222–3 n. 32.   [21] *Miscellaneous Works*, II.154.
[22] *Collected Essays*, I.118.

of this stylistic reticence: 'un stile toujours animé, toujours varié, noble et piquant'.[23] Gibbon was a dandy in dress, but not in words: 'piquant' captures well the calculation which underlies his carefulness. As well as establishing Gibbon as an authority, the historian's linguistic resources in Volume I of *The Decline and Fall* are devoted to suggesting and making plausible his explanation of the causes of Roman decline.[24]

[23] *Miscellaneous Works*, II.184.

[24] J. W. Johnson denies the intimacy of Gibbon's style with his convictions about the substance of history: 'He [Gibbon] seems to have been more concerned with style than an ultimate theory of history' (*The Formation of English Neo-Classical Thought*, p. 229). For a modern defence of the centrality of style to historiography, see Hayden White's 'Rhetoric and history' in Hayden White and F. E. Manuel, *Theories of History*, pp. 1–25.

5

Augustus

The drawing of characters is one of the most splendid, and, at the same time, one of the most difficult ornaments of Historical Composition.   Blair

It is when Gibbon turns his attention to Augustus that we first see how his command of style is instrumental in the presentation of decline. This early portrait prepares the ground for the explanation of Roman decay Gibbon advances in Volume I, while consolidating his ascendancy over his reader. He remarked on how his military experience contributed to his literary career:

The discipline and evolutions of a modern battalion gave me a clearer notion of the Phalanx and the Legion, and the Captain of the Hampshire grenadiers (the reader may smile) has not been useless to the historian of the Roman empire.[1]

But an acquaintance with military manoeuvring, 'those disciplined evolutions which harmonise and animate a confused multitude' may have helped Gibbon as much to order his narrative in Volume I as to understand his subject-matter.[2] In the portrait of Augustus, he begins to drill the felicities of his prose with a deftness of generalship which shows up strongly when set in the context of the contemporary debate on Augustus' character.[3]

In France the question of Augustus' status was influenced by Louis XIV's appropriation of Augustan values.[4] Augustan majesty was harnessed to the

[1] *Memoirs*, p. 117.

[2] *The Decline and Fall*, I.216: I.256–7.

[3] The reputation of Augustus in the eighteenth century has recently been the object of scholarly altercation. On one side there are those who, noting that there was prolific hostility towards Augustus in the eighteenth century, find no value in the term 'Augustan' when used to describe English literature from the Restoration to the early years of George III and who consequently wish to do away with it. On the other, there are those who believe that, when properly qualified, it is expressive of important characteristics in that literature. The former position is best exemplified by Howard Weinbrot's powerfully documented *Augustus Caesar in 'Augustan' England*. He argues that in the eighteenth century English opinions about Augustus were determined more by the Tacitean tradition of blame than by the Virgilian tradition of praise and that therefore 'Augustan' is an unfortunate choice of word to describe the literature of the age. The latter position is best seen in Howard Erskine-Hill's *The Augustan Idea in English Literature*. This work ranges far outside the period conventionally dubbed 'Augustan', and, while not neglecting the weight of uncomplimentary opinion about Augustus, demonstrates that the meaning and value of the term 'Augustan' is not restricted by his reputation. The debate, and the reputation of Augustus in the eighteenth century, is sensibly reviewed in Michael Meehan's *Liberty and Poetics in Eighteenth Century England*, pp. 64–78.

[4] See above, p. 17 n. 27.

glory of the Sun King, and a dominant tradition of panegyric arose. The Roman emperor became a forebear of the French king, and the two monarchs reflected to each other across the centuries ineffable power, virtue, clemency and patronage.

Thus Montesquieu's laconic handling of Augustus in the *Considérations*, on which I touched earlier, is a trenchant piece of demystification:

Voilà la clef de toute la vie d'Auguste . . . Il songea donc à établir le gouvernement le plus capable de plaire qui fut possible, sans choquer ses intérêts, et il en fit un aristocratique par rapport au civil, & monarchique par rapport au militaire: gouvernement ambigu, qui, n'étant pas soutenu par ses propres forces, ne pouvait subsister que tandis qu'il plairoit au monarque, & étoit entièrement monarchique, par conséquent . . . Toutes les actions d'Auguste, tous ses règlemens tendoient visiblement à l'établissement de la monarchie . . . Sylla, homme emporté, mène violemment les Romains à la liberté: Auguste, rusé tyran, les conduit doucement à la servitude. Pendant que, sous Sylla, la république reprenoit des forces, tout le monde crioit à la tyrannie: &, pendant que, sous Auguste, la tyrannie se fortifioit, on ne parloit que de liberté.[5]

In unmasking Augustus as a political operator distinguished only by his extraordinary prowess, Montesquieu is clearly influenced by Tacitus. But in two important respects he diverges from the senatorial historian. First, he betrays no indignation at the manipulations of the emperor; his tone is uniformly calm, subtly inquiring, and patiently analytical.[6] And secondly, he confesses to no vestigial puzzlement, no trace of arrest, in his understanding of Augustus ('Voilà la clef de toute la vie d'Auguste'). Where others might hesitate between the cowardly soldier and the intrepid statesman, the political villain and the enlightened artistic patron, Montesquieu's perspective organises the deeds of Augustus' life into a legible form ('Toutes les actions d'Auguste . . .').

Doubtless this anatomising of the father of Western despotisms carried, in the *ancien régime* of Louis XV, a political charge too powerful and too plain to require detonation by an aggressively ironic tone. Nevertheless, Montesquieu's temperate manner contrasts strongly with the strident hostility of other, 'enlightened', French commentators on Augustus:

Comme il ne marchoit que par des routes secrètes, & qu'il cachoit, sous des titres très simples, le grand pouvoir dont il étoit revêtu, il travailla aussi d'une manière couverte à changer les loix, & à accomoder à un gouvernement monarchique celles qui avoient été faites pour un Etat libre.

Ainsi le petit-neveu de César, à force de ruses & de souplesse, d'audace & de cruauté, parvint à la suprême puissance où il aspiroit des sa jeunesse. Rome perdit pour toujours la liberté.[7]

[5] *Œuvres*, III.440-1.

[6] One must, of course, remember that Montesquieu is here using 'tyran' not as a vague term of abuse, but in its technical sense, as he makes plain in a footnote: 'J'emploie ici ce mot dans le sens des Grecs & des Romains, qui donnoient ce nom à tous ceux qui avoient renversé la démocratie' (*Œuvres*, III.441 n. (g)).

[7] Louis de Beaufort, *La Republique Romaine*, II.22; *Abrégé de l'Histoire Romaine à l'Usage des Élèves de l'École Royale Militaire à Paris*, p. 181.

Such outspokenness is not confined to France. Thomas Blackwell attacks Augustus as a shrewd but malignant political conjuror:

> . . . though he preserved the old Forms and Appearances of the Magistrates, yet having wholly changed the Government and destroyed the Vitals of their Liberty . . .
>
> Nothing could be more artfully concerted, or more dexterously pursued, than his deep-laid Plan to obtain a legal Sanction of his manifest Usurpation.[8]

Chesterfield, as a Whig grandee, might be expected to have a low opinion of absolute government (though from the most selfish motives); but it raises an eyebrow to hear him denounce Augustus so roundly:

> It is a general prejudice, and has been propagated for these sixteen hundred years, that Arts and Sciences cannot flourish under an absolute government; and that Genius must necessarily be cramped where Freedom is restrained. This sounds plausible, but is false in fact . . . The number of good French authors . . . who seemed to dispute it with the Augustan age, flourished under the despotism of Lewis XIV; and the celebrated authors of the Augustan age did not shine, till after the fetters were rivetted upon the Roman people, by that cruel and worthless Emperor.[9]

It is interesting to see the firm separation Chesterfield maintains between 'Augustan' (which he uses to denote the highest artistic achievement) and that 'cruel and worthless Emperor' whose name furnishes the term: for in the clarity of that division, we can detect a confident decisiveness as untroubled as Montesquieu's.[10]

Alongside these denigrations of Augustus there was an abundance of praise. Sir Robert Filmer asserted that Rome achieved greatness only under the emperors, thereby flattering Augustus by making him the instigator of the constitution which ensured Roman majesty.[11] Basil Kennett envied the

---

[8] *Memoirs of the Court of Augustus*, I.7 and III.554.

[9] Chesterfield, *Letters*, II.141–2. Thomson (*Liberty*, III.484ff.) comes close to Chesterfield's formulation; and, of course, Thomson was linked politically with Chesterfield. It is, however, important to recognise that, even in these years, charges of political unscrupulousness and personal baseness do not comprise the totality of responses to Augustus; compare Dyer, *Ruins of Rome*, p. 20.

[10] It was generally accepted that Rome was, outwardly at least, at her most magnificent under Augustus (see, for instance, Sir William Temple, 'Of Ancient and Modern Learning' in *Works*, III.467). Even those who were hostile to Augustus, such as Mably, would admit as much: 'Rome resumed, in a manner, all its grandeur under the reign of Augustus' (*Observations on the Romans*, p. 99). They could do this by adopting the commonplace that political health and outward prosperity were not synchronised. Mills, who completed Blackwell's *Memoirs of the Court of Augustus*, is explicit: 'What we loosely term the *Stile of the Augustan Age*, was not *formed* under *Augustus*. It was formed under the Common-Wealth, during the high Struggles for Liberty against *Julius Caesar*' (III.467: see also Basil Kennett, *Romae Antiquae Notitia*, p. vi). Thus it was possible to admire 'Augustan' art without endorsing Augustus' politics.

[11] '*Rome* began her Empire under *Kings*, and did perfect it under *Emperours*; it did only encrease under that Popularity: Her greatest Exaltation was under *Trajan*, as her longest Peace had been under *Augustus*' (*Patriarcha*, pp. 56–7). Sydney (*Works*, pp. 112–16) disagrees, of course, and locates the time of Rome's greatness in the republic. Moyle, more sternly still, maintains that even by the late republic, which saw such unconstitutional events as the seven consulships of Marius and the continuation of Caesar's Gallic command, the Romans had lost their strenuous political virtue (*Essay upon the Constitution of the Roman Government, Works*, I.1–148).

Romans 'so excellent a Prince', Steele admired his palace as an asylum of politeness, and towards the end of the century Thomas Bever could still praise Augustus as 'an ornament and blessing to his country'.[12] In his *Réflexions sur les divers Génies du Peuple Romain* (1664), Saint-Evremond shuffled his terms with some finesse, and fabricated a vindication of Augustus by depreciating the quality of the material he had to work with, and by pointing out the disheartening limitations of even absolute power:

. . . il voulut enfin gouverner par la Raison un Peuple assujetti par la force; & dégoûté d'une violence, où l'avoit peut-être obligé la necessité de ses affaires, il sut établir une heureuse Sujetion, plus éloignée de la Servitude, que de l'ancienne Liberté.[13]

Yet this fine constitutional concoction is delicate, and so, for Saint-Evremond, Roman decline begins with Augustus' successor:

. . . mais si on veut remonter jusqu'à la premiere cause [of Roman decline], on trouvera que ce méchant naturel étoit autorisé par l'exemple de *Tibere*, & le Gouvernement établi sur les Maximes qu'il avait laissées . . . je maintiens que *Tibere* a corrompu tout ce qu'il y avoit de bon, & introduit tout ce qu'il y a eu de méchant dans l'Empire.[14]

Augustus emerges as a noble and traduced figure, whose generous aspirations were shackled by his circumstances, and the betrayal of whose principles by his heir is continued by the impercipience of modern historians. This almost tragic conception of Augustus is most common amongst those who believe, with Waller, that 'the vexed world, to find repose, at last / Itself into Augustus' arms did cast' and that in consequence Augustus did not take the measures at which modern republicans frown to gratify his desires, but to meet his grave responsibility of preserving the state.[15] Thomas Bever exemplifies this interpretation well. Finding that the charges of tyranny have been overstressed and that 'the reign of Augustus . . . was certainly distinguished by many strong marks of mildness and liberality', he puts the blame for the loss of republican liberty (which in his opinion was not a heavy loss) on the exhaustion of the people: 'The people themselves, indeed, were grown weary of a constitution, under which, with the form and semblance of freedom, they suffered every evil both of anarchy and despotism. They thought one tyrant more tolerable than a thousand.'[16]

---

[12] *Romae Antiquae Notitia*, p. 17; *Tatler* no. 242; *The History of the Legal Polity of the Roman State*, p. 232.

[13] *Œuvres*, I.252.

[14] *Œuvres*, I.274–5. This is a common expedient of admirers of Augustus: see Kennett, *Romae Antiquae Notitia*, p. xii.

[15] 'A Panegyric to my Lord Protector', 11. 169–70.

[16] *History of the Legal Polity of the Roman State*, pp. vi and 102. Mably and Vertot both acknowledge that in Augustus' case the maxim 'If these the times, then this must be the man' is applicable, but they see as the Romans' motive in accepting the principate not Bever's sane disgust with civil war, but depravity (*Observations on the Romans*, p. 73; *Histoire des Révolutions Arrivées Dans le Gouvernement de la République Romaine*, III.306); thus they can maintain their

Now, although these writers are divided over the verdict they bring in on Augustus, they are all in fundamental agreement on the terms and nature of the debate. They share the belief that Augustus' character is susceptible to this kind of forensic understanding; for them, Augustus is either innocent or guilty. They are also agreed on the importance of the reign of Augustus – the emperor's advocates and enemies can join in singling out the first principate for special attention:

Et à mon avis, jamais Gouvernement n'a mérité de plus particulieres Observations que le sien.

The authority of AUGUSTUS . . . forms such an aera in the ROMAN history, as is obvious to every reader.

The conduct of Octavianus . . . merits a particular attention.

. . . the Space of Years in which AUGUSTUS lived, is the Period of all the *Roman* Empire, that best deserves to be known.[17]

But one might also dwell on Augustus not because of his historical momentousness, but because he is a problematic figure who commands attention in proportion to his ability to absorb it. It is here that we find the real division between writers on Augustus. Those who straightforwardly praise or blame share a common basic understanding of the figure they are discussing; they differ only in their like or dislike of what they see. Against them we should place those writers who find Augustus irreducibly enigmatic, such as Shaftesbury.

In *Some Reflections on the Characters of Augustus, Maecenas and Horace*, Shaftesbury displays a diptych gathered from earlier writers:

Historians differ very widely in drawing the Character of *Augustus*. According to some he was a Genius of the first Form: He had large extensive Views, and laid Projects with great Judgment: He was capable not only of planning, but of executing the grandest Designs: And after the Extinction of the Triumvirate, he was humane, clement, nay full of Goodness; and in fine, one who seem'd to have been born to diffuse Happiness through the Universe.

By other Writers he is represented as an ambitious Prince without Courage; as

hostility to Augustus, as the self-serving protector of dangerous vices. In England, as Isaac Kramnick has remarked, the desire of the Romans to enslave themselves to Augustus was often used as a mirror of what the opposition held was happening under Walpole (*Bolingbroke and his Circle: the Politics of Nostalgia in the Age of Walpole*, p. 35). Lyttelton's *Dialogues of the Dead* (1760) are a prime example of this: ('Messalla Corvinus', *Works*, pp. 376 and 379); and Dialogue XXIX (added in the fourth edition of 1765), between Scipio and Caesar, centres on the question, so central to any decision as to Augustus' integrity, of whether the republic could have been restored in 44 B.C. Michael Meehan reports that the exoneration of Augustus' despotism on the grounds of the slavishness of the Roman people was styled by Warton the 'usual excuse' (*Liberty and Poetics in Eighteenth Century England*, p. 70).

[17] Saint-Evremond, *Œuvres*, I.251; Hume, 'Of the Coalition of Parties', *Essays and Treatises*, II.328; Mably, *Observations on the Romans*, p. 80; Blackwell, *Memoirs of the Court of Augustus*, I.3.

enterprising and yet timid; as treacherous to his Allies, and implacably cruel in satiating his Revenge; as superstitious; and not only without one real Virtue, but without the outward Semblance of any.

But it is easy to discern Flattery in the one and Malice in the other of these so very opposite Pictures. *Augustus*, 'tis likely, has been neither so great nor so good, so weak nor so wicked as he is described to us. Men generally are of more mixed Characters: And therefore it is probable, that if this Prince did not possess all the wonderful Qualities some ascribe to him, he was not however such a Miscreant as others have pourtray'd him.[18]

Although Shaftesbury can see the inadequacy of the two over-simplified and exaggerated portraits he holds up to view, he cannot delineate a more plausible portrait himself, but merely indicates the gaping middle ground of 'mixed character' where any more satisfactory depiction of Augustus must be situated. Shaftesbury's Augustus is a shadowy and elusive figure, neither following nor eschewing obvious courses of action, somehow contriving to produce the sweet fruit of public felicity from a form of government which was barren in the hands of his successors, and working through instruments who deflect attention (both then and now) from their master:

Augustus neither wholly rejecting , nor wholly embracing one or other of these Advices, resolv'd to retain the Sovereign Power, but gradually to inure the *Romans* to despotick Government, by gentle Usage . . .

So that if *Agrippa* made his Master triumph over a thousand publick Dangers and all his open Enemies; *Maecenas* on the other Hand disarmed his secret ones; reconciled free Men to Servitude, and rendered Monarchy, so hateful to Republicans, tolerable even to them.

The corrupting Sweets of such a poisonous Government were not indeed long liv'd. The Bitter soon succeeded: And, in the Issue, the World was forc'd to bear with Patience those natural and genuine Tyrants, who succeeded to this specious Machine of arbitrary and universal Power.[19]

Shaftesbury's tone here is unmistakably hostile: but it would be wrong to suppose that he is *merely* hostile. There is not the same clarity of denunciation here as one finds in Chesterfield; one can see Shaftesbury's antipathy towards Augustus struggling against, but not overwhelming, his awareness of mitigating considerations – for instance, in the distinguishing of Augustus from 'those natural and genuine Tyrants' or in the puzzling but not to be ignored tolerance of the republicans for his form of government. Despite seeming to have nascent thoughts of more delicate subtlety and greater penetration, Shaftesbury is trapped within the polarised vocabulary and the crude

---

[18] *Some Reflections on the Characters of Augustus, Maecenas and Horace*, sig. B2v–B3r. Compare Thomas Bever, *The History of the Legal Polity of the Roman State*, p. 232. The habit of opposing two contrasting portraits of Augustus stems, I imagine, from the two funeral speeches recorded by Tacitus (*Annales*, I.9–10). Acknowledgements of his complexity are often nothing more than the prelude to criticism, as with Vertot (*Histoire des Révolutions*, III.384).

[19] Sigs. C3r, D2r and D3r.

responses of simple praise and blame hitherto associated with Augustus. It is in *The Decline and Fall* that we find that more nuanced portrait, of the lack of which Shaftesbury was aware, but which he was impotent to create.

Over the course of his life, Gibbon's attitude to Augustus changed markedly. In 1761, details gleaned from Suetonius are indignantly expressed with Tacitean brevity:

Tyran sanguinaire, soupçonné de lâcheté, le plus grand des crimes dans un chef de parti, il parvient au trône, et fait oublier aux républicains qu'ils eussent jamais été libres.[20]

But Howard Weinbrot is wrong to suggest that this is Gibbon's final and definitive judgement on Augustus.[21] Compare this much more reserved and meditative comment – apparently the fruit of political indifference – in a letter of 1792 to Lady Elizabeth Foster: 'I remember it has been observed of Augustus and Cromwell, that they should never have been born, or never have died.'[22] The first volume of *The Decline and Fall* (1776) falls exactly midway between these two opposed positions.

There are grounds, then, for expecting more than the strident simplicities of the *Essai* when we turn to *The Decline and Fall*; and these grounds are enlarged if we look at topics naturally germane to Gibbon's estimation of Augustus. One such topic is republicanism. Not only republicans disliked Augustus, as Chesterfield shows; and we should remember that 'republican' could be used as a term of abuse in the middle decades of the eighteenth century.[23] Nevertheless, if one's dislike of Augustus were founded on his subtle despotism, that would seem to imply at least some sympathy with republican government, even were one's deepest loyalties to a mixed constitution, since both republics and mixed governments are based on the belief (which is

[20] *Essai sur l'Étude de la Littérature* (in *Miscellaneous Works*, IV.89–90). In view of Gibbon's later opinion that this work is blemished by stylistic self-consciousness (see the *Memoirs*, pp. 103–4), it is interesting to compare a parallel passage taken from the unpublished 'Sur la Succession de l'Empire Romain' of 1758: 'On connoît la politique d'Auguste. On sait avec combien d'art il présentoit toujours aux Romains l'esclavage sous l'image de la liberté' (*Miscellaneous Works*, III.171). The overheatedness of the language of the *Essai* is plain.

[21] 'Comparable remarks appear in several other essays by Gibbon and, as we shall see, culminate in the third chapter of *The Decline and Fall*' (*Augustus Caesar in 'Augustan' England*, p. 66).

[22] *Letters*, III.286. I have been unable to trace the original of this observation. A version of it concludes Blackwell's *Memoirs of the Court of Augustus*, but as a quotation: 'That memorable Saying which contains a very just Judgment of the whole Life of this Prince, – "He did so much Hurt to the *Roman* Republic, and to Mankind, that he ought never to have been born; and so much Good, that he ought never to have died"' (III.573). Mably, too, inherits it as a traditional opinion: 'It was said of a prince, who should never have been born, that he ought never to have died' (*Observations on the Romans*, p. 86). The comparison between Augustus and Cromwell was a commonplace: see Edward Greene, 'Essay on Virgil's Aeneid', *Critical Essays*, p. 228, and Waller's 'A Panegyric to My Lord Protector'.

[23] See, for instance, Fielding's election pamphlet of 1747, *A Dialogue Between a Gentleman from London, Agent for two Court Candidates, and an Honest Alderman of the Country Party*, in which it is said that 'republicans' secure the ends of Jacobites.

anathema to despotisms) that political health is produced by the conflict of competing interests.[24]

Gibbon's opinions about republics change in just the way the shift in his estimation of Augustus from outright blame to a more reflective reserve suggests might be the case: that is to say, he is a vociferous republican in his youth (when his aversion for Augustus is at its height) and a Laodicean in middle age. His comments on the Swiss cantons reveal the change most clearly. The early 'Lettre sur le Gouvernement de Berne' is an ultra-republican attack on the disguised oppression of that city's constitution, recently praised by Montesquieu, about which Gibbon taunts his imagined correspondent: 'Arretez, Monsieur; Je vous ai parlé en homme libre et vous me repondez dans la langage de la Servitude.'[25] When he returns to Lausanne in 1763, he criticises its government in terms which recall his attack on Augustus in the *Essai* of 1761:

D'ailleurs je voyois Lausanne avec les yeux encore novices d'un jeune homme qui lui devoit la partie raisonnable de son existence et qui jugeoit sans objets de comparaison. Aujourd hui j'y vois une ville mal-batie au milieu d'un pays delicieux qui jouit de la paix et du repos, et qui les prend pour la liberté.[26]

But the mature Gibbon composing his *Memoirs* in the 1790s dismisses his youthful ardour with a shrug and a sentence that might have dropped from the pen of Burke: 'While the Aristocracy of Bern protects the happiness, it is superfluous to enquire whether it be founded in the rights, of man.'[27] Political turbulence, it seems, may not be an infallible sign of political health; and in the upheavals of a republic the common felicity which Gibbon saw as the true end of government may be destroyed.

Where does *The Decline and Fall* come in this range of opinion? Gibbon's comment on the transferral of the consular elections from the people to the senate reveals his position in 1776:

The assemblies of the people were for ever abolished, and the emperors were delivered from a dangerous multitude, who, without restoring liberty, might have disturbed, and perhaps endangered, the established government.[28]

---

[24] This is a commonplace of Machiavellian thought. Gibbon alludes to it when describing how the competing interests of the consuls and the tribunes strengthened the republic: 'Their mutual conflicts contributed, for the most part, to strengthen rather than to destroy the balance of the constitution' (*The Decline and Fall*, I.67: I.80). Pope had versified the doctrine earlier in the century: 'jarring int'rests of themselves create / Th' according music of a well-mix'd State' (*Essay on Man*, III.293–4: *Works*, III.66).

[25] *Miscellanea Gibboniana*, p. 130; compare Montesquieu's *Considérations* (*Œuvres*, III.415–16). Compare Lyttelton: 'and to the eye of sober reason the poorest Swiss canton is a much nobler state than the kingdom of France, if it has more liberty, better morals, a more settled tranquillity, more moderation in prosperity, and more firmness in danger' (*Works*, p. 349). Thomson had praised Swiss constitutions in *Liberty*, IV.322–43.

[26] *Le Journal de Gibbon à Lausanne*, p. 263.

[27] *Memoirs*, p. 185.

[28] *The Decline and Fall*, I.68: I.81–2.

The care which lies behind this remark (although Gibbon would have liked to see liberty restored, he was unwilling that even the principate should be overthrown for anything less than liberty), and the fine discriminations on which it rests (between freedom and licence, between the forms of liberty and its substance), show not only Gibbon's definite, if limited, satisfaction with the principate – an important point to which I shall return – but also that he is close to Pope's conviction:

> For Forms of Government let fools contest;
> Whate'er is best administer'd is best . . .[29]

By the time Gibbon writes *The Decline and Fall*, the zeal for constitutional niceties he had betrayed in the 1750s and 60s has subsided. It would be strange were he to vilify Augustus out of republican fervour.[30]

What was the cause of this marked subsidence in the vivacity of Gibbon's political sentiments? One can only speculate. But this description of those who, in a mixed government, can check the power of a monarch is suggestive:

A martial nobility and stubborn commons, possessed of arms, tenacious of property, and collected into constitutional assemblies, form the only balance capable of preserving a free constitution against enterprises of an aspiring prince.[31]

If it is necessary to possess property and to bear arms in order to act a vigorous part in a free constitution, then Gibbon's experiences in respect of both of these qualifications were decidedly unhappy.[32] The sorry tale of mortgages and enforced sales caused by his father's dissipation of the family wealth can be traced in his correspondence.[33] His military experience, in which (together with his time in the House of Commons) republican ideals might have touched his life most nearly, and the periods of which coincide exactly with the curdling of Gibbon's youthful republican enthusiasm,

---

[29] *Essay on Man*, III.303–4: *Works*, III.67.

[30] It is appropriate to review Gibbon's attitude to monarchy here. Throughout the eighteenth century there were those who attacked the institution on grounds of its irrationality (see Walter Moyle, 'An Essay upon the Roman Government', *Works*, I.57; Mably, *Observations on the Romans*, p. 7; and Paine, *Common Sense* (1776) in *The Writings of Thomas Paine*, I.73). Gibbon quarrelled with Mably over the matter when in Paris in 1777 and 'prit généreusement la defense du gouvernement monarchique' (*Memoirs*, pp. 158 and 169–70; compare p. 5). His temperate approval of monarchy on the grounds of its beneficial consequences of political security and mild administration – solid advantages which accrue despite the superficial foolishness of the property of a nation being transmitted 'like a drove of oxen' – is best seen in *The Decline and Fall*, I.171–2: I.204–5. The classic statement of this defence of hereditary monarchy is made in Bolingbroke's *The Idea of a Patriot King* (composed 1738, published 1749) (*Works*, II.380); compare also Swift, *The Sentiments of a Church-of-England Man* (1708) (*Prose Works*, II.19).

[31] *The Decline and Fall*, I.60: I.72. First edition: '. . . the only barrier which can perpetually resist the perpetual enterprises of an aspiring prince'.

[32] The importance to a republic of a citizen militia made up of property-owning freemen is another doctrine drawn from Machiavelli (Pocock, *The Machiavellian Moment*, pp. 289–95).

[33] For an account of Gibbon's financial affairs, see *Letters*, I.402–7; also *Memoirs*, pp. 152–4.

deserves more particular comment.[34] Gibbon presents the experience in terms of defeated expectation and chastised ideals:

A young mind, unless it be of a cold and languid temper, is dazzled even by the play of arms; and in the first sallies of my enthusiasm I had seriously wished and tryed to embrace the regular profession of a soldier. This military feaver was cooled by the enjoyment of our mimic Bellona, who gradually unveiled her naked deformity. How often did I sigh for my true situation of a private gentleman and a man of letter[s]: how often did I repeat the complaint of Cicero . . .[35]

Even at the distance of some thirty years he dwells at length on the discomforts and inconveniences of militia life; and the benefit which, with the advantage of hindsight, he feels accrued as a result of his service – 'my principal obligation to the militia was the making me an Englishman and a soldier' – bears but a distant relation to the spontaneous patriotism which motivates and rewards a republican militia.[36] Indeed, Gibbon records the use of republican examples by the advocates of a militia with the distant amusement of one too learned and too aware of the reality of historical change to be convinced by these comically inapposite arguments:

The zeal of our patriots, both in, and out of, Parliament (I cannot add both in, and out of, office) complained that the sword had been stolen from the hands of the people. They appealed to the victorious example of the Greeks and Romans among whom every citizen was a soldier; and they applauded the happiness and independence of Switzerland which, in the midst of the great monarchies of Europe is sufficiently defended by a constitutional and effective militia. But their enthusiasm overlooked the modern changes in the art of war, and the insuperable difference of government and manners.[37]

'The insuperable difference of government and manners' is a phrase which should admonish those who suggest that in *The Decline and Fall* Gibbon wishes to draw tight connexions between the decay of both the Roman and British

---

[34] Gibbon took up his commission of Captain in the South battalion of the Hampshire militia on 12 June 1759 (*Memoirs*, p. 111), was demobilised on 23 December 1762 (*Memoirs*, p. 115), immediately went on a tour of Europe (reaching Paris on 28 January 1763 and returning to Buriton on 25 June 1765: *Memoirs*, pp. 124 and 137), and on his return was obliged to attend 'the monthly meeting and exercise of the militia at Southampton' every spring, rising by the indolence of his superiors from Captain to Lieutenant Colonel-Commandant (*Memoirs*, p. 137).

[35] *Memoirs*, pp. 115–16.

[36] *Memoirs*, p.117. For Gibbon's attitude to the militia, see also *Gibbon's Journal to January 28th, 1763, passim*. Richard Sher has recently drawn attention to the enthusiasm amongst the Scottish literati (of whom Robertson was one) for a Scots militia, and to their ' "civic humanist" conviction that a militia would be likely to strengthen public virtue, guard liberty, and prevent the growth of "effeminacy", selfishness, excessive luxury, and similar vices likely to afflict a modern, commercial society' (*Church and University in the Scottish Enlightenment*, p. 240). Gibbon's dry comments on the effects of the militia may be read as an implicit rejection of the shallow historical thinking which underpins such convictions; he quotes Dryden's mockery of militias with clear endorsement (*Cymon and Iphigenia*, ll. 399–408: *Memoirs*, p. 108).

[37] *Memoirs*, p. 108.

empires.³⁸ But it also suggests that Gibbon's historical learning weakened the political convictions which his remaining a mute MP indicates quickly became less than intoxicating.³⁹ A reader of *The Decline and Fall* well versed in the circumstances of Gibbon's life and conversant with his personal writings, will expect neither downright indignation nor simple praise in the pages dealing with Augustus. He will not be unprepared for the portrait's *chiaroscuro*.

Gibbon's sleight of hand in disguising meaning and blurring tone is in play from the first:

The seven first centuries were filled with a rapid succession of triumphs; but it was reserved for Augustus, to relinquish the ambitious design of subduing the whole earth, and to introduce a spirit of moderation into the public councils.⁴⁰

To couple 'relinquish' with 'reserved' seems a winsome stroke of irony, which puts Augustus unsteadily at the head of the victorious republican tradition. But the final limb of the sentence strongly qualifies that irony. We have no reason to think Gibbon considered moderation in politics anything but praiseworthy. However, the irony is merely qualified, not dismissed. Gibbon indicates a favourable and a critical view of Augustus' political conduct, but does not arbitrate between them. This reserve is sustained in what follows:

Inclined to peace by his temper and situation, it was easy for him to discover, that Rome, in her present exalted situation, had much less to hope than to fear from the chance of arms; and that, in the prosecution of remote wars, the undertaking became

---

³⁸ See J. W. Johnson, *The Formation of English Neo-Classical Thought*, pp. 238–9; Lionel Gossman, *The Empire Unpossess'd*, p. 32; and H. T. Dickinson, who gives the doctrine in its baldest and least convincing form: 'By using the example of Rome, Edward Gibbon, in his *Decline and Fall of the Roman Empire* (6 vols, 1776–88), also deliberately sought to instruct his contemporaries on the dangers of arbitrary power and corruption' (*Politics and Literature in the Eighteenth Century*, p. xiv). Rome is a reality for Gibbon, not an example, and he draws connexions between Roman and British decline only playfully, in letters. Elsewhere his conviction of the absolute reality of historical difference – a conviction which became more profound and more pregnant with the years – prevents such a facile use of history. Scepticism about applying history in this crude way was current in Gibbon's time (e.g. Chesterfield, *Letters*, III.236). It is important to gauge accurately the extent and nature of the identification an educated Englishman of the eighteenth century would feel for ancient culture. Gibbon quotes Cicero, says that from him he imbibed the public and private sense of a man, and joins 'the Roman club' (*Memoirs*, pp. 75 and 139); Gray, in a letter to Richard West while on the Grand Tour, pretends (for a while) to be an ancient Roman invited to dine in Pompey's villa (*Poems and Memoirs*, p. 89). But it is surely impossible to ignore that what underlies the playful freedom of these antique moments is a sense of being separated from the classical past, which can be approached only intermittently and through the imagination.

³⁹ Gibbon's abstention from speaking in the House (*Memoirs*, p. 156) is extraordinary given not only his literary accomplishments, but also his determination to exploit his Parliamentary position for financial advantage (*Letters*, II.56; see also II.63). Chesterfield is explicit that this can be done only through cutting a figure as an orator (*Letters*, III.43 and 124). The political importance of oratory was acknowledged by theorists as well as by practitioners: see Blackwell, *An Enquiry into the Life and Writings of Homer*, p. 45 and Blair, *Lectures on Rhetoric and Belles Lettres*, I.136.

⁴⁰ *The Decline and Fall*, I.2: I.2.

every day more difficult, the event more doubtful, and the possession more precarious, and less beneficial. The experience of Augustus added weight to these salutary reflections, and effectually convinced him, that, by the prudent vigour of his counsels, it would be easy to secure every concession, which the safety or the dignity of Rome might require from the most formidable barbarians. Instead of exposing his person and his legions to the arrows of the Parthians, he obtained, by an honourable treaty, the restitution of the standards and prisoners which had been taken in the defeat of Crassus.[41]

Gibbon is unmatched as an ironist because he so rarely surrenders his intelligence to the mode, thereby reducing irony to a gloat. There is a firm control of tone in this passage, and a fine sense of how to make a telling impact by a change of direction or the unveiling of a new perspective. 'It was easy for him to discover' seems like litotes; the knowing reader takes this as a polished circumlocution for 'it suited Augustus to be peaceful'. But this ironic reading is shaken by the adducing of 'experience' to endorse the policy we had dismissed as mere selfishness: and the conclusion of the paragraph on the word 'Crassus' is a sombre reminder of the vicissitudes of military adventuring. Irony is once more muted in a *diminuendo* which unveils the difficult complexity of Augustus' character and the consequential problems he poses for the deliberating historian.

Glancing to the next page, the reader again finds that prolonged attention does not release a single, clarified meaning from Gibbon's prose, but generates rival possibilities:

Happily for the repose of mankind, the moderate system recommended by the wisdom of Augustus, was adopted by the fears and vices of his immediate successors.[42]

There could be blame in 'the repose of mankind' (a genteelly polished version of the charge that Augustus let foreign enemies thrive, and his subjects become torpid, in the interests of his personal security). But we also know that Gibbon, once his republican ardour had waned, was sane enough always to give a properly high value to common contentment.[43] Again, 'the wisdom of Augustus' seems unambiguously favourable; although it may appear to be wisdom only because followed by the 'fears and vices' of his immediate successors.

These examples raise, but leave unsettled, the question of whether Augustus suspended the expansion of the empire in order to secure his personal safety, or because he saw that it was in the public interest to do so. This

---

[41] *The Decline and Fall*, I.2: I.2. First edition: '. . . Parthians, he satisfied himself with the restitution of the standards and prisoners which were taken . . .'.

[42] *The Decline and Fall*, I.3: I.3.

[43] Note his praise of the Antonines ('Their united reigns are possibly the only period of history in which the happiness of a great people was the sole object of government'; *The Decline and Fall*, I.78: I.94) and his disgust at political casuistry ('How far, that, or any other, consideration, may operate, to dissolve the natural obligations of humanity and justice, is a doctrine, of which I still desire to remain ignorant'; *The Decline and Fall*, II.622).

stereoscopic blending of a selfish, and a noble, image of the emperor in the equivocal wording of single sentences is matched by a studied indecision in Gibbon's account of Augustus' constitutional reforms. We saw that earlier writers could be divided into those who viewed the establishment of the principate as a guileful cheat practised on ardent republicans (for example, Montesquieu, and Gibbon himself when writing under Montesquieu's influence in the *Essai sur l'Étude de la Littérature*) and those who sympathised with it as a noble mind's expedient for governing a hopelessly degenerate people (Saint-Evremond and Thomas Bever). *The Decline and Fall* is sufficiently capacious to include both possibilities:

His [Augustus'] command, indeed, was confined to those citizens who were engaged in the service by the military oath; but such was the propensity of the Romans to servitude, that the oath was voluntarily taken by the magistrates, the senators, and the equestrian order, till the homage of flattery was insensibly converted into an annual and solemn protestation of fidelity.

Augustus was sensible that mankind is governed by names; nor was he deceived in his expectation, that the senate and the people would submit to slavery, provided they were respectfully assured, that they still enjoyed their ancient freedom.[44]

To submit to slavery is different from having a propensity to servitude; and the difference is significant, for on it depends whether Augustus is a manipulating charlatan or a high-minded patriot too firm to flinch from extreme measures. This equivocation, between noble and base alternatives, informs Gibbon's reticence and gives point to his suave refusal to be outspoken. Even passages which seem to lean towards a decided opinion about Augustus lose that inclination when considered in context. This may appear hostile:

The only accession which the Roman empire received, during the first century of the Christian Aera, was the province of Britain. In this single instance the successors of Caesar and Augustus were persuaded to follow the example of the former, rather than the precept of the latter.[45]

A man as well versed in the classics as Gibbon could not, one imagines, bring together precept and example without recalling the ancients' preference for the latter. Consequently one might argue that there was encoded blame in this passage: conquest is the better way, and Augustus a self-seeking coward.[46]

---

[44] *The Decline and Fall*, I.65–6: I.78 (first edition: '. . . service, by . . .') and I.73: I.87 (first edition: '. . . names, nor . . .').

[45] *The Decline and Fall*, I.3: I.4.

[46] Compare Seneca's 'longum iter est per praecepta, breve et efficax per exempla' (*Epistulae Morales*, VI.5), and Quintilian's 'quantum enim Graeci praeceptis valent, tantum Romani, quod est maius, exemplis' (*Institutio Oratoria*, XII.ii.30). Such sentences are not rare in eighteenth-century English literature: Fielding is particularly fond of them; see the dedication to *Don Quixote in England* (1734) and (most famously) the opening sentence of *Joseph Andrews* (1742). In his journal, we find Gibbon seeking 'to unite the exemple [sic] and the precept' (*Gibbon's Journal to January 28th, 1763*, p. 81), and it may be that in his own mind there was no automatic preference for example over precept (or vice versa).

But when Gibbon points out soon afterwards how easily historians can be deceived about the motivation of princes, the harsh judgement on Augustus entailed by the elevation of example over precept seems invidious:

Censure, which arraigns the public actions and the private motives of princes, has ascribed to envy, a conduct, which might be attributed to the prudence and moderation of Adrian.[47]

Gibbon records Diocletian's regret that a prince's perceptions are at the mercy of his counsellors: extending the insight he appreciates that the very circumstance of rule which causes Diocletian's complaint – that the prince is the object of envy and resentment – also shades a ruler from historical inquiry.[48] Men are more likely to lie about monarchs than about their subjects, just as it is more profitable to deceive a prince than a pauper. The complexity and qualification of Gibbon's portrait of Augustus thus has its prudence.

It is, however, not only prudent. It connects, as we shall see, with Gibbon's deepest aspirations in the first volume of *The Decline and Fall*; and it does so by transcending the dichotomy of a wily or a noble Augustus. This multifaceted man assumes and discards roles with a facility which defies the pat conclusions of later commentators. Gibbon records his transformations, and the tight intertwinings of personal ambition and public spirit they involve, with a scrupulousness a casual reader might mistake for ironic blame. Blair was shortly to deplore the fact that 'all languages are liable to ambiguities'; Gibbon's command of language is visible in his transformation of this liability into a strength.[49] Moreover, his patient attentiveness, his constant awareness that Augustus' successive roles are masks which conceal the man they seem to display ('A cool head, an unfeeling heart, and a cowardly disposition, prompted him, at the age of nineteen, to assume the mask of hypocrisy, which he never afterwards laid aside'), is very different from the clear-mindedness of the earlier writers we considered.[50] Gibbon preserves all the layers in Augustus' laminated character:

Every barrier of the Roman constitution had been levelled by the vast ambition of the dictator; every fence had been extirpated by the cruel hand of the Triumvir. After the victory of Actium, the fate of the Roman world depended on the will of Octavianus,

---

[47] *The Decline and Fall*, I.7: I.9.
[48] *The Decline and Fall*, I.394–5: I.469.
[49] *Lectures on Rhetoric and Belles Lettres*, I.215.
[50] *The Decline and Fall*, I.72: I.86. Gibbon takes issue with Julian the Apostate for imagining that the various overt changes in Augustus' character are signs of real changes in personality (*The Decline and Fall*, I.xii n. 26: I.86 n. 26). In 1776 Gibbon seems still to credit unity of character, which would naturally dismiss such outward volatility as a seeming; hence his frequent use of the word 'artful', implying a steady, shaping intention operating through dissimulation; and hence, too, a comment such as this about Commodus – 'A fatal incident decided his fluctuating character' (*The Decline and Fall*, I.88: I.106).

surnamed Caesar, by his uncle's adoption, and afterwards Augustus, by the flattery of the senate.

. . . according to the various dictates of his interest, he was at first the enemy, and at last the father, of the Roman world.[51]

Gibbon is pitched into the centre of this spectrum, since his subject demands that he concentrate on its indeterminate, central refractions:

It is not easy to determine whether, on this occasion, he acted as the common father of the Roman world, or as the oppressor of liberty . . .[52]

The uncertainty of which Gibbon speaks finds expression in the vagueness of the sentence. Does 'on this occasion' have a distinguishing role, separating this incident out from others in which it is easy to say whether or not Augustus was a tyrant? Or is it less stressed, serving only to locate this particular example of a general indeterminacy? Gibbon's concern in these slight obliquities, these small occlusions of meaning, is to keep the crux of Augustus' personality, the coming together within him of self-interest and genuine, perceptive statesmanship, subtly and variously before us as the constant source of a recurrent hindrance to our reading. For Gibbon's portrait suggests that it is Augustus' and the Roman world's peculiar good fortune that the emperor's temperament and circumstances led him to a true conception of the state of the empire and of the policy its safety required.[53]

It is in this context that Gibbon's fondness for syllepsis becomes something deeper than a mannerism convenient for imparting the final polish to a prose style more ornamental than expressive. Considering Augustus, Gibbon's concentration warms the figure into functional life:

The conqueror [Augustus] was at the head of forty-four veteran legions, conscious of their own strength, and of the weakness of the constitution, habituated, during twenty years civil war, to every act of blood and violence, and passionately devoted to the house of Caesar, from whence alone they had received, and expected, the most lavish rewards.[54]

The first syllepsis is unexceptional: 'conscious of their own strength, and of the weakness of the constitution'; but the second, which concludes the quotation, gives the attentive reader pause. The matter hinges on whether 'received' and 'expected' share 'from whence alone' or merely 'from whence'. If 'alone' is not included, the sentence grumbles at the rapacity of

[51] *The Decline and Fall*, I.60: I.72 and I.72: I.86. This interest in the successive phases of Augustus' character reappears in Volume II: 'In the life of Augustus, we behold the tyrant of the republic, converted, almost by imperceptible degrees, into the father of his country and of human kind' (*The Decline and Fall*, II.76–7).

[52] *The Decline and Fall*, I.164: I.197.

[53] More recently, Sir Ronald Syme has also found this accommodation between personal and public in Augustus: 'He had achieved the height of all mortal ambition and in his ambition he had saved and regenerated the Roman People' (*The Roman Revolution*, p. 524).

[54] *The Decline and Fall*, I.60–1: I.72–3. First edition: '. . . the house of Caesar; from whence alone . . .'.

the soldiery: 'whence alone they had received, and whence they expected . . .'. But if we do include 'alone', the sentence stirs with pertinence and becomes an insight into how the Augustan principate differed from its successors: 'whence alone they had received, and whence alone they expected . . .'. The legions felt as dependent on Augustus as Augustus on the legions. Later, they realised that any emperor would reward them; but for the moment it seemed that their interests were served by the Caesarian house alone:

> The military oath, and the fidelity of the troops, had been consecrated by the habits of an hundred years, to the name and family of the Caesars . . .[55]

Consequently Gibbon sees the Augustan principate occupying an area of balance between the interests of the army and civil interests arising out of the various impulses and loyalties of Augustus' character. In this poised space the unthinkable majesty of Roman peace could be established, and prolong its beneficial effects into the future: 'During a long period of two hundred and twenty years, from the establishment of this artful system [the Augustan constitution] to the death of Commodus, the dangers inherent to a military government were, in a great measure, suspended.'[56]

This recognition of the benign nature of Augustus' constitutional innovations (which nevertheless does not ignore the perils they court – Augustus and his successors contrive merely to suspend the dangers that threaten them) is reinforced as we read on through Volume I of *The Decline and Fall*. Gibbon's discussions of later emperors sometimes recall the earlier account of Augustus and reveal that, for all his reservations, he nevertheless appreciates that the first emperor set a standard for the prudent administration of empire by which those who follow him may be measured.[57] Thus Marcus Antoninus loosens the joint of public and personal interest which the political master-craftsman had fashioned:

> His excessive indulgence to his brother, his wife, and his son, exceeded the bounds of private virtue, and became a public injury, by the example and consequences of their vices.[58]

With the reign of Severus, 'the nice frame of civil policy instituted by Augustus' is dismantled.[59] But it is Diocletian who most thoroughly clarifies Augustus' stature as an imperial paradigm. Gibbon artfully suggests the comparison between the two emperors before openly taking it up himself. We learn that Diocletian possessed 'the great art of submitting his own passions,

---

[55] *The Decline and Fall*, I.75: I.90. Compare Blackwell: 'His [Augustus'] Person and Family engrossed the Thoughts and Tongues of all the Soldiery' (*Memoirs of the Court of Augustus*, III.402).

[56] *The Decline and Fall*, I.74: I.89.

[57] I thus disagree with François Furet's view that 'the emperors of the second century were his *exempla*'(*Edward Gibbon and the Decline and Fall of the Roman Empire*, p. 161).

[58] *The Decline and Fall*, I.85: I.102. First edition: '. . . passed the bounds of private virtue . . .'.

[59] *The Decline and Fall*, I.127–8: I.153.

as well as those of others, to the interest of his ambition, and of colouring his
ambition with the most specious pretences of justice and public utility': this
is far from the spontaneous coincidence of public and private that
distinguishes Augustus, but is at first sight sufficiently similar to remind us
of it.[60] It may be true that 'Like Augustus, Diocletian may be considered as
the founder of a new empire', a 'crafty prince' who 'framed a new system of
Imperial government', and adhered to the 'moderate policy of Augustus and
the Antonines': but the later prince is a mere simulacrum of his
predecessor.[61] Gibbon dwarfs Diocletian in the vocabulary that had been
tailored to Augustus:

The dislike expressed by Diocletian towards Rome and Roman freedom, was not the
effect of momentary caprice, but the result of the most artful policy.[62]

Eventually the two reigns are brought into sharp connexion, and Diocletian's
inferiority is unmistakable:

Like the modesty affected by Augustus, the state maintained by Diocletian was a
theatrical representation; but it must be confessed, that of the two comedies, the former
was of a much more liberal and manly character than the latter. It was the aim of the one
to disguise, and the object of the other to display, the unbounded power which the
emperors possessed over the Roman world.[63]

'Liberal and manly': it is clear that Gibbon is as far from pure disparagement
of the princeps as he is from pure adulation. And in his recognition of the
merits of Augustus and of the form of government he instituted, we can see
his measured dissociation from those who pilloried the first emperor as the
author of the empire's decline.

We are now in a position to suggest how the intricacies of Gibbon's account
of Augustus contribute to his strategy in Volume I of *The Decline and Fall*. The
portrait of Augustus is a fine example of the method of this first volume. The
'facts' of the past are presented to us in language rich in coherent,

---

[60] *The Decline and Fall*, I.357: I.424.
[61] *The Decline and Fall*, I.357: I.424; I.385: I.458. First edition: '. . . imperial government . . .';
I.379: I.451.
[62] *The Decline and Fall*, I.385: I.458. Compare the phrases used of Augustus: 'the crafty tyrant'
(*The Decline and Fall*, I.62: I.75), 'that subtle tyrant' (*The Decline and Fall*, I.72: I.86. First edition: '. . . subtile . . .').
[63] *The Decline and Fall*, I.389: I.463. Gibbon frequently indicates the mimicry of power as a
symptom of decline (*The Decline and Fall*, I.199: I.236; III.496: V.485: VI.36: VI.156). Imagery drawn from the theatre (e.g., *The Decline and Fall*, II.491) reinforces the theme. Lionel
Gossman, in *The Empire Unpossess'd*, makes much of this connexion between mimicry and
decline, and draws from it the conclusion that for Gibbon all power is irremediably flawed.
In so doing, he fails to make the necessary distinction between those administrations whose
only power is mimicry, and those different governments (of which Augustus' is one) that use
theatre to advance their policy; see the comparison between Augustus and Charles IV (*The
Decline and Fall*, V.167–9). One might also note that Gibbon praises 'the admirable policy of
the senate' (*The Decline and Fall*, III.195 n. 10) for using theatre as an instrument of government at the gravest crisis of the second Punic war.

embedded comment; and the cumulative effect of this comment is to predispose us in favour of a particular interpretation of Roman decline. In this way, the significance Gibbon finds in Augustan poise is deftly woven into the volume's overall argument. By positioning himself to one side of the republican, Tacitean tradition of blame for Augustus, and yet by moulding his prose so that this interpretation of the emperor's character and achievement is not baldly repudiated, but assimilated into what seems a more profound and plausible reading of the past, Gibbon questions the traditional explanation of Roman decline which located the cause of the empire's decay in the loss of civic virtue attendant on the establishment of the principate.[64] Gibbon admits that a widespread loss of civic virtue played a part in the decline of the empire, but he does not attribute that loss to the effects of the change of government instituted by Augustus. Discussing the gradual increase of success enjoyed by the barbarian armies against the imperial troops, he alights briefly and inexplicitly on what he takes to be the root cause of Roman effeteness:

When we recollect the complete armour of the Roman soldiers, their discipline, exercises, evolutions, fortified camps, and military engines, it appears a just matter of surprise how the naked and unassisted valour of the barbarians could dare to encounter in the field, the strength of the legions, and the various troops of the auxiliaries, which seconded their operations. The contest was too unequal, till the introduction of luxury had enervated the vigour, and a spirit of disobedience and sedition had relaxed the discipline, of the Roman armies.[65]

The 'introduction of luxury' is a reference to the originally Polybian notion of success inevitably entailing decline, recently restated by Montesquieu in his *Considérations* and popular amongst the opposition as a monitory historical parallel during the years of Walpole's ascendancy.[66] Yet the very political applicability of this explanation of Roman decline seemed to make its

---

[64] That the supersession of republican government by a despotism weakened the Roman people and brought about the eventual collapse of their empire was not a new argument in the eighteenth century; it can be traced back to *Paradise Regained* (IV.125-45). It had most recently been advanced by Robertson. In the 'View of the Progress of Society in Europe' which prefaces the *History of Charles V* (1769), he attributed the waning military vigour of the Romans to their no longer being 'freemen' (*The History of the Reign of the Emperor Charles V*, I.7): in his earlier sermon, *The Situation of the World at the Time of Christ's Appearance*, preached in 1755, he had maintained that the principate had poisoned private morality, and thus occasioned the fall of Rome (there was no copy of this work in Gibbon's library: Robertson, *Works*, I.cxvi).

[65] *The Decline and Fall*, I.237: I.283.

[66] Polybius, Book VI; *Œuvres*, III.414-16; Johnson, as one might expect, is an uncompromising spokesman for the inevitability of political decline: 'The Romans, like others, as soon as they grew rich, grew corrupt, and, in their corruption, sold the lives and freedoms of themselves, and of one another' (*Works*, VI.11) – there is no suggestion here that decline can be fended off by some nice constitutional tinkering. Isaac Kramnick suggests that those opposed to Walpole held that 'The decline of Rome, and of an unaware England, began with the extinguishing of ancient honor by luxury, ambition, and a careless and profligate reign', and that these ideas, though never extinct in the eighteenth century, were powerfully revived at the time of publication of *The Decline and Fall* (*Bolingbroke and his Circle*, pp. 239 and 169).

supporters casual about vindicating it historically – it is as if it were too obvious to require explanation.[67] Gibbon gives luxury a place in the decay of the Romans' military force; it 'enervated the vigour' of the soldiery. But its influence is closely circumscribed because Gibbon has already suggested that the effects of luxury have been exaggerated. One might expect the historian of Roman decline to seize on oriental trade as a notable and early symptom of decay:

The annual loss is computed, by a writer of an inquisitive but censorious temper, at upwards of eight hundred thousand pounds sterling. Such was the style of discontent, brooding over the dark prospect of approaching poverty.

But Gibbon has a larger view:

And yet, if we compare the proportion between gold and silver, as it stood in the time of Pliny, and as it was fixed in the reign of Constantine, we shall discover within that period a very considerable increase. There is not the least reason to suppose that gold was become more scarce; it is therefore evident that silver was grown more common . . . that the produce of the mines abundantly supplied the demands of commerce.[68]

Trade in silk and spices, the commerce of luxury, was thus no intolerable financial burden on the empire; Gibbon has brought the slack explanation of politicians to the bar of history and found it wanting.[69] When even the simple magnitude of the phenomenon has been so casually assumed, instead of investigated, what credibility should we extend to large claims made for the still less definable moral effects supposed to flow from it? However, the second factor Gibbon discusses, the 'spirit of disobedience and sedition', seems more enigmatic, and too widespread or general a phenomenon to be laid at

---

[67] This is true of Kennett (*Romae Antiquae Notitia*, pp. xvi and 62) and Warburton (*The Divine Legation of Moses Demonstrated*, Book I, Sect. 6). The vagueness which seems to overtake most eighteenth-century historians when discussing Roman decline arises from their inability to exert strict control over the figurative language in which they describe the phenomenon (see Robertson, *The Situation of the World at the Time of Christ's Appearance*, *Works*, I.civ and Thomas Bever, *The History of the Legal Polity of the Roman State*, p. 107). Those who assert that Rome fell because of a coincidence of concurrent causes elevate this vagueness to the status of an explanation (see particularly Thomas Blackwell, *Memoirs of the Court of Augustus*, I.194–5). Amongst opposition figures, only Lyttelton cites the idea of luxury with any precision, and gives thought to how it might fit in with the other factors instrumental in Rome's decline. Given his adversity to Walpole, it is not surprising to find that he gives luxury priority among the developments which seem to have promoted the collapse of the empire, but he does not do so unscrupulously (*Works*, pp. 5, 349–50 and 598–9). The depth to which these ideas soaked into society can be gauged by Thomas Turner's wringing his hands over 'that bane of private property LUXURY' (*The Diary of Thomas Turner 1754–1765*, p. 245).

[68] *The Decline and Fall*, I.56: I.67–8. Wotton had maintained that trade with the East was responsible for the Romans' taste for luxury (*The History of Rome from the Death of Antoninus Pius to the Death of Severus Alexander*, p. 8). Robertson implied that the financial effects of this craving crippled Rome ('A View of the Progress of Society in Europe', *Charles V*, I.7).

[69] For examples of such easy assumptions, see e.g. Swift's *Some Arguments against Enlarging the Powers of Bishops* (Dublin, 1723) (*Prose Works*, IX.48) or Hume's 'Of Refinement in the Arts'. Gibbon's scepticism about the harmful effects of luxury persists into the instalment of 1781, as J. G. A. Pocock has noticed (*Virtue, Commerce and History*, p. 148).

Augustus' door. Moreover, sedition and disobedience seem unlikely consequences of despotism. Thus the blame for Roman decline is shifted away from
the principate. On cool inspection, the effects of the prevalence of luxury, to
which Augustus *may* have contributed, have been exaggerated; and there seem
to have been other factors at work, too large for any individual to be indicted and
out of harmony with the supposed effects of absolute government, which changed the manners of the Romans. There are further sound reasons for this partial
exoneration of the emperor. Prompted by Tacitus' 'et laudatorum principum
usus ex aequo quamvis procul agentibus: saevi proximis ingruunt', Gibbon
depicts the creation of the principate as an administrative revolution whose
effects would inevitably be confined for the most part to Rome:

It had hitherto been the peculiar felicity of the Romans, and in the worst of times their
consolation, that the virtue of the emperors was active, and their vice indolent.
Augustus, Trajan, Hadrian, and Marcus, visited their extensive dominions in person,
and their progress was marked by acts of wisdom and beneficence. The tyranny of
Tiberius, Nero, and Domitian, who resided almost constantly at Rome, or in the
adjacent villas, was confined to the senatorial and equestrian orders.[70]

The question immediately arises: how large a role could a factor operating on
such a restricted stage assume in a process as vast as the sapping of an empire?
   The twists, turns and reverses of Gibbon's account of Augustus have as
their deepest purpose not to rescue the emperor from the polarised caricatures
of his admirers and detractors, but to indicate, through its careful and convincing rehabilitation of Augustus as a statesman of definite if not absolute integrity, that we should inquire for the cause of the slackening of the strenuous
Roman civic spirit in a phenomenon approximately coeval with the principate, but acting far more uniformly across the population of the empire.[71]
Gibbon's subtly revisionist account of Augustus' reign thus engages with
existing causal explanations of Roman decline, but not to endorse them. He
administers a check to both the constitutionalist explanation of Roman
decline, which located the original cause of the collapse of the empire in the
establishment of the principate, and the moral explanation, which attributed
Rome's decline to the corrupting influence of inordinate wealth. In their
place, the early chapters of *The Decline and Fall* hint at an explanation of
decline – what *does* Gibbon mean by 'a spirit of disobedience and sedition'?
– they do not enunciate and create a vacancy for the reader who, attuned
to modern, philosophic historiography, would have opened *The Decline and
Fall* in quest of causal enlightenment. Throughout the first volume Gibbon
quietly reminds us of this vacancy, this causal absence, without filling it; until
in the final two chapters he unmasks the villain in Rome's decline.

[70] *Historiae*, IV.74 (not IV.75, as Gibbon gives it in *The Decline and Fall*, I.xxi n. 33: I.166 n. 33). *The
Decline and Fall*, I.139: I.166. The same point had been made by Gibbon's friend Chastellux (*De
la Félicité Publique*, I.196) and by Blackwell (*Memoirs of the Court of Augustus*, III.560).
[71] A manuscript note in the margins of his own copy of *The Decline and Fall* indicates that Gibbon
dated Roman decline from the death of Augustus (*The English Essays of Edward Gibbon*, p. 338).

6

Tacitus

Those oft are stratagems which errors seem   Pope

From the first, it was realised that *The Decline and Fall* was in some respect 'Tacitean'. Mme Necker wrote to her old lover in September 1776 that

> . . . la nature, qui n'avoit d'abord refusé qu'un Tacite à Aurélien ou Zénobie, n'a pu se résoudre à laisser son ouvrage imparfait; si vous avez moins de précision que cet historien, en revanche vous avez cent fois plus d'idées, et de variétés dans les idées.[1]

There is something both amusing and touching in the would-be bluestocking's determination to show Gibbon that she can still converse with him on literary topics as an equal, as she had done in the 'societé du printemps' at Lausanne.[2] Certainly, the connexion with Tacitus seems well calculated to flatter Gibbon, and modern criticism has singled out his consanguinity with the author of the *Annales* and *Historiae* as a profound truth.[3] However, we saw in the portrait of Augustus that Gibbon is no bondman of the senatorial historian. Although he has a great respect for Tacitus, the substance of what he has to say in *The Decline and Fall* is different from while being thoroughly informed by the Tacitean perspective on Roman history.

This careful separation of *The Decline and Fall* from Tacitus, the gravitational pull of whose work Gibbon acknowledges but to which he does not succumb, is visible once more in Chapter IX, where he assesses the magnitude of the barbarian threat to the empire.[4] In his handling of Augustus, Gibbon had questioned the narrowly constitutional explanation of Roman decline (namely, that Rome fell because it abandoned republican government) and diminished the importance of the moral explanation, which found the seeds of decay in luxury. In Chapter IX, he trims another traditional explanation of the collapse of the empire – that it fell because of the external pressure

---

[1] *Miscellaneous Works*, II.177.
[2] *Memoirs*, pp. 129–30.
[3] See David Jordan, *Gibbon and his Roman Empire*, p. 182.
[4] It is here, where he is thrown into close contact with the *Germania*, that Gibbon most nearly touches the subject-matter of a Tacitean work. Gibbon gives no narrative account of the periods that lie behind the *Annales*, the *Historiae* and the *Agricola*. The theme of the *Dialogus de Oratoribus* – the relation between political health and literary creativity – is, of course, of perennial importance to Gibbon and to eighteenth-century English literature generally; see Michael Meehan, *Liberty and Poetics in Eighteenth Century England*, *passim*.

exerted by barbarians – thus further widening the causal vacancy he had opened up in the volume's early chapters.[5]

In *Paradise Lost* Milton had used the overrunning of the empire by the barbarians to figure the 'bad Angels' alighting on the 'firm brimstone' of Hell:

> A multitude, like which the populous North
> Pour'd never from her frozen loyns, to pass
> *Rhene* or the *Danaw*, when her barbarous Sons
> Came like a Deluge on the South, and spread
> Beneath *Gibraltar* to the *Lybian* sands.[6]

It is a simile which reveals how deeply Milton's subject troubles his categories of thought: the fallen angels are compared to the murderers of the classical culture to which at other times they are also approximated. But although the simile shows Milton's equivocal feelings about the classics, there seem to be no such doubts about the barbarians. They are imagined as a straightforwardly destructive 'deluge'. This idea of the empire being overrun by devastating inundations of barbarians recurs throughout the eighteenth century in the work of men as diverse as Temple, Steele, Swift, Boulainvilliers, Collins and Robertson.[7] The issue thickened, however, as the implications of the political taste for the Gothic worked their way into the historiography of the decline of Rome. Instead of wanton destroyers of art and culture, the primitive Germans were transformed into turbulent but freedom-loving peoples who easily overwhelmed the slavish inhabitants of the empire.[8] The rehabilitation of the barbarians was complete when, at the end of the eighteenth century, Milton's image of destructive inundation was used by

---

[5] J. G. A. Pocock has argued that in Chapter IX 'Gibbon is systematically if not avowedly destroying the myth of Gothic agrarian virtue' (*Virtue, Commerce and History*, p. 151). The argument that the influence of the barbarians in the dilapidation of the *city* of Rome had been exaggerated dates from at least the sixteenth century and Angeli da Barga's *Epistola* (Florence, 1589), a work which Gibbon had read and on which he commented (*Journal de Gibbon à Lausanne*, pp. 82–3). He in his turn is unconvinced by the conventional 'idée trop outrée des ravages de ces barbares' ('Nomina Gentesque Antiquae Italiae', *Miscellaneous Works*, IV.221). His scaling down of the role of the barbarians in the undoing of the empire seems to be an extension of this argument.

[6] *Paradise Lost*, I.351–5.

[7] Sir William Temple, 'Of Heroic Virtue', *Works*, III.351; Steele and Swift, *Tatler* no. 31, I.87; Boulainvilliers, *La Vie de Mahomed*, p. 2; Collins, 'Ode to Liberty', ll. 18ff.; Robertson, 'A View of the Progress of Society in Europe', *Charles V*, I.8ff.

[8] The political argument which saw in the Goths the originators of eighteenth-century liberty, and in particular of limited monarchy, was expressed most forcibly by Bolingbroke in *Remarks on the History of England* (serialised in the *Craftsman*, 1730–1) (*Works*, II.124: see also Joseph Sterling, *Poems*, p. 31 and Montesquieu's *Esprit des Loix*, where the English constitution is traced back to the German woods). It has received considerable attention from modern scholars; J. G. A. Pocock, *The Ancient Constitution and the Feudal Law*; S. J. Kliger, *The Goths in England*; Isaac Kramnick, 'Augustan politics and English historiography'; and Quentin Skinner, 'The principles and practice of opposition; the case of Bolingbroke versus Walpole'. For a sampling of the idiom in which the subject was discussed in the eighteenth century, see Thomson, *Liberty*, III.529–38; Blackwell, *Memoirs of the Court of Augustus*, II.371; Stuart, *A View of Society in Europe*, p. 23; Joseph Sterling, 'The Rhapsodist', *Poems*, p. 22.

Herder to express his conviction of the powerfully creative contribution to civilisation made by barbarian violence in its overthrowing of empire and establishment of nationhood:

As when mountain torrents, swelled to a flood in some lofty valley, at length burst down it's feeble dam and inundate the plains below, wave breaks on wave, stream follows stream, till all becomes one wide sea, which, slowly subsiding, leaves every where traces of devastation, obliterated in time by flourishing pastures animated with fertility; so followed the celebrated irruptions of the northern nations into the provinces of the roman empire, and such were their effects.[9]

But if one sees Roman imbecility as the counterpart to barbarous violence, and the barbarians as victors over only a degenerate race, is one not then obliged to moderate one's ideas about the awfulness of the barbarian onslaught? For to see a political exemplum in the Goths is to complicate one's ideas of the fall of Rome; it demands that one posit an internal weakness to match the external pressure. The ruinous consequences of a despotism cravenly endured by the luxurious Romans – the inverse of the boisterous liberty of the Goths – were most often chosen as that inner flaw. But upholders of this explanation of Roman decline seem never to allocate the respective shares of responsibility for the collapse of the empire between the internal flaw and the external pressure; and the result is that the vagueness which enwraps the causes of Rome's decay is increased. Gibbon avails himself of this vagueness in another subtle variation on the language in which the decline of the empire was discussed. He denies the terrific destructiveness imputed to the barbarians by Milton, thereby suggesting that the success of the barbarian invasions was attributable to the feebleness of the Romans; but by also doubting the, for him, mythical political soundness of the barbarians, and thus not seeing the confrontation between Goths and empire as a duel between different political principles, he implies that the root of the Roman weakness is not to be found in its form of government. In adopting this carefully chosen ground, he once again throws our attention on to the as yet anonymous fundamental cause of the empire's weakness.

The pressure of choice behind the language in which Gibbon discusses the barbarians is apparent if we compare a passage from *The Decline and Fall* dealing with the impact of the barbarians on the empire with two others (one from Rousseau and another from Hume) on the same subject and of approximately the same date. All three men are addressing the question of the decay, and then regrowth, of European culture, in the light of the Gothic invasions. Rousseau is the earliest of the three, and the most straightforward:

Nos Peintres & nos Sculpteurs se plaignent de ne plus trouver de modeles comparables à ceux de l'antique. Pourquoi cela? L'homme a-t-il dégénéré? L'espece a-t-elle une décrépitude physique, ainsi que l'individu? Au-contraire: les Barbares du nord, qui ont, pour ainsi dire, peuplé l'Europe d'une nouvelle race, étoient plus grands & plus

---

[9] *Outlines of a Philosophy of the History of Man*, p. 525.

forts que les Romains qu'ils ont vaincus & subjugués. Nous devrions donc être plus forts nous-mêmes qui, pour la plûpart, descendons de ces nouveaux venus; mais les premiers Romains vivoient en hommes, & trouvoient dans leurs continuels exercices la vigueur que la Nature leur avait refusée . . .[10]

'Vaincus et subjugués' calls to mind the military successes of the barbarians, but also suggests that in defeating Rome they did away with the worn-out race; indeed, the barbarians 'ont . . . peuplé l'Europe d'une *nouvelle* race'. Traces of the old Roman stock remain ('nous . . . pour la plûpart, descendons de ces nouveaux venus'), but are almost invisible beneath the vigorous, new, barbarian graft. Writing in 1761, Hume is less decided about the nature and extent of the barbarians' influence:

. . . Europe, as from a new epoch, rekindled her antient spirit, and shook off the base servitude to arbitrary will and authority, under which she had so long laboured. The free constitutions then established, however impaired by the encroachments of succeeding princes, still preserve an air of independence and legal administration, which distinguish the European nations; and if that part of the globe maintain sentiments of liberty, honour, equity, and valour, superior to the rest of mankind, it owes these advantages chiefly to the seeds implanted by those generous barbarians.[11]

Hume was convinced that, in the realm of letters and arts, the irruption of the barbarians was a catastrophe.[12] Nevertheless, he is prepared to concede, despite his steepening doubts about the existence of ancient constitutions, that the barbarians may have benefited mankind politically.[13] Notwithstanding his residual uncertainties ('however impaired', 'an air of' and 'if that part of the globe' all diminish the sentence's decisiveness), he still says that we owe our 'sentiments of liberty, honour, equity and valour' chiefly to the barbarians. However, although Hume's barbarians are 'generous', he does not make them generating. They are the agents of progress, in that they plant the seeds of future benefits, but none of their own barbarous nature is contained in those seeds. By keeping his metaphor vegetable and thus making the barbarians only the propagators of progress, Hume reveals his stubborn doubts as to how civilisation can arise out of barbarism. Gibbon concludes his second chapter with similar reservations:

This diminutive stature of mankind, if we pursue the metaphor, was daily sinking below the old standard, and the Roman world was indeed peopled by a race of pygmies; when the fierce giants of the north broke in, and mended the puny breed. They restored a manly spirit of freedom; and after the revolution of ten centuries, freedom became the happy parent of taste and science.[14]

[10] *Lettre à d'Alembert*, pp. 191–2.

[11] *History*, I.217–18.

[12] Compare 'The irruption of the barbarous nations, which soon followed, overwhelmed all human knowledge, which was already far in its decline; and men sunk every age deeper into ignorance, stupidity, and superstition; till the light of antient science and history, had very nearly suffered a total extinction in all the European nations' (*History of England*, III.318).

[13] See above, p. 26 n. 24.

[14] *The Decline and Fall*, I.59: I.71.

Gibbon's image is not of conquest, but of rape: 'the fierce giants of the north broke in . . .'. Yet instead of predominating over and obscuring the puny breed, as Rousseau had suggested, Gibbon's barbarians 'mended' it; that is to say, they were a means whereby the Roman race could once more attain 'the old standard' and have restored to it qualities (such as 'a manly spirit of freedom') which it had once possessed, but now lacked. The barbarians con- tributed no new qualities to mankind, but merely replaced certain vital elements which had been eroded. Thus the potency of the barbarians as a causal influence on history is diminished. Their actions have effects, but those effects are far removed from barbarousness: 'After the revolution of ten cen- turies, freedom became the happy parent of taste and science.' Like Hume, Gibbon rejects the extravagance of those who derive modern politeness from ancient barbarism; but unlike Hume, who seems in the grip of doubts he can neither dismiss nor organise into a more probable reading of the past, Gibbon as we shall see makes his scepticism about the importance of the barbarians functional in his dissimulating presentation of Rome's decline.

By the end of Chapter II, then, Gibbon's view of the effectiveness of the barbarians in overthrowing the Roman empire is already slightly different from that of his eminent contemporaries. But it is only in Chapter IX that he gives any detailed justification of this shift in perspective. In a footnote Gibbon has gently reproved Pope for unfaithful translation:

The rights, powers, and pretensions of the sovereign of Olympus, are very clearly described in the xvth. book of the Iliad: in the Greek original, I mean; for Mr. Pope, without perceiving it, has improved the theology of Homer.[15]

Yet in Chapter IX he is himself more calculatingly disloyal, since he systematically traduces Tacitus' *Germania*.[16] Taken together, the infidelities to the Latin constitute a coherent and deliberate slanting of the Roman's text in the interests of the Englishman's argument. Gibbon 'improves' Tacitus and, unlike Pope with Homer, also perceives that he does so; but he judges that it is in his best interest to disguise his departures from Tacitus' meaning, and to make his portrait of the Germans appear a faithful rendition of the *Germania*. Some inquirers into the use Gibbon makes of other writers have spectacularly come to grief. His crushing reply to Davis' charge of plagiarism – 'According to the opinion which he has conceived of literary property, to *agree* is to *follow*, and to *follow* is to *steal*' – admonishes those who examine his use of sources.[17] My own intention, however, is not to level a charge of plagiarism against Gibbon, but to uncover the distortions of the Latin which underlie moments when he makes a point of noting his indebtedness to

---

[15] *The Decline and Fall*, I.v n. 4: I.36 n. 4.
[16] There is coolness in handling with such freedom a book which in some quarters was the object of veneration: Gilbert Stuart held that 'Antiquity has not given to the kingdoms of Europe a present more valuable' than the *Germania* (*A View of Society in Europe*, p. 2).
[17] *The English Essays of Edward Gibbon*, p. 276.

Tacitus and which conspire to make the Englishman's belittling view of the Germans seem that of the senatorial historian. Gibbon is not awed by his proximity to Tacitus, and is sufficiently confident to depart from the Roman's intentions while at the same time calling on his words for support.[18] His infidelities to Tacitus show him deploying the writer he so much admired, not deferring to him.

Gibbon acknowledges that Tacitus has come to this subject before him: 'In their primitive state of simplicity and independence, the Germans were surveyed by the discerning eye, and delineated by the masterly pencil, of Tacitus, the first of historians who applied the science of philosophy to the study of facts.'[19] Because so many other writers have preceded him, he will content himself 'with observing, and indeed with repeating, some of the most important circumstances of climate, of manners, and of institutions, which rendered the wild barbarians of Germany such formidable enemies to the Roman power'.[20] We have here a more than Tiberian degree of dissimulation. Gibbon does not simply repeat Tacitus, and the tendency of this chapter is to diminish the barbarian threat to Rome to the point of insignificance.

Gibbon achieves this covert end by exploiting the idiom of philosophic historiography. He styles his argument after Montesquieu: 'To a mind

---

[18] The extent of Gibbon's unacknowledged reliance on Tacitus in Chapter IX is large, and I shall set out those moments when he simply adopts the Latin as expeditiously as possible. 'Peopled by the various tribes of one great nation, whose complexion, manners, and language, denoted a common origin and preserved a striking resemblance' (*The Decline and Fall*, I.218: I.260) looks back to 'unde habitus quoque corporum, quamquam in tanto hominum numero, idem omnibus' (*Germania*, IV). 'The eastern frontier was faintly marked by the mutual fears of the Germans and the Sarmatians' (*The Decline and Fall*, I.218: I.260) recalls 'a Sarmatis Dacisque mutuo metu aut montibus separatur' (*Germania*, I). 'The spontaneous production of the earth' (*The Decline and Fall*, I.220: I.263) echoes 'Tuistonem deum terra editum' (*Germania*, II). 'The care of the house and family, the management of the land and cattle, were delegated to the old and infirm, to women and slaves' (*The Decline and Fall*, I.225: I.268–9) reminds one of 'delegata domus et penatium et agrorum cura feminis sensibusque et infirmissimo cuique ex familia' (*Germania*, XV). The long passage beginning 'As soon as a youth . . .' and ending with '. . . more violent and seditious' (*The Decline and Fall*, I.228–9: I.273–4) is a sly blend of material from the eleventh and thirteenth chapters of the *Germania*. 'The Germans treated their women with esteem and confidence, consulted them on every occasion of importance, and fondly believed, that in their breasts resided a sanctity and wisdom, more than human' (*The Decline and Fall*, I.232: I.277) is a recollection of 'inesse quin etiam sanctum aliquid et providum putant, nec aut consilia earum aspernantur aut responsa neglegunt' (*Germania*, VIII). 'The wretch, who had lost his shield, was alike banished from the religious and the civil assemblies of his countrymen' (*The Decline and Fall*, I.235: I.280) relies on 'scutum reliquisse praecipuum flagitium, nec aut sacris adesse aut concilium inire ignominioso fas' (*Germania*, VI). 'Though the horses of Germany were neither beautiful, swift, nor practised in the skilful evolutions of the Roman manage' (*The Decline and Fall*, I.237: I.282) is a dandified version of 'equi non forma, nec velocitate gyros in morem nostrum docentur' (*Germania*, VI). 'Each barbarian fixed his independent dwelling on the spot to which a plain, a wood, or a stream of fresh water, had induced him to give the preference' (*The Decline and Fall*, I.223: I.266) is a rendering of 'colunt discreti ac diversi, ut fons, ut campus, ut nemus placuit' (*Germania*, XVI). It is clear that Tacitus haunts Gibbon's chapter.

[19] *The Decline and Fall*, I.217: I.259. First edition: '. . .pencil of Tacitus, . . .'.

[20] *The Decline and Fall*, I.218: I.260. First edition: '. . . Germany, such . . .'.

capable of reflection, such leading facts convey more instruction, than a tedious detail of subordinate circumstances.'[21] He fabricates a description of the ancient Germans from such 'leading facts', and then invites us to consider how daunting such a nation was likely to be. He allows that 'The strength of ancient Germany appears formidable, when we consider the effects that might have been produced by its united effort.'[22] But the chapter's final maxim is, in all respects, the last word: 'The most splendid appellations have been frequently lavished on the most inconsiderable objects.'[23] In its pruning of extravagance, Chapter IX is closer to Hume's 'Of the Populousness of Ancient Nations' than to the *Germania*.

As part of his diminution of the Germans, Gibbon suggests that they were illiterate:

But all this well-laboured system of German antiquities [that of Olaus Rudbeck] is annihilated by a single fact, too well attested to admit of any doubt, and of too decisive a nature to leave room for any reply. The Germans, in the age of Tacitus, were unacquainted with the use of letters . . .[24]

A footnote quotes a relevant passage of the *Germania*: 'litterarum secreta viri pariter ac feminae ignorant.'[25] Taken out of context, the Latin may bear the construction Gibbon places on it: but in context it is clear that Tacitus is discussing the abstention by both sexes of the Germans from conducting liaisons in correspondence. The implied contrast is with the turpitude of Rome; and for the contrast to have any weight, it is necessary that the Germans should have been able to read and write, otherwise the abstention can carry no merit. Rightly understood, then, Tacitus is suggesting the reverse of what Gibbon makes him say.[26]

We find a different kind of mistranslation, involving not a shade of interpretation but the ignoring of a construction, in what the inverted commas and parenthesis suggest is a precise rendition:

'The Bructeri (it is Tacitus who now speaks) were totally exterminated by the neighbouring tribes, provoked by their insolence, allured by the hopes of spoil, and perhaps inspired by the tutelar deities of the empire.'[27]

It is in fact Gibbon who is now speaking. What Tacitus gives as three

---

21 *The Decline and Fall*, I.224: I.268. Gibbon makes a similar point in the *Essai sur l'Étude de la Littérature*, the indebtedness of which to Montesquieu he later considered its greatest blemish: 'Que ce contraste est parlant pour un homme instruit dans l'antiquité!' (*Miscellaneous Works*, IV.31); see also *The Decline and Fall*, I.xxiv n. 69: I.185 n. 69.

22 *The Decline and Fall*, I.238: I.284.

23 *The Decline and Fall*, I.241: I.288.

24 *The Decline and Fall*, I.222: I.265.

25 *Germania*, XIX.

26 Later in the chapter (*The Decline and Fall*, I.xxxiv n. 56: I.276 n. 56) Gibbon shows that he realises that this passage of the *Germania* refers to sexual morality and not to general literacy. Compare also Gilbert Stuart, *A View of Society in Europe*, p. 190. Murphy translates the Latin correctly, and in a note gives examples of German literacy (*The Works of Cornelius Tacitus*, IV.23 and 250).

27 *The Decline and Fall*, I.238–9: I.285. First edition: '. . . tribes provoked . . .'.

alternative motives ('seu superbiae odio seu praedae dulcedine seu favore quodam erga nos deorum'), Gibbon portrays as cumulative incitements.[28] Tacitus is unsure about barbarian psychology. But Gibbon (even when the full concessive force of 'perhaps' is allowed) makes the Germans a prey simultaneously to superstition, avarice and false pride.

A more intricate misrepresentation occurs in another passage punctuated with inverted commas:

'Among the Suiones, says Tacitus, riches are held in honour. They are *therefore* subject to an absolute monarch, who, instead of intrusting his people with the free use of arms, as is practised in the rest of Germany, commits them to the safe custody not of a citizen, or even of a freedman, but of a slave. The neighbours of the Suiones, the Sitones, are sunk even below servitude; they obey a woman.'[29]

This seems a translation of one continuous piece of Latin. But in fact it comprises two separate passages. Down to 'of a slave', it is an elegant compression of the concluding sentence of Chapter XLIV; from 'The neighbours . . .', it is an elegant compression of the concluding sentence of Chapter XLV. The footnote directs the reader to both these chapters of the *Germania*: but Gibbon's slyness lies in his placing of these two passages together so as to imply that Tacitus gives a connected account of German servitude rather than the isolated *aperçus* we in fact find in the *Germania*. The matter impinged on Tacitus' mind infrequently and adventitiously, but Gibbon sees that his thesis will be advanced by the implication that the spectacle of barbarian slavery drew the concentrated and scornful attention of the senator.

The revolt of Civilis prompts Gibbon's most sustained dissimulation. In a footnote he tells us where we may find Tacitus' account and passes judgement: 'The relation of this enterprise occupies a great part of the fourth and fifth books of the History of Tacitus, and is more remarkable for its eloquence than perspicuity.'[30] Once more Gibbon 'improves' the Latin. One notices immediately how Tacitus' presentation of this episode is very much more complex than Gibbon's. This is in part a function of space: Tacitus discusses Civilis at length, Gibbon in a page. But it is the *nature* of the complexity of which Gibbon gives us no hint that is so striking. In *The Decline and Fall* we hear nothing of the confusion and disorder amongst the barbarians that Tacitus alludes to in *Historiae*, IV.lxx, and nothing of the loyalty of places such as Cologne. So the translation of 'caesos exercitus, capta legionum hiberna' by 'He . . . defeated the legions, destroyed their fortified camps' is more than an innocent replacement of the passive by the active. Gibbon's whole account is slanted towards enhancing Civilis' despatch and success as a commander.[31]

[28] *Germania*, XXXIII.
[29] *The Decline and Fall*, I.227: I.271–2.
[30] *The Decline and Fall*, I.xxxv n. 74: I.283 n. 74.
[31] *Historiae*, IV.xii; *The Decline and Fall*, I.238: I.284.

Nowhere is this quiet magnification of Civilis clearer than in Gibbon's final sentences:

When, at length, after an obstinate struggle, he yielded to the power of the empire, Civilis secured himself and his country by an honourable treaty. The Batavians still continued to occupy the islands of the Rhine, the allies not the servants of the Roman monarchy.[32]

Gibbon gives the impression that the Batavian status as 'the allies not the servants of the Roman monarchy' was a result of Civilis' rising, an extra concession wrung from the Romans, in addition to the maintenance of their territories. Tacitus, however, is explicit, and Gibbon certainly knew, that the Batavi enjoyed this privilege before the revolt:

Batavi, donec trans Rhenum agebant, pars Chattorum, seditione domestica pulsi extrema Gallicae orae vacua cultoribus simulque insulam iuxta sitam occupavere, quam mare Oceanus a fronte, Rhenus amnis tergum ac latera circumluit. nec opibus (rarum in societate validiorum) attritis viros tantum armaque imperio ministrant . . .[33]

The reason for this magnification of Civilis, which seems at first glance to be at odds with Gibbon's general strategy of running down the barbarians, becomes clear when we appreciate that it follows his laying bare of the underlying weakness and confusion of the Germans. The reader can interpret this sudden and puzzling appearance of resolute forces under Civilis only as a sign of how decadent the Romans seemed to the provinces on the death of Nero. Tacitus has Civilis admit that he is inspired to revolt by Roman distraction: 'dum alii Vespasianum, alii Vitellium foveant, patere locum adversus utrumque.'[34] Gibbon notes that Civilis' rising takes place during the 'civil wars that followed the death of Nero', but he does not suggest that this dissension incited Civilis.[35] Rather, by stressing that the success and duration of the revolt was caused by the slothful Roman policy of employing and training barbarian auxiliaries he indicates that, far from being an opportunistic exploitation of the unprecedented events of A.D. 69, Civilis' uprising was a response to a weakness in Rome which, even had it not happened now, was going to happen sooner or later.[36] It was an internal decay which precipitated the political and military decline of Rome, not barbarian onslaughts. Gibbon still refuses to state what causes that sapping of civic resolve (to use the language of Rhédi in *Lettres Persanes*, he keeps it veiled as a 'venin secret et caché'); but this vagueness is the product of ironic calculation, not incomprehending wonder.

[32]   *The Decline and Fall*, I.238: I.284. First edition: '. . . island of the Rhine . . .'.
[33]   *Historiae*, IV.xii; compare *The Decline and Fall*, I.iii n. 55: I.18 n. 55.
[34]   *Historiae*, IV.xvii.
[35]   *The Decline and Fall*, I.237: I.283.
[36]   Civilis 'employed against the Romans the military knowledge which he had acquired in their service' (*The Decline and Fall*, I.238: I.284). The calamitous policy of employing the barbarians as auxiliaries had already been much commented on (Mably, *Observations on the Romans*, p. 215; Chastellux, *De la Félicité Publique*, I.225). See also Robertson's 'A View of the Progress of Society in Europe' (*Charles V*, I.8).

7

Narrative

We have considered how Gibbon's style, and his handling of central issues, such as the character of Augustus and the barbarian irruptions, further the dissimulated design of the first volume of *The Decline and Fall*. By indirectly questioning the traditional explanations of Roman decline – that Rome fell through luxury, or that it fell because of the erosion of civic vigour following the establishment of the principate, or that it collapsed under the onslaughts of the Goths – Gibbon teases his reader about what he sees as the most important cause of the empire's decay. Addison had found the main pleasure of historiography in its creation of suspense:

It is the most agreeable talent of an Historian, to be able to draw up his armies and fight his battles in proper expressions, to set before our eyes the divisions, cabals, and jealousies of great men, and to lead us step by step into the several actions and events of his history. We love to see the subject unfolding itself by just degrees, and breaking upon us insensibly, so that we may be kept in a pleasing suspence, and have time given us to raise our expectations, and to side with one of the parties concerned in the relation.[1]

Gibbon's innovation is to transfer this 'pleasing suspence' from narrative to argument. But before proceeding to discuss how and where Gibbon unveils what he takes to be the key cause of Roman decline, we might pause to notice how even Gibbon's demeanour as an historian furthers his manipulation of his reader.

Gibbon is famous as an ironist; but it should by now be apparent that, even when one can discern no ironic *tone*, the prose of Volume I of *The Decline and Fall* tends to the ironic in its creation of a disingenuous relationship between writer and reader. Lionel Gossman has suggested that Gibbon is always concerned to win the reader's trust: 'the historian continually weighs the evidence before the reader's eyes, as though to show him all his cards', and so the 'narrator of the *Decline and Fall* is ingratiating, infinitely cautious, and

---

[1] *Spectator*, no. 420 (originally 'that so we'); Joseph Addison, *Works*, III.479. Giarrizzo believes that Gibbon's purpose in dealing with so many possible causes of decline was to 'innervare le azioni particolari nel corso generale della decadenza organica' (*Edward Gibbon e la Cultura Europea del Settecento*, p. 260 n. 102; compare also pp. 266–7). But to adopt this argument is to overlook the nice discriminations Gibbon makes between these various causes which effectively rank them into major and minor.

deferential'.[2] As a description of Gibbon's courtly manner, this is exact; but there is naivety in Gossman's assumption that Gibbon's manners are the straightforward expression of his desires and that the appearance of candour on the surface of *The Decline and Fall* indicates an underlying candour. As we have seen in his handling of the *Germania* in Chapter IX, Gibbon is most deeply dissimulating when he seems most confiding – the reader of *The Decline and Fall* is never more likely to be manoeuvred and positioned than when he imagines his hand is being cordially shaken. In Volume I of his history Gibbon practises the art of artlessness and the craft of candour in a narrative style whose implications are central to any understanding of his intentions in this first volume.

Gibbon's narrative values in Volume I are not in doubt; by preserving 'a clear and unbroken thread of narration' he hopes to attain 'some degree of order and perspicuity'.[3] In philosophic vein, Gibbon proclaims the artistic spirit with which he approaches the past, searching for a wholeness in its shapes which he can then transpose into the proportioned and interpretable forms of his own narrative:

The imperfect historians of an irregular war do not enable us to describe the order and circumstances of his [Claudius'] exploits; but, if we could be indulged in the allusion, we might distribute into three acts this memorable tragedy.[4]

Even where his material is defective, Gibbon applies an artistic finish; and this vigilance over the decorum of his work, over the seemly and luminous arrangement of its elements, is a product of his firm grasp of *design* in Volume I:

The general design of this work will not permit us minutely to relate the actions of every emperor after he ascended the throne, much less to deduce the various fortunes of his private life.[5]

This eschewal of mere particularity is nourished by the example of Montesquieu, from whom Gibbon was only at length to wean himself. Gossman has eloquently described the selfless civility which seems to prompt this constant pruning away of unmeaning luxuriance: 'This tedium of the mere unconnected particular is the enemy the historian must continually combat in order to secure for the reader the order and perspicuity, the intellectual and esthetic well-being, that are the principal object of his reading.'[6] But whose interests are in fact served by this thorough direction of the narrative? If you believe that reading *The Decline and Fall* gives you access to an ideal *salon* of

---

[2] *The Empire Unpossess'd*, pp. 90 and 118.
[3] *The Decline and Fall*, I.242: I.289 and I.161: I.193. This lucidity seems to have been a connotation of the word 'philosophic'; compare James Harris' *Hermes*: 'He has endeavoured to treat his subject with as much order, correctness, and perspicuity as was in his power' (p. vii).
[4] *The Decline and Fall*, I.294: I.350–1. First edition: '. . . war, do . . .'.
[5] *The Decline and Fall*, I.296: I.353.
[6] *The Empire Unpossess'd*, p. 95.

politesse and learning in which historian and reader meet on terms of equality to impart and receive knowledge, then everybody is gratified by this literary version of the common good manners of always speaking to the point. But Gibbon's own life gave him ample opportunities to observe that the civility of the eighteenth century merely rested above, and did not do away with, the shrewdness and calculation of an instrumental attitude to those whom weakness or circumstance had placed within your power.[7] In its draping of intent with the tissue of ingenuousness, Volume I of *The Decline and Fall* duplicates the doubleness of eighteenth-century society. It is no accident that Gibbon prefers the word 'design' to its near-synonyms 'plan' or 'intention'; 'the general design of this work' is as much a design on its readers as a sketch of what is to be undertaken.

Previous critics have willingly taken Gibbon's fabrication of the shadow of candour for its substance. To go further, one might inquire as to the price of the narrative order and perspicuity, the adherence to design, which Gibbon displays as the tokens of his good faith. The opening of Chapter X is revealing:

From the great secular games celebrated by Philip, to the death of the emperor Gallienus, there elapsed twenty years of shame and misfortune. During that calamitous period, every instant of time was marked, every province of the Roman world was afflicted, by barbarous invaders and military tyrants, and the ruined empire seemed to approach the last and fatal moment of its dissolution. The confusion of the times, and the scarcity of authentic memorials, oppose equal difficulties to the historian, who attempts to preserve a clear and unbroken thread of narration. Surrounded with imperfect fragments, always concise, often obscure, and sometimes contradictory, he is reduced to collect, to compare, and to conjecture: and though he ought never to place his conjectures in the rank of facts, yet the knowledge of human nature, and of the sure operation of its fierce and unrestrained passions, might, on some occasions, supply the want of historical materials.[8]

From the dizzying array of various particularity which constitutes the past ('every instant of time . . . every province') the historian must spin a single and sequential thread of narration. If he is to avoid being mired in his material and forced to give up the raised point of vantage which, as we saw in Hume's historiography, is the proper position for the philosophic historian, and if he is not to remain 'surrounded with imperfect fragments', then he must supplement his normal habits of collection and comparison with that of conjecture. Here Gibbon comes even closer to Hume, for the historian's guide in his conjectures is 'the knowledge of human nature, and of the sure

---

[7] For example, this studied choice of metaphor dresses, but does not heal, the bruise Gibbon received on meeting the hard reality of political ingratitude (which is given a subtle prominence by the contrary motive which animates his own conduct): 'From a principle of gratitude I adhered to the coalition: my vote was counted in the day of battle; but I was overlooked in the division of the spoil' (*Memoirs*, p. 165).

[8] *The Decline and Fall*, I.242: I.289. First edition: '. . . afflicted by . . .'.

operation of its fierce and unrestrained passions'; that is to say, the notion of a constant and regular human nature which has such a central and problematic position in Hume's work. Thus the order and perspicuity of philosophic history is more created in despite of historical evidence than released from it. The conjectures which cement the imperfect fragments of the past, because they are the product of assumed conclusions, suggest that the legible form of philosophic history is not so much the past restored to its pristine shape, as the past moulded until it satisfies the expectations of the observer.

The philosophic historian seems to be serving his reader by maintaining a distinct and unbroken view of a scene which is naturally shaded and incessantly shifting. But, far from facilitating a vision with which he does not interfere, in Volume I of *The Decline and Fall* Gibbon is always choosing our ground and defining our prospect. His deference cloaks his dominance:

I shall not, however, enter into a minute narrative of these military operations; but as the two civil wars against Niger and against Albinus, were almost the same in their conduct, event, and consequences, I shall collect into one point of view, the most striking circumstances, tending to develope the character of the conqueror, and the state of the empire.[9]

Gibbon here poses as the *cicerone* of the past; but his implication that particulars can be collected 'into one point of view' without being altered by that collocation, although apparently endorsed by the practice of an historian such as Montesquieu, is disingenuous. As the careful rearrangements of circumstances 'collected' from the *Germania* in Chapter IX demonstrate, Gibbon is well aware of how thoroughly the face of the historical landscape can be transformed by the seemingly innocent juxtapositions involved in 'collection'. The expressions he uses to describe his handling of material all imply the scrupulously neutral endeavours of the ideal editor:

It is not without some attention, that we can explain and conciliate their imperfect hints.

However these historians differ in names . . . it is evident that they mean the same people, and the same war, but it requires some care to conciliate and explain them.[10]

Attentively and carefully to unfold and reconcile one's material seems a selfless task. But is it not utopian to imagine that truth is located where sources overlap and confirm one another?

I have endeavoured to blend into one consistent story the seeming contradictions of the two writers.

The circumstances of this war, and the death of Severus are very doubtfully and variously told in our ancient fragments . . . I have endeavoured to extract from them a consistent and probable narration.[11]

---

[9] *The Decline and Fall*, I.119: I.143.
[10] *The Decline and Fall*, I.xl n. 123: I.323 n. 123 and I.xliv n. 25: I.357 n. 25.
[11] *The Decline and Fall*, I.xvii n. 14: I.132 n. 14 and I.lix n. 23: I.489 n. 23.

The venerable maxim of interpretation – that truth is single, whole and therefore self-consistent – was seized on by historiographic theorists in the decades preceding the publication of *The Decline and Fall* as a principle of historical criticism which would enable one to distinguish false (and therefore self-contradictory) evidence from true.[12] Here, as elsewhere, Gibbon shows his investment in this principle.[13] But how does he decide where contradiction ends and consistency begins? Extreme contradictions (such as the self-contradiction of material which alleges that someone was in two places at once) are obvious; but in the twilit areas with which Gibbon has most to do, how does he know, by reference to what 'truth' does he decide, that he has sufficiently blended the fragments with which he is surrounded? Presumably, when a 'consistent and probable narration' can be extracted from them. But that 'narration' is not a collection of simple facts; at its root is an hypothesis or interpretation of the past which enables it to be recognised as consistent. Gibbon contrives in Volume I to give his narrative the appearance of induction. But the interpretation of the significance of Roman decline in which it seems to issue has from the first shaped the book and governed Gibbon's critical decisions. In *The Decline and Fall* Gibbon seems to be almost surprised by his conclusions about why Rome fell. In fact that appearance of surprise is a finely calculated stroke of rhetoric.

Gibbon manipulates his material in order to produce a clean narrative line purged of mere, unmeaning particularity – such as 'the trifling details preserved in the compilation of Lampridius'.[14] He thereby attains the 'expressive conciseness' of a philosophic style composed of truly telling facts which persuade through a brilliant economy of demonstration:

But a single fact, the only one indeed of which we have any distinct knowledge, erases, in a great measure, these monuments of vanity and adulation.[15]

Such moments of ostentatious revision, which have the effect of a conjuring trick despite their tone of sober intelligence, gladden the heart of the philosophic historian, as we saw in the case of Montesquieu. But elsewhere the philosophic urge to conciseness, when joined to a conviction of the sure operation of the constant elements of human nature, justifies a discounting of historical variation. When reading Guischardt as a youth, Gibbon had been made aware of the variety which can be subsumed under a single word:

---

[12] The antiquity of this principle can be judged from its appearance in the *Summa Theologica*, i, q.5, a.4, *apud* 1. Amongst later writers, see for instance Bayle: '*Il n'y a que la verité qui soit uniforme*, comme le remarque fort bien le P. Maimbourg dans son Histoire des Iconoclastes, *l'erreur & le mensonge estant trop foibles pour se soutenir par une conduite suivie et mesurée*' (*Critique Generale*, p. 464); Locke, 'Of the DEGREES of ASSENT', *Essay Concerning Human Understanding*, IV.16; and Bolingbroke's *Letters to M. de Pouilly* (*c.* 1720).

[13] E.g. 'These two relations are consistent with each other, and with probability' (*The Decline and Fall*, I.lxxxi n. 79: I.656 n. 80).

[14] *The Decline and Fall*, I.156: I.186.

[15] *The Decline and Fall*, I.217: I.259 (the phrase is not used in the first edition; it is an interesting revision); *The Decline and Fall*, I.260: I.311; see also I.221–2: I.265.

The fourth [chapter of the *Memoires Militaires*], on the battle of the Adda, is a compleat treatise on the Roman legion, very satisfactory as to the times of Polybius; very little so as to those of Caesar.[16]

That knowledge is present in *The Decline and Fall*: 'The legions, as they are described by Polybius, in the time of the Punic wars, differed very materially from those which atchieved the victories of Caesar.'[17] Nevertheless, his own portrait of the legion is a conjectural average: describing the point of the pilum as 'eighteen inches' in length, he notes that this is a 'medium' between the assessments of Polybius and Vegetius.[18] Such averages are only permissible if you take historical change to be accidental, not substantial. In Volume I of *The Decline and Fall* Gibbon finds the substance of history, as had Hume, in the *congeries* of passions, liabilities and impulses which for him comprise human nature; and that model of human nature is restated in the volume's conclusions as to why Rome fell, as well as shaping the narrative as a critical principle.

The major means whereby Gibbon preserves the pertinence of his narrative is the footnote. Gibbon's use of the footnote changes as *The Decline and Fall* progresses, but in Volume I it is part of his commitment to the philosophic idea of historiography, in which material can be winnowed into the essential and illuminating facts to be placed in the narrative, and the unmeaning chaff. His footnotes are repositories of those 'singular' facts which cannot be assimilated into the clean lines of a narrative dedicated to the exemplification of an hypothesis of Roman decline, but which Gibbon the scholar can yet not ignore. In one respect, this shows that from the first Gibbon was an imperfect *philosophe*; Montesquieu uses his footnotes ruthlessly to confirm the contentions of his narrative and banishes all evidence that contradicts his hypothesis. Gibbon's footnotes, on the other hand, contain scholarly *trouvailles* which question the swift probabilistic suppositions of philosophic historiography:

It is natural enough to suppose, that Arragon is derived from Tarraconensis, and several moderns who have written in Latin, use those words as synonymous. It is however certain, that the Arragon, a little stream which falls from the Pyrenees into the Ebro, first gave its name to a country, and gradually to a kingdom.[19]

One way in which the magnitude of the change *The Decline and Fall* undergoes over the period of its publication can be assessed is to plot the steady elevation of these awkward insights from the footnotes to the text: the initially well-policed frontiers of the historian's empire eventually become permeable and are overrun by hordes of distracting and opaque particulars. Even in Volume I Gibbon is not so much a victim of the besetting vice of the philosophic

---

[16] *Gibbon's Journal to January 28th, 1763*, p. 72.

[17] *The Decline and Fall*, I.12: I.15. First edition: '. . . described by Polybius, and commanded by the Scipios, differed very materially . . .'.

[18] *The Decline and Fall*, I.12: I.16.

[19] *The Decline and Fall*, I.iv n. 70: I.24 n. 70; see also, e.g., *The Decline and Fall*, I.v n. 89: I.33 n. 89.

historian, 'esprit de système', as to exclude such details, but he is adept at finding forms of words which protect as far as possible the integrity of his text. The feeble, because fantasising, ambition of Galerius aligns itself happily with what Gibbon presents as the Roman propensity to be self-defeating:

In the full confidence, that the approaching death of Constantius would leave him sole master of the Roman world, we are assured that he had arranged in his mind a long succession of future princes, and that he meditated his own retreat from public life, after he should have accomplished a glorious reign of about twenty years.[20]

It is just this puerile and groundless confidence in the certainty of effortless and continued imperium which, Gibbon implies, permits the cause of Roman decline to take root. This detail of Galerius' psychology thus is, in terms of Gibbon's hypothesis, a speaking fact; and the phrase 'we are assured' seems to state that Gibbon takes it as a fact. Yet we are referred to a footnote:

These schemes, however, rest only on the very doubtful authority of Lactantius . . .[21]

We now realise that 'we are assured' means not 'I am confident of this' but 'my source is confident of this'. With a philosophic dedication to his hypothesis, to the 'système' of his explanation of Roman decay, Gibbon wants to keep this comely detail in his text: as a scholar, he cannot prevail on himself to leave unrecorded his doubts about Lactantius' reliability, no matter how muted or incidental his acknowledgement of them must be.

It would be wrong, however, to lay too much emphasis at this stage on the latent divergency of Gibbon's double loyalty to accuracy and to philosophy, since his open commitment to precision is an important part of his strategy; it is through his scruple that he hopes to secure for himself the credibility to gain acceptance for his thesis. In sighing over the unreliability of his sources, Gibbon at the same time makes public his aspirations to the highest accuracy:

The general complaints of intense frost, and eternal winter, are perhaps little to be regarded, since we have no method of reducing to the accurate standard of the thermometer, the feelings, or the expressions, of an orator, born in the happier regions of Greece or Asia.[22]

Such a comment is quite consonant with the depreciation of written evidence liable to personal bias and the corresponding elevation of impersonal evidence current since the historical pyrrhonism of the late seventeenth century. But Gibbon goes on to cite 'two remarkable circumstances of a less equivocal nature' – the retreat of the reindeer from Germany and the fact of the Rhine and the Danube no longer freezing over – from which he draws untainted conclusions about the climate of ancient Germany.

[20] *The Decline and Fall*, I.403: I.479.   [21] *The Decline and Fall*, I.lviii n. 7: I.479 n. 7.
[22] *The Decline and Fall*, I.218: I.261.

This desire to supplement written evidence with impersonal information and thereby bring historiography closer to the condition of a science accounts for the statistical emphasis of *The Decline and Fall*. The historian of 1776 must replace eulogy with measurement:

. . . they [the Romans] gradually usurped the licence of confounding the Roman monarchy with the globe of the earth. But the temper, as well as knowledge, of a modern historian, require a more sober and accurate language. He may impress a juster image of the greatness of Rome, by observing that the empire was above two thousand miles in breadth, from the wall of Antoninus and the northern limits of Dacia, to mount Atlas and the tropic of Cancer; that it extended, in length, more than three thousand miles from the Western Ocean to the Euphrates; that it was situated in the finest part of the Temperate Zone, between the twenty-fourth and fifty-sixth degrees of northern latitude; and that it was supposed to contain above sixteen hundred thousand square miles, for the most part of fertile and well-cultivated land.[23]

Yet this instance of apparently impersonal (and therefore 'juster') description shows well how easily what seems to be mere accuracy can glide into and reinforce the surreptitious strategies whereby the philosophic historian coerces his reader. This measurement of the extent of the empire places Gibbon alongside Hume's Stoic on that lofty eminence which is at once a point of precise vision and a point of dominant vantage: indeed it is its dominance of the past which makes the precision possible.[24]

What, however, is it in the position of the philosophic historian which is denoted by that quality of dominance, which is after all only a metaphor? Disengagement, independence, a certain loftiness of intellect – certainly: but, further than this, it also suggests the philosopher's position in time. In Montesquieu's *Considérations* it was the 'presentness' of the historian's vision, his standpoint on the raised ground of the eighteenth century, which threw the past into legible relief.[25] Gibbon, too, sees the fall of Rome through his knowledge of intervening history. This filtered vision leaves various traces: in the allusions which bespeak a mind ranging freely over world literature and

---

[23] *The Decline and Fall*, I. 27–8: I.33. First edition: '. . . assumed the licence . . .'; '. . . a juster image, by . . .'. Other examples of the fashionable statistical interest of Volume I of *The Decline and Fall* are the following footnotes; I.xviii n. 37: I.141 n. 37, I.xxii n. 38: I.167 n. 38, I.xxix n. 1: I.238 n. 1, I.xxxi n. 48: I.253 n. 49 and I.xxxii n. 1: I.260 n. 1. It also sharpens Gibbon's regret for the loss of Augustus' accounts (*The Decline and Fall*, I.162–3: I.194) and dictates such phrases as 'our ready imagination instantly computes and multiplies . . .' (*The Decline and Fall*, I.269: I.322) or 'the melancholy calculation . . .' (*The Decline and Fall*, I.286: I.341).

[24] In this context the eighteenth-century desire to include maps in works of history is important (see Chesterfield, *Letters*, I.125–6). Gibbon is a great admirer of d'Anville and is delighted at the promise (alas, it remained only a promise) that he might draw some maps for *The Decline and Fall* (*Letters*, II.152). Maps enable one to form a clearer idea of the action of history; but they are also, in the way that they seem to unfold the scene of history beneath us, an image of how the world appears from the Olympian standpoint of the philosophic historian. Just as that point of vantage *organises* history and turns it from a chaotic throng of particular details to a prospect within which legible patterns can be discerned, so do maps: on this point, see Chesterfield, *Letters*, II.336.

[25] See, for example, *Œuvres*, III.363.

making intelligent connexions with a perfect liberty of movement;[26] in the dry urbanity with which the eighteenth-century historian will narrate the excesses of antiquity – the perspective of centuries he enjoys in his library in Cavendish Square shading him from violence and lunacy, but illuminating moral deformity;[27] most straightforwardly in his references to later history or customs.[28] Moreover, because Gibbon conceives of decline as 'insensible', it is visible only from this standpoint in the present:

It was scarcely possible that the eyes of contemporaries should discover in the public felicity the latent causes of decay and corruption. This long peace, and the uniform government of the Romans, introduced a slow and secret poison into the vitals of the empire. The minds of men were gradually reduced to the same level, the fire of genius was extinguished, and even the military spirit evaporated. The natives of Europe were brave and robust. Spain, Gaul, Britain, and Illyricum supplied the legions with excellent soldiers, and constituted the real strength of the monarchy. Their personal valour remained, but they no longer possessed that public courage which is nourished by the love of independence, the sense of national honour, the presence of danger, and the habit of command. They received laws and governors from the will of their sovereign, and trusted for their defence to a mercenary army. The posterity of their boldest leaders was contented with the rank of citizens and subjects. The most aspiring spirits resorted to the court or standard of the emperors; and the deserted provinces, deprived of political strength or union, insensibly sunk into the languid indifference of private life.[29]

This is obviously a crucial passage. Gibbon once more seems to endorse the constitutional, political argument which maintains that Rome fell because of the stifling of republican virtue under the emperors, but in fact subtly departs from it. The imperial government of the Romans, and the peace which ensues, *introduces* a slow and secret poison into the vitals of the empire, but the principate is not *itself* that poison. Compare Blackwell's conventional use of the same image for the organic nature of political change:

---

26 Amongst a plethora of examples, consider: 'and however he might applaud the deed, we may candidly presume that he was innocent of the knowledge of it' (*The Decline and Fall*, I.290: I.347), which glances at *Macbeth* ('Be innocent of the knowledge, dearest chuck, / Till thou applaud the deed' III.ii). Gibbon was a connoisseur of allusion.

27 Once more, examples are plentiful. But perhaps the most striking occur when Gibbon, faced with a particularly gross enormity, seems to play along, and adopts, the vocabulary engendered by the event; see *The Decline and Fall*, I.149: I.178 and I.355: I.422.

28 This is patent in the volume's opening chapter, which discusses the provinces of the Roman empire with an eye to the states into which they have subsequently developed, but other, more local, examples pepper the narrative: 'Such, at least, is the practice of the modern Turks' (*The Decline and Fall*, I.266: I.318); 'To navigate the Euxine before the month of May, or after that of September, is esteemed by the modern Turks the most unquestionable instance of rashness and folly' (*The Decline and Fall*, I.269: I.321).

29 *The Decline and Fall*, I.57: I.69. Gibbon's fondness for the word 'insensible' is discussed by F. E. Manuel in his contribution to Bowersock et al., eds., *Edward Gibbon and the Decline and Fall of the Roman Empire*, p. 169. David Jordan accurately defines the term: 'Gibbon frequently speaks of the 'insensible' development. What he means by this is that the development was 'insensible' to contemporaries' (*Gibbon and his Roman Empire*, p. 104).

This Defect in their Constitution [an insufficiently clear distinction between the power of the senate and the power of the people] like a secret Poison in a wholesome Body, lay lurking a long time, while great Exercise abroad and Temperance at home preserved its Vigour: But no sooner was it pampered with Ease and Luxury, than the Distemper appeared in all its Virulence, infected the neighbouring Parts, and in [the] end brought Death and absolute Dominion.[30]

Blackwell is specific about what he is likening to 'a secret Poison'. Adopting Blackwell's vocabulary without adopting his argument, Gibbon avoids pinning down his image of 'slow and secret poison'; and he goes on to discuss the symptoms of the malaise (the waning of civic pride which opens the way for the poison by reducing, extinguishing, evaporating and depressing all that might withstand it), still without saying what the poison is. (Those readers who recollect the patristic justification of the Roman empire – that God permitted it to become so mighty in order that the spread of Christianity might thereby be facilitated – may prick an ear at this juncture.)[31] The absolute command (of material, of narrative and of prose) which enables Gibbon to suggest the subsidiary nature of the traditionally accepted causes of Roman decline, and to indicate the presence of a single villainous cause without as yet naming it, is conferred by his situation in the present, and by the incisive perception, far keener than that enjoyed by 'the eyes of contemporaries', such a situation makes possible. It is to that single villainous cause, and the circumstances of its unmasking, that we must now turn.

[30] *Memoirs of the Court of Augustus*, I.131. Compare also Mably and Hume (*Observations on the Romans*, p. 90; *History*, III.317).
[31] See above, p. 17 n. 30.

8

Chapters XV and XVI

Will you set up profane reason against sacred mystery? No punishment is great enough for your impiety. And the same fires, which were kindled for heretics, will serve also for the destruction of philosophers.

Hume

Whenever I hear the current running against the Characters of my Friends I never think them in such Danger as when Candour undertakes their Defence.

Sheridan

Volume I of *The Decline and Fall* is set apart from the later instalments of the history because it is the only instalment which has a perceivable structure (by which I mean an ordonnance of parts calculated to create a sense of wholeness through the careful admission of variety or change). The first three chapters are general surveys, addressing themselves to the extent and military force, the union and internal prosperity, and the constitution of the empire in the age of the Antonines. There follow four chapters of narrative, in which the course of decline is deduced from Commodus to the secular games of Philip.[1] Then come two interleaved chapters (Chapters VIII and IX) which review the state of both the Persian and German barbarians and thus constitute a pause in the flow of narrative (although not, as we have seen, in the development of Gibbon's implicit argument). They are succeeded by a further five chapters of narrative which take the history of the empire from the accession of Decius to Constantine's reunion of the empire after the divisions introduced by Diocletian. The volume is concluded by the notorious two chapters in which Gibbon assesses the spread of Christianity through the empire, and the attitude of the Roman government towards the new religion.[2]

---

[1] See *Memoirs*, p. 156, where Gibbon deplores 'the concise and superficial narrative of the first reigns from Commodus to Alexander' (i.e. Chapters IV to VI): he eventually regrets the *philosophe* keenness which led him to shape his material in accordance with his covert argument, rather than according to the forms it seems intrinsically to require and merit. It is often in such unobtrusive remarks as this that Gibbon's *Memoirs* bear quiet witness to the subtle development of his ideas.

[2] Gibbon vaunts the structural perfection of his first volume in a letter to Sheffield (*Letters*, II.81); Walpole, who is much the most suggestive of Gibbon's contemporary critics, finds a good word to express that perfection; 'Gibbon's first volume is enamelled' (*Correspondence*, XV.328). Harold Bond was the first to notice the structure of Volume I (*The Literary Art of Edward Gibbon*, pp. 62–4); Michel Baridon's interesting discovery of the generally shorter length of the paragraph in 1776, by testifying to the pressure of Gibbon's attention, seems to me to confirm Bond's insight (*Edward Gibbon et le Mythe de Rome*, p. 757).

Thus the narrative sections of Volume I are framed by, or placed within, groups of chapters cast more as essays or dissertations than as narrative, which attempt not to trace the thread of chronology, but to analyse a particular phenomenon or to display the face of affairs at a certain time. The placing of these essay-like chapters so that they occupy the beginning, middle and end of the volume is a clear sign of the shaping care Gibbon expended on this first instalment of his history.[3] The symmetry they create might suggest this by itself; but as we saw in Montesquieu's *Considérations*, to control the impulse to narrative (which might be represented as a naive recounting of the past without any attempt to understand it), even to the point of eliminating narrative altogether, was a characteristic of the 'enlightened' writing of Gibbon's time.[4] Nor was it just a fashion among historians. Chesterfield offers it to Philip Stanhope as a maxim of how to please in society:

Tell stories very seldom, and absolutely never but where they are very apt, and very short. Omit every circumstance that is not material, and beware of digressions. To have frequent recourse to narrative, betrays great want of imagination.[5]

One reason why the first volume of *The Decline and Fall* pleased when, in 1776, it was on the desk of every philosopher and the toilette of every hostess may have been its simultaneously enlightened and well-bred holding in check of its necessary recourses to narrative, pinioning them with rewarding reflection.[6] Gibbon's suave management of narrative enables him to skirt the pitfall of being a mere button-holer and to observe the principle of good manners Chesterfield seeks to inculcate; namely that you should impose on people's attention only when you have something of profit to communicate, and only for a period proportionate to the value of what you have to impart. By courteously dividing his narrative into two, and by framing it with reflection and analysis, Gibbon satisfied the demands of both philosophy and politeness, and fulfilled the obligations laid on him by being both a gentleman and an historian.[7] But in the same gesture with which Gibbon signals his

---

[3] By the same token, the growing preponderance of narrative over such 'review' chapters in the later volumes of *The Decline and Fall*, which Michel Baridon has so interestingly demonstrated (*Edward Gibbon et le Mythe de Rome*, p. 836), suggests to me a waning of architectonic vigilance in the historian.

[4] It is present also, I suppose, in the eighteenth-century vogue for 'historical retrodiction'; that is to say, the tracing of the outline of the past by inference from known principles or characteristics but without reference to actual events. Hume's *Natural History of Religion* is an example of this form of historiography. See F. J. Teggart, *Theory and Processes of History*, pp. 82–98; R. A. Nisbet, *Social Change and History*, pp. 139–58; and J. W. Burrow, *Evolution and Society*.

[5] *Letters*, II.86.

[6] *Memoirs*, p. 157. For Gibbon's relishing of the female response to *The Decline and Fall*, see *Letters*, II.106.

[7] In the 1760s Gibbon piqued himself on his gentility more than on his literary merits; note his comments on his reception in Paris in 1763 (*Miscellanea Gibboniana*, pp. 105–6). Gray, too, is reported to have had 'a certain degree of pride, which led him, of all other things, to despise the idea of being thought an author professed' (*Poems and Memoirs*, p. 335). By the time of the *Memoirs*, Gibbon's ideas had changed – presumably his estimation of the difficulty of literary composition had been deepened (*Memoirs*, pp. 4–6).

community with his readers we can also see his ironic and manipulative intentions. The sculpting of Volume I is as much a means whereby Gibbon increases the impact of his covert, suspended explanation of Roman decline as
a discharging of his authorial obligations. The features of *The Decline and Fall*
a contemporary reader might take as guarantees of his cordial welcome also
allow Gibbon to ambush him most effectively with the revelation of the root
cause of Roman decline for which he has prepared from the first stroke of his
portrait of Augustus, and which has governed the shaping of Volume I.

When the reader of *The Decline and Fall* reaches Chapters XV and XVI he
is likely, because of the arrangement of the previous chapters, to feel a
heightened sense of structural fulfilment; not only has he reached the end of
the book, but in that end he can also see the completion of an ordering pattern.[8] However, the conclusion of a work raised other expectations in Gibbon's contemporaries. Chesterfield reveals the literary habits and assumptions of his time with the acuity of an insider wishing to initiate an innocent
into the unspoken conventions of *le monde*:

As for the reflections of Historians, with which they think it necessary to interlard their
Histories, or at least to conclude their chapters . . .[9]

'Interlard' is an interesting choice of word, given Gibbon's placement of his
two general chapters on the barbarians: but it is on the association between
reflection and conclusion that I wish for the moment to dwell. The kind of
reflection on which a philosophic historian would choose to rest at the end of
a chapter was that of a paradoxical insight into the functional essence of human
affairs. The conclusions of his chapters thus tend to be pregnant with consequences for his discussion of causation. The final paragraph of Chapter VII
of Montesquieu's *Considérations* is a good example:

Ce fut alors que Pompée, dans la rapidité de ses victoires, acheva le pompeux ouvrage
de la grandeur de Rome. Il unit au corps de son empire des pays infinis; ce qui servit
plus au spectacle de la magnificence Romaine, qu'à sa vraie puissance: &, quoiqu'il
parût, par les écriteaux portés à son triomphe, qu'il avait augmenté le revenu du fisc
de plus d'un tiers, le pouvoir n'augmenta pas, & la liberté publique n'en fut que plus
exposée.[10]

By acknowledging but then discarding the traditional, unreflective admiration of the achievements of Pompey, Montesquieu suggests that this apparent
prosperity disguised and nurtured the seeds of debility which were already
germinated in the republic; and this reflection then flows quietly into Montes-

---

[8] Readers after 1788, for whom *The Decline and Fall* has always existed as a work of six
volumes, have naturally tended to overlook this structural wholeness; especially because the
volume divisions of later reprintings, such as those of Bury and Smith, have not observed the
frontiers between the original instalments, and indeed seem not to have considered them of
significance.

[9] *Letters*, II.46.

[10] *Œuvres*, III.404.

quieu's vindication of what he takes to be the real cause of Roman decline,
that its political forms, outstripped by its growth, eventually collapsed.

If one now turns to Volume I of *The Decline and Fall*, one will see that Gibbon, too, habitually ends his chapters on such causally resonant notes.[11] But
in Chapters XV and XVI he transfers this connexion between closure and
causal insight from the level of the chapter to that of the volume. The
reader's expectation, built up and gratified by Gibbon in his chapters, of moving through narrative or analysis to be ultimately rewarded with a conclusion
which is not merely a termination but also a judgement, is satisfied in
Chapters XV and XVI, where the real villain of the fall of the Roman empire
is revealed. In Chapter XV Gibbon discovers in Christianity the historical
factor which, arising just before the decay of Rome became visible, and affecting a body of the empire's inhabitants increasing in proportion with the
precipitancy of decline, exposed Rome to the otherwise ineffectual blows of
the barbarians and exacerbated the debilitating effects of luxury and
despotism, thus becoming the radical cause of its decline. Christianity undermines the empire by the uncivic tendency of its values and the unmanly
pusillanimity of what it requires its adherents enthusiastically to believe. Gibbon discusses the rise and progress of the new religion so as to bring out what
he sees as its intrinsic poverty and the fatal wound it inflicts on the empire
through its corruption of the minds and hearts of its population. Even in his
Memoirs, written long after the first volume of *The Decline and Fall* and when
he has thoroughly recognised that the attribution of effects to causes is not the
end of historical inquiry, he insists on the role of Christianity in the decline
of the empire:

As I believed, and as I still believe, that the propagation of the gospel and triumph
of the Church are inseparably connected with the decline of the Roman Monarchy,
I weighed the causes and effects of the Revolution . . .[12]

'Weighed' suggests well the pondering, placing and ranking of causes
whereby Gibbon makes his volume and his argument culminate in his indictment of the Christian religion.

As we have seen, Gibbon has deftly depreciated the traditional causes of the
decline of Rome, and thus created a vacancy at the heart of *The Decline and
Fall*. The magnitude of that vacancy is revealed by Shaftesbury's thoughts on
the fall of the empire in his 'Soliloquy: or, Advice to an Author':

And now that I am fall'n unawares into such profound Reflections on the Periods of
Government, and the Flourishing and Decay of *Liberty* and *Letters*; I can't be contented
to consider merely of the Inchantment which wrought so powerfully upon Mankind,
when first this Universal Monarchy was establish'd. I must wonder still more, when
I consider how after the extinction of this CAESAREAN and CLAUDIAN Family, and a

---

[11] Consider, for instance, the conclusions to Chapters II, V, VI, VII, X, and XI.
[12] *Memoirs*, p. 147; see also *A Vindication* (*The English Essays of Edward Gibbon*, p. 232).

short interval of Princes rais'd and destroy'd with much disorder and publick Ruin, the ROMANS shou'd regain their perishing Dominion, and retrieve their sinking State, by an after-Race of wise and able Princes successively adopted, and taken from a private State to rule the Empire of the World. They were Men who not only possess'd the military Virtues, and supported that sort of Discipline in the highest degree; but as they sought the interest of the World, they did what was in their power to restore *Liberty*, and raise again the perishing *Arts*, and decay'd *Virtue* of Mankind. But the Season was now past! The fatal Form of Government was become too natural: And the World, which had bent under it, and was become slavish and dependent, had neither Power nor Will to help it-self. The only Deliverance it cou'd expect, was from the merciless hands of the *Barbarians*, and a total Dissolution of that enormous Empire and despotick Power, which the best Hands cou'd not preserve from being destructive to human Nature. For even *Barbarity* and *Gothicism* were already enter'd into Arts, ere the Savages had made any Impression on the Empire. All the advantage which a for-tuitous and almost miraculous Succession of good Princes cou'd procure their highly favour'd Arts and Sciences, was no more than to preserve during their own time those perishing Remains, which for a-while with difficulty subsisted, after the Decline of *Liberty*. Not a Statue, not a Medal, not a tolerable Piece of Architecture cou'd shew it-self afterwards. Philosophy, Wit and Learning, in which some of those good Princes had themselves been so renown'd, fell with them: and Ignorance and Darkness overspread the World, and fitted it for the *Chaos* and Ruin which ensu'd.[13]

Pursuing his theme of the necessary connexion between the form of a government and the quality of the art those it governs will produce, Shaftesbury traces Roman decline directly to the 'fatal Form of Government' initiated by Augustus; it is this which eats away the strength of the Romans, weakening them to the point where they are an easy prey for the barbarians. In many respects, *The Decline and Fall* echoes this concise, yet subtle, analysis of the fall of Rome. Gibbon like Shaftesbury notes how the empire continues to decline despite the stewardship of men as virtuous as the Antonines (whom I presume Shaftesbury has primarily in mind when he speaks of 'an after-Race of wise and able Princes' and 'a fortuitous and almost miraculous Succession of good Princes'). Gibbon, too, notes and deplores the collapse of taste and artistic achievement in the empire; although he is eventually more puzzled than the brief 'even *Barbarity* and *Gothicism* were already enter'd into Arts' suggests Shaftesbury is by the separation in time of political and artistic decline. And Gibbon also echoes Shaftesbury in making the proximate cause of the empire's fall the sapping of civic vigour amongst its inhabitants:

Such princes [Nerva, Trajan, Hadrian, and the Antonines] deserved the honour of restoring the republic, had the Romans of their days been capable of enjoying a rational freedom.[14]

Gibbon accepts that the weakness of 'the generous but enervated youth of

[13] *Characteristicks*, I.220–2. Milton is an important English source of this ultimately republican analysis of decline (*Samson Agonistes*, II.268–71; *Paradise Regained*, IV.130–45). Closer to Gibbon's own time, Thomson had voiced similar ideas (*Liberty*, III. 372–89).

[14] *The Decline and Fall*, I.80: I.96.

Italy', and 'the patience of the Romans', may both plausibly be traced back
to the effects of the monarchy, since they were directly affected by that revolution.[15] But, like those of a philosophic cast of mind who lived at the time,
Gibbon feels that the real cause of Roman decline must touch a larger number
of the empire's denizens:

At the same time when Decius was struggling with the violence of the tempest, his
mind, calm and deliberate amidst the tumult of war, investigated the more general
causes, that, since the age of the Antonines, had so impetuously urged the decline of
the Roman greatness. He soon discovered that it was impossible to replace that
greatness on a permanent basis, without restoring public virtue, ancient principles and
manners, and the oppressed majesty of the laws.[16]

It is typical of Gibbon's coquetry over the cause of Roman decline that he
should not state directly what those 'more general causes' are, but should
invite us to infer their nature from the qualities Decius tries to revive. What
current element in society undermined public virtue, overturned ancient principles and manners, and disregarded the laws? Not the principate, which as
Gibbon has pointed out was carefully created to incorporate at least the form
of the ancient Roman state.[17] And our search for this 'more general' cause
will be quickened when we think on the role of the soldiery in the empire.
Gibbon states that

. . . the Roman emperors defended their extensive conquests, and preserved a military
spirit, at a time when every other virtue was oppressed by luxury and despotism.[18]

The relaxing of the valour and civic virtue of the native Romans by the
monarchy has shifted the balance of responsibility within the empire:

The rich and luxurious nobles, sinking into their natural character, accepted, as a
favour, this disgraceful exemption from military service; and as long as they were indulged in the enjoyment of their baths, their theatres, and their villas; they cheerfully
resigned the more dangerous cares of empire, to the rough hands of peasants and
soldiers.[19]

What is it that softens the rough hands of peasants and soldiers? The patricians' strenuous liberty is the victim of the despotism which they accept and
of the taste for luxury which cushions their servitude. But what could erode
the more hardy, if less refined, commitment of these new guardians of
empire?

Gibbon continues, then, to qualify, place or subordinate analyses of the
causes of Roman decline which other men of letters had found satisfactory.
At the same time, he drops hints as to the cause he finds at the root of the

---

[15] *The Decline and Fall*, I.189: I.225 and I.141: I.169.
[16] *The Decline and Fall*, I.252: I.301. First edition: '. . . discovered, that . . .'.
[17] See above, p. 72.
[18] *The Decline and Fall*, I.16: I.20. First edition: '. . . virtue was almost extinguished by the progress of despotism'.
[19] *The Decline and Fall*, I.263: I.314.

Roman decay. The fecklessness of Valerian and Gallienus leads almost annihilation of the empire:

It was saved by a series of great princes, who derived their obscure origin from martial provinces of Illyricum. Within a period of about thirty years, Claudius, Aureli Probus, Diocletian and his colleagues, triumphed over the foreign and domestic enemies of the state, re-established with the military discipline, the strength of the frontiers, and deserved the glorious title of Restorers of the Roman world.[20]

The vigilant reader, mindful of Diocletian's persecutions, will understand whom Gibbon is indicating with the phrase 'domestic enemies'; and once he has replaced it with the word 'Christians', it is clear that what underlies the passage is the antinomy between martial and Christian values.[21]

Before Gibbon composed *The Decline and Fall* there was already a long tradition of enlightened blame of Christianity which drew attention to its deleterious social consequences.[22] During the eighteenth century there were repeated attempts, made by the polite rather than the enthusiastic, to refute this view and to award Christianity a central place in civil society.[23] Thus *The Decline and Fall* enthrones Christianity as the *prime* cause of the fall of Rome at a time when a substantial body of contemporary thought was moving in the opposite direction.[24] Only here, according to Gibbon, do we find a solvent of civic

---

[20] *The Decline and Fall*, I.287: I.343. First edition: '. . . princes who . . .'.

[21] The subtlety of Gibbon's procedure in Volume I raises stubborn critical problems. When he describes Christianity as 'an independent and increasing state in the heart of the Roman Empire' (*The Decline and Fall*, I.451: I.537), does he intend us to recall, however subliminally, his earlier and echoing words describing the cause of decay initiated by the principate, which introduced 'a slow and secret poison into the vitals of the empire' (*The Decline and Fall*, I.57: I.69)? The span of attention such an effect demands is large; but the intention would be to create a worrying and vague disquiet in the reader, not a precise link. Certainly Gibbon's command of style, which is the fruit of exercise, has such effects within its scope.

[22] This tradition goes back at least to Machiavelli's *Discorsi* and *Dell'Arte della Guerra*. In 1697 it is restated by Bayle in his *Dictionaire Historique et Critique* (art. 'Junius', rem. 'B'), and in 1762 it recurs in Rousseau's *Du Contrat Social*. For other examples see Montesquieu, *Œuvres*, III.509; Boulainvilliers, *La Vie de Mahomed*, pp. 101–2 and 242; Pope, *Essay on Criticism*, ll. 681–96 and *The Dunciad Variorum*, III.91–104; Thomson, *Liberty*, II.250, 395–6, and IV.69–83; and Hume, *The Natural History of Religion*, in *Essays and Treatises*, IV.307–8.

[23] In *Paradise Regained* Milton depreciates classical oratory on grounds of social utility, preferring the Old Testament (IV.356–64). Later writers defended the centrality of Christianity to civil society less on grounds of the excellence of the Bible as a primer for statesmen, than on those of the importance of its tenets to the regular operation of society; see Kennett, *Romae Antiquae Notitia*, p. 61; Steele, *Tatler*, no. 130, III.170; and Warburton, *Julian, or a Discourse concerning the Earthquake and Fiery Eruption*, p. xliii. Warburton's *Divine Legation of Moses Demonstrated*, written 'to shew the necessity of RELIGION in general, and of the doctrine of a FUTURE STATE in particular, to civil Society, from the nature of things and the universal consent of Mankind' ('Preface'), is perhaps the century's most heroic attempt to place Christianity at the centre of earthly life. On this subject, see 'Orthodox Anglican Political Theology' in J. C. D. Clark's *English Society 1688–1832*, pp. 216–35.

[24] Montesquieu situates the damage Christianity did to the fabric of the empire after the process of decline was under way; consequently it cannot be a cause of that decline (*Œuvres*, III.514). Chesterfield juxtaposes the ruin of antiquity with the guile of the Church, but without suggesting that they are causally linked (*Letters*, II.156). Bacon's 'De Interpretatione Naturae Proemium' gives 'malignitas sectarum' a prominent place in the causes of the 'declinatio . . . et ruina' of states, and explicitly discounts 'barbarorum incursiones' (*Works*, V.194–6).

virtue of which the operation was sufficiently widespread to bring about the decline of the empire. Bishop Douglas, writing to Alexander Carlyle in 1783, recognised that Gibbon had made his 'Narrative only a vehicle for attacking the Religion of his Country'; the sharpness of the complaints which arose after the publication of the first volume of *The Decline and Fall* from those who presumably thought that they were winning the fight against infidelity show the accuracy and energy with which Gibbon struck.[25]

It is because he is working in a hostile environment that Gibbon chooses to express himself through irony; with him, as with others, ''tis the persecuting Spirit has rais'd the *bantering* one'.[26] In part, he hopes thereby to implant his unsettling views more deeply within the minds of those who might deny them – to render them less dismissable by virtue of their never being baldly stated, but always kept as immanent implications of a narrative otherwise amply graced by scholarship and urbanity – and moreover, as we shall see, closely echoing the language and arguments of the pious. But there is also a motive of discretion. In *A Project for the Advancement of Religion* (1709), Swift had asked 'why a law is not made for limiting the Press; at least so far as to prevent the publishing of such pernicious Books, as under Pretence of *Free-Thinking*, endeavour to overthrow those Tenets in Religion, which have been held inviolable almost in all Ages'.[27] Gibbon, however, had applied himself to Blackstone's *Commentaries* ('the excellent commentaries of Sir William Blackstone'), and so would have been fully aware of the still current statute law dealing with crimes against God and religion.[28] Moreover, he would also have been aware of the change in the temper of the age which was bringing this legislation out of the desuetude in which Swift had overlooked it.

---

[25] Quoted in Richard Sher, *Church and University in the Scottish Enlightenment*, p.201 n. 119.
[26] Shaftesbury, *Characteristicks*, I.72.
[27] *Prose Works*, II.60.
[28] *Memoirs*, p. 66. See *The English Essays of Edward Gibbon*, pp. 59–87: the problem of the date of the 'copious and critical abstract' (*Memoirs*, p. 148) Gibbon made of the first volume is discussed on p. 55 and in n. 3, p. 557. Although this abstract is confined to the first volume, it is reasonable to assume that Gibbon would have read the work in its entirety (there were two copies in his library), and that consequently he would have read of the crime of apostasy, which 'offence can only take place in such as have once professed the true religion': 'To this end it was enacted by statute 9 and 10 W. III. c. 32 that if any person educated in, or having made profession of, the christian religion, shall by writing, printing, teaching or advised speaking, deny the christian religion to be true, or the holy scriptures to be of divine authority, he shall upon the first offence be rendered incapable to hold any office or place of trust; and, for the second, be rendered incapable of bringing any action, being guardian, executor, legatee or purchaser of lands, and shall suffer three years imprisonment without bail' (Blackstone, *Commentaries on the Laws of England*, IV.44; see also J. C. D. Clark, *English Society 1688–1832*, pp. 284ff.). *The Decline and Fall* clearly falls within the scope of this law; indeed, after the religious tumult of his youth Gibbon might be said to have more consciously professed Christianity than one who had not undergone the same crisis of faith. Moreover, prosecution under this statute would have beggared Gibbon. By 1773 his letters already speak of hopes of a seat in Parliament, and since he turned out to be one of those MPs known more by their feet than by their voice, it seems likely that his motive for entering the House was a narrowly financial one. By becoming an MP he hoped to put himself in line for a lucrative sinecure

The last years of the seventeenth and the early years of the eighteenth century saw much wringing of hands over the profanity of the age.[29] But as the
century progressed, more defenders of Christianity appeared, many fighting
on the front of social utility, but others apparently motivated by an inner
piety.[30] And there is evidence to suggest that the early decades of the reign
of George III saw a growth of concern over profanity and irreligion. The
keener moral edge of the new reign is already evident when, in his 'Address
of the Painters, Sculptors and Architects to the King', Johnson urges George
to 'make the Arts of Elegance subservient to Virtue and Religion'.[31] Hume
also observes this change (which to him is a decline). In 1747 he could write
to James Oswald with calm assurance: 'I see not what bad consequences
follow, in the present age, from the character of an infidel; especially if a
man's conduct be in other respects irreproachable.'[32] In 1763, and after the
campaign of 1755–6 to censure himself and Kames for infidelity, that
assurance is diminished when he notes the vestigial powers of coercion at the
disposal of the Church: 'The liberty of the press is not so secured in any country, scarce even in this, as not to render such an open attack on popular prejudices somewhat dangerous.'[33] And by 1765 his confidence is evaporating
under the pressure of his dismayed recognition that the English 'are relapsing

(such as the seat on the Board of Trade he eventually obtained) and thereby to ease the financial embarrassments in which he had been enmeshed since the death of Edward Gibbon senior
in 1770 (see *Memoirs*, pp. 149–50). Were he convicted as an apostate, he would be debarred
from such positions of trust. With that hope removed, his only chance of financial security
lay in the possibility of his being the legatee of, as he puts it, 'old Ladies' (*Letters*, II.32). As
an apostate it would be impossible for him to inherit property, and so this hope, too, would
disappear. William Hone, the publisher, was prosecuted three times in 1817 under this
act.

[29] See William Cave, *Primitive Christianity*, sigs. A6v and A7r; William Wotton, *Reflections upon
Ancient and Modern Learning*, sig. a5v; Swift, *A Project for the Advancement of Religion* and *Letter
to a Young Gentleman*, in *Prose Works*, II.45 and IX.79, and *A Defence of Natural and Revealed
Religion*, I.278, II.60, III.584. In 1755 Robertson would still style the eighteenth century 'a
degenerate age' (*The Situation of the World at the Time of Christ's Appearance*; *Works*, I. cxxiii).

[30] In 1753 Blackwell had suggested that Britain was secure from reverses of fortune such as
those which had overtaken Rome because of 'the Support given to *Religion*, and if I may so
term it, the PUBLIC LEADING taken in *Probity and Virtue*' (*Memoirs of the Court of Augustus*,
I.195). In the same year Lyttelton, speaking 'on the Repeal of the Act called the JEW Bill',
had taken comfort from the integration of religion into the life of the nation (*Works*, p. 566).
In 1766 Thomas Bever had found in religion the cornerstone of society (*A Discourse on the Study
of Jurisprudence and the Civil Law*, p. 7). These men all take the high ground of the great utility
of religion to society as a whole, irrespective of its truth. On the personal level this position
is duplicated in the admission by even scoffers such as Lady Mary Wortley Montagu of the
comforts of religious belief (*Complete Letters*, III.57). Gibbon expressed similar sentiments at
the end of his life (*Letters*, III.118). Not surprisingly, then, Richard Sher has found that a
'spirit of reconciliation between Christianity and the Enlightenment' flourished in mid-
century (*Church and University in the Scottish Enlightenment*, p. 64).

[31] *London Gazette*, 6–10 January 1761.

[32] *Letters*, I.106. In 1737 he had written to Henry Home, fearing that 'Of Miracles' would give
offence 'even as the world is disposed at present' (*Letters*, I.24–5).

[33] *Letters*, I.374.

fast into the deepest Stupidity, Christianity & Ignorance'.[34] In 1776, he warned Gibbon about the 'prevalence of superstition' in England which 'prognosticates the Fall of Philosophy and Decay of Taste'.[35] Nor did this change in national manners spend its force in the 1760s and 70s. In 1787 George III issued *A PROCLAMATION for the Encouragement of PIETY and VIRTUE, and for preventing and punishing of VICE, PROFANENESS and IMMORALITY*, in which he urged his magistrates

. . . to suppress all loose and licentious prints, books and publications, dispersing poison to the minds of the young and unwary, and to punish the publishers and venders thereof; and to put in execution . . . an act of parliament made in the ninth year of the reign of the late King William the Third, intitled 'An Act for the more effectual suppressing of Blasphemy and Profaneness'.[36]

By this time, of course, Gibbon was living in Lausanne; but it is nevertheless important to acknowledge that the years of publication of *The Decline and Fall* were also years in which an attempt was made to purify public morals and in which (at least to the mind of one intelligent observer) there was a new piety abroad. We should not forget that in 1790, only two years after *The Decline and Fall* was completed, Burke was to draw attention to the outmodedness of infidelity.[37] Furthermore, Gibbon's chosen realm of historiography was particularly influenced by this change of disposition. From mid-century onwards, there is a rash of providentialist history, in which the finger of God makes frequent appearances.[38] Only when one uncovers this development in Gibbon's intellectual milieu can the extraordinariness of the first volume of *The Decline and Fall*, and of Chapter XV in particular, be clearly seen. In addition, an acquaintance with the literature of Christian apology in the eighteenth century is necessary if one is to appreciate the skill with which Gibbon transforms the hostility of his environment to his own account by imitating the accents and discussing the topics which had been used to comfort the faithful, but which in his hands assume a threatening aspect.

Gibbon felt the sharpness of this religious wind. Even the security of his position as a literary celebrity could not efface (although it might disguise) his

---

[34] *Letters*, I.498. For the campaign against Hume and Kames, see Richard Sher, *Church and University in the Scottish Enlightenment*, pp. 65ff.

[35] *Letters*, II.310; also reprinted in *Miscellaneous Works*, I.224–6.

[36] Leon Radzinowicz, *A History of English Criminal Law*, III.489.

[37] In *Reflections on the Revolution in France*: see J. C. D. Clark, *English Society 1688–1832*, p. 329.

[38] In 1755 Robertson had preached that 'there is no employment more delightful to a devout mind, than the contemplation of the divine wisdom in the government of this world. The civil history of mankind opens a wide field for this pious exercise' and went on to restate the providentialist explanation of the purpose of the Roman Empire (*The Situation of the World at the Time of Christ's Appearance*; *Works*, I.xciii and ci; see above, p. 17 n. 30). In 1769, he published his *History of Charles V*, which offers a providential explanation of the Reformation; see also James Tunstall, *Lectures on Natural and Revealed Religion*, p. 130 and Thomas Bever, *The History of the Legal Polity of the Roman State*, p. 33.

memory of what must have been a genuine anxiety in the weeks following publication of the first volume of *The Decline and Fall* in 1776. The contradictoriness of his remarks when he came to record this chapter of his life in his *Memoirs* is revealing. He begins with the injured dignity of one who has trusted too generously in his fellows:

I had likewise flattered myself that an age of light and liberty would receive without scandal, an enquiry into the *human* causes of the progress and establishment of Christianity.[39]

This quickly degenerates into a more straightforward bafflement, and its loftiness is replaced by satisfaction at the impotence of the enraged clergy (although even here we might feel that when Gibbon suggests the timid and the prudent feigned outrage, he is indicating the existence of pressure to assume at least an outward piety):

Had I believed that the majority of English readers were so fondly attached even to the name and shadow of Christianity; had I foreseen that the pious, the timid and the prudent would feel or affect to feel with such exquisite sensibility; I might, perhaps have softened the two invidious Chapters, which would create many enemies, and conciliate few friends. But the shaft was shot, the alarm was sounded, and I could only rejoyce, that if the voice of our priests was clamorous and bitter, their hands were disarmed of the powers of persecution.[40]

But as we have seen, if the hands of the clergy were disarmed, those of the magistrate were not; in fact, they were being encouraged to wield more vigorously the trenchant, if rusty, weapons already in their grasp. Gibbon ever found majesty of deportment congenial, in both life and letters, and we should not be surprised to find him choosing phrases which depict in the most becoming light the dignity which it seems he actually was able to muster in the face of the implacable tribe of his enemies. But he is also sufficiently honest not to strike from the record the unease which he felt and managed to disguise; 'Let me frankly own that I was startled at the first vollies of this Ecclesiastical ordnance.'[41] And a note which describes his response to the Arian Taylor's contribution to the controversy betrays his awareness of the laws and penalties which could be brought against him; 'The stupendous title, *Thoughts on the causes of the Grand Apostacy* at first agitated my nerves.'[42] The term 'apostasy' is used by Blackstone to denote the crime against God and religion, for which Gibbon had such good reason to fear conviction. In the work Gibbon wrote in the midst of the controversy surrounding his first volume, we find a much more direct acknowledgement, unsmoothed by retrospection, of the hornets' nest he was stirring up:

When I delivered to the world the First Volume of an important History, in which I

[39] *Memoirs*, p. 157.
[40] *Memoirs*, pp. 159–60; compare Shaftesbury, *Characteristicks*, I.149.
[41] *Memoirs*, p. 160.
[42] *Memoirs*, p. 171.

had been obliged to connect the progress of Christianity with the civil state and revolutions of the Roman Empire, I could not be ignorant that the result of my inquiries might offend the interest of some and the opinions of others.[43]

There are thus strong prudential motives for Gibbon's veiling with irony the explanation of Roman decline he wished to impart in Volume I. The cogency of those motives might be seconded by other considerations which suggested the appropriateness of irony when discussing religion. Shaftesbury had maintained that wit was a 'Remedy against Vice, and a kind of Specifick against Superstition and melancholy Delusion', and in *The Decline and Fall* Gibbon eruditely shows how venerable is the tradition of irony in religious dispute:

Against such unworthy adversaries [the mythologising poets], Cicero condescended to employ the arms of reason and eloquence; but the satire of Lucian was a much more adequate, as well as more efficacious weapon.

In his circular letters, which were addressed to the several cities, Constantine employed against the heretics the arms of ridicule and *comic* raillery.[44]

In addition, Antony Collins had suggested that religion demanded an ironic response not on grounds of remedial aptness, but simply because folly should always be rewarded by mockery: 'In a word, the Opinions and Practices of Men in all Matters, and especially in Matters of Religion, are generally so absurd and ridiculous that it is impossible for them not to be the Subjects of Ridicule.'[45] Thus a wide range of disparate considerations – considerations of rhetorical efficacy, of protective self-interest, and of traditional appropriateness – seem to have combined to impel Gibbon towards the irony which saturates Volume I of *The Decline and Fall*, soaking far below its verbal surface to stain even its form. Gibbon's irony consists not of an accent or an idiom, the 'prophane Scoffs and Jests' of the free-thinker pilloried by the Boyle lecturers; only its subordinate aims are secured through felicities of style.[46] It is the medium of a strategy whose covert ambitions determine every aspect of the first volume.

Chapter XV has long been recognised as one of the finest examples in the language of sustained irony, and an orthodoxy has arisen to explain how the irony works. F. R. Leavis, comparing Gibbon's irony with Swift's, gives the keynote: 'The decorously insistent pattern of Gibbonian prose insinuates a solidarity with the reader . . . establishes an understanding and habituates to certain assumptions.'[47] This belief that Gibbon creates a relationship of seamless confidence between himself and his reader was developed, again in comparison with Swift, by A. E. Dyson; 'Swift is concerned to betray his

---

[43] *A Vindication: The English Essays of Edward Gibbon*, p. 232.
[44] *Characteristicks*, I.128; *The Decline and Fall*, I.31: I.37 and II.262 n. 82.
[45] *Discourse Concerning Ridicule and Irony in Writing*, p. 19.
[46] See, for example, *A Defence of Natural and Revealed Religion*, II.863.
[47] *The Common Pursuit*, p. 75.

readers, but Gibbon's betrayal is of targets that he and the reader have in common'; and it has been adopted by some of Gibbon's more recent critics.[48]

Such toothless irony indeed existed in the eighteenth century. Chesterfield urges Philip Stanhope to cultivate 'genteel irony', the use of which comprised 'one great part of the knowledge of the world', since it was the correct and prompt pronunciation of this shibboleth which distinguished the true inhabitant of that charmed circle of privilege called 'the world' from the interloper; and John Barrell has recently suggested how this particular badge of belonging is part of a whole array of such marks which defined the gentleman in terms of a comprehensive point of view and the verbal idiom which seemed naturally to accompany that expansive, even vision.[49] However, the cutting edge of Gibbon's ironic treatment of Christianity is honed by the perfection with which, in the chapters preceding Chapter XV, he has confected a style apparently consonant with the polite badinage of genteel irony, which then becomes hostile to those who had found it companionable. In these last two chapters of Volume I that style is replaced by prose which, instead of exhaling a sense of assured community with its readers, is vivified by Gibbon's awareness of how separate he really is from the society in which he may seem perfectly to inhere. As we have seen, on the score of religion at least Gibbon had little reason to feel at home in the England of George III.

After announcing the importance of a 'candid but rational inquiry into the progress and establishment of Christianity', Gibbon begins Chapter XV by distinguishing two different kinds of religious discussion:

The scanty and suspicious materials of ecclesiastical history seldom enable us to dispel the dark cloud that hangs over the first age of the church. The great law of impartiality too often obliges us to reveal the imperfections of the uninspired teachers and believers of the gospel; and, to a careless observer, *their* faults may seem to cast a shade on the faith which they professed. But the scandal of the pious Christian, and the fallacious triumph of the Infidel, should cease as soon as they recollect not only *by whom*, but likewise to whom, the Divine Revelation was given. The theologian may indulge the pleasing task of describing Religion as she descended from Heaven, arrayed in her native purity. A more melancholy duty is imposed on the historian. He must discover the inevitable mixture of error and corruption, which she contracted in a long residence upon earth, among a weak and degenerate race of beings.[50]

This all seems very fair (if loftily phrased); but we shall quickly discover that Gibbon's disingenuousness is often a case of temporarily veiling discon-

---

[48] 'A note on dismissive irony', p. 222. See also David Jordan ('Gibbon takes his readers into his confidence', *Gibbon and his Roman Empire*, p. 152) and Lionel Gossman ('Every reader of the *Decline and Fall* reoccupies . . . the same impregnable position . . . as Gibbon's philosopher', *The Empire Unpossess'd*, p. 82).

[49] Chesterfield, *Letters*, II.32; John Barrell, *English Literature in History, 1730–80: An Equal, Wide Survey*, *passim*. On the coherence of the aristocratic vision, see 'The social theory of elite hegemony' in J. C. D. Clark, *English Society 1688–1832*, pp. 93–118.

[50] *The Decline and Fall*, I.449: I.535; I.449–50: I.535–6.

certing complexity with disarming simplicity. The assumption that the realms of doctrine and history are quite separate and that the historian's discoveries could be taken by only a careless observer to impugn the verities celebrated by the theologian seems to be made in all sincerity. But it is an assumption to which the ensuing discussion will prove fatal. For as this particular historian sifts among 'the secondary causes of the rapid growth of the Christian church' which with feigned reverence he has selected as his province, he uncovers traces of error and corruption which lead straight to Christianity's central mysteries.[51] Gibbon may scrupulously confine his attention to the faith's historical record, but the implications of his account are not so restricted.[52]

The passage thus has a depth which its appearance of candour belies; and our presumption of dissimulation on Gibbon's part will be strengthened when we inquire into the passage's verbal resonances.[53] Milton had considered the contamination of truth in *Areopagitica*:

Truth indeed came once into the world with her divine master, and was a perfect shape most glorious to look on; but when he ascended, and his apostles after him were laid asleep, then strait arose a wicked race of deceivers, who . . . took the virgin truth, hewed her lovely form into a thousand pieces, and scattered them to the four winds.[54]

This closeness of subject-matter is multiply suggestive. On the one hand, it is a crucial part of Gibbon's strategy to gain audience for his irony that he should initially seem at least politely pious, and this respectful handling of an established religious topic clearly contributes to the desired appearance of at least respect if not devoutness. But the ultimate tendency of Chapters XV and XVI is to vilify the ways of God to men, and one can only guess at the private

---

[51] *The Decline and Fall*, I.450: I.536. In *The Reason of Church Government* (1642), Milton had ranked 'that knowledge that rests in contemplation of natural causes and dimensions' as necessarily 'a lower wisdom, as the object is low' (*The Works of John Milton, Historical, Political and Miscellaneous*, I.60). But in *The Advancement of Learning* (1605), Bacon had been more specific and had suggested that scrutiny of secondary causes led to atheism (*Works*, I.5: see also Hobbes, *Leviathan* (1651), Part IV, Chapter 44). Thus to the sharp-sighted Christian Gibbon's interest in examining only secondary causes may have seemed ominous.

[52] Gibbon later acknowledges the intimate reliance of Christianity on history, but only at a safe distance from Chapter XV: 'a religion [Christianity], which depends on the laborious in vestigation of historic evidence' (*The Decline and Fall*, III.566). An awareness of how thoroughly the establishment and vindication of Christianity is bound up with the examination and settling of historical questions did not suddenly dawn on Gibbon at some time in between 1776 and 1781: the intellectual struggles lying behind his conversion to Catholicism and reconversion to Protestantism in the early 1750s had made such knowledge inescapable.

[53] We should not forget that this is the most revised and deliberate part of *The Decline and Fall*: '. . . the fifteenth and sixteenth Chapters have been reduced by three successive revisals from a large Volume to their present size; and they might still be compressed without any loss of facts or sentiments' (*Memoirs*, p. 156). Compare also *Memoirs*, p. 180; 'I will add two facts which have seldom occurred in the composition of six or at least of five quartos. 1 My first rough manuscript, without any intermediate copy has been sent to the press' – the correction 'or at least of five' suggests that there was at least one 'intermediate copy' of Volume I.

[54] *Works*, I.166. On the subject of the contamination of holy truth, see also Dryden, *Religio Laici*, ll. 258–9.

satisfaction it may have given Gibbon to appear to be following in Milton's footsteps while in fact taking the directly opposite path. As with so much of Gibbon's irony, the more one delves into and meditates on this passage, the more clearly one realises that the regular form of one's response to his disingenuity is that of sensing innocence dissolve to reveal knowingness.

Gibbon goes on to shoulder the burden of the historian's 'melancholy duty':

> Our curiosity is naturally prompted to inquire by what means the Christian faith obtained so remarkable a victory over the established religions of the earth. To this inquiry, an obvious but satisfactory answer may be returned; that it was owing to the convincing evidence of the doctrine itself, and to the ruling providence of its great Author. But as truth and reason seldom find so favourable a reception in the world, and as the wisdom of Providence frequently condescends to use the passions of the human heart, and the general circumstances of mankind, as instruments to execute its purpose; we may still be permitted, though with becoming submission, to ask, not indeed what were the first, but what were the secondary causes of the rapid growth of the Christian church. It will, perhaps, appear, that it was most effectually favoured and assisted by the five following causes: I. The inflexible, and, if we may use the expression, the intolerant zeal of the Christians, derived, it is true, from the Jewish religion, but purified from the narrow and unsocial spirit, which, instead of inviting, had deterred the Gentiles from embracing the law of Moses. II. The doctrine of a future life, improved by every additional circumstance which could give weight and efficacy to that important truth. III. The miraculous powers ascribed to the primitive church. IV. The pure and austere morals of the Christians. V. The union and discipline of the Christian republic, which gradually formed an independent and increasing state in the heart of the Roman empire.[55]

Because critics have hitherto concentrated so exclusively on the 'proportioned elegance' of Gibbon's style, qualities which are revealed only when a sentence is viewed as a shape in time, rather than as an instantaneous order of balancing masses, have been neglected.[56] Yet this passage depends, as do so many in *The Decline and Fall*, on Gibbon's Jamesian sense of timing. As we move from the happy simplicities of those whose faith is so absolute that they are untroubled by the circularity of explaining the worldly success of Christianity by reference to its undoubted truth (while at the same time vindicating its truth by reference to its undoubted worldly success) the prose is thickened by punctuation which seems calculated to create a sense of deferential hesitation and disabling scruple; the early placing of parenthetic phrases such as 'though with becoming submission' are particularly decisive in generating the impression of a writer anxious to meet and remove any objection before it arises.

This circumspection is akin to the flaunted scrupulousness with which the *philosophes* preface their ironic attacks on Christianity, colouring their mischievous designs with the fairest appearances of truth and candour and

---

[55] *The Decline and Fall*, I.450–1: I.536–7. First edition: '. . . returned, That . . .'.

[56] See Michel Baridon, *Edward Gibbon et le Mythe de Rome*, pp. 841–2 and Lionel Gossman, *The Empire Unpossess'd*, pp. 99–101 for examples of such analysis.

veiling their inward contempt with outward reverence. Comparisons with Voltaire's *Essai sur les Mœurs* (1769) are particularly interesting, since propinquities of phrasing suggest that Gibbon may have called this work to mind when, in his own way, he responded to the call 'Écrasez l'infâme!':[57]

Au moins nous est-il permis de peser les probabilités, et de nous servir de notre raison dans ce qui n'intéresse point nos dogmes sacrés, supérieurs à toute raison, et qui ne cèdent qu'à la morale.

C'était [the parting of the Red Sea to allow the passage of the Jews] assurément le plus grand évènement dans l'histoire du monde: comment donc ni Hérodote, ni Manéthon, ni Ératosthène, ni aucun des Grecs, si grands amateurs du merveilleux et toujours en correspondance avec l'Égypte, n'ont-ils point parlé de ces miracles qui devaient occuper la mémoire de toutes les générations? Je ne fais pas assurément cette réflexion pour infirmer le témoignage des livres hébreux, que je révère comme je dois: je me borne à m'étonner seulement du silence de tous les Égyptiens et de tous les Grecs. Dieu ne voulut pas sans doute qu'une histoire si divine nous fût transmise par aucune main profane.[58]

But to juxtapose these passages from the *Essai sur les Mœurs* with that from *The Decline and Fall* is to see that, in contrast to Gibbon, the energy of Voltaire's irony comes from its volatility, from the way that it seems always on the point of evaporating and thereby depositing in a pure state the straightforward and indignant accusation of which it is the vehicle. Voltaire's restlessness – the feeling we have that he might at any moment lose patience with the game of irony and lapse into simple denunciation – explains the small scale on which his irony operates. It tends to be bounded by a paragraph; for instance, the *Essai sur les Mœurs* has the general character of an ironic work simply because it is made up of a large number of ironic sentences, and not because the *shape* of the work is ironic. Gibbon, however, is an ironist *de longue haleine*, whose disingenuousness is more deeply matured and emerges in a larger form. Thus, although it is inconceivable that anyone should not notice Voltaire's irony, it is of the essence of Gibbon's irony that its slight profile, the way it presents itself thin side foremost, as it were, to its readers, means that even the most intelligent and careful reader – indeed, especially the most intelligent and careful reader – may be unsure of its borders, or overlook it completely. Herder is a fine example of this:

[57] While exiled in Lausanne Gibbon made the acquaintance of Voltaire ('whom I then rated above his real magnitude'), and attended the dramas put on at Monrepos (*Memoirs*, pp. 82–4). Gibbon there records his feat of memorising Voltaire's Ode, 'O Maison d'Aristippe! . . .' after only two readings: we should never underestimate the power of the historian's mind to retain and order what he has read.

[58] *Œuvres Complètes*, XI.41 and XI.62; for the second quotation, see *The Decline and Fall*, I.517–18: I.618–19. This ostentatious circumspection is not, of course, restricted to Voltaire: it is also to be found in Montesquieu (see particularly Book XXIV of the *Esprit des Loix*) and Boulainvilliers' *Vie de Mahomed* (p. 247). Its sweetness as a tactic in the struggle against the Church springs from the fact that in employing it, the *philosophes* were turning the weapons of Christian apologists back upon themselves: Gibbon notes Bossuet's ability to assume 'with consummate art, the tone of candour and simplicity' (*Memoirs*, p. 59).

With heartfelt pleasure we can here cite the third classical British historian, the rival of Hume, and of Robertson, whom sometimes perhaps he excels, Gibbon; whose *History of the Decline and Fall of the Roman Empire* is a finished masterpiece . . . The cry that has been raised in England, however, against this learned and truly philosophical work, as if the author were an enemy to the Christian religion, seems to me unjust: for Gibbon has spoken of Christianity, as of other matters in his history, with great mildness.[59]

Herder's response may provoke a smile, since Gibbon's skill as an ironist is for us such a familiar critical notion; but it is, of course, the fact that Herder's response speaks to us from a time before this critical orthodoxy was in place which makes it so valuable, so revealing an indication of the way in which the extraordinarily fine grain of Gibbon's irony necessarily makes *The Decline and Fall* susceptible to this misreading. It may seem puzzling that on the one hand, Herder could ignore Gibbon's irony, while on the other, Chapters XV and XVI could provoke such a violent response. But the delicacy of Gibbon's irony goes hand in glove with its potent insidiousness. That Herder should overlook it is quite consonant with the inability of others to forget it. It is precisely because Gibbon's irony is so perfectly controlled and because, despite the absolute unwaveringness of his ironic intent, its linguistic surface is exactly situated at the point where irony becomes invisible, that the reception afforded it by those of an outward and unreflective Christian conformity was so energetically hostile. The twin sources of that energy are frustration and annoyance: frustration at the historian's deft shielding of himself behind irony, annoyance at the way Gibbon's deferential demeanour also imparts a disguised violence which fixes the poisoned dart of what he has to say about the role of Christianity in history unerringly in its once complacent but now goaded victims.

So much for the effect and ancestry of Gibbon's manner. The real bite of his irony in this chapter, however, springs from the way he engages with and transforms topics drawn from the Christian apologetics of his age.[60] In addressing the question of the Christian faith's remarkable victory over all the religions of the earth, Gibbon was rehearsing a circumstance of the history of the early Church offered by many divines as a proof of the truth of their faith. Robertson had touched on this subject in his sermon of 1755, *The Situation of the World at the Time of Christ's Appearance*.[61] The Boyle

---

[59] J. G. v. Herder, *Reflections on the Philosophy of the History of Mankind*, p. 302. Cardinal Newman was another obviously competent reader who, in *The Grammar of Assent*, found Gibbon actually ambiguous rather than ironic (see Empson's discussion in *Seven Types of Ambiguity*, p. x).

[60] In what follows, I discuss Gibbon's adoption and twisting of the arguments of the Christian apologists. I would also like to think that Gibbon's selection of five secondary causes with which to explain the success of Christianity is a mischievous allusion to Woodward's ascription of the luxuriant growth of profanity to 'Five general Causes' in the Boyle lectures (*A Defence of Natural and Revealed Religion*, I.541).

[61] *Works*, I.xciv.

lectures – of which Gibbon owned a copy – return to it frequently. Stanhope laboured to 'prove the Success this Religion hath met with in the World, an unanswerable Evidence, that its Doctrines are of God'.[62] Bradford believed that

The Attestation it [Christianity] hath received from without, *viz.* from Prophecies compared with Events; from Miracles wrought in Confirmation of it; from the surpriz-ing Success of its being published to the World, is of great Use, both for the exciting Men seriously to consider it, and the persuading them to believe it.[63]

As we shall see, in the course of Chapter XV Gibbon examines all these proofs (prophecies, miracles and worldly success) and finds them insufficient.

The triumph of Christianity was, to the eyes of the faithful, evidence that it had been planted by God not only because it flourished despite the hostility of its environment, but because it made no appeal to those base desires which normally ensure an easy reception for whatever favours them.[64] Soame Jenyns, writing in the same year as that in which Gibbon published his first volume, argues that Christianity's success is miraculous, given that it works 'in opposition to the interests, pleasures, ambition, prejudices, and even reason of mankind'.[65] Others shrank from the invidiousness of making the demands Christianity made on men's beliefs and inclinations so uncom-promising, and introduced the idea of man's depraved appetite to reconcile the naturalness of the Christian faith's doctrines with their not pandering to men's desires:

The Precepts of Christianity are all of them so perfectly good in their own Nature, and so thorowly agreeable to the Understanding of a reasonable Creature, that every Man to whom they are made known, would readily comply with them, if it were not for the seeming Pleasures of Sin, and the Difficulties with which some instances of Virtue seem to be attended . . .[66]

Now, when Gibbon considers the success of Christianity, he acknowledges that this providential explanation is 'obvious and satisfactory'; but as he

---

[62] *A Defence of Natural and Revealed Religion*, I.644; see also I.737. Compare also Leng's fifth Ser-mon (III.49), or his fifteenth, in which he rejoices that 'the wonderful Manner in which Chris-tianity was so speedily propagated, and the Effects which for a long time followed it, are a standing Argument of its Truth and Divinity, and give a more than human Testimony to the Revelation contained in Holy Scripture' (III.139).

[63] *A Defence of Natural and Revealed Religion*, I.440.

[64] In *Letters from a Persian in England* (1735), Lyttelton gives this as the advice of a cunning minister (presumably a Walpole figure) to the king of the Troglodytes (*Works*, p. 139). Leng had argued for the truth of Christianity on the grounds of its eschewal of such tactics (*A Defence of Natural and Revealed Religion*, III. 134–5). Mahomet was usually cited as an example of such a cheat; see Sir William Temple, 'Of Heroic Virtue', *Works*, III.370 and John Adams, *The Flowers of Modern History*, pp. 8–9.

[65] *A View of the Internal Evidence of the Christian Religion*, p. 106; this work was also in Gibbon's library. Compare William Cave: 'The genius and nature of its *Doctrine* was such, as was almost impossible to escape the frowns and displeasure of men' (*Primitive Christianity*, p. 4). See also Dryden, *Religio Laici*, ll. 158–63.

[66] *A Defence of Natural and Revealed Religion*, I.505.

delves into the secondary causes of its triumph, they eventually so sufficiently explain the spread of Christianity that the need for the providential cause vanishes. Gibbon thus brings Christianity within the scope of the natural history of religion and finds that, far from being miraculous, its success was only to be expected. Leng had asserted that a purely human inquiry could never account for the rise and progress of the Christian faith:

They therefore, who look no farther than Human Nature and Human Means, may well enough be allowed to lie under great Surprize, when they see the Foundations of a Religion, designed to be universal, laid in the Disgrace of a crucified Master, the Poverty and Simplicity of illiterate Publicans and Fishermen, and the Blood and Sufferings of the much greater part of them, who, at its first setting out into the World had the Hardiness to embrace it upon such forbidding Terms.[67]

But Gibbon is not distracted by the severity of Christianity's moral injunctions and its apparent worldly disabilities from the fact that, as his careful choice of secondary causes shows, it gratifies man's propensity to enthusiasm, assuages his fear of death and desire for eternal life, and feeds his taste for prodigies with an unequalled generosity. Even the pure morals of the Christians, considered in the light of their motives, are base.[68] Gibbon's apparently pious restriction of his attention to secondary causes thus has the effect of depicting Christianity in the same colours as a natural religion such as Islam.[69]

It is necessary to lay stress on the element of camouflage in Gibbon's irony, its ability initially to present itself as something far more innocent than it turns out to be, because to respond fully to Chapter XV is to trace how the courtesy and respectfulness of its opening shades into the calm effrontery of its conclusion, where the historian questions the truth of the darkness at noon and thereby finally dispels the illusion that the doctrinal is insulated from the historical. The trenchancy of Gibbon's irony derives from the joining of this final effrontery to the initial shadowing of the orthodox by a seamless exposition. Gibbon's words about the advance of corruption in the Catholic Church apply well to his own argument in Chapter XV:

From the first of the fathers to the last of the popes, a succession of bishops, of saints, of martyrs, and of miracles, is continued without interruption, and the progress of

[67] *A Defence of Natural and Revealed Religion*, I.823.

[68] 'As it is my intention to remark only such human causes as were permitted to second the influence of revelation, I shall slightly mention two motives which might naturally render the lives of the primitive Christians much purer and more austere than those of their Pagan contemporaries or their degenerate successors; repentance for their past sins, and the laudable desire of supporting the reputation of the society in which they were engaged' (*The Decline and Fall*, I.479: I.572).

[69] The exactness with which Gibbon has feigned the dialect of piety can be seen if we juxtapose a passage from Bever's *History of the Legal Polity of the Roman State*: 'the Almighty; who, having once manifested his glory to the world, and established the worship of himself by signs and wonders, hath, in later times, more usually chosen to effect his gracious purposes, by the ordinary, though not less providential, operations of secondary causes' (pp. 421–2).

superstition was so gradual and almost imperceptible, that we know not in what particular link we should break the chain of tradition.[70]

The bemused Christian reader of these final chapters, for whom the historian's ostentatious scruple is but an added irritation, cannot see where the all-too-evident poison of the final paragraphs was introduced. Trapped with their heretical implications, the believing reader is compelled either to accept those implications, or to deny the whole chapter and the virtues of politeness, erudition and reasonableness which are inscribed there with such deceitful clarity.

By throwing a shade of doubt over the darkness at noon, and thus questioning the Passion as a whole, Gibbon opposes history to doctrine in the sense that the lowly historian, through diligent research, is able to discomfit the most seraphic doctors. Truly, the last shall be first. But there is another tension between history and doctrine informing Chapter XV. Gibbon archly admonishes the historian 'not to dissemble the difficulty of adopting such a theory as may reconcile the interest of religion with that of reason'.[71] He himself poses as one sincerely involved in a similar endeavour: that of bringing together history and religion, actions and principles. But throughout, the effect of his writing is in fact to tease Church doctrine and historical truth, Christian professions and Christian deeds gradually apart; and the delicacy with which the scale of this disjunction is increased until they finally and irreconcilably diverge, testifies to prose of remarkable and sustained control. The Christian reader is confronted with a series of dilemmas, of varying aspect but constant substance and steepening gravity, in which he is required to decide between the claims of his faith and the findings of the historian, and on which Gibbon does not arbitrate but which he is content merely to indicate.[72] This covert aggression is present even in the formalities of the introductory paragraphs:

While that great body [the Roman empire] was invaded by open violence, or undermined by slow decay, a pure and humble religion gently insinuated itself into the minds of men, grew up in silence and obscurity, derived new vigour from opposition, and finally erected the triumphant banner of the cross on the ruins of the Capitol.[73]

---

[70] *The Decline and Fall*, I.477: I.570.

[71] *The Decline and Fall*, I.477: I.569–70. The possibility of reconciling reason and religion is a perennial topic, but it was debated with great force in the eighteenth century, when the reasonable was so commonly taken as the creditable; hence Locke's *Reasonableness of Christianity* (1695), the numerous attempts to bring revealed and natural religion together, and Addison's writing *The Evidences of the Christian Religion* in opposition to 'Our modern Scepticks and Infidels [who] are great Pretenders to Reason and Philosophy, and are willing to have it thought that none who are really possess'd of those Talents, can easily assent to the Truth of Christianity' (p. iv).

[72] Gibbon silently confronts us with the choice Bayle nakedly offered his reader: 'Il faut renoncer aux maximes les plus sûres selon lesquelles on juge des faits, ou convenir que Jean Barclai ne renonça point en Angleterre à la profession du Catholicisme' (*Dictionaire Historique et Critique*, art. 'Barclai', rem. I, I.448).

[73] *The Decline and Fall*, I.449: I.535. First edition: '. . . capitol'.

The piety of 'pure and humble' is exemplary, but the sensitive Christian might be unsettled by the solecism in presenting the triumph of the Church in military terms: and that unease is amplified when Gibbon, speaking as if from the time of Caligula, expresses surprise at the present 'inflexible perseverance' of the Jews, given that 'when the tides of the ocean, and the course of the planets were suspended for the convenience of the Israelites', God's chosen people were incorrigibly wayward.[74] Devout suspicions may be aroused further by the historian's strange unconcern to draw any conclusions from the incoherence he has found between Biblical and secular accounts of the Jews – and this despite the incoherence being heavily pregnant with possible consequences. Does it suggest that the Old Testament prodigies are themselves frauds? Or does it point merely to later falsification of the attitude of the Jews, as zealous then as now, to those prodigies – the peccadilloes of rabbis wishing to write a history which would sustain Jewish religious fervour by painting a vivid picture of divine favour and disgrace? Or is the whole business a miracle at which it is seemly only to marvel? Gibbon's blandness is superb:

The contemporaries of Moses and Joshua had beheld with careless indifference the most amazing miracles. Under the pressure of every calamity, the belief of those miracles has preserved the Jews of a later period from the universal contagion of idolatry; and in contradiction to every known principle of the human mind, that singular people seems to have yielded a stronger and more ready assent to the traditions of their remote ancestors, than to the evidence of their own senses.[75]

Of course, the Christian reader is likely to set these questions to one side as at most academic, since the discrepancies the apparently engrossed Gibbon is uncovering concern only the Jews and the Old Testament. The tenets of his own faith are surely untouched.[76]

That repose is unsettled when it becomes clear that Gibbon is considering the Jewish faith as a natural religion, viewing it as just as much an institutionalising of the desires of its adherents as an object of their veneration. This attitude releases his comments from applying merely to the Jews and makes them particular exemplifications of flaws to which all religions are prone (excluding Christianity, which, as the special creation of God, proceeds, in the eyes of the faithful, according to its own laws):

The conquest of the land of Canaan was accompanied with so many wonderful and with so many bloody circumstances, that the victorious Jews were left in a state of irreconcilable hostility with all their neighbours. They had been commanded to extirpate some of the most idolatrous tribes, and the execution of the Divine will had seldom

---

[74] *The Decline and Fall*, I.452: I.538–9.

[75] *The Decline and Fall*, I.452: I.539.

[76] Chastellux, whose *De la Félicité Publique* anticipates Gibbon's work in many respects, simply states the propinquity of Christianity and Judaism (I.250). Gibbon prefers to restrain his thoughts so that the reader sees them as disturbing possibilities.

been retarded by the weakness of humanity. With the other nations they were forbidden to contract any marriages or alliances, and the prohibition of receiving them into the congregation, which in some cases was perpetual, almost always extended to the third, to the seventh, or even to the tenth generation. The obligation of preaching to the Gentiles the faith of Moses, had never been inculcated as a precept of the law; nor were the Jews inclined to impose it on themselves as a voluntary duty.[77]

Does this passage really suggest, in the vein of the later comment that 'the situation of the first Christians coincided very happily with their religious scruples', that the principles of the Jewish faith – and the suggestion would of course be equally valid for any faith – were not the product of revelation, but merely an expression of the bloodthirsty and solitary character of the Jewish race?[78] Or is its upshot the easier thought, that through an act of grace God had made the actions he required from the Israelites peculiarly congenial to them? Gibbon does not arbitrate between these rival possibilities, and so in that respect at least they are both equally probable. However, the second, pious possibility involves a fatal begging of the question. You can adopt that reading only if you assume what is at stake – namely that Judaism is a divine, and not merely human, institution. Beneath their variety of subject, the interpretative cruces with which Gibbon confronts his reader all share this form. In his studied reticence, his well-bred refusal to be dogmatic, Gibbon always provides the pious reader with a way out of these dilemmas. But the price of egress is an outrageous privileging of his own beliefs and a casting aside of probability and all he knows of human nature:

It was with the utmost difficulty that ancient Rome could support the institution of six vestals; but the primitive church was filled with a great number of persons of either sex, who had devoted themselves to the profession of perpetual chastity.

The government of the church has often been the subject as well as the prize of religious contention. The hostile disputants of Rome, of Paris, of Oxford, and of Geneva, have alike struggled to reduce the primitive and apostolic model, to the respective standards of their own policy. The few who have pursued this inquiry with more candour and impartiality, are of opinion, that the apostles declined the office of legislation, and rather chose to endure some partial scandals and divisions, than to exclude the Christians of a future age from the liberty of varying their forms of ecclesiastical government according to the changes of times and circumstances.[79]

Are we able to believe that the Apostles were this prescient and considerate, and that the sexual morality of the Christians was indeed so extraordinary? If you assume the divine origin of Christianity, all these problems disappear and are transformed into sure tokens of its heavenly extraction.

But the effect of being so often required to smuggle in the desired conclusion as an axiom, and of supposing what the study of history was, according

---

[77] *The Decline and Fall*, I.453: I.539–40.
[78] *The Decline and Fall*, I.487: I.581.
[79] *The Decline and Fall*, I.485: I.578–9; I.488: I.582–3. first edition: '. . . as well as the instrument . . .'; '. . . have each of them strove . . .'.

to thinkers such as Leibnitz, intended to demonstrate, is that the Christian reader is made aware of how slender are the evidences of his religion.[80] He is repeatedly obliged to suppose the truth of his faith in order to wring from the past the testimony that faith requires to vindicate its truth: while Gibbon, calmly reviewing the past and indicating still more of these dilemmas, courteously abstains from pronouncing upon the questions which he must merely present to his reader, since the 'duty of an historian does not call upon him to interpose his private judgment'.[81] Like the prose in which Gibbon discusses the secular history of the empire, we can feel this writing shifting and sliding beneath us. But whereas before Gibbon was concerned to establish his authority as a guide to the past, he now pretends to abandon that dominant role the better to manoeuvre his hapless reader.

We have considered the general structure of Gibbon's irony, its typical forms and underlying assumptions. However, its success is produced not just by the sureness with which he has grasped how well placed the historian is to damage Christianity, but also by the way in which that underlying intentness is disguised by a style that seems to belong to one whose only concern is to smooth the path of the believing reader:

While the orthodox church preserved a just medium between excessive veneration and improper contempt for the law of Moses, the various heretics deviated into equal but opposite extremes of error and extravagance. From the acknowledged truth of the Jewish religion, the Ebionites had concluded that it could never be abolished. From its supposed imperfections the Gnostics as hastily inferred that it never was instituted by the wisdom of the Deity. There are some objections against the authority of Moses and the prophets, which too readily present themselves to the sceptical mind; though they can only be derived from our ignorance of remote antiquity, and from our incapacity to form an adequate judgment of the divine œconomy. These objections were eagerly embraced and as petulantly urged by the vain science of the Gnostics. As those heretics were, for the most part, averse to the pleasures of sense, they morosely arraigned the polygamy of the patriarchs, the gallantries of David, and the seraglio of Solomon. The conquest of the land of Canaan, and the extirpation of the unsuspecting natives, they were at a loss how to reconcile with the common notions of humanity and justice. But when they recollected the sanguinary list of murders, of executions, and of massacres, which stain almost every page of the Jewish annals, they acknowledged that the barbarians of Palestine had exercised as much compassion

---

[80] '*Historiae* ipsius praeter delectationem utilitas nulla est, quam ut religionis Christianae veritas demonstretur, quod aliter quam per historias fieri non potest' (Leibnitz, *Opera*, VI.297). This awareness that Christianity can be grounded, in the end, only on history explains the repeated attempts by pious historians in the eighteenth century to locate and describe a providential shape in the past.

[81] *The Decline and Fall*, I.477: I.569. I would therefore suggest that Lionel Gossman's account of Gibbon's irony, in which he says that 'the narrator continually assumes or points to a position of detachment and invites the reader to join him in it' (*The Empire Unpossess'd*, p. 75) tells only half the story. Gibbon knows that it is impossible for the Christian reader to join him in the calm and secluded regions of philosophy without ceasing to be a Christian. It is this poison in Gibbon's smoothness and civility which enraged his contemporaries (see *The English Essays of Edward Gibbon*, p. 231, and *Boswell's Life of Johnson*, II.448).

towards their idolatrous enemies as they had ever shewn to their friends or countrymen.[82]

The reader is manipulated and disarmed by the first sentence, a sentence so inoffensive that it could have been lifted from the most partisan Church history. As, however, the damaging evidence creeps in – the objections against Moses and the flouting of the 'common notions of humanity and justice' – we learn that Gibbon is never more dangerous than when he is defending his victims and making a show of removing or solving problems. The objections 'too readily present themselves to the sceptical mind'; and, in any case, they must (must they not?) have their roots in 'our incapacity to form an adequate judgment of the divine œconomy'. Gibbon seems to make an honest attempt to guide us round the problems of Christian belief, and to minimise their importance, but in the process makes them loom larger; the doubts of the Gnostics cease to be amusingly shallow when Gibbon shifts disconcertingly from the sexual peccadilloes of the Old Testament worthies to the substantial moral transgression of genocide. This reassurance is masterly in its unsettlingness. Perusing what is apparently 'a simple narrative of authentic facts', the Christian reader is adroitly made to create his own doubts without, it seems, the interference of the historian.[83] This irony is at once Socratic and dramatic: Gibbon feigns ignorance of his object, while the pious are momentarily ignorant of being that object. And even when they subsequently sense Gibbon's bad faith, the curiously unironic surface of the prose – the absence of any aphoristic edge to the phrasing, the dilution of Gibbon's intentness in the grave prolixity of the paragraph – offers them no target for their baffled resentment.[84]

As Gibbon progresses in his account of the establishment of 'the Christian empire', and as the abuses of Christianity assume a broader aspect, so too his irony coarsens; yet this is no genuine relaxation, only a feint which aims the more effectively to wrong-foot the reader.[85] As these broader strokes of irony concentrate on that traditional topic of satire, the worldliness of the Church, there is a desperate comfort for the Christian: it seems that Gibbon is concerned only to expose the corruptions of the earthly institutions of Christi-

---

[82] *The Decline and Fall*, I.459–60: I.547–8.

[83] *Letters*, II.321. For similar tactics in other writers, see Swift, *Gulliver's Travels* (*Prose Works*, XI.276) and Paine, *The Age of Reason*, (*Writings*, IV.28).

[84] It is striking that in the controversy succeeding publication of Volume I of *The Decline and Fall* in 1776, Gibbon's opponents are unable to attack him directly on the subject which gives rise to the dispute (to wit the demonstration of Christianity by means of history) and are reduced to frantic assaults on the outworks of his position, such as impugning his accuracy. Concerning the dilution of his irony, we should remember that in the same breath as he says how assiduously he has revised these chapters he reveals that he did not pare them to the bone: 'But the fifteenth and sixteenth Chapters have been reduced by three successive revisals from a large Volume to their present size; and they might still be compressed without any loss of facts or sentiments' (*Memoirs*, p. 156).

[85] *The Decline and Fall*, I.495: I.591; see also I.501: I.598).

anity and is content to respect the doctrines of the faith itself.[86] This merely masks the tremendous irony on which the chapter closes. Defending the Church against 'the imputation of ignorance and obscurity which has been so arrogantly cast on the first proselytes of Christianity', he turns the 'occasion for scandal into a subject of edification':[87]

Our serious thoughts will suggest to us, that the apostles themselves were chosen by Providence among the fishermen of Galilee, and that the lower we depress the temporal condition of the first Christians, the more reason we shall find to admire their merit and success.[88]

This apparent endorsement of Providence must seem conciliatory to the pious reader; especially since the lowliness of the disciples was a circumstance which had been seized on by defenders of Christianity, in a refinement of the argument from the worldly disadvantages under which it had suffered, as a clear sign of the truth of their religion.[89] But Gibbon characteristically turns this salutation into a blow when he inverts the issue to consider those whom Christianity excluded:

We stand in need of such reflections to comfort us for the loss of some illustrious characters, which in our eyes might have seemed the most worthy of the heavenly present. The names of Seneca, of the elder and the younger Pliny, of Tacitus, of Plutarch, of Galen, of the slave Epictetus, and of the emperor Marcus Antoninus, adorn the age in which they flourished, and exalt the dignity of human nature.[90]

The obvious Christian retort is that the pride of these pagans blinded them to the truth of the new religion; but Gibbon, as if foreseeing this rejoinder, then tauntingly inquires how great the effects of this blindness were. Was it

---

[86] Even this would be sufficiently shocking at a time when the purity of primitive Christianity was still credited: see William Cave, *Primitive Christianity* (1675) and D. Dobel, *Primitive Christianity* (1755). Bradford concluded his ninth sermon as a Boyle lecturer with the prayer '*May Almighty god revive the Spirit of Primitive Christianity, in those who take upon them the Christian name*' (*A Defence of Natural and Revealed Religion*, I. 524). Robertson had celebrated the purity and virtue of the early Christians (*The Situation of the World at the Time of Christ's Appearance*, *Works*, I.cv). This is yet another casual belief of the time which Gibbon finds history will not substantiate.

[87] *The Decline and Fall*, I.515–16: I.616. This may be a slap at Warburton who (like Fielding's magistrate in *Amelia*, who 'had too great an honour for truth to suspect that she ever appeared in sordid apparel, nor did he ever sully his sublime notions of that virtue, by uniting them with the mean ideas of poverty and distress') in the *Divine Legation of Moses Demonstrated* had argued that 'when God sees fit, in an extraordinary way, to give a new revelation of his WILL to man, we may conclude, from the very nature of things, that he will not disgrace his own DISPENSATION, by the use of unworthy Instruments' (Book IX, n. G, II).

[88] *The Decline and Fall*, I.516: I.616. First edition: 'providence'.

[89] Gibbon could have found such providential arguments about the lowliness of the apostles in his copy of William Cave's *Primitive Christianity*, (p. 49) or in his copy of the Boyle lectures (Leng's fifteenth sermon, *Defence of Natural and Revealed Religion*, II.134 and 135–6). In 1776 Soame Jenyns had once more tried to prove the divine origin of Christianity from the low station of the first Christians (*A View of the Internal Evidence of the Christian Religion*, pp. 9–10). See also Dryden, *Religio Laici*, ll. 140–5.

[90] *The Decline and Fall*, I.516: I.616.

a literal blindness, and can its effects thus explain the pagan ignorance of the miracles of the early Church?

But how shall we excuse the supine inattention of the Pagan and philosophic world, to those evidences which were presented by the hand of Omnipotence, not to their reason, but to their senses?[91]

In this context, the providentialist phrase 'the hand of Omnipotence' offers no balm, but inflicts another wound – how much less disturbing this observation would be if the prodigies in question were not the work of God. This would indeed allow the Christian reader to escape from the trap Gibbon has constructed; but only at a dreadful cost, which becomes clear when Gibbon reminds us that the miracles in question comprise not only the raising of the dead and the healing of the blind and lame, but the darkness at noon:

Under the reign of Tiberius, the whole earth, or at least a celebrated province of the Roman empire, was involved in a praeternatural darkness of three hours. Even this miraculous event, which ought to have excited the wonder, the curiosity, and the devotion of mankind, passed without notice in an age of science and history.[92]

Once again, Gibbon is touching on a favourite topic of the defenders of Christianity; and, once again, he transforms what had been used as a shield into sword. The darkness of the Passion was held to be a strong argument for the Christian religion because it was a miracle gracing the faith's central act;[93] because it was recorded by pagan writers;[94] and because it fulfilled prophecies.[95] Gibbon innocently relates it as if he takes it for a fact, but in so doing he also indicates the reasons for disbelieving it. The *coup de grâce* for the bemused Christian, mischievously brought face to face with the full magnitude of the consequences of his beliefs, comes when Gibbon concludes by politely offering for consideration one final but ruinous way out of his

---

[91] *The Decline and Fall*, I.517: I.618. first edition: '. . . explain or excuse . . .'.

[92] *The Decline and Fall*, I.518: I.618–19. Gibbon's training of irony on this central miracle of Christianity is an extreme application of Anthony Collins' position, outlined in *A Discourse Concerning Ridicule and Irony in Writing*, in which, following Shaftesbury, he asserts that irony is most proper to free us from religious imposture and that it is of peculiar efficacy against the false miracles which festoon the later history of the Church: 'Are these, or such as these the *clearest Miracles God ever wrought?* Do such Miracles deserve a serious Regard? And shall the *Gravity* with which Mankind is thus banter'd out of their common Sense, excuse these Matters from *Ridicule?*' (p. 9). Collins' irony is much closer to invective than to Gibbon's sustained and grave irony, which is so much more than a tone of voice; and Gibbon's recognition that the central miracles of Christianity are, to the historian's eye, no different from the peripheral ones is a recognition of which Collins stops short.

[93] See, for instance, Stanhope's fifteenth sermon (*A Defence of Natural and Revealed Religion*, I.817; see also II.161).

[94] See, for instance, Addison's *Evidences of the Christian Religion*, p. 11; the only authority he can adduce, however, is Phlegon, whose evidence according to Gibbon 'is now wisely abandoned' (*The Decline and Fall*, I.lxxvi n. 194: I.619 n. 196).

[95] Gibbon could have read a detailed correlation of the Passion with the prophecies it fulfilled in his copy of Houtteville's *La Religion Chrétienne Prouvée par les Faits*, pp. 282–3.

embarrassments and draws to his attention the darkness which is supposed to have followed the assassination of Caesar:

This season of obscurity, which cannot surely be compared with the praeternatural darkness of the Passion, had been already celebrated by most of the poets and historians of that memorable age.[96]

The pagan ignorance of the darkness of the Passion can be readily explained if one assumes that all such prodigies are not actual events, but stories the faithful, of whatever persuasion, tell themselves. It is the triumph of Chapter XV that this extraordinary conclusion, so fatal to Christianity, is presented in such a plausible form that it is impossible for it to be dismissed out of hand. Indeed, in the repose it offers, it may even seem attractive to a reader weary after the struggles and shocks of the preceding eighty-four pages.

Gibbon's undermining of the darkness of the Passion is experienced by the reader as a dramatic shift in the profundity of Chapter XV. Its sceptical gaze moves disorientingly and without pause from the transgressions of bishops to the Son of God. But from another point of view, Gibbon's taunting equation of a Christian and pagan prodigy is merely an extreme example of the general point he has been making throughout, that the doctrine of the Church is not divine in origin, but has been created on earth, by men, in response to worldly pressures and out of motives of expediency.[97] It is a point Gibbon insinuates throughout the chapter when he figures the progress of Christianity as a military campaign or as a successful business.[98] This subjection of Christianity to the regard of a disinterested eye is part of the change in the relation between history and religion in the eighteenth century noted by Momigliano: 'Gibbon followed Voltaire in boldly sweeping away every barrier between sacred history and profane history.'[99] In essence, this is true; but it is unfor-

---

[96] *The Decline and Fall*, I.518: I.619. Blackwell gives a natural explanation for the darkness following the death of Caesar and seems blithely unaware that it applies with equal force to the darkness of the Passion: 'For *natural Appearances*, in Heaven or Earth, if they co-incide with any remarkable Event, are *consecrated* by Credulity, and transformed into *Miracles*. About the vernal Equinox, the Air is frequently thick with vapours, that dim the Sun's radiancy by intercepting his beams. The Destroyer of the *Roman* Liberty met with his fate on the *Ides of March*. It happened to be a moist Season. THE SUN, said the Flatterers of his Successor, *hid his face from the horrid Deed* – and who will venture to call in question the Sun's testimony?' (*Memoirs of the Court of Augustus*, II.433).

[97] Gibbon's erudite account of the origins of episcopacy is a clear example of this strand of thought (*The Decline and Fall*, I.489–90: I.584–5). One might also instance here his careful tracing of the idea of the immortality of the soul, which quietly and steadily brings this crucial item of Christian doctrine within an historical perspective of formidable erudition and judgement (*The Decline and Fall*, I.466–71: I.556–62).

[98] E.g. 'To the first of these . . .' (*The Decline and Fall*, I.502: I.600) and 'When the promise of eternal happiness . . .' (*The Decline and Fall*, I.470: I.561). This may have the ring of obvious impiety to us, but once again Gibbon is adopting the accents of piety. Consider Stanhope's fourteenth sermon; 'We have the good Providence and unalterable Promises of God to insure our Venture: so that the return of this Commerce is certain, and the Prime cost cannot miscarry' (*A Defence of Natural and Revealed Religion*, I.810).

[99] *Studies in Historiography*, p. 52.

tunately phrased. Gibbon indeed strips Christianity of the historiographic privileges it enjoyed in, say, Bossuet's *Discours sur l'Histoire Universelle* (1681), where the whole course of history is subordinated to, and made to demonstrate the truth of, the Christian religion.[100] But Gibbon does not stop at levelling the sacred with the secular and allowing the two to mingle on conditions of equality (as Momigliano's expression 'sweep away every barrier' suggests). He aims at nothing less than a subjection of the sacred to the secular; not just at an undoing, but at a *reversal*, of the previous state of affairs. For Gibbon, Church history is a department of secular history – nothing more than a sector of that spacious stage on which the same passions are everywhere displayed:

In the church as well as in the world, the persons who were placed in any public station rendered themselves considerable by their eloquence and firmness, by their knowledge of mankind, and by their dexterity in business, and while they concealed from others, and perhaps from themselves, the secret motives of their conduct, they too frequently relapsed into all the turbulent passions of active life, which were tinctured with an additional degree of bitterness and obstinacy from the infusion of spiritual zeal.[101]

The history of the Church thus has no cardinal position in Gibbon's view of the past. It reveals the same human depravity and weakness which run throughout secular history; and the prominence it receives in Volume I is not only of a distinctly equivocal kind (Gibbon's relegation of Christianity to the end of the volume both suits his ironic argument, and is a cool affront), it is also a prominence arising solely from the bad eminence of the Church in the secondary causes which sap the empire. As the chapter progresses and Gibbon's irony steadily exerts ever more pressure on the reader, we find what seem to be quite open assertions of the propriety of this 'candid but rational' exposure: 'But neither the belief, nor the wishes of the fathers can alter the truth of history.'[102] But even this is not without its mocking guardedness, for the importance of history to Christianity had been evident since the controversy over miracles earlier in the century.[103] If miracles 'are the adequate and sole Foundation of a Christian's Faith', then that faith is necessarily grounded on historical evidence.[104] It is this putting of religion into the pocket of history by the religious themselves which made Chapter XV so disconcerting; in this, as well as in his adoption of the vocabulary and topics of reverence, Gibbon might say that he was simply taking the Anglicans at their word. Yet as he does so, he turns a classic defence of Protestantism – most vigorously stated by Tillotson, who argues against transubstantiation on

---

[100] See above, p. 17.

[101] *The Decline and Fall*, I.488: I.582. first edition: '. . . motive of their actions . . .'.

[102] *The Decline and Fall*, I.449: I.535 and I.512: I.611.

[103] This was, of course, a controversy in which the young Gibbon had read widely if not wisely: *Memoirs*, pp. 58–9.

[104] Stanhope's eighth sermon: *A Defence of Natural and Revealed Religion*, I.731. Consider also the opening of Butler's sermon 'Upon Human Nature'.

the grounds that the scepticism it entails concerning the evidence of our senses undermines faith by making it impossible simultaneously to credit the miracles which he asserts are the cornerstone of Christianity – into a means of attacking the faith as a whole.[105] The trench Tillotson dug to protect what he took to be the true faith against the Roman Church turns out to have opened up the citadel of Christianity to the depradations of the infidel. Thus in its own way Chapter XV is an historiographic example of the ruinousness of schism; a dry case in point to underline the insanity of the dissensions which, in Gibbon's understanding of the fall of the empire, combined with the powerful solvents of civic virtue inherent in Christianity to weaken Rome.

This historicising of the Church, and its dislodgement from the pivotal position in history awarded it by apologists such as Bossuet, shows Gibbon combining within himself, as Momigliano has famously argued, the *érudit* and the *philosophe*.[106] He shares the indignation of the latter, and, more resolutely and firmly determined than Voltaire that the barbs he launches against the Church should be not only sharp, but also stick, he weights that indignation with a scholarly accuracy which ensures that it cannot be dismissed as mere apostasy. Anglican readers, whose faith was grounded on history by virtue of the importance they accorded miracles, could not reject the historiographic values Gibbon deployed in Chapter XV without bringing ruin down upon their heads; their fortress has become the site of an ambuscade. They had appealed to history, and now Gibbon obliges them to abide its arbitration. Even the most galling aspects of the chapter – for instance, Gibbon's quoting Tacitus far more often than the gospels in this 'inquiry into the progress and establishment of Christianity' – are easily defensible on grounds of historiographic propriety; here, Gibbon is merely following the impeccable historiographic principle of not allowing historical agents to be witnesses in their own cause.[107] And the cumulative effect of this deposition of layer after layer of scrupulously weighed evidence is that the historical indictment of Christianity assumes an awful gravity. It emerges as a religion both corrupt in itself and, through its appeal to those elements in human nature which the civic humanist most despises, as well as the mental decay fostered by its encouragement of enthusiasm and hostility to sceptical inquiry, a source of corruption in what was otherwise healthy. The fundamental question is taken from the mouth of Celsus, who urged the point 'with great force and candour':

This indolent, or even criminal, disregard to the public welfare, exposed them [the Christians] to the contempt and reproaches of the Pagans, who very frequently asked,

---

[105] *The Rule of Faith*, Part III, Section 10, p. 598.
[106] This celebrated argument is developed in two classic essays, 'Ancient history and the antiquarian' and 'Gibbon's contribution to historical method', both to be found in *Studies in Historiography*.
[107] *The Decline and Fall*, I.449: I.535. Compare Bayle (*Critique Generale*, p. 221).

what must be the fate of the empire, attacked on every side by the barbarians, if all mankind should adopt the pusillanimous sentiments of the new sect?[108]

The historian knows, but does not need to utter, the melancholy answer to Celsus' question; and once that unspoken truth is shared by writer and reader, Gibbon's explanation of the cause of the decline and fall of the Roman empire is complete.

Chapter XV deferentially and indeflectibly leads the reader to a position from which he can see Christianity in history, as opposed to history in Christianity. Chapter XVI focuses on a particular area of the past on which this perspective throws a new light, that of persecutions.

The two chapters complement one another powerfully. In Chapter XV Gibbon, motivated by indignation and aided by imagination and scholarship, reorients history so that Christianity comes within its purview as an object of scrutiny instead of being the determining, and therefore invisible, ground from which the historian surveys the past. This new angle of vision reveals a startling corruption and hypocrisy not just in the abuses of Christianity, but lurking at its very heart. By narrowing his vision in Chapter XVI to the question of the persecution of the early Christians, and by insinuating that the Church exaggerated the scale of the persecutions it suffered in order to secure its worldly success, Gibbon suggests how thoroughly the early Church poisoned history in order to perpetuate its poisoning of the sources of the virtue which supports healthy civil society.[109] The historiographic question addressed in Chapter XVI (on which Gibbon, as a practitioner, might be expected to feel deeply) is therefore continuous with the larger cultural considerations raised by Chapter XV.[110]

The keynote of the chapter is the dependence of the dignity and utility of history on the impartiality of the historian:

History, which undertakes to record the transactions of the past, for the instruction of future, ages; would ill deserve that honourable office, if she condescended to plead the cause of tyrants, or to justify the maxims of persecution.[111]

The cutting edge of this remark is veiled by Gibbon's deft phrasing of it as a rebuke to himself: he would ill deserve the title of historian were he, in his

---

[108] *The Decline and Fall*, I.486: I.580–1. Compare his earlier comment, that 'the discipline of the legions, which alone, after the extinction of every other virtue, had propped the greatness of the state, was corrupted by the ambition or relaxed by the weakness of the emperors' (*The Decline and Fall*, I.199: I.236). It is Christianity which furthers the ambition of the emperors and which they tolerated through weakness.

[109] In depreciating the number of martyrs, Gibbon follows Dodwell in his *Dissertationes Cyprianicae*, dissertation 11. Dodwell, however, says that the paucity of martyrs is no argument against the truth of Christianity. More recently, in Chapter VIII of his *Essai sur les Mœurs*, Voltaire had questioned the extent of the persecution of the early Church (*Œuvres Complètes*, XI.224–30).

[110] Gibbon's earnest solicitude for his 'moral and literary character' appears most clearly in the opening pages of *A Vindication* (*The English Essays of Edward Gibbon*, pp. 229–313, p. 234).

[111] *The Decline and Fall*, I.529: I.633. First edition: '. . . future ages . . .'.

attempt to look afresh at the question of the persecution of the early Christians, to become the apologist of oppression and intolerance. But it is not only pagan oppression and intolerance which must be shunned; and at the end of Chapter XVI, when we have seen how little averse were the Fathers to the use of fraud when it was employed in the service of religion, it is clear that Christianity suffers rather than profits under the great law of impartiality.

As he did in Chapter XV, Gibbon is directing his attention at a field of history from which the faithful had reaped a rich harvest. The persecutions endured by the early Christians under emperors such as Nero and Diocletian had been cited by Christian apologists as examples of the extraordinary worldly handicaps which the early Church had nevertheless overcome, thereby demonstrating its divine origin. Only a religion protected by God, it was urged, could have not merely survived but prospered under such onslaughts.[112] Thus Thomas Church will carelessly assume and argue from the conviction (which he takes, if not to be self-evident, at least to require no evidence) that the pagan world had 'an unreasonable Prejudice against, and an extravagant Contempt of, the Christians'.[113] Stanhope announces confidently that 'Christianity hath never wanted Enemies in Abundance', Guthrie yet more carelessly says that the conversion of Constantine delivered the Church 'from the cruel persecution under which it had groaned for near three hundred years', and Warburton (never one to spoil a point with qualification) asserts that 'CHRISTIANITY [was] persecuted indifferently by the Good and Bad [emperors]'.[114] It is exactly this kind of assumption and the argument it commonly supports, made so slackly and yet so big with consequences flattering to Christianity, which Gibbon dismantles in Chapter XVI.

If the substance and fundamental strategy of both chapters are similar, Gibbon's demeanour has, however, changed slightly in Chapter XVI. The chapter's early paragraphs show his familiar command of the feint by attacking the impious without, in themselves, becoming actually pious:

The author of a celebrated dialogue, which has been attributed to Lucian, whilst he affects to treat the mysterious subject of the Trinity in a style of ridicule and contempt, betrays his own ignorance of the weakness of human reason, and of the inscrutable nature of the Divine perfections.[115]

This contrives to seem respectful of the doctrine of the Trinity while yet not possessing the substance of respect, for although the superficial pagan is chastised, the terms of the rebuke are not ultimately reassuring for the

---

[112] See *A Defence of Natural and Revealed Religion*, I. 823 and 830–1.

[113] *A Vindication of the Miraculous Powers*, p. 329.

[114] *A Defence of Natural and Revealed Religion*, I.813; *A General History of the World*, IV.576; *The Divine Legation of Moses*, Book II, n. QQ. For another sceptical consideration of the subject of persecutions, see Hume's essay 'Of Parties in General' (*Essays and Treatises*, I.39–105).

[115] *The Decline and Fall*, I.525: I.627.

Christian. As Hume had suggested in the as yet unpublished *Dialogues Concerning Natural Religion*, those who, like Demea, defend Christianity by reference to its ineffability are obliged to retire early and ignominiously from religious dispute. On the next page, Gibbon praises Jesus for his great human qualities, but even this is not without its sting:

> The Pagan multitude, reserving their gratitude for temporal benefits alone, rejected the inestimable present of life and immortality, which was offered to mankind by Jesus of Nazareth. His mild constancy in the midst of cruel and voluntary sufferings, his universal benevolence, and the sublime simplicity of his actions and character, were insufficient, in the opinion of those carnal men, to compensate for the want of fame, of empire, and of success; and whilst they refused to acknowledge his stupendous triumph over the powers of darkness and of the grave, they misrepresented, or they insulted, the equivocal birth, wandering life, and ignominious death, of the divine Author of Christianity.[116]

The outward allegiances of this writing are at variance with its true loyalty, for on close inspection the words of apparently greatest meekness contain a core of mockery. The genuflection of 'inestimable', viewed from a different angle, is a gesture of derision which suggests not that a mere mortal cannot value the rewards of Christianity, but rather that they have no value. A smile of well-bred contempt for enthusiasm plays beneath the tear Gibbon drops over Jesus' 'voluntary sufferings'. And 'stupendous', with its etymological implications of suspended or stunned judgement, is a word which moves from seeming to marvel at the Passion to commenting quietly but precisely on the significance of its provoking such a response. In Chapter XV Gibbon's dissimulation was deep. In Chapter XVI his hostility to Christianity takes the form of a less disguised disingenuousness which is seen through more quickly – indeed, which sometimes hardly disguises itself at all:

> The first of these examples [of imperial clemency cited by Tertullian] is attended with some difficulties which might perplex a sceptical mind. We are required to believe, *that* Pontius Pilate informed the emperor of the unjust sentence of death which he had pronounced against an innocent, and, as it appeared, a divine, person; and that, without acquiring the merit, he exposed himself to the danger, of martyrdom; *that* Tiberius, who avowed his contempt for all religion, immediately conceived the design of placing the Jewish Messiah among the gods of Rome; *that* his servile senate ventured to disobey the commands of their master; *that* Tiberius, instead of resenting their refusal, contented himself with protecting the Christians from the severity of the laws, many years before such laws were enacted, or before the church had assumed any distinct name or existence; and lastly, *that* the memory of this extraordinary transaction was preserved in the most public and authentic records, which escaped the knowledge of the historians of Greece and Rome, and were only visible to the eyes of an African Christian, who composed his apology one hundred and sixty years after the death of Tiberius.[117]

[116] *The Decline and Fall*, I.525–6: I.628.   [117] *The Decline and Fall*, I.556: I.666–7.

This passage is ironic only because Gibbon refrains from straightforwardly saying that Tertullian is a liar. The iteration of the emphatic '*that*', which makes the sacrifice of probability necessary to believe Tertullian typographically clear, has none of the serpentine strength of, for instance, the guileful paragraph on the Gnostics and Ebionites discussed above.[118] Yet this loss of stylistic finesse is not, when judged in terms of the impact of the volume as a whole, evidence of a loss of control – quite the reverse. It is because Gibbon has previously tiptoed so fastidiously towards positions from which Christianity appears in an unflattering light that he can now take up his position there more boldly.

Gibbon states his purpose in this chapter in terms which suggest that he is merely shouldering the least escapable of a historian's responsibilities:

To separate (if it be possible) a few authentic as well as interesting facts from an undigested mass of fiction and error, and to relate, in a clear and rational manner, the causes, the extent, the duration, and the most important circumstances of the persecutions to which the first Christians were exposed, is the design of the present Chapter.[119]

This would perhaps not seem ominous to a readership for whom the idea that Christianity could be vindicated through history (and in particular through the historical investigation of miracles) was familiar. But it soon becomes clear that, for Gibbon, a truly historical perspective can never coincide with a Christian perspective. Careful and dispassionate investigation regularly results in the discarding of traditions dear to the faithful:

If indeed we were disposed to adopt the traditions of a too credulous antiquity, we might relate the distant peregrinations, the wonderful atchievements, and the various deaths of the twelve apostles: but a more accurate inquiry will induce us to doubt, whether any of those persons who had been witnesses to the miracles of Christ were permitted, beyond the limits of Palestine, to seal with their blood the truth of their testimony.[120]

As the fine silt of Gibbon's patient riddling of the evidence accumulates, the candid equability shown (for the most part) by the empire to the new religion bulks large.[121] And this reformed and purified view of the past, in which the improper conflations and confusions both tolerated and propagated by the Church are undone by Gibbon's determination to acquire 'a just and distinct idea' of this important topic, is expressed in an idiom which flaunts its

---

[118] See above, pp. 121–2.
[119] *The Decline and Fall*, I.520: I.621.
[120] *The Decline and Fall*, I.531–2: I.635.
[121] Consider 'But the wisdom of the emperors protected the church from the danger of these tumultuous clamours and irregular accusations, which they justly censured as repugnant both to the firmness and to the equity of their administration' (*The Decline and Fall*, I.543: I.650). See also Hume's *Enquiry Concerning Human Understanding*, Section XI.

emancipation from the Christian perspective which had hitherto dominated history.[122]

In this respect the style of Chapter XVI may seem similar to the style which a Churchman like Warburton would stigmatise as typical of free-thinkers. What sets Gibbon's writing apart, however, is the immensely strong skeleton of scrupulous scholarship and criticism by which it is informed. It is this skeleton which vindicates his claim to be, not an apostate gadfly, but a spokesman for the 'sober discretion of the present age'.[123] And in the end it is Gibbon's sobriety, his refusal to be betrayed into any bantering style, which is his most damaging weapon because it means that his irony cannot be dismissed as persiflage. Unlike the Church Fathers, who fouled history by relating whatever might redound to the glory, and suppressing whatever might tend to the disgrace, of religion, Gibbon's position is characterised by principled restraint: 'But I cannot determine what I ought to transcribe, till I am satisfied how much I ought to believe.'[124] That being so, the essence of the chapter – that the Christians have grotesquely exaggerated the scale of the persecutions they suffered under the empire – appears almost of its own accord, as do other revealing but hitherto suppressed aspects of history. For instance, Gibbon's holding back of his consideration of Christianity until the end of the first volume means that we initially meet Diocletian, not as the enemy of Christianity, but as the restorer of the empire. His attack on Christianity is quite transformed by appearing against the backdrop of his civic probity rather than stifling it – particularly when juxtaposed with the calm Christianity enjoyed under the most vicious and abandoned emperors.

The irony of Chapter XVI thus depends on Gibbon's careful assembly of all the historical evidence required to muddy the clear outlines of the simple picture drawn by Christian apologists, in which the true faith triumphs despite having the awesome worldly force of the pagan world trained on it. Gibbon blurs that speciously sharp focus and restores a proper shade to those areas which have been invaded by a falsifying, Christian light. He introduces facts 'of a more distinct and stubborn kind', which not only refuse to be massaged into a Christian form, but which disclose the effects of such manipulation.[125] Gibbon takes the part of one on whose, if not reluctant, at least independent, mind the melancholy truth has obtruded itself; and it is with this chastened manner that he produces his final reflection. Noting that even Grotius, 'a man of genius and learning, who preserved his moderation

---

[122] *The Decline and Fall*, I.575: I.690. An example of this determination in action is to be found in note 74 (*The Decline and Fall*, I.lxxxi n. 73: I.654). For an example of the second point, consider the phrase 'those unfortunate sectaries' (*The Decline and Fall*, I.570: I.684).

[123] *The Decline and Fall*, I.551: I.661. The conclusion of the chapter, in its powerfully coercive blend of mathematical calculation, thorough information and intellectual acuteness, shows by how much *The Decline and Fall* exceeds mere raillery.

[124] *The Decline and Fall*, I.582: I.699.

[125] *The Decline and Fall*, I.584: I.701.

amidst the fury of contending sects, and who composed the annals of his own age and country, at a time when the invention of printing had facilitated the means of intelligence' seems to have done more than justice to the persecution of the Reformed Church in the Netherlands by Charles V, he concludes that:

. . . we shall be naturally led to inquire, what confidence can be placed in the doubtful and imperfect monuments of ancient credulity; what degree of credit can be assigned to a courtly bishop, and a passionate declaimer, who, under the protection of Constantine, enjoyed the exclusive privilege of recording the persecutions, inflicted on the Christians by the vanquished rivals or disregarded predecessors of their gracious sovereign.[126]

The unavoidable historiographical imperative – to consider the possible influence that the provenance of evidence and the circumstances of the witnesses may have had on what is asserted – is but the coping stone of an historical narrative of some six hundred pages in which Christianity is gradually brought to the bar of history and found guilty, impeached by the unexceptionable testimony of stubborn facts.

There is, however, one final irony. For in the two subsequent instalments of *The Decline and Fall*, Gibbon is himself overtaken by the fate which he has here artfully contrived for the Christian religion. The stubborn facts which he wielded as a tool of argument eventually unsettle and overturn the ideas on which he had confidently relied in 1776. Just as in Volume I he charges Christianity with simplifying history in its own interest, so in 1781 and 1788 he is obliged to level the same charge against himself. In 1776 he can, as Momigliano has suggested, unite the characters of the *érudit* and *philosophe*, because erudition is essential to his irony, and his irony is the necessary vehicle of his philosophic understanding of the past. But he finds it steadily more difficult to combine these two essentially contradictory characters when he is obliged to study centuries in which the findings of scholarship quarrel with, rather than support, the ambitions of the philosopher.

[126] *The Decline and Fall*, I.586: I.704. First edition; '. . . which Christianity had experienced from the vanquished rivals . . .'.

Gibbon among the philosophers

The phrase 'the reaction to *The Decline and Fall*' calls immediately and perhaps exclusively to mind the hostile response the first volume of Gibbon's history provoked among the pious; so successfully has the uproar from the orthodox drowned quieter, but equally revealing reactions. One such reaction comes from Hume. In his *Memoirs*, Gibbon quotes his letter of congratulation on the publication of Volume I, in which his fellow historian writes suggestively of the volume's concluding chapters:

> When I heard of your undertaking (which was some time ago) I own, that I was a little curious to see how you would extricate yourself from the subject of your two last chapters. I think you have observed a very prudent temperament: but it was impossible to treat the subject so as not to give grounds of suspicion against you, and you may expect that a clamour will arise.[1]

It is the second sentence which, in its precision of response, is the more arresting. The recognition of Gibbon's prudence in his handling of Christianity, and the simultaneous prediction of the controversy which would arise, show Hume the practitioner's awareness of how Gibbon's irony is a weapon both sharp and, as far as possible, safe.[2] But on deeper reflection, it is the first sentence which is more fraught with interest in its suggestion that, for a philosophic historian (as Hume most surely was), the question of the influence exerted by a burgeoning Christianity on the fabric of the empire would disengage itself promptly and distinctly from the more general topic of the fall of Rome.[3] For in the clarity of Hume's expectation, and in the fullness with which the first volume of *The Decline and Fall* meets that expectation by being organised around a conviction about the role played by Christianity in the fall of Rome, there is evidence not only that in 1776 Gibbon was recognisably a philosophic historian, but also of what it meant to study history philosophically.

---

[1] *Memoirs*, p. 168.

[2] This warning of Hume's, of course further exposes the disingenuousness of Gibbon's pretence, in the *Memoirs*, of being surprised when there was an outcry against his handling of Christianity (p. 159: also discussed on pp. 108–10 above).

[3] That Gibbon should refer to Hume simply as 'our philosophic historian' (*The Decline and Fall*, VI.525) is evidence that he, at least, felt that Hume was unmistakably Britain's one true philosophic historian.

Definitions of the phrase 'philosophic history' have normally focused on intellectual style. Philosophic historians, it has been suggested, approach the past with the aim of ascending to the most simple ideas through the analysis of causality.[4] Thus a philosophic historian is recognisable more by his manner of thought than by his style of writing.

But, as we have seen, Gibbon held that style was an image of mind, and in his considerations of what it means to be a literary *philosophe* we find close attention paid to the way the characteristic intellection of a philosophic historian imparts a distinctive quality of literary finish. Gibbon's understanding of how the philosophic historian signs his work both intellectually and stylistically deepens our apprehension of Volume I of *The Decline and Fall* as 'philosophic' and helps us see why the later volumes cannot be so called.[5] We need not bluntly to say that Gibbon either was or was not a philosophic historian, but to think about how, where, and why Gibbon writes *en philosophe*.[6]

Addison, who boasted that he had brought philosophy into the drawing room, uses the term in the *Spectator* to denote informed conversation on topics worthy of a gentleman's attention.[7] This is not as casually patrician as it may seem, given that Locke had recently suggested that his *Essay Concerning Human Understanding* arose easily and naturally out of the informal discussions of the polite.[8] But in the later decades of the century this definition of philosophy in social terms and its installation as the idiom of a particular social class, must have seemed increasingly untenable. Hume's thought (in print by 1739, but influential only several years later) sunders the philosophic from the quotidian; and as the work of the French *philosophes* became known in England around the middle of the century, its characteristics may be assumed further to have particularised the word 'philosophic'.[9]

Whatever the causes, when Gibbon first examines the philosophic character in literature it is clear that he is using *philosophique* with a restriction which is striking after Addison's expansiveness.[10] The *Essai sur l'Étude de la Littérature*

---

[4] John Burrow gives the most pithy definition of 'philosophic': 'the critical use of reason and the search for the underlying causes or "principles" of things' (*Gibbon*, p. 17).

[5] Gibbon's relation with the *philosophes* is a vexed issue. Michel Baridon holds that Gibbon is a pure product of the *philosophes* (*Edward Gibbon et le Mythe de Rome*, p. 929). David Jordan champions the view that 'Gibbon was no *philosophe*' (*Gibbon and his Roman Empire*, p. xiv: see also p. 71). More recently, John Burrow has made suggestions at once more subtle and more probable (*Gibbon*, pp. 17–19).

[6] Throughout this section I, like Gibbon, use *philosophe* and 'philosophic' as synonyms.

[7] *Spectator*, no. 10: *Works*, II.397.

[8] See 'The Epistle to the Reader', *An Essay Concerning Human Understanding*, I.xi–xii.

[9] The influence of the *philosophes* in England is shown by, for instance, Gray's prompt response to the publication of the *Esprit des Loix*: see the headnote to 'The alliance of education and government' in Roger Lonsdale's edition of *The Poems of Gray, Collins and Goldsmith*, pp. 85–92.

[10] Gibbon uses 'philosophic' in its large sense, denoting tolerance, acceptance of one's human nature, and a secular coolness of mind, in a phrase like 'philosophic repose' (*The Decline and Fall*, IV.vi; see also V.539 n. 39): although we should remember that Gibbon charges the

(1761) is intended as a defence of *belles lettres* and of *littérature* in its precise eighteenth-century sense of the study of antiquity against the scorn of the ascendant *philosophes* and their amazement that one could spend a lifetime 'à se charger la mémoire au lieu de s'éclairer l'esprit'.[11] But although Gibbon argues against the *philosophes* in the *Essai*, he is not hostile to them – indeed, in later life he was to sigh over the *philosophe* allegiances of that work: 'Alas how fatal has been the imitation of Montesquieu!'[12] Gibbon is primarily referring to his stylistic affectations, but the *Essai* is also informed by a more general admiration for 'cet esprit philosophique qui . . . fait le caractère du siècle où nous vivons': 'C'est la chose du monde la plus prônée, la plus ignorée et la plus rare.'[13] Gibbon's enthusiasm leads him to be much more concerned with the ideal than the practical, as his image of the *philosophe* (reminiscent of Hume's image of the Stoic) reveals:

Placé sur une hauteur, il embrasse une grande étendue de païs, dont il se forme une image nette et unique, pendant que des esprits aussi justes, mais plus bornés, n'en découvrent qu'une partie.[14]

This typifying of the *philosophe* in terms of an intellectual elevation which makes possible a focused, single and penetrating vision of what to lesser minds is a baffling multiplicity accords well with what we might call the intellectual programme of *philosophes* such as Montesquieu and Hume; but it says nothing of the impediments which arise, or the areas of blindness which emerge, when this programme is put into practice.[15] The *Essai* testifies to the ideals of the youth, not to the mature writer's beliefs.[16]

There is, however, a work – roughly contemporary with the *Essai* – in which Gibbon exposes *l'esprit philosophique* to just the testing scrutiny from which he elsewhere protects it. In the neglected essay 'Sur la Monarchie des Mèdes', Gibbon considers at length the practical consequences of writing

philosophes with imaginative and scholarly indolence in their historiography, so 'philosophic repose' may also comment quietly on the more specific area of historical writing. When Gibbon calls himself a 'philosopher' (as he does in *The Decline and Fall*, VI.599 n. 65), it is only in this large sense that he does so. Certainly by 1788 he has discarded many of the most central tenets of philosophic history.

[11] *Miscellaneous Works*, IV.20. On the meaning of the word *littérature*, see R. A. Leigh's article, 'The loss of Gibbon's literary maidenhead', pp. 323–34. In his *Memoirs*, Gibbon deplores his loose usage of the term (p. 103).

[12] *Memoirs*, p. 103.

[13] *Miscellaneous Works*, IV.57.

[14] *Miscellaneous Works*, IV.58.

[15] See above, pp. 24–5.

[16] Lord Dacre believes that the *Essai* was Gibbon's 'historical *credo*' (H. R. Trevor-Roper, 'The historical philosophy of the Enlightenment', p. 1674). Gibbon knew that 'at the end of twenty eight years, I may appreciate my juvenile work, with the impartiality, and almost with the indifference of a stranger' (*Memoirs*, p. 103).

history *en philosophe* and in so doing suggests the likely literary effects of a philosophic posture.[17]

Gibbon begins by unfolding an important implication of the dominant *philosophe* interest in the analysis of causality when he states that the *philosophes* accord only an illustrative role to facts:

Aux yeux d'un philosophe, les faits composent la partie la moins intéressante de l'histoire. C'est la connoissance de l'homme, la morale, et la politique qu'il y trouve, qui la relèvent dans son esprit. Tâchons de suivre cette idée, et de voir jusqu'à quel point elle conduiroit un écrivain, qui ne voit dans les faits particuliers que la preuve de ses principes généraux.[18]

There are four major consequences. The first is that the philosophic historian inscribes himself into his work:

Tout homme de génie qui écrit l'histoire, y répand, peut-être sans s'en appercevoir, le caractère de son esprit. A travers leur variété infinie de passion et de situation, ses personnages semblent n'avoir qu'une façon de penser et de sentir; et cette façon est celle de l'auteur.[19]

It is this impatience with difference and intolerance of the foreign that Gibbon, with his pleasure in paradox, would later refer to as the 'zeal' of a philosophic historian.[20] It connects with the second consequence. Because of his zealous preconceptions about the subject of his history, wherever possible the philosophic historian favours only that evidence which concurs with his preconceptions:

Lorsqu'il s'agit d'une histoire, dont les variations permettent quelque liberté à la critique, et même à la conjecture; l'historien philosophe choisira parmi les faits contestés, ceux qui s'accordent le mieux avec ses principes, et ses vues. Le désir de les employer, leur donnera même un dégré d'evidence qu'ils n'ont pas; et la logique de cœur ne l'emportera que trop souvent sur celle de l'esprit.[21]

The third consequence also springs from the *philosophes* favouring their preconceptions. In order to procure a greater credibility for their contentions, they elevate their conjectures to the level of facts, thereby composing a seamless narrative from which those contentions then appear naturally to arise:

---

[17] The *Essai* was published in 1761: but its stance was adopted and 'the first pages or chapters' composed before Gibbon left Lausanne on 11 April 1758 (*Memoirs*, pp. 87 and 99). Sheffield dates the hand of 'Sur la Monarchie des Mèdes' between 1758 and 1763 (*Miscellaneous Works*, III.vii); it is thus probably coeval with the *Essai*, and possibly subsequent to it.

[18] *Miscellaneous Works*, III.126. J. G. A. Pocock has commented that 'the late medieval and Renaissance intellect found the particular less intelligible and less rational than the universal' (*The Machiavellian Moment*, p. 4) It is important to acknowledge the traditional, as well as the modern, elements in the *philosophe*. Lionel Gossman holds that Gibbon shares this distaste (*The Empire Unpossess'd*, p. 95). This strikes me as true for the instalment of 1776, but a distortion of Gibbon's thought thereafter.

[19] *Miscellaneous Works*, III.126.

[20] *The Decline and Fall*, II.305.

[21] *Miscellaneous Works*, III.128.

Les histoires les plus particulières laissent beaucoup à désirer au lecteur curieux. Lorsqu'elles décrivent les faits, il souhaiteroit de connoître les causes les plus cachées qui les ont produit. Il voudroit pénétrer dans les conseils, et jusqu'à dans la pensée de leurs auteurs, pour y voir les circonstances qui ont fait éclorre les plus grands desseins, le but qu'ils se proposoient, les obstacles qu'ils ont rencontré, et les arts par lesquels ils les ont vaincu. Un esprit philosophique se plaît à suppléer tous ces termes intermédiaires; et à tirer du vrai, le vraisemblable et le possible. S'il donne à ses réflexions la forme d'une histoire, il est obligé de prendre un ton plus ferme. Ses hypothèses deviennent des faits, qui semblent découler des faits généraux et avérés.[22]

The fourth and final consequence is simply the strongest form of the unscrupulousness which runs through them all. The philosophic historian will connive at untruth and distortion in order to support and protect the system he has undertaken to demonstrate:

L'historien d'un grand homme est presque toujours son ami. Le sculpteur se prosterne devant son ouvrage. Ce raffinement d'amour-propre est aussi connu qu'il paroît singulier. Lorsque l'historien philosophe se propose un systême de politique, ou de morale, les exceptions particulières qu'une vérité odieuse lui montre, l'accablent de leur poids importun; il les affoiblit, il les dissimule, il les fait enfin disparoître, pour ne voir que le genre de faits qui convient à son but. On est en droit de supposer cette foiblesse au philosophe. Ce philosophe est homme et écrivain. Mais en s'écartant de la vérité, il la respecte toujours; il ne s'en éloigne qu'à regret; il ne se permet que des erreurs douces, insensibles et nécessaires.[23]

It is presumably this indeflectible, even bigoted, desire to vindicate a point of view which Gibbon has in mind when, at the end of his life, he says paradoxically that 'the Philosopher may preach'.[24]

Given these insights into the nature of philosophic historiography, the grounds for calling the first volume of the history 'philosophic' should be clear. Although the period of *The Decline and Fall* had been 'neglected by a philosophic age', falling in between two of Voltaire's 'Quatre Âges Heureux' and comprising for the most part 'des avantures barbares, sous des noms barbares', and although the more common object of philosophic scrutiny was the grandeur and decline of a state, rather than merely the half of the political

---

[22] *Miscellaneous Works*, III.128–9. In the *Advancement of Learning* Bacon comments on the puzzlingness of mere particularity, and the luminousness of connexion: 'For it is the harmony of a philosophy in itself which giveth it light and credence; whereas if it be singled and broken, it will seem more foreign and dissonant. For as when I read in Tacitus the actions of Nero or Claudius, with circumstances of times, inducements, and occasions, I find them not so strange; but when I read them in Suetonius Tranquillus . . . they seem more monstrous and incredible' (*Works*, I.63).

[23] *Miscellaneous Works*, III.130.

[24] *Memoirs*, p. 4. As Giarrizzo has rightly commented, 'Gibbon aveva trovato molti anni prima che i *philosophes* erano tutti, a modo loro, degli insopportabili bigotti' (*Edward Gibbon e la Cultura Europea del Settecento*, p. 303). In *The Decline and Fall* we find just the criticisms of the *philosophes* which 'Sur la Monarchie des Mèdes' might have led us to expect: their attentiveness to facts is impugned (*The Decline and Fall*, II.61: II.574 n. 15: II.304–5) and their bigotry asserted (*The Decline and Fall*, VI.442 n.13). Later Gibbon even goes so far as restrainedly to suggest that Montesquieu is a liar (*Memoirs*, p. 135).

parabola comprised by decline and fall, Volume I of *The Decline and Fall* is a truly philosophic history in its subtle promotion and protection of a distinctive view of the past, a particular interpretation of Roman decline.[25] Most of the foregoing discussion has been concerned with tracing the slight but decisive adjustments and selections of material – what Gibbon called 'ces erreurs qui éclairent l'esprit en le trompant' – entailed in philosophic history.[26]

If the determined sculpture of Volume I of *The Decline and Fall* makes up the surest grounds for styling it 'philosophic', we should note that this first instalment also shows its nature in other, more obvious ways. In 1776 Gibbon subscribes to the philosophic desire, most plainly visible in Voltaire's *Siècle de Louis XIV* (1751), to redirect the attention of the historian away from the military and diplomatic and towards the social: or, as Gibbon puts it, to move 'from the splendid to the more useful parts of history'.[27] His hostility towards Christianity is also, though different in origin, an attitude he shares with the *philosophes*. And throughout *The Decline and Fall* Gibbon shows a fondness for the 'historical retrodiction', the deduction of history from manners or principles occasionally practised by, for instance, Montesquieu, Hume and Mably.[28]

Yet Gibbon himself warns us that 'On mature consideration, I am perhaps less selfish or less philosophical than I appear at first sight.'[29] From the very beginning of *The Decline and Fall* he criticises the shallowness in the *philosophes* to which his own scholarship continually alerts him. Montesquieu is as much rebuked as praised when Gibbon credits him with 'a lively fancy'.[30] Voltaire, who casts a 'keen and lively glance over the surface of history', is

[25] *Memoirs*, p. 99; Ian White, 'The subject of Gibbon's History', pp. 299–309; Voltaire, 'Histoire', *Encyclopédie*, VIII.223. D'Alembert recommends 'l'histoire approfondie et raisonnée, qui a pour but de développer dans leur principe les causes de l'accroissement et de la décadence des Empires' (*Réflexions sur l'Histoire*, in *Œuvres Complètes*, II.7). The same attention to prosperity as well as to calamity is present in Montesquieu's *Considérations*.

[26] *Miscellaneous Works*, III.174.

[27] *The Decline and Fall*, I.163: I.194. This redirection of historiography lies behind the debate between Usbek and Rhédi in Montesquieu's *Lettres Persanes* on how one should contemplate the vicissitudes of empires (letters cxii–cxxii), and it shapes Voltaire's formulation of the enlightened historian's task (*Œuvres Complètes*, XVI.140). At the time when he was writing the *Essai sur l'Étude de la Littérature*, Gibbon followed the *philosophe* line with the precision of a disciple ('Relation des Noces de Charles Duc de Bourgogne', dated by Sheffield as 1758–61, *Miscellaneous Works*, III.203–3). Invocations of it recur as late as 1781 (*The Decline and Fall*, II.23). But by 1788, and as part of his general questioning of the assumptions of philosophic history, Gibbon understands the value of what the *philosophes* discarded: 'the paths of blood, and such is the history of nations' (*The Decline and Fall*, V.649). Although it was acknowledged that this redirection of attention was the hobby-horse of enlightened French historians, especially Voltaire, its justice was generally recognised: see Lyttelton, *Dialogues of the Dead, Works*, p. 415; Warburton, *A Critical and Philosophical Enquiry into the Causes of Prodigies and Miracles*, p. 46; Adams, *The Flowers of Modern History*, sig. a2r.

[28] See, for example, *The Decline and Fall*, V.502, or the account of the Turks in Chapter XXVI. For a discussion of historical retrodiction, see above, p. 27 n. 26.

[29] *Letters*, III.159.

[30] *The Decline and Fall*, I.xliii n. 11: I.349 n.11.

in plainer terms a trifler, whose vivacity must be underpinned by the more solid labours of others: 'The lively scepticism of Voltaire is balanced with sense and erudition by the French author of the Esprit des Croisades.'[31] Even Hume may be *'Ingenious but superficial'*.[32]

Gibbon comes gradually to see in the weakness of the philosopher's passions not the basis of equanimity, or an independence and stability of judgement which could underwrite historiographic accuracy, but rather the expression of a disabling narrowness of temperament. Even in his earliest writings Gibbon had noted that the *sang froid* of 'cold philosophy' was a numbness betrayed by a vacancy in the mother tongue of the *philosophes*: 'En effet il faut un esprit, bien ferré a Glace par la bonne Philosophie pour n'y pas sentir un certain tremoussement, un certain – (en Anglois je dirois Awe)'.[33] And when Deyverdun dies, Gibbon uses 'philosophy' to denote a shameful and regrettable unfeelingness, a callousness:

. . . his amiable character was still alive in my remembrance; each room, each walk was imprinted with our common footsteps, and I should blush at my own philosophy if a long interval of study had not preceded and followed the death of my friend.[34]

Lionel Gossman misreads this passage when he glosses it as ' "and if I had not thrown myself into study both before and after his death, I do not know if all my philosophy would have enabled me to overcome my grief" '.[35] Gibbon was a remorseless autodidact, and so one cannot, as Gossman does here, construe 'interval of study' as time *spent* studying: Gibbon studied all the time. 'Interval of study' here surely means a break from study; Gibbon would have been coldly philosophical had his friend's death not prevented him from following his usual pursuits. Gibbon makes substantially the same point less equivocally when his father dies: 'My quiet was gradually disturbed by our domestic anxiety: and I should be ashamed of my unfeeling philosophy, had I found much time or taste for study in the last fatal summer (1770) of my father's decay and dissolution.'[36]

When the philosopher turns to history, the insensitivity which diminishes his humanity prevents him from properly appreciating certain areas of the past. His placid smile indicates an unshakeable equanimity close to incomprehension:

. . . a philosophic smile will not disturb the triumph of the priest or the happiness of the people.[37]

The equipoise of philosophic coolness is proof against the disturbing energy

[31] *The Decline and Fall*, V.301 n.55 and VI.58 n.106.
[32] *Gibbon's Journal to January 28th, 1763*, p. 42.
[33] *Miscellanea Gibboniana*, p. 28.
[34] *Memoirs*, p. 184.
[35] *The Empire Unpossess'd*, p. 127. n. 72.
[36] *Memoirs*, pp. 148–9.
[37] *The Decline and Fall*, VI.559–60.

of the past; but in being so protected it is also deprived of the baffling yet (as Gibbon ever more clearly appreciates) valuable insights which come only as a result of struggling with the past's turbulent, embarrassing and awkward vitality. The price of the philosopher's impressive security of judgement is, for an historian, ruinously high, since it is to be imprisoned in your own time. Gibbon admired Tacitus and saw in him the 'first of historians who applied the science of philosophy to the study of facts'.[38] But even he has the characteristic weakness of the philosophic historian:

At the distance of sixty years, it was the duty of the annalist to adopt the narratives of cotemporaries; but it was natural for the philosopher to indulge himself in the description of the origin, the progress, and the character of the new sect, not so much according to the knowledge or prejudices of the age of Nero, as according to those of the time of Hadrian.[39]

One way of explaining the evolutions of *The Decline and Fall* might be to say that the changes this great history goes through all ultimately arise from this originally philosophic historian's sharpening awareness of how the philosophic and historical characters are ultimately incompatible. In a letter to Malcolm Darling, E. M. Forster writes of Gibbon with appreciation and incomprehension:

What a giant he is – greatest historian & greatest name of the 18th century *I* say; whether it is his greatness or his remoteness that makes his goings on with religion so queer I do not know. That such a nature should be preoccupied at all with it personally puzzles me.[40]

It is too late to remove Forster's puzzlement, but we may now suggest at least why Gibbon's indictment of Christianity stands at the centre of the first volume of *The Decline and Fall*. Gibbon, his youthful mind moulded by Giannone's indictment of the Catholic Church's political activities in the *Istoria civile del regno di Napoli*, had seen how the 'progress and abuse of Sacerdotal power' had made the Church's role in the decline and fall of the empire not only a neglected area of the past but an invisible one.[41] To explain the collapse of the empire by reference to the Church was an hypothesis difficult to entertain, let alone assess. In Volume I of *The Decline and Fall* he rectifies the twist Christianity had given history by applying its *philosophe* opposite. In the five subsequent volumes, he is obliged to acknowledge and drawn to explore those portions of the past which philosophic history in its turn renders invisible.

---

[38] *The Decline and Fall*, I.217: I.259.
[39] *The Decline and Fall*, I.536: I.640–1. First edition: 'contemporaries'. J. G. A. Pocock implies that Gibbon's attitude to Tacitus was one of unreserved approval (*Virtue, Commerce, and History*, pp. 125 and 147). But, as we have seen, Gibbon's undoubted admiration for Tacitus is not incompatible with critical reservations.
[40] *Selected Letters of E. M. Forster: Volume One 1879–1920*, p. 107.
[41] *Memoirs*, p. 79.

He is compelled to heed the 'vérité odieuse', with its 'poids importun', on which he had turned his back in 1776.[42]

[42] *Miscellaneous Works*, III.130.

Volumes II and III – 1781

. . . l'art n'y a pas pu vaincre la nature tout à fait . . .

. . . the more he thought, the less he comprehended; and the more he wrote, the less capable was he of expressing his thoughts. In every step of the enquiry, we are compelled to feel and acknowledge the immeasurable disproportion between the size of the object and the capacity of the human mind. Gibbon

9

'The more rational ignorance of the man' [1]

With a fine sense of the piquant, Gibbon chose as the epigraph for Volume I of *The Decline and Fall* a quotation from the historian who had recounted the foundation and prodigious growth of the Roman state:

Jam provideo animo, velut qui, proximis littori vadis inducti, mare pedibus ingrediuntur, quicquid progredior, in vastiorem me altitudinem, ad velut profundum invehi; et crescere pene opus, quod prima quaeque perficiendo minui videbatur. [2]

There is, of course, a becoming modesty in an author's confessing his inadequacy before the majesty of his subject. [3] Nevertheless, the controlled shapeliness of Volume I is so striking that it cannot but seem surprising to have this indication of overwhelming immensity standing at its head. Nowhere is Gibbon less at sea than in the first volume of his history.

An historian may encounter different kinds of difficulty. On the one hand, he may feel burdened by a mass of meaningless particularity from which nothing of value can be extracted, and for which he feels little sympathy; a philosophic historian (if Gibbon has rightly taken the measure of the man in 'Sur la Monarchie des Mèdes') will be especially liable to this, because he will have such a well-defined idea of what it is he has to say. On the other hand, the historian may feel oppressed by evidence too weighty and plentiful for him to dismiss as meaningless, and yet determinedly resistant to his efforts to read and understand it.

The impediments Gibbon acknowledges in 1776 are of the former kind. In decorous understatement he submits that he has managed to overcome the deficiencies of his witnesses and to produce an elegant narrative with minimal and insignificant wastage:

As far as the barrenness of materials would permit, we have attempted to trace, with order and perspicuity, the general events of that calamitous period. There still remain some particular facts . . . [4]

---

[1] *Memoirs*, p. 56.
[2] *Ab Urbe Condita*, XXXI.i.5. The text is as transcribed and printed by Gibbon.
[3] Gibbon's anxiety about his competence to match his subject is not a mere authorly flourish. It surfaces in the correspondence he wrote immediately before publication of Volume I (see above, p. 48).
[4] *The Decline and Fall*, I.283: I.338.

It is important to recognise that, at the outset of his endeavour, Gibbon believes that any resistance to his historical intelligence derives solely from the inadequacy of his sources, 'the barrenness of materials'. There is no suggestion that the past itself might be so foreign to an Englishman of the eighteenth century as to be opaque. Holding fast to the central tenet of the philosophic historian – that mankind is everywhere and at all times the same – Gibbon infers that all historiographic problems can be reduced to critical problems of how correctly to understand deficient evidence. His self-deprecating manner cannot disguise his confidence that he is gifted in this task of seeing past his sources:

The imperfect historians of an irregular war, do not enable us to describe the order and circumstances of his exploits; but, if we could be indulged in the allusion, we might distribute into three acts this memorable tragedy.[5]

There is perhaps the playfulness germane to a consciousness of mastery in Gibbon's request for indulgence; nevertheless, his confidence that the past is like a work of art in its intelligibility has serious implications, since this faith that history can ultimately be understood because essentially ordered is a necessary supposition of his conviction that any obscurity arises in transmission and is not intrinsic to the past. The conventional language of decline, which Gibbon uses straightforwardly in 1776, gives figurative expression to this idea that historical darkness is not a quality of past centuries, but is interposed between the historian and a past which he would otherwise find familiar:

This obvious difference [the linguistic separation of East and West] marked the two portions of the empire with a distinction of colours, which, though it was in some degree concealed during the meridian splendor of prosperity, became gradually more visible, as the shades of Night descended upon the Roman world.

A cloud of critics . . . darkened the face of learning . . .

. . . the noxious weed . . . darkened the Roman world with its deadly shade.[6]

This darkness is not a challenge to the historian's powers of comprehension, merely a tax on his patience rendered unimportant by the Olympian point of vantage which gives him a commanding prospect over the vast bulk of historical evidence. The Livyan epigraph to Volume I is thus not a perplexed acknowledgement of the unwieldiness and intractability of Gibbon's subject, more a delighted confession of the deluge of intelligible material by which he

[5] *The Decline and Fall*, I.294: I.350–1.
[6] *The Decline and Fall*, I.38: I.45 (third edition: 'shades of night'); I.58: I.70; I.169: I.202. The *Dunciad* is, of course, replete with this idiom (e.g. IV.248 and 627–56). Compare, too, Warburton's *Julian, or a Discourse concerning the Earthquake and Fiery Eruption*, pp. xxxvii and 319. Gibbon owned a copy of the 1751 edition of this work (Keynes, p. 281), had himself written an essay defending the truth of this miracle (*Memoirs*, p. 79) and in his *Critical Observations on the sixth book of the Aeneid* (1770) had jousted with Warburton ('the Dictator and tyrant of the World of Litterature'; *Memoirs*, pp. 144–5) over the Eleusinian mysteries.

has been overtaken. It is Gibbon's experience in 1776, as it was Montes-quieu's in 1748, that merely to adopt the correct, philosophic, stance towards the past is to be in a position to see and be overwhelmed by its legibility: 'Mais, quand j'ai découvert mes principes, tout ce que je cherchois est venu à moi.'[7]

In Volumes II and III, however, Gibbon's understanding of the difficulties he is encountering changes. He comes to see them not as accidental, but as substantial – as an aspect of the past itself, and not of its transmission. As Gibbon is obliged to struggle with increasingly recalcitrant material, the uniformitarian certainties of the philosophic historian are eroded. This erosion has marked literary consequences.

Gibbon's comments on the second instalment of *The Decline and Fall* are in places contradictory. He recalls his stylistic ease and his feelings of authority:

. . . when I resumed my task I felt my improvement. I was now master of my style and subject: and while the measure of my daily performance was enlarged, I discovered less reason to cancel or correct.[8]

But this is almost immediately followed by an admission that these feelings were deceptive:

. . . the second and third volumes insensibly rose in sale and reputation to a level with the first. But the public is seldom wrong; and I am inclined to believe, that especially in the beginning they are more prolix and less entertaining than the first: my efforts had not been relaxed by success and I had rather deviated into the opposite fault of minute and superfluous diligence.[9]

On looking back, Gibbon realises that his sensations of progress and achieve-ment were subtly illusory, and that the areas of the past with which he was dealing in the five years between 1776 and 1781 were in fact much more absorbent of his attention than were those he had covered in Volume I.[10] In Volumes II and III of *The Decline and Fall* Gibbon's critic must pay close atten-tion to the literary consequences of the increasing resistance the past offers to the historian's intelligence.

The figure of Constantine straddles the divide between Volumes I and II: Chapter XIV takes us from his birth to the reunion of the empire after the death of Licinius, and Chapters XVII, XVIII and XX complete Gibbon's ac-count of his reign. In the work of historians writing from a firmly Christian point of view, such as Tillemont and Bossuet, the reign of Constantine has

---

[7] *Esprit des Loix*; *Œuvres*, I.lxii.
[8] *Memoirs*, p. 159.
[9] *Memoirs*, p. 163.
[10] This can be verified by a simple calculation. In Volume I Gibbon gives us not only the initial review of the empire from Augustus to Marcus Antoninus, but a circumstantial narrative of 132 years (A.D. 192 to A.D. 324). Volume III concludes with the fall of the western empire in A.D. 476; and so in the second instalment of *The Decline and Fall* Gibbon requires two volumes of the same size as Volume I to narrate the history of only 152 years.

a pivotal importance reflected in structural prominence.[11] Thus for Gibbon so to carve up Constantine's reign and pay it only interrupted attention may be read as yet more evidence of his determination to dislodge Christianity from the sovereign position by virtue of which it was able to organise history. Once Christianity has been reduced to the level of an historical phenomenon like any other, and is no longer the lens through which history is viewed, the reign of Constantine is no longer the jewel in the crown of history it was for Bossuet and Tillemont. Nothing could better show Gibbon's nonchalance before Bossuet's 'Constantin le Grand, Prince sage & victorieux' than his episodic rendering of this hitherto epochal reign.[12]

This affront has an air of imperturbable stylishness; but it is only an air. In his *Memoirs*, Gibbon records how this period taxed him:

It is difficult to arrange with order and perspicuity the various transactions of the age of Constantine: and so much was I displeased with the first Essay that I committed to the flames above fifty sheets.[13]

The expedient Gibbon hits on is made plain in the opening pages of the second instalment of *The Decline and Fall*:

The age of the great Constantine and his sons is filled with important events; but the historian must be oppressed by their number and variety, unless he diligently separates from each other the scenes which are connected only by the order of time.[14]

This analytic arrangement of narrative, which frees it from the obligation to follow the broadly advancing front of chronology and thus gives the historian much greater mobility, is, as we have seen, a state towards which philosophic historiography is always aspiring and which is formalised in the topical arrangement of a work such as Voltaire's *Siècle de Louis XIV*.[15] Hence, when Gibbon introduces his analytic account of the reign of Constantine, he notes

---

[11] For instance, Constantine's adoption of Christianity is the eleventh of Bossuet's 'époques': the tenth is the birth of Christ, the twelfth, the establishment of the new empire under Charlemagne.

[12] *Discours sur l'Histoire Universelle*, p. 114.

[13] *Memoirs*, p. 159. Sir Ronald Syme felt that Gibbon was in trouble over the age of Constantine (in Ducrey et al. eds., *Gibbon et Rome*, p. 53). For other discussions of Gibbon's handling of the reign of Constantine, see J. Straub, 'Gibbons Konstantin-Bild' in Ducrey et al., eds., *Gibbon et Rome*, pp. 159–85 and Chapter VI of David Jordan's *Gibbon and his Roman Empire*, pp. 191–212.

[14] *The Decline and Fall*, II.1–2. Others found the period of Constantine a problematic area. Chastellux confesses to carving up his subject, thus acknowledging its difficulty (*De la Félicité Publique*, I.290). Bever deplores the inadequacy of his material (although his providential viewpoint has no trouble in assimilating the substance of Constantine's reign) (*History of the Legal Polity of the Roman State*, p. 421).

[15] Gibbon criticises Voltaire's plan on grounds of oversimplification: 'His method (of treating every article in a distinct chapter) I think vicious, as they are all connected in human affairs, and as they are often the cause of each other, why seperate them in History?' (*Gibbon's Journal to January 28th, 1763*, p. 129). When a similar topical arrangement, which however gave far greater acknowledgement to chronology, was adopted by Henry in his *History of Great Britain* (1771–85) Gibbon pronounced it 'excellent' (*Letters*, III.223).

that the narrative will be interrupted and that this will be deplored only by those who are out of sympathy with the values of philosophic historiography:

This variety of objects will suspend, for some time, the course of the narrative; but the interruption will be censured only by those readers who are insensible to the importance of laws and manners, while they peruse, with eager curiosity, the transient intrigues of a court, or the accidental event of a battle.[16]

Gibbon is no slave to chronology in 1776: for instance, in Chapter X he recounts the inroads of the barbarians under Valerian and Gallienus ('one uninterrupted series of confusion and calamity') nation by nation rather than sequentially; and the relegation of the discussion of Christianity to the two final chapters may also be taken as an example of this philosophic ordering of narrative.[17] The important difference, however, is that in Volume I this manipulation of the narrative is discreet. Indeed, explicitly to state that narrative must dominate the past and that the demands of argument will be preferred to the fact of sequence, would have been death to Gibbon's masked intentions in Volume I, which depend on the narrative's appearing 'easy and natural', rather than artificial. When the principles of narrative order find expression in the text, instead of being kept back as anonymous agents working in the decent obscurity of the study, it is tempting to read this change as evidence of a less guarded attitude on the part of the historian. When it is accompanied by signs of intellectual impediment, it is plausible to attribute this less guarded attitude to the new stubbornness of the historian's material.

Gibbon's changing understanding of the nature and origin of the resistance the past offers to his intelligence entails a fresh sense of its significance. In 1781 we find for the first time a recognition of the possibility of positive value in difficulty, and an admission that in difficulty may lie the life of the past. Discussing a textual emendation, Gibbon comments that:

Dom. Bouquet . . . by substituting another word, ενομισε, would suppress both the difficulty and the spirit of this passage.[18]

The awkwardness of the past can be a guarantee of its authenticity and vitality. In Volumes II and III, Gibbon agrees with Bacon that 'the most corrected copies are commonly the least correct', and finds that independent life is the touchstone for distinguishing true narration from falsehood:

The *Cyropaedia* is vague and languid: the *Anabasis* circumstantial and animated. Such is the eternal difference between fiction and truth.[19]

A scrupulous fidelity to the past is now likely to be found not in narratives which possess the synthetic smoothness of an emulsion, but in those which are

[16] *The Decline and Fall*, II.23.
[17] *The Decline and Fall*, I.258: I.309. First Edition: '. . . uninterrupted period of . . .'.
[18] *The Decline and Fall*, II.170 n. 81.
[19] *Works*, I.89. *The Decline and Fall*, II.467 n. 115; see also *Letters*, I.336–7.

gritty both with the indissoluble particularity of history and the fitful and interrupted comprehension it alone permits.[20] Despite having applied his talents in Volume I to the creation of a deceptive, emulsive contexture, Gibbon now shuns the smooth artistic finish which disguises, rather than reveals, its material.

This shift in Gibbon's ideas about the nature of the past is matched, then, by a movement in his ideas concerning the appearance of reliable historiography. It is also accompanied by a new interest in the affectiveness not of the verbal surface of narrative, but of the material (or in eighteenth-century terms the 'fable') behind or beneath it. The ironic, philosophic organisation of Volume I was born of a conviction that the choices and juxtapositions of the literary artist could guide, and perhaps even ultimately determine, the reader's response. That belief is not so much repudiated as set to one side while Gibbon explores the consequences of his freshened awareness that 'a plain narrative of facts is much more pathetic, than the most laboured descriptions of epic poetry'.[21] The plainness of Volume I was a manoeuvre of the ironist, a feint to elicit undeserved trust from his reader. In the later volumes, Gibbon's ambitions for a transparent handling of the past are not attempts to ambush his readership, but a part of his intention to translate history into language. His cunning is directed not at us but at the shifting and elusive past.

It would be wrong to suggest that, having completed Chapter XVI, Gibbon made a clean break with all his previous ideas of history and historiography by abruptly adopting this new position. There are moments in Volume II when we can see the historian undecided between the philosophic assumptions he has held since 1776 and the new insights which are disrupting those assumptions:

When Tacitus describes the deaths of the innocent and illustrious Romans, who were sacrificed to the cruelty of the first Caesars, the art of the historian, or the merit of the sufferers, excite in our breasts the most lively sensations of terror, of admiration, and of pity.[22]

The most important word here is 'or'. Gibbon is unsure whether the artist or his material is the major source of literary emotion. In this passage, we

---

[20] Hence the greater trust Gibbon is prepared to extend to those historians who are visibly embarrassed by their task of transposing the past into language: 'We may observe, that the rumour is mentioned by Tacitus with a very becoming distrust and hesitation, whilst it is greedily transcribed by Suetonius, and solemnly confirmed by Dion' (*The Decline and Fall*, I.lxxviii n. 30: I.637 n. 30).

[21] *The Decline and Fall*, III.221 n. 75.

[22] *The Decline and Fall*, II.498–9. Sir Ronald Syme has suggested that Gibbon uses alternatives such as these to communicate firm opinions (in Ducrey et al., eds., *Gibbon et Rome*, p. 71). This may be true earlier in *The Decline and Fall*, although I disagree with his reading of the quotation he uses to support his point. In the later volumes, however, such alternatives suggest doubt in the historian and uncertainty in the past: see *The Decline and Fall*, IV.9, V.666, and VI.34.

can see the historian pausing reflectively at an important fork in his develop-ing ideas of historical narrative. For to hesitate between attributing literary affectiveness to subject-matter or to verbal embodiment is also to hesitate, if you yourself happen to be an historian, between giving priority to the order and perspicuity of your narrative or to the texture of the past which an ordered and perspicuous narrative may traduce. The joint reigns of Valenti-nian and Valens prompt Gibbon to make the dilemma explicit:

Perhaps the method of annals would more forcibly express the urgent and divided cares of the two emperors; but the attention of the reader, likewise, would be distracted by a tedious and desultory narrative. A separate view of the five great theatres of war . . . will impress a more distinct image of the military state of the empire under the reigns of Valentinian and Valens.[23]

The choice Gibbon must make is between annals, in which chronology is dominant and forcible expression given to what we might call the surface of the past at the expense of narrative shapeliness, and a more philosophic mode, in which the principle of order is analytic, not chronological, and which is calculated to display not the surface of the past but its efficient causal structure. What is at stake is whether *The Decline and Fall* should continue in the philosophic manner of Volume I or change register and become a history in which the historian is more passive before the past, and the reader is closer to the historian – a fellow observer of the past, and not the historian's pupil.

In dealing with Valentinian and Valens, Gibbon persists with the analytic and philosophic manner. But in Volume III it is clear that the price exacted by orderly and perspicuous narrative in terms of what it obliges the historian to omit is rising steeply. The narrative decorums which became Gibbon so handsomely in 1776 now chafe in tender places by forbidding him to expatiate on rewarding areas of the past:

Their [the Roman senators'] luxury, and their manners, have been the subject of minute and laborious disquisition: but as such enquiries would divert me too long from the design of the present work . . .[24]

And yet despite this adherence on Gibbon's part, the increasing fissi-parousness of his subject-matter prevents him from recreating the illusion of seamlessness which had been so strong in Volume I:

The distinction of two governments, which soon produced the separation of two

---

23 *The Decline and Fall*, II.515.
24 *The Decline and Fall*, III.202. Lionel Gossman speaks accurately of at least Volume I of *The Decline and Fall* when he says that 'The aim of historiography, however, is to sew together into a harmonious and extensive design as many of the pieces and patches of the historical record as possible' (*The Empire Unpossess'd*, p. 98); but after 1776 Gibbon not only finds that such har-mony and extensiveness is more difficult to achieve, but that to require that the past yield a harmonious and extensive narrative is to make possibly blinding presuppositions about the nature of the past.

nations, will justify my design of suspending the series of the Byzantine history, to pro-secute, without interruption, the disgraceful, but memorable, reign of Honorius.[25]

When considering Valentinian and Valens Gibbon at least had the choice of persevering with a philosophic narrative. But the material Gibbon encounters in Volume III sets the various demands of philosophic historiography at war with one another. Gibbon had known since he was twenty-six that the pro-bable, so crucial to the *philosophes*, does not necessarily coincide with the true.[26] But now the *philosophe* programme is not simply open to error, but self-contradictory. In order to provide the 'distinct image' the philosophic reader demands Gibbon must abandon the comprehensive view which Voltaire and Montesquieu, who in the *Essai sur les Mœurs* and the *Esprit des Loix* take the whole of history for their province, had made the outward sign of the capacity of the *bravura* intelligence of the *philosophe*:

It is not the purpose of the present chapter, or even of the present volume, to continue the distinct series of the Byzantine history; but a concise view of the reign and character of the emperor Leo, may explain the last efforts that were attempted to save the falling empire of the West.[27]

If he is seriously to attempt to show how effects arise from causes, he cannot at the same time preserve the literary shapeliness and economy which had accompanied the incisive perceptions of other philosophic historians:

These controversies were first agitated under the reign of the younger Theodosius: but their important consequences extend far beyond the limits of the present volume.[28]

In Volume I there was a visible conflict between the moulding hand of the historical artist and his material. But now the tension between the narrative considerations of form, order and emphasis, and the past and the insights it provokes, is too great to be eased by simply giving priority to the demands of narrative, as Gibbon did in the case of Valentinian and Valens; since it is clear that to do so is not innocently to set a high value on literary form, nor even to make a decision about how the past is to be presented. It is to decide which areas of the past are presented. The philosophic values of order and perspicuity ultimately limit the attention of the historian to certain areas of the past.[29] Because Gibbon has moved into centuries and regions inimical to philosophic history, he is obliged to evolve new decorums and narrative strategies. To persist as a philosophic historian would be to exclude what now

---

[25] *The Decline and Fall*, III.122.
[26] 'Le fait n'est pas vraisemblable, mais il est vrai' (*Miscellanea Gibboniana*, p. 104). The same thought recurs in Volume I of *The Decline and Fall* (*The Decline and Fall*, I.323: I.384).
[27] *The Decline and Fall*, III.469.
[28] *The Decline and Fall*, III.554.
[29] Voltaire suggested as much when he formulated the 'Quatre Âges Heureux'; the ages of Pericles, Augustus, of the Medici and of Louis XIV are not just the only periods of history in which enlightened values were in the ascendant, but the only periods which are transparent, and thus fully legible, to the philosophic historian.

seems the essence of the troubled and contradictory age he has taken for his own.[30]

The indeterminacy of this period ruffles the pages of *The Decline and Fall*. Tracing the rift between Constantine and Crispus, the historian is discomposed:

The public favour, which seldom accompanies old-age, diffused its lustre over the youth of Crispus. He deserved the esteem, and he engaged the affections, of the court, the army, and the people. The experienced merit of a reigning monarch is acknowledged by his subjects with reluctance, and frequently denied with partial and discontented murmurs; while, from the opening virtues of his successor, they fondly conceive the most unbounded hopes of private as well as public felicity.[31]

One's attention is caught by the phrase 'the experienced merit of a reigning monarch', together with the generalisation Gibbon introduces to explain the jealousy of the emperor for his son and thus assimilate that jealousy to the principles of human nature. It draws attention to itself because it is at odds with what Gibbon has said about Constantine immediately beforehand. We have just been told that, when emperor, Constantine lost the virtues of the youth he had expended in achieving his ambition:

In that [the life] of Constantine, we may contemplate a hero, who had so long inspired his subjects with love, and his enemies with terror, degenerating into a cruel and dissolute monarch, corrupted by his fortune, or raised by conquest above the necessity of dissimulation.[32]

Gibbon locates this decay in the last fourteen years of Constantine's reign (i.e. A.D.. 323 to 337). The estrangement between the emperor and his son lies wholly within this period, beginning in October 324 and reaching its consummation with the death of Crispus in July 326. Thus the 'experienced merit' of Constantine, which Gibbon invokes when trying to explain the 'dangerous popularity' of Crispus, was by his own account already disappearing. The divergence is all the more striking because the earlier comment, that Constantine's reign degenerated into an undisguised tyranny, removes the need for the later supposition that he was a monarch more sinned against than sinning, whose known and extant virtues were overlooked by the feckless masses eager for novelty. We have Gibbon's own word for it that he found the reign of

[30] Gibbon would not have subscribed to the division between the 'critical' and 'speculative' kinds of philosophy of history, the former dealing with the process of historical thinking, the latter with the actual course of historical events, which George Dennis O'Brien sees as the hallmark of modern thought about philosophy of history ('Does Hegel have a philosophy of history?', pp. 174–6). Gibbon comes to understand that a historian's critical thought about the process of historical thinking is intertwined with his thought about the course of historical events, and that each influences the other. As he moves into areas of the past which are unphilosophic in character – that is, inimical to philosophic historiography – he is made aware of how rich in presuppositions about the nature of the past are the critical principles of the philosophic historian.

[31] *The Decline and Fall*, II.80–1.

[32] *The Decline and Fall*, II.77.

Constantine problematic: this slight contradiction is valuable because it shows us the nature of at least one of the problems it posed the historian. It suggests that Gibbon found it difficult to reconcile the various reflections about the past which his task stimulated in him once he was engaged. From different stand-points the shape and significance of the past alters slightly and yet decisively. With such elusive subject-matter, the philosophic ideal of a single point of vantage from which the whole of the past would be truthfully displayed to the historian is becoming harder to discover, and also less desirable. In small con-tradictions such as this we find the beginnings of the mobility in Gibbon's nar-rative which will assume a much greater prominence in 1788.

The historian must be as flexible as the past itself in his attempts to catch it in the net of words; but his language, too, must respond to its volatility. Words make statements, but Gibbon has more delicate ends in view: 'I owe it to myself, and to historic truth, to declare, that some *circumstances* in this paragraph are founded only on conjecture and analogy. The stubbornness of our language has sometimes forced me to deviate from the *conditional* into the *indicative* mood.'[33] It is more and more Gibbon's experience that language slides towards what is, for his purposes, a false definition or a spurious in-dicative. Thus we find that one of the major achievements of Gibbon's style in the later volumes of *The Decline and Fall* is its truth to both the vagueness of our knowledge of the past and the vagueness of the past itself:

The Roman troops had less degenerated from the industry, than from the valour, of their ancestors; and if the servile and laborious work offended the pride of the soldiers, Tuscany could supply many thousand peasants, who would labour, though, perhaps, they would not fight, for the salvation of their native country.[34]

This sentence does not so much describe facts as outline possibilities. Either the soldiers dug the earthworks or they dragooned the peasants into doing so. Gibbon entertains both these hypotheses, each of which supposes the character of Stilicho's army to be quite different from the character supposed in the other. He indicates and negotiates this lacuna in our knowledge of the past; and in so doing demonstrates his growing understanding that the historian of the declining empire should preserve, and not triumph over, the incompleteness of his material.

We can now appreciate a major respect in which the narrative of the later volumes of *The Decline and Fall* differs from that of Volume I. In 1776 the whole volume was presented as an interpretation of the past acquired at the end of a process of thought. It possessed the kind of unity that springs from having reached a conclusion. In Volumes II to VI we find increasingly that the process of thought, which in Volume I we had to infer, floats upon the

---

[33] *The Decline and Fall*, III.275 n. 178.   [34] *The Decline and Fall*, III.166–7.

surface of the prose. A turn of phrase which in Chapter XV had served ironic ends is now employed with different purposes in mind:

In the midst of his apparent prosperity, Alaric was conscious, perhaps, of some secret weakness, some internal defect; or perhaps the moderation which he displayed, was intended only to deceive and disarm the easy credulity of the ministers of Honorius.

This supernatural gift of the African confessors, who spoke without tongues, will command the assent of those, and of those only, who already believe, that their language was pure and orthodox. But the stubborn mind of an infidel is guarded by secret, incurable, suspicion; and the Arian, or Socinian, who has seriously rejected the doctrine of the Trinity, will not be shaken by the most plausible evidence of an Athanasian miracle.[35]

In Volume I, such hesitant sentences overlaid pits prepared for the credulous. Now, they announce moments when Gibbon takes his reader into his confidence and exposes to our view the pits which surround the historian; the unity of style disguises a difference of intent. In Chapter XV Gibbon embarrassed those who believed even the most holy and tremendous miracle. Here he separates himself from those whose minds are 'guarded by secret, incurable, suspicion', just as he also distances himself from the 'easy credulity' of Honorius' counsellors. Gibbon has left the chorus of those who mock and has realised that the historian has more difficult tasks than to pillory or to praise.

A glorious moment in the career of Stilicho might serve as an emblem of Gibbon's educated sense of the nature of this part of history, and of the use historians have made of it:

The triumph of Stilicho was compared by the poet, and perhaps by the public, to that of Marius; who, in the same part of Italy, had encountered and destroyed another army of northern Barbarians. The huge bones, and the empty helmets, of the Cimbri and of the Goths, would easily be confounded by succeeding generations; and posterity might erect a common trophy to the memory of the two most illustrious generals, who had vanquished, on the same memorable ground, the two most formidable enemies of Rome.[36]

'Succeeding generations', philosophically presupposing that history is integrated and orderly, place a confused, partial and erroneous construction on the arresting, impressive, yet also disordered and fragmentary, traces of the past. Alternatively, the philosophic historian may be simply repelled by the inability of the records of these centuries to supply an answer to any question he thinks worth asking:

. . . the battle of Châlons can only excite our curiosity, by the magnitude of the object; since it was decided by the blind impetuosity of Barbarians, and has been related by partial writers . . .[37]

Values in history other than the philosophic must be found. The rest of *The Decline and Fall* is taken up by their discovery and celebration.

[35] *The Decline and Fall*, III.225 and 547.   [36] *The Decline and Fall*, III.152.
[37] *The Decline and Fall*, III.413.

10

Julian the Apostate

. . . for you must know, that next to new-invented characters, we are fond of new lights upon ancient characters; I mean such lights as shew a reputed honest man to have been a concealed knave; an illustrious hero a pitiful coward, &c. . . .   Lyttelton

Cet empereur élevé jusqu'aux nues par les ennemies du nom chrétien, a mérité que de nos jours un auteur célebre prit la peine d'écrire son histoire, & s'efforçat de rectifier le jugement qu'on devoit en porter.   Chastellux

The way in which Gibbon's allegiance to the *philosophe* assumptions with which he had begun *The Decline and Fall* is shaken, and the consequences of that disturbance, are shown with great clarity in his handling of Julian the Apostate.[1]

Julian's most recent historian has found that it is possible only to 'grope towards the facts about the man and his reign'.[2] Michel Baridon has argued that Gibbon did not share this tentativeness. While acknowledging that his portrait of Julian is not a simple panegyric – after all, the historian himself speaks of 'my impartial balance of the virtues and vices of Julian' – Baridon suggests that *The Decline and Fall* astutely blends criticism of Julian with praise in order to confuse those who, aware of Gibbon's aversion to Christianity, expected him to make a hero of the Apostate.[3] Nevertheless, the wise and sympathetic are not deceived and understand that the account is 'implicitement' favourable:

Tout son portrait de Julien est peint dans l'espoir de faire admettre qu'avec lui, l'empire romain avait retrouvé à la fois un chef et un serviteur dans la grande tradition des Antonins . . .[4]

The mingling of praise and blame to which Baridon refers is unmistakable; but we are not therefore required to accept his sophisticated reading of it.

---

[1] On Gibbon's portrait of Julian, see R. J. Ziegler, 'Edward Gibbon and Julian the Apostate', G. W. Bowersock, 'Gibbon and Julian' in Ducrey et al., eds., *Gibbon et Rome*, pp. 191–217, and Michel Baridon, *Edward Gibbon et le Mythe de Rome*, pp. 693–8.

[2] G. W. Bowersock, *Julian the Apostate*, p. xii.

[3] *Memoirs*, p. 162.

[4] Baridon, *Edward Gibbon et le Mythe de Rome*, p. 697. G. W. Bowersock agrees that this is the effect Gibbon's portrait of Julian has on the reader, although he argues that it is a product of the different sources Gibbon relied on, not of design (in Ducrey et al., eds., *Gibbon et Rome*, p. 191).

Assuming that Gibbon's values were as philosophic in 1781 as in 1776, Baridon is obliged to find the portrait of Julian covertly philosophic, since it is obviously not overtly so. However, I shall argue that it is simply not philosophic; that it neither secretly nor openly shares the admiring view of the Apostate common among the *philosophes*. In this case, the appearance is the reality. Gibbon's judgement is genuinely suspended between opposed possibilities, as the phrase 'impartial balance' in his *Memoirs* – written, we must remember, when the need for dissimulation was past and when Gibbon was fêted on his visits to London – implies.[5]

Gibbon does not know quite where he stands with Julian:

When we inspect, with minute, or perhaps malevolent attention, the portrait of Julian, something seems wanting to the grace and perfection of the whole figure. His genius was less powerful and sublime than that of Caesar; nor did he possess the consummate prudence of Augustus. The virtues of Trajan appear more steady and natural, and the philosophy of Marcus is more simple and consistent. Yet Julian sustained adversity with firmness, and prosperity with moderation.[6]

The controlled vagueness of 'something' has, in Volume I, so often disarmed the reader before a thrust of irony, that it is not surprising to find Baridon convinced that the same ironic intelligence is at play here as there. But when we look at the passage as a whole we find it to be a genuine expression of an indeterminacy in Gibbon's thoughts about Julian for which 'something' is the literal and straightforward word. Revolving his predecessors in turn, no other emperor can provide Gibbon with a point of entry into the opaque figure whom comparison can define, but not illuminate. Gibbon achieves a sharp silhouette, while leaving Julian's dark essence untouched.

Gibbon's reserve contrasts strongly with previous discussion devoted to Julian. Momigliano has called the Apostate 'an obvious test case for the Enlightenment'.[7] Certainly the *philosophes* seem to have recognised that here history was offering them an opportunity to create a hero who, if not quite in their own image, at least shared their values. By ignoring his aggressive militarism and his superstition, the *philosophes* could make Julian embody all the secular ideals of social betterment they held dear, so that his apostasy would emerge as clear evidence of the incompatibility of Christianity with a firm commitment to the humane. Thus Pierre Bayle hoped to indict the intolerance of Catholicism by praising Julian as 'un des plus grands Empereurs qui ayent jamais regné, et outre cela tres-honnête homme, chaste, sobre, vigilant, ennemi du luxe et des voluptez'.[8] Montesquieu singles Julian out for special praise in the *Considérations*:

[Julian] par sa sagesse, sa constance, son économie, sa conduite, sa valeur, & une

[5] For Gibbon's reception in London during the late 1780s, see *Memoirs*, pp. 180–2.
[6] *The Decline and Fall*, II.354.
[7] 'Eighteenth-century prelude to Mr. Gibbon' in Ducrey et al., eds., *Gibbon et Rome*, p. 63.
[8] *Critique Generale*, p. 296.

suite continuelle d'actions héroïques, rechassa les Barbares; & la terreur de son nom les contint tant qu'il vecut.[9]

It is, however, Voltaire who pays most regular and extravagant tribute to Julian. He supplied the notes to d'Argens' translation of the *Discours de l'Empereur Julien contre les Chrétiens* (1768) and provocatively asserts what he feels ought to be as what is:

La saine critique s'étant perfectionnée, tout le monde avoue aujourd'hui que l'empereur Julien était un héros et un sage, un stoicien égal à Marc-Aurèle.[10]

If polite opinion were indeed united in admiration of Julian, then the work of the *philosophes* would be done. But while Churchmen such as Warburton could propose alternative, providentialist readings of Julian's career, in which the Apostate's persecution of Christianity is tolerated by God in order to show the impotence of even the greatest worldly power against the true faith, Voltaire's unanimity is more a consummation devoutly to be wished than a fact.[11]

Certainly if we look back to the polemical literature spawned by the Exclusion Crisis, in which Julian plays a leading role, we shall not find unanimous admiration.[12] The reason why Julian is introduced as an historical example to illuminate the issues underlying the uncertainties of the 1680s is revealed by Samuel Johnson in his *Julian's Arts to Undermine and Extirpate Christianity* (1689). Johnson explains that 'The Design of my Book [*Julian the Apostate* (1682)] was to shew, that the Primitive Christians would have been for a Bill of Exclusion'; to this end he uses the resistance of the early Christians to the Apostate's attempts to reintroduce paganism as an illustration of the principle that it is legitimate to resist a monarch's proposed changes in religion.[13] The pagan Julian's succession to the devout Constantius is offered as the image of a Popish succession and as a demonstration that secular loyalty to one's sovereign need not imply obedience in matters of religious conscience. Johnson uses history to show that a loyal Protestant Englishman would be bound to resist any attempt to change his country's religion. Consequently prudence and conscience unite in the realisation 'that we are bound, in order to the keeping out the Pope's Power, which we have utterly renounced, humbly to beg of his Majesty to foreclose a Popish Successor, who will infallibly let it in'.[14]

Johnson's pamphlet of 1682 provoked a plentiful response, in which counterexamples are advanced, or the pertinence of the example of Julian to

---

[9] *Œuvres*, III.477.

[10] *Œuvres Complètes*, XVII.317: see also XI.241, XI.323, XVII.321 and XIX.546. In his dismissal of Julian's apostasy as a peccadillo, and his redirection of our attention to his moral virtues, Voltaire echoes Spanheim (*Juliani Opera*, I.sig. c2v; note also the language of the dedication). Julian cuts a minor figure in English literature, too: see Fielding's *Journey from this World to the Next* (1743) and Shaftesbury's *A Letter Concerning Enthusiasm* (1708).

[11] *Julian, or a Discourse concerning the Earthquake and Fiery Eruption*, pp. 27–8.

[12] For an interesting account of how Julian infiltrates the iconography of this period, see Edgar Wind, 'Julian the Apostate at Hampton Court'.

[13] *Julian's Arts to Undermine and Extirpate Christianity*, p. 156.

[14] *Julian's Arts to Undermine and Extirpate Christianity*, pp. 141–2.

England in the late seventeenth century questioned and 'the disparity of the Cases of *Julian*, and the *D. of Y.*' explored.[15] What is striking, however, is the large measure of agreement there is about the character of Julian on both sides of the dispute. Although these writers disagree violently about the significance of Julian, they are united in an untroubled loathing of him as a consummate and impious dissimulator. He poses no problems of understanding, merely problems of interpretation. Thus, he is controversial only in the subordinate sense of figuring in controversy. That he could be the *subject* of controversy, that anyone might find him intrinsically controversial, is unthinkable for these writers, since any possible ambiguity or uncertainty in his character and actions is swiftly reduced to yet another example of 'his treacherous Malice'.[16]

Johnson and his adversaries skip over Julian's complexities because he is merely a pawn in their argument and not the ultimate object of their attention; they are writing parallel history, which allowed political criticism to masquerade as historical analysis.[17] But even in the work of the classical scholars and historians who might be supposed to have no ulterior aim in considering Julian, we find that he causes an arrest in thought. Ezechiel Spanheim, who published the *Juliani Opera* in 1696, acknowledges the various facets of Julian's character, but simultaneously contrives to minimise their tendency to pull in different directions by arranging them so that there is a smooth graduation from the emperor's virtues to his vices:

verum a quo felici auspicatoque laudum curriculo, alia eum longe abduxerunt: praeceps nempe ingenium; inquies animus; testata in incessu, sermone, obtutu lenitas; cupido laudis immodicae; vanissima insuper abdita quaeque, etsi nefaria, perscrutandi libido; ac nata inde paullatim a pietate, a religione, cui innutritus fuerat, abalienatio primum, tum clandestina, mox aperta desertio; & quae subsequi vulgo eadem solent, acerrimum illinc odium, ac immanis tandem insectatio.[18]

To arrange the different elements of Julian's character in the form of the different refractions of the spectrum is to imply a fundamental unity beneath this diversity and to camouflage or make invisible what Gibbon would later respond to as a paradox.

One finds a similar regularising of the disparate components which made up Julian's personality in Fleury's *Histoire Ecclésiastique*. Fleury is troubled by the contrast between Julian's stoic virtues and his religious vindictiveness, but resolves the contradiction by assuming that the former were simply a pretence

---

[15] William Hopkins, *Animadversions on Mr. Johnson's Answer to Jovian*, p. 12. Other duellists in this controversy are: Anon., *Constantius the Apostate* (1683); Edward Meredith, *Some Remarques Upon a Late Popular Piece of Nonsense Call'd Julian the Apostate &c* (1682); George Hickes, *Jovian or, an Answer to Julian the Apostate* (1683).

[16] *Julian's Arts to Undermine and Extirpate Christianity*, p. 36.

[17] I borrow this accurate and brief description of 'parallel history' from David Nokes's *Jonathan Swift: A Hypocrite Reversed*, pp. 54–5.

[18] *Juliani Opera*, sig. a2r.

which allowed Julian the more plausibly to indulge his hatred of Christianity:

Plusieurs Chrétiens furent envellopez dans cette recherche & dans la réforme des officiers du palais imperial, que Julien chassa, sous prétexte d'en bannir le luxe & de vivre en philosophe.[19]

Thus Fleury can sum Julian up in the phrase 'la douceur apparente & la dérision de l'évangile'.[20] The complexity of the historical evidence concerning Julian is dissolved when one subordinates everything to his hatred of Christianity.

The book which exerted the most powerful influence over Gibbon's understanding of the Apostate – which was, indeed, one of the three seminal books of his youth – was Bleterie's *Vie de l'Empereur Julien*.[21] Bleterie is aware that Julian has been misrepresented: 'Les Historiens mêmes cessent d'être historiens, des qu'ils parlent de Julien, & deviennent des accusateurs ou bien des panégyristes.'[22] He advances beyond his contemporaries and predecessors, however, when he grasps that something within Julian himself precipitates this polarised response, and that it is not simply a product of the disputatiousness of later commentators:

. . . Julien étoit lui-même un amas de contradictions. M. Fleury observe judicieusement, *qu'il y avoit dans ce prince un tel mélange de bonnes & de mauvaises qualités, qu'il étoit facile de le louer & de le blâmer, sans altérer la vérité.*[23]

Thus in Bleterie's own account of Julian we find hints of the ineffable and the opaque. The vocabulary in which Julian demands to be discussed is rich in words denoting the anomalous. He is 'merveilleux', 'singulier' and 'monstrueux':

Plus j'ai étudié Julien, soit dans ses propres écrits, soit dans les autres monumens de l'antiquité, plus il m'a paru intéressant. Le contraste de ses vices réels & de ses vertus apparentes, joint à la diversité de ses situations & de ses avantures, forme un morceau d'histoire, où l'on trouve, avec la plus exacte vérité, le merveilleux des fictions.

. . . après avoir distingué avec précision l'apostat du philosophe & de l'empereur, je trouve qu'il ne fut point un grand homme, mais un homme singulier.

Ainsi faisant un mélange monstrueux de folie & de sagesse, il honoroit la débauche en Payen, & s'en abstenoit en philosophe.[24]

Instead of denying the prodigiousness of Julian's character and reducing it to caricature, as does Fleury, Bleterie recognises its fractures. Julian is, in the

---

[19] *Histoire Ecclésiastique*, IV.2.
[20] *Histoire Ecclésiastique*, IV.10.
[21] First published in Paris, 1735; see *Memoirs*, p. 79.
[22] *Vie de l'Empereur Julien*, p. ix. No copy of this work is recorded in Gibbon's library. Others commented on the polarised opinions Julian provoked: see William Guthrie, *A General History of the World*, V.30 and Chastellux, *De la Félicité Publique*, I.252).
[23] *Vie de l'Empereur Julien*, pp. ix–x.
[24] *Vie de l'Empereur Julien*, pp. vi, 2 and 305.

strict sense, eccentric: 'Il n'eut point ce fonds de bon sens, qui doit être le centre & le point fixe des vertus.'[25] But Bleterie's own writing is fractured, since the conclusions he reaches about Julian are not informed by the apparently irreducible complexity he has identified within the emperor's character. With abrupt inconsequence Bleterie styles Julian 'ce prince hypocrite', acquiescing in Fleury's hypothesis of real vices and merely apparent virtues:

J'ai representé celles [the virtues] de Julien dans le vrai, c'est-à-dire, toujours défigurées par quelque défaut: & d'ailleurs il les a tournées contre leur auteur; ce qui doit nous les rendre odieuses.[26]

One could argue that Bleterie intends us to see through his meek endorsement of the Christian perspective on Julian by making its inconsequence unmistakable. The problem is that it is not unmistakable in the way that, say, Voltaire's ironic inconsequences are. It seems more likely that Bleterie reaches for a conclusion and forecloses on the debate he has aroused within himself by adopting Fleury's explanation of Julian's character, however uneasily it sits alongside his own complicating intuitions. Thus Gibbon's predecessors 'solve' the enigma of Julian the Apostate by either ignoring it or dismissing it. They either see no difficulty in his character because they are too intent on their real objects, for which Julian is but an illustration; or, if they are aware of the complexity of Julian's character, they refuse to explore it and bring their discussions swiftly to a close.

Gibbon's account of Julian has the marks of neither abbreviation nor cursoriness. G. W. Bowersock has noted that Julian is given a prominent place in *The Decline and Fall*, and that the amplitude of the portrait 'emphasizes the significance he attached to a ruler whose uncontested reign lasted but a year and a half'.[27] Gibbon himself notes that Julian enjoyed only 'a reign of one year and about eight months', but that the prince's virtue made time elastic: 'By this avarice of time, he seemed to protract the short duration of his reign.'[28] Thus, the extended consideration Gibbon pays Julian seems not the result of his own narrative requirements, a pointing up of an area of the past on which he wants to lay particular emphasis: it has the air rather of a response to Julian's intrinsic arrestingness. It is the density of this material which slows the course of Gibbon's narrative.

The impediment Gibbon encountered in Julian is all the more striking since, if one looks at the arrangement of the chapters in Volume II, it appears that he originally intended to present Julian in *philosophe* style as an Enlightenment hero and martyr. Chapter XIX deduces Julian's career down to the period of his successful administration in Gaul. Then, echoing the paired fifteenth and sixteenth chapters which conclude Volume I, Chapters XX and

[25] *Vie de l'Empereur Julien*, p. 2.
[26] *Vie de l'Empereur Julien*, pp. 153 and x.
[27] See Ducrey et al., eds., *Gibbon et Rome*, p. 191.
[28] *The Decline and Fall*, II.459 and 340.

XXI recount the progress of Christianity through the empire, and it is only in Chapter XXII, after an interval of one hundred and thirty-two pages, that we return to Julian. The order of chapters – presumably decided on before the detailed work of composition – suggests a reading of Julian's historical significance at variance with what Gibbon actually gives us. The empire's more or less wholesale capitulation to Christianity in Chapters XX and XXI seems intended as a backdrop of pusillanimity against which the apostasy of Julian will stand out boldly. The firm-mindedness of the individual is to be placed against the general, vicious servility – a contrast also made, but in a different way, by the inevitable comparison between Julian and his predecessor in the purple, the Arian Constantius.[29]

Why does Gibbon stray from the smooth path he has mapped out for himself? We can appreciate the stubborn cross-grainedness of Julian for Gibbon if we recall the conviction which organised his account of decline in Volume I. There Gibbon had urged that it was pre-eminently Christianity, rather than the effects of luxury or the change in constitution from republic to principate that had sapped the civic virtue on which the safety of the empire depended. In terms of this argument Julian is an unmanageable figure. He can be used without reservation as an historic flail with which to lash the Christian religion; from this point of view he really does seem the lonely hero whose apostasy is a gesture of solitary defiance to the rising tide of monkishness and credulity which was to overwhelm the empire. But Gibbon's precision as an historical scholar will not allow him (unlike those lesser scholars but better *philosophes* Voltaire and Montesquieu) to suppress all the evidence which indicates that, from the point of view of civic virtue, Julian is a very equivocal character. Gibbon's sharp eye discerns that Julian gives us the appearance but not the substance of such virtue, and that his adherence to the pristine forms of the constitution is an elaborate mime which gratifies his vain and enthusiastic nature.[30] Gibbon characterises the philosophic

---

[29] It may seem that the sequence of monarchs is an aspect of the past the historian simply has to accept, and that it consequently cannot form part of his design. But an historian might nevertheless choose to begin his narrative so that suggestive contrasts between monarchs are made prominent: for instance, Wotton begins his *History of Rome from the Death of Antoninus Pius to the Death of Severus Alexander* with a justification of his choice of period: 'These particular Emperors of whom here is some Account given, were pitch'd on by Your Lordship [Gilbert Burnet, Bishop of Salisbury] as the properest Examples in the whole *Roman* History, to Instruct a Prince how much more Glorious and Safe it is, and Happier both for Himself and for his People, to govern well than ill' – and the reason for this is that 'A very Bad Prince who immediately succeeded a very Good one; and a most extraordinary Prince, who came after one of the most Profligate of Men; were thought the properest Instances to set Virtue and Vice, and the Consequences of them both in a clear and a full Light' (sigs. A2v and A5r). It seems possible to me that Gibbon had a similar end in mind when he began the circumstantial narrative of *The Decline and Fall* with the reign of Commodus (but for a different view, see Giarrizzo, *Edward Gibbon e la Cultura Europea del Settecento*, p. 230).

[30] Gibbon's insistence that Julian merely acts out the typical forms of civic virtue does not prevent his acknowledging that even this sham sometimes has beneficial effects, enabling Julian for instance 'to revive and enforce the rigour of ancient discipline' (*The Decline and Fall*,

perspective as one of 'partial ignorance', and then proposes a 'more accurate' alternative:

Our partial ignorance may represent him [Julian] as a philosophic monarch, who studied to protect, with an equal hand, the religious factions of the empire; and to allay the theological fever which had inflamed the minds of the people, from the edicts of Diocletian to the exile of Athanasius. A more accurate view of the character and conduct of Julian, will remove this favourable prepossession for a prince who did not escape the general contagion of the times.[31]

As expressed in Julian, the 'general contagion' which, far from silhouetting him against a general depravity, blends him into it, is the pretence of virtue and power and the reduction of civic virtue to a *coup de théâtre*:

During the games of the Circus, he had, imprudently or designedly, performed the manumission of a slave in the presence of the consul. The moment he was reminded that he had trespassed on the jurisdiction of *another* magistrate, he condemned himself to pay a fine of ten pounds of gold . . .[32]

Even Julian's reluctance to mimic a contrary, depraved tradition of imperial behaviour is spiced with affectation, as the word 'vanity' suggests: 'Julian . . . who placed his vanity, not in emulating, but in despising, the pomp of royalty.'[33] This weakness for unseasonable imitation contributes to his death, displaying all his contradictory complexity in 'the inflexible firmness of a hero, who remembered, most unfortunately for himself, and for his country, that Alexander had uniformly rejected the propositions of Darius'.[34] Eventually Julian's infatuation prompts Gibbon to mingle rebuke, elegy and amusement in an utterance as hybrid as its subject:

. . . he resolved to imitate the adventurous spirit of Alexander, and boldly to advance into the inland provinces, till he forced his rival to contend with him, perhaps in the plains of Arbela, for the empire of Asia.[35]

In the phrase 'perhaps in the plains of Arbela' one can hear the tone change, see the eyebrow slightly raised. This ambition is both heroic and of a comic preposterousness. And the risible elements of fraud in Julian's character disturb Gibbon because they challenge the firm opposition of Christianity and civic virtue which occupied a commanding position in his ideas in 1776. They force him to contemplate the ungrateful fact that the greatest enemy of Christianity in the ancient world also accelerated the process of decline by trivialising what little remained of the political forms of the republic; that because of

II.439). But of course Gibbon is fascinated throughout *The Decline and Fall* by the palpable consequences of illusions.

[31] *The Decline and Fall*, II.355.   [32] *The Decline and Fall*, II.349.
[33] *The Decline and Fall*, II.342.   [34] *The Decline and Fall*, II.448.
[35] *The Decline and Fall*, II.448.

his intemperate craving for military glory and his inability to distinguish the consummate skill of generals such as Caesar and Alexander from impetuosity, he steered the empire towards disaster.

Not only is Julian divided in himself; he also divides his historian. For, from the point of view of Gibbon's understanding of what he is about when writing history, the problem Julian poses is that the antinomy of his character (he is both stalwart opponent of Christianity and agent in the political enfeeblement of the empire) cracks the union between the *philosophe* and the *érudit* forged in Volume I of *The Decline and Fall*. In 1776 Gibbon found that his philosophic leanings and his scholarly accuracy complemented one another. In 1781 his philosophic liking for Julian – his 'partial ignorance' – is brought up short by his scholarly awareness of all there is to be said against such a flattering reading of the historical significance of the Apostate. Thus Gibbon begins Chapter XXIII with the words 'His [Julian's] motives, his counsels, and his actions, as far as they are connected with the history of religion, will be the subject of the present chapter.'[36] For Voltaire, Julian's rejection of Christianity was an integral part of his paradigmatic value: it was the union of his secular values and his rejection of the Church which made him such a potent figure for the *philosophes*. Thus Voltaire never lets us forget the conjunction of these two aspects of Julian's life. Gibbon, however, is obliged to separate them, since they coincide exactly with the ambivalence he finds so problematic in Julian.

The suspension of judgement in Gibbon's impartial balance of Julian's virtues and vices imparts an oscillation to his writing. We find him noting the attempts of contemporaries to 'read' Julian, and there are frequent occasions when Gibbon approximates the emperor to his predecessors; but he never achieves a commanding and satisfactory perspective.[37] Instead, we see the mobility of a fine historical intelligence trying to find a point of entry into this indistinct and contradictory figure:

The functions of a judge, which are sometimes incompatible with those of a prince, were exercised by Julian, not only as a duty, but as an amusement; and although he might have trusted the integrity and discernment of his Praetorian praefects, he often placed himself by their side on the seat of judgment. The acute penetration of his mind was agreeably occupied in detecting and defeating the chicanery of the advocates, who laboured to disguise the truth of facts, and to pervert the sense of the laws. He

---

[36] *The Decline and Fall*, II.356.

[37] As an example of the former, one might cite 'the slaves who would not dare to censure his defects, were not worthy to applaud his virtues' (*The Decline and Fall*, II.348). Concerning the latter, it is remarkable that Julian is most often juxtaposed with the emperor who sold the pass of empire to the Christians. Chrysanthius' refusal to visit Julian at Constantinople recalls Athanasius' similar behaviour towards Constantine (*The Decline and Fall*, II.272). Gibbon explains the dreams of both men as the product of waking anxieties (*The Decline and Fall*, II.320 n. 13 and II.197). Julian's false humility in the lawcourts recalls Constantine's affected humility in synods (*The Decline and Fall*, II.352 and 229). Both emperors adopt the Sun as their tutelar deity (*The Decline and Fall*, II.182 and 372).

sometimes forgot the gravity of his station, asked indiscreet or unseasonable questions, and betrayed, by the loudness of his voice, and the agitation of his body, the earnest vehemence with which he maintained his opinion against the judges, the advocates, and their clients. But his knowledge of his own temper prompted him to encourage, and even to solicit, the reproof of his friends and ministers; and whenever they ventured to oppose the irregular sallies of his passions, the spectators could observe the shame, as well as the gratitude, of their monarch. The decrees of Julian were almost always founded on the principles of justice; and he had the firmness to resist the two most dangerous temptations, which assault the tribunal of a sovereign, under the specious forms of compassion and equity. He decided the merits of the cause without weighing the circumstances of the parties; and the poor, whom he wished to relieve, were condemned to satisfy the just demands of a noble and wealthy adversary. He carefully distinguished the judge from the legislator; and though he meditated a necessary reformation of the Roman jurisprudence, he pronounced sentence according to the strict and literal interpretation of those laws, which the magistrates were bound to execute, and the subjects to obey.[38]

As Gibbon adjusts his angle of vision on Julian, each change or extension of perspective is also a change of estimation. We find no cumulative weight of careful discrimination leading to a perhaps subtle, but pondered and stable conclusion (note that the paragraph ends not with a definitive judgement, but by revealing the incompatibility of Julian's intentions and his practice). Rather, we have a collage of fragmentary and equivocal insights. 'Sometimes incompatible' suggests that Julian brings off the difficult combination of being both judge and prince, but 'amusement' weakens that praise with its connotations of levity, just as 'agreeably' lightens and diminishes 'acute penetration'. The ambiguity of 'might have trusted' (undecided between meaning 'could safely have trusted' and 'would have entrusted, were he a lesser prince') vibrates between describing a prince who is a charlatan, and one who is an exemplar. 'Encourage' reinforces the good impression made on us by Julian's self-forgetful zeal for justice, but 'his knowledge of his own temper' prompts us to question the depth of that self-forgetfulness, just as 'solicit' hints that it might all be affectation. 'Almost always' is tantalisingly half-hearted, while the apparent wisdom of attending solely to the merits of the cause is shaken by its paradoxical outcome.

That these qualifications and reservations are the product of perplexity (rather than of artfulness, as was the case with the portrait of Augustus) is indicated by the way the experience of coming to grips with Julian's character is a watershed in Gibbon's understanding of character generally. In the early pages of his account of Julian, Gibbon talks of the Apostate's 'ruling passion' or 'ruling principle':

A tender regard for the peace and happiness of his subjects, was the ruling principle which directed, or seemed to direct, the administration of Julian.

---

[38] *The Decline and Fall*, II.352–3. A long quotation is necessary to register the complexity of Gibbon's attitude, which would naturally not appear in a short quotation.

A devout and sincere attachment for the gods of Athens and Rome, constituted the ruling passion of Julian . . .[39]

But this idiom soon crumbles under the pressure of trying to cope with the elusiveness of this emperor, who was so at home in multiplicity that he could 'pursue at once three several trains of ideas'.[40] The inflection to a plural form, as much as the variety of the ruling passions Gibbon at different times finds convincing, confesses his inability to reduce Julian's character to a single principle:

The acquisition of new proselytes gratified the ruling passions of his soul, superstition and vanity . . .

In his last moments he displayed, perhaps with some ostentation, the love of virtue and of fame, which had been the ruling passions of his life.[41]

Since Gibbon persists with the plural form in later volumes, this would seem to mark a permanent complication and enrichment of his ideas of what human nature, and thus history, can encompass.[42]

Chapter XXIV, the final chapter of Gibbon's account of Julian and the place where we might expect whatever conclusions he will provide, in fact furnishes simply more vivid signs of indecision and reservation. It begins by paraphrasing 'the philosophical fable which Julian composed under the name of the CAESARS'.[43] In this work, the gods must choose the greatest of the Roman emperors, and their choice alights on Marcus Antoninus. It is a felicitous stroke for Gibbon to open a chapter in which he will be called on to judge an emperor by considering that prince's judgements on his fellows. But it also suggests that Gibbon is going to judge Julian severely. His review of Julian's fable concludes with the reflection that 'A prince, who delineates with freedom the vices and virtues of his predecessors, subscribes, in every line, the censure or approbation of his own conduct.'[44] Thus we must judge Julian in the light of his own avowed preference for a prince 'who had practised on the throne the lessons of philosophy'; and Gibbon has already done enough to suggest that Julian will not find this a flattering light.

However, as was the case with the portrait of Julian as a whole, matters refuse to move along their preallotted paths. Despite having created what seemed a settled framework within which to judge Julian, Gibbon is still beset with ambiguous and shimmering evidence which resists his urge to clear judgement by occluding Julian's motives and thoughts:

---

[39] *The Decline and Fall*, II.174 and II.355–6: see also *The Decline and Fall*, I.259: I.310. Patricia Craddock reprints an early manuscript comment of Gibbon's on the theory of the ruling passion in *The English Essays of Edward Gibbon*, pp. 90–1.
[40] *The Decline and Fall*, II.339.
[41] *The Decline and Fall*, II.379 and II.459.
[42] E.g. *The Decline and Fall*, V.303 and VI.15.
[43] *The Decline and Fall*, II.412.
[44] *The Decline and Fall*, II.414.

In the cool moments of reflection, Julian preferred the useful and benevolent virtues of Antoninus: but his ambitious spirit was inflamed by the glory of Alexander; and he solicited, with equal ardour, the esteem of the wise, and the applause of the multitude.

. . . the severe simplicity with Julian always maintained, and sometimes affected.

. . . the ranks, from a motive either of use or ostentation, were formed in such open order, that the whole line of march extended almost ten miles.[45]

Moreover, as Julian's Persian campaign proceeds, the isolation of the central figure becomes more pronounced. Julian moves through a contrasting landscape which teems with precise information docile to the philosophic historian, but he remains an elusive cynosure, who both grips and frustrates attention.[46]

It is hardly surprising, then, that Julian's death is not a moment of pure elegy. When Julian receives the fatal blow, Gibbon distractingly alludes to the title of the history:

Julian led the van, with the skill and attention of a consummate general; he was alarmed by the intelligence that his rear was suddenly attacked. The heat of the weather had tempted him to lay aside his cuirass; but he snatched a shield from one of his attendants, and hastened, with a sufficient reinforcement, to the relief of the rear-guard. A similar danger recalled the intrepid prince to the defence of the front; and, as he galloped between the columns, the centre of the left was attacked, and almost overpowered, by a furious charge of the Persian cavalry and elephants . . . The Barbarians fled; and Julian, who was foremost in every danger, animated the pursuit with his voice and gestures. His trembling guards, scattered and oppressed by the disorderly throng of friends and enemies, reminded their fearless sovereign that he was without armour; and conjured him to decline the fall of the impending ruin.[47]

This oddity is worth dwelling on because it suggests an unusual lack of control of tone on Gibbon's part. It cannot but strike a flippant or *dégagé* note on this occasion when we expect him either to keen over the demise of a hero or to rebuke the impetuous youth for his folly. It is revealing to turn back to the very similar death of Gallienus in Volume I, which is, however, embellished by a very different allusion:

At a late hour of the night, but while the emperor still protracted the pleasures of the table, an alarm was suddenly given, that Aureolus, at the head of all his forces, had made a desperate sally from the town; Gallienus, who was never deficient in personal bravery, started from his silken couch, and, without allowing himself time either to put on his armour, or to assemble his guards, he mounted on horseback, and rode full speed towards the supposed place of the attack. Encompassed by his declared or concealed enemies, he soon, amidst the nocturnal tumult, received a mortal dart from an uncertain hand.[48]

[45] *The Decline and Fall*, II.414, II.416 and II.430.
[46] See *The Decline and Fall*, II.433–4 for Gibbon's comments on the Persian landscape.
[47] *The Decline and Fall*, II.455–6.
[48] *The Decline and Fall*, I.288–9: I.345.

Gallienus is no hero of Gibbon's, but that does not prevent him, aware that the 'great art of a writer shews itself in the choice of pleasing allusions', from echoing Virgil's 'incertum qua pulsa manu' on the wounding of Aeneas.[49] There is no large resonance behind the allusion. Gibbon is not implying that Gallienus was a second Aeneas. This is simply the casual reminiscence, the easy perception of a limited congruence, which comes almost without thought to a man of broad literary culture. As such, it marks a composure quite lacking in the narrative of Julian's death.

The chapter closes with Julian's funeral, and Gibbon notes that 'It was an ancient custom in the funerals, as well as in the triumphs, of the Romans, that the voice of praise should be corrected by that of satire and ridicule.'[50] The scorn of the comedians and Christians is placed alongside the regret of the philosophers and soldiers, but no synthesised judgement arises. Aptly enough, the last word in Gibbon's frustrated study of 'that extraordinary man' is 'competition'.[51]

[49] *Spectator*, no. 421; Addison, *Works*, III.482. *Aeneid*, XII.318–20.
[50] *The Decline and Fall*, II.475.
[51] *The Decline and Fall*, II.476.

11

Ammianus Marcellinus

For to all the observations of the Ancients, *wee have our owne experience: which, if wee will use, and apply, wee have better meanes to pronounce. It is true they open'd the gates, and made the way that went before us; but as guides, not Commanders . . .*

                                                                                    Jonson

Gibbon's relationship with Ammianus Marcellinus, by far the most important of his sources in the second instalment of *The Decline and Fall*, also reveals the transitional nature of Volumes II and III. The Englishman's attitude to his Roman guide betrays his anxieties and concerns about narrative, while revealing the change in his view of historiography from seeing it as an exercise in authoritative orchestration to appreciating it as an undertaking in which the control and composure of the historian are jeopardised. In the various use Gibbon makes of Ammianus, we find once more, as we found in the portrait of Julian, the vestigial allure of philosophic historiography together with an appreciation of all the aspects of these difficult centuries which ever more peremptorily challenge that idiom.

The reader of *The Decline and Fall* is likely to be most aware of Gibbon's reliance on 'the military historian' in a passage which occurs long after his most extended use of the *Res Gestae* (a section of *The Decline and Fall* bounded by Chapters XIX and XXVI). This passage is the description of the luxurious and effete Roman nobles in Chapter XXXI. J. W. Johnson, pursuing his idea that 'Gibbon's history of Rome owed much of its acclaim to classicists who read it in order to profit from Roman example and thus forestall English decline and fall', has written of this cameo that it is an 'ironic representation of eighteenth century London and its society in crypto-Roman terms', and that 'no eighteenth century reader could fail to get Gibbon's point'.[1] But no hard evidence is offered for this reading, and the notion that Gibbon desired obliquely to snipe at aristocratic luxury is more unconvincing the more one looks into it. Setting aside his depreciation of luxury as a cause of decline in

---

[1] J. W. Johnson, *The Formation of English Neo-Classical Thought*, pp. 67, 237 and 239. Such parallel history as Johnson discovers (erroneously, to my mind) in *The Decline and Fall was* written in the eighteenth century; for instance, Blackwell makes no bones that the *Memoirs of the Court of Augustus* is a cautionary tale for his fellow-Britons. But not all eighteenth-century historiography was of this nature; and J. G. A. Pocock is surely right when he says of Gibbon that 'his historical intellect was a good deal stronger than its ideological promptings' (*Virtue, Commerce and History*, p. 149).

Volume I, we need only recollect how keenly Gibbon enjoyed such luxury as he was able to muster in his life for doubts to take shape. Gibbon smiles briefly and coldly at his father's foolish affectation of being a new Cincinnatus.[2] Such thespianism was not for him, in either literature or life. If we examine in some detail the way Gibbon has 'translated' Ammianus, we will be able to propose a more plausible account of his intentions.[3]

In a footnote, Gibbon explains how he has rendered the original:

It is incumbent on me to explain the liberties which I have taken with the text of Ammianus. 1. I have melted down into one piece, the sixth chapter of the fourteenth, and the fourth of the twenty-eighth, book. 2. I have given order and connection to the confused mass of materials. 3. I have softened *some* extravagant hyperboles, and pared away some superfluities of the original. 4. I have developed some observations which were insinuated, rather than expressed. With these allowances, my version will be found, not literal indeed, but faithful and exact.[4]

Gibbon arranges his amendments under these four heads: amalgamation, organisation, refinement and elucidation. Examples of all these transformations can be found, yet Gibbon is disingenuous in suggesting that this fully describes the effects of his adjustments.[5] The ethics of translation in the eighteenth century permitted a degree of freedom, provided it was employed in the service of a higher fidelity; but in writing what Ammianus ne'er so well

---

[2] *Memoirs*, p. 111.

[3] In the Appendix I give the two relevant sections of the *Res Gestae*, the text of Gibbon's version in Chapter XXXI divided into sections in accordance with how he has drawn on the Latin, and a table showing the passages from Ammianus on which the various sections of the English rely. References to Gibbon's 'translation' are given by volume, page and section. Interestingly enough, in 1772 Chastellux had also translated Ammianus' character of the Roman nobles in his *De la Félicité Publique*, I.345–50.

[4] *The Decline and Fall*, III.202 n. 34.

[5] To give such examples expeditiously: when Gibbon writes 'their long robes of silk and purple float in the wind' (*The Decline and Fall*, III.204, sect. 5), there is a glance at *Res Gestae* XXVIII.iv.8 in a section which predominantly relies on *Res Gestae* XIV.vi.9. In the sixth section, the details of the patricians' behaviour in the streets of the city (*The Decline and Fall*, III.204, sect. 6) condenses *Res Gestae* XIV.vi.8–10. Thus Gibbon does not simply shuffle sections of the two chapters of Ammianus to form a mosaic. Widely separated passages of the Latin may be blended together, long passages may be purified and reduced, and so Gibbon's foundry metaphor ('I have melted down') is quite accurate. His claim to have imparted 'order and connection' is justified when we see that the easy transition he effects between sections six and seven is produced by his perceiving the congruent subject-matter of *Res Gestae* XXVIII.iv.8–10 and XXVIII.iv.19 – to wit, bathing. In sections nineteen and twenty, three consecutive sections of the Latin (*Res Gestae* XXVIII.iv.25–7) are rearranged as 26–27–25 to yield an order which, although it misses Ammianus' hint of the chaotic prevalence of Roman decline, nevertheless gives forcible expression to the original's spirit of denunciation through its smoother articulation. When it comes to softening Ammianus, occasionally Gibbon simply ignores damaging details: 'maximeque sinistra' and 'detestantes ut venena' (*Res Gestae* XIV.vi.9 and XXVIII.iv.14) both find no place in his English, while 'they express their affection by a tender embrace (*The Decline and Fall*, III.205, sect. 6) is a welcome toning-down of 'palpantesque advenam' (*Res Gestae* XXVIII.iv.9). Concerning elucidation, one might note that a phrase such as 'and appropriate to their own use the conveniences which were designed for the Roman people' (*The Decline and Fall*, III.205, sect. 6) has no antecedent in Ammianus' Latin, but is nevertheless in perfect accord with the aberrations he wishes to record there.

expressed, Gibbon changes not only his manner, but also his matter.[6] As François Paschoud has remarked,'Ammien a été systématiquement exploité.'[7] Throughout this 'translation', Gibbon is striving to produce a single, heightened and vivid evocation of decline from the separate sketches he finds in Ammianus. He attempts to overcome the disparate, the fragmentary, the equivocal, and the nuanced, and to coerce his material into a simplicity which, far from being the pure essence to which it could without harm be reduced, is imposed at the expense of significant complexity.

To begin with sections four and five: the two passages of Ammianus on which they rely (XIV.vi.9–10) are also contiguous, but Gibbon reverses their order, so that section four looks back to XIV.vi.10 and section five to XIV.vi.9. He thus allows himself an easeful transition from section to section through a contrast between 'antiquus rigor' and modern morals ('But the modern nobles . . .').[8] However, the price of this adjustment is an accentuation of the contrast between present degeneration and past virtue which is only fleetingly present in Ammianus.

Other infidelities support this binary view of political demise – for instance, the elucidatory sentence which opens section ten:

In the exercise of domestic jurisdiction, the nobles of Rome express an exquisite sensibility for any personal injury, and a contemptuous indifference for the rest of the human species.[9]

This is about the most extreme rendering of the Latin which nevertheless stays on the right side of falsehood. That Gibbon should choose to express the original so markedly in terms of public and private, personal and general, shows how concerned he is to figure decline through sharp oppositions, whether historical (then and now) or social.

This process of amplifying oppositions only murmured in the *Res Gestae* begins with Gibbon's adjustment of the Polybian image in which Ammianus encapsulates the whole trajectory of the Roman state.[10] The Latin image is shaded with some care and intricacy: 'ab incunabilis primis ad usque pueritiae tempus . . . aetatem ingressus adultam . . . in iuvenem erectus et virum . . . iamque vergens in senium'. Gibbon, eager to trim away what he perhaps sees as excrescent detail detracting from clarity of outline, discards Ammianus' scrupulous modifying terms ('ingressus', 'erectus', 'vergens') and keeps only three stages; infancy, youth and old age. This removal of the

---

[6] For the tolerance of freedom in a translation, see William Wotton, *The History of Rome from the Death of Antoninus Pius to the Death of Severus Alexander*, sig. A7v; Gray, *Poems and Memoirs*, p. 145; and Cowley, *Works*, I.sigs. N1r–N1v. The classic statement of the relative merits of metaphrase, paraphrase and imitation is to be found in Dryden's 'Preface' to *Ovid's Epistles* (1680), which Gibbon could have read in his copy of *The Miscellaneous Works*, IV.71–80.

[7] In Ducrey et al., eds., *Gibbon et Rome*, p. 222.

[8] *The Decline and Fall*, III.204, sect. 5.

[9] *The Decline and Fall*, III.207, sect. 10.

[10] XIV.vi.4.

graduating terms in which Ammianus' account is comparatively rich goes a
stage further when Gibbon renders 'post superbas efferatarum gentium
cervices oppressas' by 'which had trampled on the necks of the fiercest
nations'.[11] Once again, this translation lies close to the edge of the spectrum
of possibility. 'Trampled', as a version of 'oppressas', draws the English away
from the Latin, and not in order to 'soften' it; 'trampled' is a very strong word.
However, the infidelity resides not in that strength, but in the replacement
of a subtle possibility in the Latin by a cruder statement. Ammianus suggests,
largely through the connotations of 'efferatarum', that the relationship
between Rome and the captive provinces is like that between a wild animal
and the man who bridles it: although hardly an equal relation, it is possibly
of mutual benefit. Gibbon's 'trampled' removes that benign possibility by
eliding the openness of 'cervices' to mean the necks of animals, and thus portrays the Romans hubristically enforcing a thorough subjugation. The
beneficial relation between Rome and the provinces which Ammianus had
whispered is rejected for a vision that sees only oppressors and oppressed.
Whether Gibbon or Ammianus is closer to the truth is, for the moment,
beside the point. What it is important to recognise, is that here Gibbon is
gravitating towards a view of the past which tends to reduce its intricacy to
simple oppositions.

This reduction continues when Gibbon translates 'suscipitur' by 'was still
adored'.[12] Ammianus chooses not only a present tense (Rome is even now
venerated in all parts of the earth), but also a verb which reacts interestingly
with the surrounding vocabulary. 'Suscipio' may denote the act of picking up
a child to acknowledge its legitimacy; and, in context, this meaning becomes
live through the prior occurrence of 'parens', 'liberis' and 'domina'.[13]
Through the various meanings of 'suscipitur' – the provinces both
venerating Rome and acknowledging her as their offspring – an *arcanum imperii* is touched. As the empire aged, power relations between the capital and
the provinces were modified. Political authority remained in the *urbs*, especially when the emperor was present; but with the larger numbers of provincials
in high military office and even assuming the supreme magistracy, and with
the founding of Constantinople, the direction of patronage and protection had
in some respects been reversed. One could, without impropriety, picture
Rome under the guardianship of the provinces. Elsewhere in this volume Gibbon shows that he is aware of these finer details, although in this set piece he
chooses to ignore them, since such subtleties would blur the definition he
desires.[14] The multiple possibilities of 'suscipitur' keep in play and confirm

---

[11] XIV.vi.5 and *The Decline and Fall*, III.203, sect. 1.
[12] XIV.vi.6 and *The Decline and Fall*, III.203, sect. 1.
[13] Lewis and Short, IIb; XIV.vi.5–6.
[14] A substitution shows Gibbon's alertness to this political shift: 'In the civil war between
     Theodosius and Eugenius, the count, or rather the sovereign, of Africa, maintained a haughty
     and suspicious neutrality . . . [and] condescended, as a proof of his moderation, to abstain

the range of meaning established by the earlier image of the bridled animal, where the complexity of Rome's relationship with the provinces was also touched on. It would have been a superhuman translation had Gibbon been able to preserve and transfer all that resonance in his rendering of 'suscipitur'. But given that his slight mistranslations of 'oppressas' and 'suscipitur' are both untrue to the Latin in the same way and to the same end, we seem here to be dealing with intention rather than with accident.

If we compare Gibbon's sly manipulations of Ammianus with the apparently similar operations he performed on Tacitus' *Germania* in Chapter IX, important differences emerge. Gibbon's exploitation of Tacitus came as part of a large and subtle design to prepare, imply and eventually to enunciate an explanation of the causes of Roman decline. Gibbon's infidelities to Ammianus are close in character to his amendments of the *Germania*; their purpose, however, is crucially different. In their coarsening of the Latin, they minister to no explanation of decay, but seek instead almost sensationally to accentuate its magnitude. Gibbon's ambitions have been chastened by the recalcitrance of his material to the extent that the lesser aspiration of making decline visible is replacing the high philosophic aim of making decline legible. Clarity is no longer the kernel of truth the historian must release from the past, but the simple and reductive strokes of the caricature he is condemned to draw should he persist, as Gibbon does in this set piece, with the philosophic aim of a unified and perspicuous narrative.

However, this portrait of the Roman nobles is anomalous in the second and third volumes precisely because it is a set piece and thus, much like a digression, is not fully part of the flow of narrative. It is in some measure isolated from the distending, deforming pressures which, as we saw in the portrait of Julian, the contradictory and elusive past Gibbon is obliged to handle in these volumes exerts on his narrative. Gibbon's relation with Ammianus outside the limited, protected area of this sketch of the Roman nobles is rather different. That portrait revealed the remains of Gibbon's philosophic loyalties, and also displayed the resistance to that loyalty his material now puts up even in what seem the most advantageous circumstances. Elsewhere, his turbulent relation with Ammianus discloses the quite new possibilities and problems which face an historian once he is no longer the imperial author of a

---

from the use of the diadem, and to supply Rome with the customary tribute, or rather subsidy, of corn' (*The Decline and Fall*, III.124). A tribute is demanded, a subsidy more freely given, as Gibbon's usage elsewhere indicates: ' "The payment of a subsidy, which had excited the indignation of the Romans, ought not (such was the language of Stilicho) to be considered in the odious light, either of a tribute, or of a ransom, extorted by the menaces of a Barbarian enemy" ' (*The Decline and Fall*, III.180); 'they must no longer insult the majesty of Rome, by the mention of a tribute' (*The Decline and Fall*, III.392). The same new volatility in the respective dignity of *urbs* and provinces is shown by the development that 'a discontented Roman might freely aspire, or descend, to the title and character of a Barbarian' (*The Decline and Fall*, III.603).

philosophic narrative, and is instead involved with – even mired in – his material, so that the past is less his subject than his element.

When, in the cameo of the Roman nobles, Gibbon inserts the parenthesis '(which may be interpreted the game of dice and tables)' as a gloss on the more technical and more faithful phrase 'the *Tesserarian* art', it is clear that he has momentarily ceased to translate Ammianus in the interests of explanation.[15] Elsewhere in the cameo such clarifying interjections are not so overt and seem less like interruptions than moments when Gibbon's voice merges with that of Ammianus. This seems to be the case with such small amplifying phrases as 'mixed and general resort' applied to the Roman baths, or 'and the other ensigns of their dignity', appended to a comment about the distinguishing rings of the patricians.[16] Gibbon unobtrusively blends into the Latin the information an English reader may require, but which Ammianus had no need to provide for his Roman counterpart.

These occasions when Gibbon allows his voice to mingle with that of Ammianus hint at the complex relation of companionship as well as exploitation which can arise between an historian and a source he uses over a long period of time. The protracted commerce with Ammianus Gibbon's theme enjoins turns their relationship into a forum in which the developing pressures on the English historian are displayed.

From Constantius' suspicion and cruelty towards Gallus in Chapter XIX to Theodosius' assumption of the Gothic war in Chapter XXVI, Ammianus is Gibbon's chief support. Such reliance poses difficulties. At the end of the *Res Gestae* Ammianus looked forward to the historians of the future:

scribant reliqua potiores, aetate et doctrinis florentes. quos id (si libuerit) aggressuros, procudere linguas ad maiores moneo stilos.[17]

Gibbon's comment does not meet his source's conclusion quite head on:

Ammianus Marcellinus, who terminates his useful work with the defeat and death of Valens, recommends the more glorious subject of the ensuing reign to the youthful vigour and eloquence of the rising generation. The rising generation was not disposed to accept this advice, or to imitate his example . . .[18]

But the men in the prime of life and learning to whom Ammianus left the continuation of his labours were not only his near-contemporaries. His conclusion was an address to all the historians of posterity, not just 'the rising generation'. Gibbon steps forward to assume the mantle that Ammianus has let fall, but is reluctant to acquiesce in the pedagogic relation Ammianus posits between himself and any future continuer of his history – especially, perhaps, because Ammianus is pontificating about historiographic tone,

---

[15] *The Decline and Fall*, III.209, sect. 14.
[16] *The Decline and Fall*, III.205, sect. 6 and sect. 7.
[17] XXXI.xvi.9.
[18] *The Decline and Fall*, II.627.

concerning which Gibbon was so careful.[19] The expedient Gibbon adopts is to limit the audience to whom the closing words of the *Res Gestae* are addressed: Ammianus was thinking solely of 'the rising generation'. Thus Gibbon can complete the task Ammianus bequeaths without feeling trammelled by the terms of the bequest.

Gibbon's dealings with Ammianus are strongly marked by this desire to keep their relationship supple, to prevent it from setting into a firm mould within which he will then be confined; and this desire is given urgency by the prolonged contact Gibbon has with Ammianus. All historians have to vindicate their right to pronounce, and must convince us that their voice ought to be heard, that it comprises a range of accents not hitherto brought together. Should their narrative ever become simply a recapitulation of an earlier writer's, then their voice is extinguished in his.[20] This is the danger which Gibbon's prolonged reliance on Ammianus poses, which his simultaneous loss of philosophic dominance renders more threatening, and against which he guards not only by his adjustment of the conclusion of the *Res Gestae* but also by intriguing manoeuvres that help preserve an independence no longer secured by the philosopher's impregnable position overlooking and dominating the past.

Perhaps the most obvious of such manoeuvres is indicated by the variety of language in which Gibbon talks about Ammianus. Praise is plentiful: 'Ammianus adds, with a nice distinction'; 'Ammianus expresses himself with cool and candid hesitation'; 'His death and character are faithfully delineated by Ammianus'; 'Ammianus . . . has impartially stated the merits and defects of his judicial proceedings'; 'The curiosity and credulity of the emperor . . . are fairly exposed by Ammianus'; 'Ammianus very justly remarks'; 'Ammianus, an intelligent spectator'; 'The modest and judicious historian'; 'Ammianus and Eutropius may be admitted as fair and credible witnesses of the public language and opinions'; 'Ammianus observes, with more candour and judgment'; 'Ammianus, who makes a fair report'; and finally 'Ammianus, who acknowledges the merit, has censured, with becoming asperity, the oppressive administration of Petronius Probus.'[21] The great historiographic virtues of style, judgement and attitude are accorded Ammianus; but only to be cancelled by criticism which sits alongside the praise and quarrels with it irreconcilably. Ammianus is inaccurate: 'Ammianus has marked the chronology of this year by three signs, which do not perfectly coincide with each other, or with the series of the history'; 'The chronology of Ammianus is obscure and imperfect'; 'The memory of Ammianus must have been inaccurate, and his language incorrect';

---

[19] See *Memoirs*, p. 155. On the subject of historiographic tone see also Johnson, *Rambler* no. 152.

[20] It was doubts over whether he could find an independent voice which scotched Gibbon's projected history of Ralegh (*Memoirs*, p. 121). For a more modern comment on this problem, see Collingwood (*The Idea of History*, p. 256).

[21] *The Decline and Fall*, II.141 n. 36; II.332 n. 36; II.335 n. 42; II.352 n. 83; II.377 n. 44; II.420 n. 21; II.459 n. 99; II.461 n. 100; II.470 n. 122; II.499 n. 54; II.514 n. 86; and II.555 n. 151.

and 'Obsidionalibus coronis donati. Ammian. XXIV.4. Either Julian or his historian were unskilful antiquaries. He should have given *mural* crowns.'[22] His judgement is defective: 'This unquestionable evidence may correct the hasty assertion of Ammianus'; and 'Ammianus, who unwarily deviates into gross flattery'.[23] His failures of judgement alternatively and inappropriately either bloat or cramp his narrative: 'Ammianus declares . . . that he means only, ipsas rerum digerere *summitates*. But he often takes a false measure of their importance; and his superfluous prolixity is disagreeably balanced by his unseasonable brevity.'[24] The flawed whole is couched in a style for which the fastidious Gibbon feels strong disdain: 'The coarse and undistinguishing pencil of Ammianus'; 'Such is the bad taste of Ammianus . . . that it is not easy to distinguish his facts from his metaphors'; and 'those turgid metaphors, those false ornaments, that perpetually disfigure the style of Ammianus'.[25]

We are faced here by more than Gibbon simply responding with proper discrimination to areas of excellence and error, since the praise and blame are rarely tied to particular details of the *Res Gestae*, but are expressed as generalisations which cannot fail to interfere with one another. Indeed, Gibbon's delight in the slyness of ambiguity occasionally allows him to unite praise and blame in a single stroke:

I give this speech as original and genuine. Ammianus might hear, could transcribe, and was incapable of inventing, it.[26]

Gibbon awards Ammianus the virtue of honesty while simultaneously stripping him of the modicum of imagination demanded by lying. By so complicating his judgements Gibbon is establishing a latitude of response which, through its deliberate evasion of any settled view of Ammianus, allows the historian a mobility and an independence which might otherwise easily be surrendered to such a major source.

Gibbon's desire for intellectual space in which to manoeuvre and evade is shown in the bafflingly fine degrees of credibility he finds, or affects to find, in Ammianus. Speaking of Julian's attempts to raze the temple in Jerusalem, Gibbon notes that the prodigies which greeted the emperor's efforts have been attested by Christian writers, and continues:

The last of these writers [Gregory Nazianzen] has boldly declared, that this praeternatural event was not disputed by the infidels; and his assertion, strange as it may seem, is confirmed by the unexceptionable testimony of Ammianus Marcellinus. The philosophic soldier, who loved the virtues, without adopting the prejudices, of his master, has recorded, in his judicious and candid history of his own times, the

22 *The Decline and Fall*, II.157 n. 59; II.591 n. 63; II.314 n. 4; and II.440 n. 62.
23 *The Decline and Fall*, II.371 n. 34 and II.414 n. 7.
24 *The Decline and Fall*, II.594 n. 65.
25 *The Decline and Fall*, II.499; II.561 n. 1; and II.605 n. 81.
26 *The Decline and Fall*, II.441 n. 63.

extraordinary obstacles which interrupted the restoration of the temple of Jerusalem
. . . Such authority should satisfy a believing, and must astonish an incredulous, mind.
Yet a philosopher may still require the original evidence of impartial and intelligent
spectators.[27]

The effect of taking such deft exception to unexceptionable testimony is that
our own sense of security in this passage is troubled by the fluidity and eventual suspension of Gibbon's point of judgement. It seems initially as if the
'unexceptionable testimony' of Ammianus will settle the issue, but in place
of a conclusion we find an inscrutable sentence peopled with pure notions (the
believing and incredulous minds) and the shadowy figure of the philosopher.
We learn that evidence may be unexceptionable and also inconclusive; but we
also appreciate how determined Gibbon is to preserve the purity and independence of his own judgements.

Concerning the prodigy at the temple, Gibbon separates himself from
Ammianus by laying claim to a fineness of scepticism absent from his source.
On other occasions he releases himself from the disagreeable obligation of
merely agreeing with Ammianus by using the 'double freedom' of text and
footnotes.[28] In the text, Gibbon accepts Ammianus' suggestion that Eusebia
was responsible for the suspicious deaths of Julian's children:

. . . even the fruits of his marriage-bed were blasted by the jealous artifices of Eusebia
herself, who, on this occasion alone, seems to have been unmindful of the tenderness
of her sex, and the generosity of her character.[29]

But the footnote murmurs the following technical and compassionate reservations: 'Our physicians will determine whether there exists such a poison. For
my own part, I am inclined to hope that the public malignity imputed the
effects of accident as the guilt of Eusebia.'[30] In Volume I Gibbon had used
his footnotes as a means of tidying the text of any excrescent detail which
might disrupt its otherwise clean lines. Now it seems that the note does not
so much serve the text as provide space in which the full amplitude of
Gibbon's judgement, too large for the text alone, can spread itself.

Gibbon's airing of the large complexity of his understanding is, as I have
suggested, a means of resisting the strong pull of the *Res Gestae* and thus of
maintaining the independence of his own narrative. The same end is secured
in a different way by this account of a surprise attack by Jovinus on a band
of Alemanni:

Jovinus . . . could distinctly perceive the indolent security of the Germans. Some were
bathing their huge limbs in the river; others were combing their long and flaxen hair;

---

[27] *The Decline and Fall*, II.389. This 'miracle' was much debated in the eighteenth century, and
Warburton's *Julian* (1750) is the most exhaustive, if not the most satisfying, account; see also
Memoirs, p. 79.

[28] Gibbon uses this phrase of Bayle's *Dictionaire* (*Gibbon's Journal to January 28th, 1763*, p. 110).

[29] *The Decline and Fall*, II.142–3.

[30] *The Decline and Fall*, II.143 n. 39.

others again were swallowing large draughts of rich and delicious wine.[31]

The interest of the passage appears when one looks at the original Latin:

exsultantes innoxii proelii gloria milites, ad alterius globi perniciem ducens, sensimque incedens rector eximius, speculatione didicit fida, direptis propius villis, vastatoriam manum quiescere prope flumen, iamque adventans, abditusque in valle densitate arbustorum obscura, videbat lavantes alios, quosdam comas rutilantes ex more, potantesque non nullos.[32]

At first glance the English seems amplified ('indolent security', 'huge limbs', 'long and flaxen', 'large draughts of rich and delicious wine'), but accurate. Yet there is an important deviation from the Latin. Ammianus says that the Germans are dying their hair red 'ex more'.[33] Gibbon renders this with 'combing', an evident mistranslation which we cannot ascribe to ignorance of either the Latin or the custom. The reason lies in the seventh book of Herodotus when a Persian scout approaches the Spartan position at Thermopylae:

There he saw some of the men at exercise, and others combing their hair. Marvelling at the sight, and taking exact note of their numbers, he rode back unmolested . . . [34]

One way of preventing a single source from dominating a narrative is to make the references to it also allusions to other writers; thus Gibbon can, in this instance, momentarily alleviate the galling sense of restriction and deep indebtedness against which he is struggling in his dealings with Ammianus.

One might say, however, that instead of serving that recondite and private purpose, Gibbon's glance at Herodotus has in fact an open and rhetorical function. By giving the barbarians the role of the Spartans, Gibbon is indicating both the degeneracy of the empire and the positive contribution made by the barbarians to civilisation in their destruction of that impediment to human progress. It is now the empire which manacles advancement, and the barbarians who are its defenders and martyrs. Such a reading is tempting, but in fact untenable, because the encounter between Jovinus and the Alemanni is not a second Thermopylae. The Persian scout is amazed by the sang-froid of the Spartans, while the ease of the Alemanni springs from only ignorance; and in the engagement which follows they show none of the disciplined heroism of Leonidas and his men: 'Astonishment produced disorder; disorder was followed by flight and dismay; and the confused multitude of the bravest warriors was pierced by the swords and javelins of the legionaries and auxiliaries.'[35]

---

[31] *The Decline and Fall*, II.517. The similar phrasing of a later passage (*The Decline and Fall*, III.248) shows well how Gibbon's style is, in parts, formulaic.
[32] *Res Gestae*, XXVII.ii.2.
[33] This custom is also mentioned by Suetonius (*Caligula*, 47) and Tacitus (*Historiae*, IV.lxi).
[34] *Herodotus*, tr. Godley, VII.208.
[35] *The Decline and Fall*, II.517.

Moreover, Gibbon's allusion to Herodotus, though a snug fit, is extremely brief and limited: it has none of the extended parallelism which distinguishes those moments when Gibbon actually does use allusion for such rhetorical purposes. An example of this occurs, as one might expect, in Volume I, where the manipulation of the reader is one of Gibbon's prime concerns. Galerius' Persian campaign of A.D. 296 is checked, as was that of Crassus, at Carrhae. The air of palimpsest is extended beyond the realm of the geographical when Gibbon recounts the exploits of Tiridates, Galerius' ally:

The king of Armenia had signalized his valour in the battle, and acquired personal glory by the public misfortune. He was pursued as far as the Euphrates; his horse was wounded, and it appeared impossible for him to escape the victorious enemy. In this extremity Tiridates embraced the only refuge which he saw before him; he dismounted and plunged into the stream. His armour was heavy, the river very deep, and in those parts at least half a mile in breadth; yet such was his strength and dexterity, that he reached in safety the opposite bank.[36]

In the footnote Gibbon appends to this passage he admits that he has massaged his material: 'Hist. Armen. I.ii.c.76. I have transferred this exploit of Tiridates from an imaginary defeat to the real one of Galerius.'[37] Gibbon's scruple in noting this transposition raises some questions. How does he know that this exploit is a true pearl set in the false metal of the 'imaginary defeat'? If we grant that Gibbon somehow could so distinguish it, on what grounds does he attach it to this particular battle, rather than to another? Above all, what is Gibbon's motive for including this heroic feat?

We can, of course, only conjecture about these secrets of the study, but we may give our conjectures some basis of probability if we note how close this anecdote is to Livy's account of Horatius Cocles' swimming the Tiber after defending the Sublician bridge against the Etrurians:

tum Cocles 'Tiberine pater,' inquit, 'te sancte precor, haec arma et hunc militem propitio flumine accipias.' ita sic armatus in Tiberim desiluit multisque super-incendentibus telis incolumis ad suos tranavit, rem ausus plus famae habituram ad posteros quam fidei.[38]

By fashioning this allusion of circumstance, if not of phrasing, Gibbon brings this famous moment of Roman heroism into the classically educated reader's mind when he introduces its later simulacrum. A barbarian, Gibbon insinuates, has taken the place of one of Rome's primal heroes; and so, despite Rome's frontier being now the Euphrates rather than the Tiber, the Eternal City is in fact more feeble than it was in its Herculean infancy. Its vigour dwarfed by its possessions, Rome is consumed by an inner malaise which has rotted the empire's core.

---

[36] *The Decline and Fall*, I.376: I.447. First edition, 'saw before him . . .'.
[37] *The Decline and Fall*, I.lv. n. 67: I.447 n. 67.
[38] *Ab Urbe Condita*, II.x.11.

Thus Gibbon retains the dubious anecdote of Tiridates' swimming the Euphrates in order to form an ironic contrast. The myth of Horatius' swimming the Tiber (the hero gathered back into the city whose inviolability he has guaranteed) stressed the irreducible, central strength of Rome: its arms-bearing citizens. Under the empire that cardinal function is gradually being handed over to barbarians free from the uncivic pacificism of Christianity; and so this paralleling of Livy is a small brick in the large edifice of the explanation of Roman decline Gibbon advances in his first volume. This echo of Livy is therefore distinguished from the later momentary allusion to Herodotus by the coherence and extent of the motivation which appears once we begin to excavate it. The subsequent echo, as a local solution to Gibbon's constant aim of maintaining a slight but saving distance between his narrative and that of Ammianus, is far more isolated.

We have seen how the prolonged truck Gibbon is obliged to have with 'the military historian' arouses his care lest the sustained reliance he has on the earlier writer turn this part of *The Decline and Fall* into a shadow of the *Res Gestae*. But that sustained reliance also furnishes Gibbon with opportunities of a more positive kind. Ammianus' abiding presence occasionally comforts, as well as threatens, Gibbon. Moving more deeply into areas of the past he finds steadily more ungrateful, he finds in Ammianus a guide whose proximity, if at times imperilling, can also be relieving. There are moments of true fellowship between the two writers when Gibbon reposes on Ammianus as on a kindred spirit, finding in him his own taste and even his own literary tactics in a period which was predominantly foreign or irksome. This is one such moment:

The ecclesiastical historians, Socrates . . . and Theodoret . . . ascribe to Jovian the merit of a confessor under the preceding reign; and piously suppose, that he refused the purple, till the whole army unanimously exclaimed that they were Christians. Ammianus, calmly pursuing his narrative, overthrows the legend by a single sentence. hostiis pro Joviano extisque inspectis, pronuntiatum est, &c. xxv.6.[39]

Ammianus overthrows a fiction erected by later writers, although necessarily unaware of its existence; Gibbon's note hides the fact that Ammianus wrote before Socrates and Theodoret. 'Calmly' is placed so as to counter 'piously', the trace of blame attaching to the latter balanced by the mild approbation of the former; but 'calmly' can have this commendatory force only if Ammianus is aware of the pious fictions he is exploding – calm in the face of opposition is admirable, but the calm of ignorance is surely neutral. Ammianus, of course, wrote in ignorance of Socrates and Theodoret, but by making him seem calmly to discredit them, Gibbon turns him into an image of himself. For do we not find just the feigned inadvertence and ignorance which Gibbon here groundlessly awards to Ammianus in the fifteenth chapter

---

[39] *The Decline and Fall*, II.461 n. 102.

of *The Decline and Fall*? The same manipulation occurs in the peculiar choice of verb in this footnote:

Three lines of Ammianus (xxxi.14) countenance a whole oration of Themistius (viii. p. 101–120), full of adulation, pedantry and commonplace morality.[40]

In place of 'countenance', one might have expected 'comprise' or 'say as much as'. Gibbon's choice, however, contains an ambiguity to which it draws attention by virtue of its own oddity. The most obvious gloss of 'countenance' is 'bear out'; Ammianus shows that Themistius' speech, however disgraceful in other ways, is at least not a pack of lies.[41] But there is also a secondary meaning in play, in which 'countenance' has the meaning of 'set off'; and Ammianus may be said to 'set off' Themistius because his brevity reveals the mere language which subsequently passed for oratory.[42] Gibbon portrays this as a silent piece of demolition akin to that carried out on Socrates and Theodoret, thereby once more creating an antecedent for his ironic tactics out of the unironic prose of his predecessor. By forging these anticipations of his own practice, Gibbon fashions for himself in the alternative society of books he esteemed so highly an imaginative asylum insulated against both his indocile material and the contemporary attacks of Davis et al.[43]

Gibbon's relationship with Ammianus repays attention, especially when compared with his relationship with Tacitus, because of the sharpness with which it shows how his theory and practice as an historian were changing. Working with fragmentary, ambiguous and opaque material over which he is unable to wield the imperial authority of the first volume, Gibbon finds that his narrative is now less an instantaneously conceived argument than a moving point of perception, the past less a country to be surveyed than a terrain through which to journey, and composition a process in which the historian is more shaped than shaping. Gibbon's crumbling authorial *imperium* and increasing vulnerability are both made visible in his dealings with Ammianus.

---

[40] *The Decline and Fall*, II.504 n. 63.
[41] OED, 5b.
[42] OED, 4. Sheridan's *Dictionary* gives the meaning 'make a shew of'.
[43] 'At home I occupied a pleasant and spacious apartment; the library on the same floor was soon considered as my peculiar domain; and I might say with truth that I was never less alone than when by myself' (*Memoirs*, pp. 95–6). This Ciceronian adage, to be found in *De Officiis*, III.1 and attributed originally to Scipio Africanus, was a commonplace in the eighteenth century: see *Spectator*, no. 4.

12

'The nice and secret springs of action'

So far in this second instalment of *The Decline and Fall* we have chiefly examined the changing surface of Gibbon's writing. Beginning with his acknowledgement of the greater difficulties his material posed for him in the years between 1776 and 1781, we considered, in his portrait of Julian the Apostate and his relationship with Ammianus Marcellinus, some of the literary consequences of this new historical terrain; consequences which stood out more clearly when we juxtaposed parallel elements of Volume I, such as the portrait of Augustus or the use made of Tacitus. We have, however, left untouched the question of the extent to which these new difficulties affected *The Decline and Fall* at the level of argument. How far and in what way does the stubbornness of the past influence Gibbon's explanation of the causes at work in history?

We might begin by recalling two innovations in Gibbon's historiographic practice which emerged in his dealings with Ammianus Marcellinus: first, that in his characterisation of the Roman nobles he seemed more concerned to depict the magnitude of decline than to explain it, and secondly, that over the long term the uneasy parity between Gibbon and Ammianus indicates that Gibbon is more immersed in the past than overlooking it. As we consider the handling of causality in 1781, the deep connexion between these two innovations will become clear.

As we saw in Montesquieu's *Considérations*, the philosophic urge to discover causal principles in the past was also a desire to make the study of history 'scientific'; philosophic historians as well as natural philosophers were in quest of timeless and unchanging laws of motion. The historiography of causes hopes to dissolve the surface of historical change and thereby reveal the unchanging principles governing human society and action which, so the philosophic historian assumes, underlie mere events. In 1781, however, Gibbon does not deny change, but draws our attention to it:

Within the space of fifty years, a philosophic spectator of the vicissitudes of human affairs might have contemplated Tacitus in the senate of Rome, and Constantine in the council of Nice.[1]

This passage has some of the turbidity of oxymoron in its bringing together of intrinsically opposed elements. The spectator is 'philosophic', and to

---

[1] *The Decline and Fall*, II.229. This is not, of course, Tacitus the historian, who died (it is thought) around A.D. 117, but Tacitus the emperor, a champion of republican values elected by the senate in A.D. 275. The council of Nice was held in A.D. 325.

juxtapose an advocate of pristine republican values with the first Christian emperor is to hint at the explanation of decline around which Gibbon, himself at that time a philosophic spectator, had organised his first volume. But at variance with these emphases is the adverbial clause which introduces the sentence, 'within the space of fifty years'. For the keynote of the sentence is the astonishing rapidity of decline and the immensity of the change that so few years brought about, rather than any philosophic erasure of historical change. The sudden collapse of values and institutions seemingly so well grounded in time is dumbfounding; it is suggestive that the philosophic spectator is mute, and that we are not told what sense, if any, he can make of this vicissitude.

Such turbid moments are symptoms of a deep change in ideas. The language of past conviction remains, but sits alongside the insights that will eventually combine to displace it, and that force their way into words despite the absence of a vocabulary in which they might be clearly enunciated. For these comparisons of individual moments which, when brought together, reveal the magnitude of historical change are hostile to philosophic historiography. They are the work of an historian who finds it easier (or preferable) to describe and evoke than to explain, and who – unable (or unwilling) to attain the synoptic, philosophic view of the past in which causes become obviously visible – instead brings together strikingly opposed moments he has encountered in his journey through history. Such moments may adumbrate an explanation of causality, but they can never constitute such an explanation.

The most prominent example of such an evocation of magnitude is 'the memorable fable of the SEVEN SLEEPERS' which Gibbon singles out from 'the insipid legends of ecclesiastical history'.[2] To escape persecution by the emperor Decius, seven Ephesians hid in a cave and were subsequently immured by the tyrant. They promptly fell asleep for one hundred and eighty-seven years, until during the reign of Theodosius the cave was opened in a search for building materials, and the sleepers awoke. This, it was soon realised, was a miracle, and the sleepers expired after they had blessed Theodosius and related their story.

Gibbon has no doubt that this tale is 'imaginary', and he assembles evidence of the wide dispersal of similar traditions amongst the most diverse cultures and religions.[3] However, the fable recommends itself on just these grounds of its ubiquity. It speaks with uncommon directness of a common paradox in our apprehension of time's lapse:

This easy and universal belief, so expressive of the sense of mankind, may be ascribed to the genuine merit of the fable itself. We imperceptibly advance from youth to age, without observing the gradual, but incessant, change of human affairs; and even in

---

[2] *The Decline and Fall*, III.350
[3] *The Decline and Fall*, III.350 and 352. Compare also *The English Essays of Edward Gibbon*, p. 324.

our larger experience of history, the imagination is accustomed, by a perpetual series of causes and effects, to unite the most distant revolutions.[4]

In trying to think rigorously about the processes we assume are embedded within time, we run the risk of being untrue to the ordinary facts of change and duration to which the seven sleepers are inescapably alerted but to which the philosophic quest for uniform causality is liable to pay insufficient attention. Thus the fable of the seven sleepers culminates not in an analysis of causes, but in an image of calamitous vicissitude whose origins are inscrutable:

The union of the Roman empire was dissolved: its genius was humbled in the dust; and armies of unknown Barbarians, issuing from the frozen regions of the North, had established their victorious reign over the fairest provinces of Europe and Africa.[5]

As we move towards the conclusion of the second instalment of *The Decline and Fall* we are repeatedly reminded that the shifting surface of events in time has a reality from which we should not allow an analysis of causality to distract us.

Gibbon now chooses to evoke the scale of decline, rather than to explain it, because he has a sober sense of both the difficulty and the possible undesirability of obtaining the 'clear and comprehensive view' of the past in which causality appears:

There are few observers, who possess a clear and comprehensive view of the revolutions of society; and who are capable of discovering the nice and secret springs of action, which impel, in the same uniform direction, the blind and capricious passions of a multitude of individuals.[6]

Gibbon's uncertainty about causal explanation is revealed here by the contrast of singular with plural, of uniformity with variety. The philosophic historian seeks to reduce the plural variety of events to the uniform singularity of causal principles. But Gibbon reverses this; behind the 'uniform direction' of each event lurks the vertiginous prospect of a multiplicity of intricate and occult causes ('nice and secret springs') corresponding to the random and unorganised plurality of 'the blind and capricious passions of a multitude of individuals'.

We have here the obverse of the distant view of the philosopher. Behind each 'fact' of history Gibbon is aware that there may be a swarming mass of causes on which he could turn his historical microscope. Take, for instance, the inevitable calamity which overtakes the Romans who allow the Goths to cross the Danube:

. . . as their patience was now exhausted, the townsmen, the soldiers, and the Goths,

---

[4] *The Decline and Fall*, III.352. [5] *The Decline and Fall*, III.353.
[6] *The Decline and Fall*, III. 66–7.

were soon involved in a conflict of passionate altercation and angry reproaches. A blow was imprudently given; a sword was hastily drawn; and the first blood that was spilt in this accidental quarrel, became the signal of a long and destructive war.[7]

Gibbon is gripped by the sharp disjunctions and disproportions in this fragment of the past. In this drama of passions the largest effects flow from the most minute and indistinct causes ('a blow . . . a sword'). Montesquieu might interject that these slight events are not the causes of what ensues, merely the triggers through which the larger, proportionate causes take effect. But this can never be more than an hypothesis; and Gibbon might reply that it is genuinely intriguing that the past should move forward through such minute causality. The investigation of historical causes, once the medium of cool, unmoved philosophic intelligence, now provokes the wonder and admiration against which the *philosophes* had used it as a specific.

Pascal had famously pointed out the disproportion of historical causation: 'Le nez de Cléopâtre s'il eût été plus court toute la face de la terre aurait changé.'[8] The Christian ironist offers this as a warning both risible and disturbing that we should place no faith in the world and its ways. But the theme was susceptible of lighter treatment, and in 1764 Richer aroused ripples of amusement and gallantry by showing, in his *Essai sur les Grands Événements par les Petites Causes*, the power wielded by love. Later, in the *Essai sur les Mœurs* of 1769, Voltaire would stress the paradoxical intimacies of historical causation:

C'est ainsi que les événements sont enchaînés: un pilote génois donne un univers à l'Espagne: la nature a mis dans les îles de ces climats lointains un poison qui infecte les sources de la vie; et il faut qu'un roi de France en périsse.[9]

But he does so only in order that lesser considerations would not distract the reader's attention from the large significance he finds in history as the stage on which enlightenment makes its progress. However, what separates Gibbon from Pascal, Richer and Voltaire is his dawning understanding that minute causality is not an oddity at which to smile, or a trick of historical perspective which one can use rhetorically, but a primary and perplexing fact about the past.

Thus Gibbon's sensitivity to minute causality accompanies a tentative revaluation of the marvellous and wonderful, against the vulgar weakness for which the *philosophes* had directed much scorn, and which they identified as one of the great obstacles to mature historiography.[10] That tentative revaluation can also be seen in a new idiom Gibbon uses to express historical causality:

[7] *The Decline and Fall*, II.599.
[8] *Pensées*, no. 143, p. 173.
[9] *Œuvres Complètes*, XII.271.
[10] See above, pp. 9–10; and also Bayle, *Dictionaire Historique et Critique*, I. 62, art.'Achillea', rem. H.

The original principle of motion was concealed in the remote countries of the North; and the curious observation of the pastoral life of the Scythians, or Tartars, will illustrate the latent cause of these destructive emigrations.

. . . a furious tempest was excited among the nations of Germany, who yielded to the irresistible impulse, that appears to have been gradually communicated from the eastern extremity of the continent of Asia.[11]

It was a commonplace to notice the vast numbers of barbarians who infested the empire:

During the whole Remainder of his Reign, it [the empire] was almost continually molested with those barbarous Nations; which often crossing the *Danube* in *Hungary* and *Austria* in incredible Numbers, would under any other Emperor than *Marcus*, have put the Empire into almost insuperable Distresses.[12]

What is peculiar to Gibbon, however, is the scientific flavour of 'original principle of motion' and 'irresistible impulse'. It might be thought, therefore, that there was a new rigour in Gibbon's analysis of causes. But in fact the opposite is true. Philosophic historiography was 'scientific' only in that it aspired to reach the lofty level of powerful generalisation (capable of explaining at the same moment the most mundane and the most celestial events) which the example of Newton had established as the proper orbit of natural philosophy. Philosophic historiography acknowledged natural science as the model of rational inquiry, but was not especially responsive to the imaginative impact which scientific discovery can make.

Yet it seems to me that it is precisely from this angle – from the point of view of how science can transform our imaginative apprehension of the world – that Gibbon appreciates science and uses its language. We know that during the two years of furlough he permitted himself after completing his first volume he refreshed himself with a change of discipline:

After a short holyday, I indulged my curiosity in some studies of a very different nature; a course of Anatomy which was demonstrated by Dr Hunter, and some lessons of Chemistry which were delivered by Mr Higgins: The principles of these sciences, and a taste for books of Natural history contributed to multiply my ideas and images; and the Anatomist or Chemist may sometimes track me in their own snow.[13]

The effect these new studies had on Gibbon's historiography, then, was to broaden his vocabulary ('may sometimes track me in their own snow') by extending his imagination ('multiply my ideas and images').

---

[11] *The Decline and Fall*, II.563 and III. 160.

[12] William Wotton, *The History of Rome from the Death of Antoninus Pius to the Death of Severus Alexander*, p. 55; see also Basil Kennett, *Romae Antiquae Notitia*, p. xiv; Sir William Temple, 'Of Heroic Virtue', *Works*, III. 351 and Thomson, *Liberty*, III.533–8.

[13] *Memoirs*, p. 159; Gibbon takes the phrase from Dryden's *Of Dramatic Poesy: An Essay*. It is interesting that Johnson, who held so few ideas in common with Gibbon, also recognised the interest and value of chemistry and admired Watson, the chemical bishop of Llandaff (*Boswell's Life of Johnson*, IV.118–19 and 232; see also *Rambler* no. 25). Watson published three volumes of *Chemical Essays* (1781–2) which Gibbon possessed and praised (*Memoirs*, p. 171).

If we now glance back at the examples of this scientific idiom I give above, we shall note that they both deal with emigrations, with huge numbers of individuals moving in a uniform direction, and that the scientific language Gibbon employs does not so much explain these events as offer an analogy which allows their extraordinariness to be voiced. Addison had opined that

We often find eminent writers very faulty in this respect; great scholars are apt to fetch their comparisons and allusions from the sciences in which they are most conversant, so that a man may see the compass of their learning in a treatise on the most indifferent subject. I have read a discourse upon Love, which none but a profound Chymist could understand, and have heard many a Sermon that should only have been preached before a congregation of *Cartesians*.[14]

But Gibbon's scientific diction is not merely ostentatious; it is the register of what has recently been well expressed as 'a purified, truthful marvellous'.[15] It holds out the promise of rescuing from the vicious alternatives of philosophic dismissal or dumb astonishment the unignorable and marvellous elements of history, to which Gibbon is becoming gradually more responsive as they come steadily to occupy more central positions in his chosen centuries.

Philosophic historiography is not concerned with historical causality as a phenomenon which is itself intrinsically interesting. Rather, it wishes to discover the causes of recurrent conditions, such as prosperity and decline. In other words, its concern is sociological, not metaphysical. In Volume I of *The Decline and Fall* Gibbon had provided a philosophic and sociological explanation of Roman decline when he attributed the enfeeblement of the empire to the advent of Christianity. As we have seen, Gibbon never loses faith in this explanation. In the *Memoirs* he says firmly: 'I believed, and . . . I still believe, that the propagation of the gospel and triumph of the Church are inseparably connected with the decline of the Roman Monarchy.'[16] And so in 1781 we still find teasing hints of the ruinous effects of Christianity. We move from Chapter XXVII, which concludes with the observation that 'The enervated soldiers abandoned their own, and the public, defence; and their pusillanimous indolence may be considered as the immediate cause of the downfal of the empire', to the headnote to Chapter XXVIII, *Final Destruction of Paganism. – Introduction of the Worship of Saints, and Relics, among the Christians.*[17] It is hard not to suspect some connexion between the quickening pace of decline and the quickening progress of the new faith, especially when elsewhere one comes across statements such as these:

. . . the abuse of religion dangerously undermined the foundations of moral virtue.

The abuse of Christianity introduced into the Roman government new causes of

[14] *Spectator*, no. 421; *Works*, III. 483.
[15] D. L. Patey, *Probability and Literary Form*, p. 149.
[16] *Memoirs*, p. 147.
[17] *The Decline and Fall*, III. 68–9.

tyranny and sedition; the bands of civil society were torn asunder by the fury of religious factions . . .[18]

But these ideas, which had occupied a sovereign position in Volume I, now seem increasingly marginal. The reason for this change is that Gibbon is moving from a sociological, philosophic interest in historical causality to a more metaphysical (for want of a better word) interest in the fact of historical change and the often dumbfounding means whereby it comes about. The question in his mind seems less to be 'What are the causes of this event?' than 'What sort of thing is a cause?'

This change of emphasis is nowhere more visible than in the *General Observations on the Fall of the Roman Empire in the West* which brings the second instalment of *The Decline and Fall* to a close.[19] Volume I of *The Decline and Fall* concluded with chapters which completed that volume's explanation of the cause of Roman decline, just as so many of its chapters were punctuated with an insight into causality.[20] The reader may expect that the *General Observations* will perform a similar function for the second and third volumes; but his expectation will not be gratified. For in its modesty, its suggestion of a plurality of provisional and limited ideas, the phrase *General Observations* expresses accurately the incoherence of this 'puzzling and disappointing' postscript.[21]

The *General Observations* begins with a brief résumé of Polybius' discussion of the causes of Rome's greatness. Gibbon then unexpectedly (and with a tacit rebuke to Montesquieu) says that his own subject is not susceptible of such philosophic treatment:

The rise of a city, which swelled into an empire, may deserve, as a singular prodigy, the reflection of a philosophic mind. But the decline of Rome was the natural and inevitable effect of immoderate greatness. Prosperity ripened the principle of decay; the causes of destruction multiplied with the extent of conquest; and as soon as time or accident had removed the artificial supports, the stupendous fabric yielded to the pressure of its own weight. The story of its ruin is simple and obvious; and instead of enquiring *why* the Roman empire was destroyed, we should rather be surprised that it had subsisted so long.[22]

This frank admission of the banality of sociological explanation in the case of Rome's decline (the 'why' of the event), and the redirection of the historian's attention towards the truly extraordinary facts which a philosophic concentration on sociological factors tends to mask, is just what we can see the changes

---

[18] *The Decline and Fall*, II. 207 and 293.
[19] *The Decline and Fall*, III. 629–40. Gibbon drafted this section before 1774, although the references to earlier passages in *The Decline and Fall* demonstrate that it was reworked for publication in 1781 (see *Memoirs*, p. 175 n. 48).
[20] See above, pp. 101–2 ff.
[21] The phrase is J. G. A. Pocock's: *Virtue, Commerce and History*, p. 149.
[22] *The Decline and Fall*, III.631. This seems to be a reminiscence of Petrarch: 'iam non Orbem ab hac urbe domitum, sed tam sero domitam, miror.' Chastellux had agreed that it was the growth of Rome which attracted philosophic attention (*De la Félicité Publique*, I. 89).

in Gibbon's thought about historical causality earlier in the second and third volumes have been leading up to. This new indifference about the kind of historical explanation which had stood at the heart of his first volume allows Gibbon, now with a less engaged eye, to treat Christianity more dispassionately and to admit that if it had weakened Rome, there was nevertheless some truth in Robertson's thesis that it had also been a humanising factor in history:

If the decline of the Roman empire was hastened by the conversion of Constantine, his victorious religion broke the violence of the fall, and mollified the ferocious temper of the conquerors.[23]

Gibbon's ebbing interest in sociological explanation here has a beneficial effect by properly complicating his historical understanding and allowing him to appreciate the probability of suggestions he might earlier have denied out of a desire for argumentative victory.

But the corollary of this more relaxed attitude on Gibbon's part is that the coherence of his argument suffers badly. When one recalls the care with which Gibbon arranges the hierarchy of causes in Volume I, culminating in Christianity, it is remarkable that in the space of two pages he can advance as a cause of decline both the rapacity of the soldiery 'who, in distant wars acquired the vices of strangers and mercenaries' and also the wastage of money which could have been used to pay for additional legions on 'the useless multitudes of both sexes' who lived in monasteries and convents.[24] Does Gibbon imagine there would be less rapacity with more soldiers? It seems that he is no longer thinking with full attentiveness about these questions.

That this is so is borne out by the fact that well over half the *General Observations* is taken up with a discussion of the likelihood of further barbarian inundations overrunning Europe. J. G. A. Pocock attributes the assumption on Gibbon's part that Europe could decline only as a result of barbarian invasion, rather than through internal corruption, to his 'developing ideas on the sociology of barbarism'.[25] We might also explain it in terms of the historian's growing interest in the immense tidal movements of history and their source in minute springs; an interest which goes hand in hand with his diminishing interest in sociological explanation and his rising sensitivity to the marvellous.

Gibbon adduces four arguments to support his conclusion that modern Europe is not threatened by a repetition of the calamity which overtook the Roman empire: first, that civil society has spread to the areas from which the barbarians came ('The plough, the loom, and the forge are introduced on

---

[23] *The Decline and Fall*, III.633. Compare Defoe, *General History of Discoveries and Improvements*, p. 171, and Robertson, *The Situation of the World at the Time of Christ's Appearance*, *Works*, I.cxx.
[24] *The Decline and Fall*, III.631 and 633.
[25] *Virtue, Commerce and History*, p. 150.

the banks of the Volga, the Oby, and the Lena'); secondly, that the national spirit of the various European countries, which was stifled by the empire, would now make Europe very difficult to conquer; thirdly, that the military proficiency of the Europeans renders them unassailable by barbarian methods; and finally that history reveals man's steady progress:

We may therefore acquiesce in the pleasing conclusion, that every age of the world has increased, and still increases, the real wealth, the happiness, the knowledge, and perhaps the virtue, of the human race.[26]

This complacency is intriguing, given that Gibbon has shown us in the over-turning of the deep foundations of Rome's greatness so many reasons for not feeling complacent. But what it is ultimately most important to grasp is the implication in Gibbon's conviction of the unrepeatableness of barbarian invasion that the present is sundered from the past. Philosophic historio-graphy had assumed that, in essence and beneath the deceptive, distracting surface of events, the past and the present were the same because they were informed by the same causes, which would always produce the same effects. Montesquieu makes this point on the very subject of barbarian invasions. We may seem to be separate from the past, but in reality were we to act as they did, we would have to endure the same consequences:

Ces essaims de barbares, qui sortirent autrefois du nord, ne paroissent plus aujourd'hui. Les violences des Romains avoient fait retirer les peuples du midi au nord: tandis que la force qui les contenoit subsista, ils y restèrent; quand elle fut affoiblie, ils se répandirent de toutes parts. La même chose arriva quelques siècles après. Les conquêtes de Charlemagne, & ses tyrannies, avoient une seconde fois fait reculer les peuples du midi au nord: si-tôt que cet empire fut affoibli, ils se portèrent une seconde fois du nord au midi. Et, si aujourd'hui un prince faisoit en Europe les mêmes ravages, les nations, repoussées dans le nord, adossées aux limites de l'univers, y tiendroient ferme jusqu'au moment qu'elles inonderoient & conquerroient l'Europe une troisième fois.[27]

It seems likely that Gibbon has this passage at the back of his mind when writing the *General Observations*, for he counters Montesquieu's philosophic supposition of causal regularity with an alternative interpretation of exactly the same example. Some events, he claims, are unique; and this uniqueness

---

[26] *The Decline and Fall*, III.635 and 640. We may, incidentally, note that Coleridge's attribution of the decline of the empire to its denial of national spirit, which he says Gibbon ignores, is in fact borrowed from Gibbon (*Table Talk and Omniana*, pp. 263–4). Gibbon might have encountered assertions of the durability of modern Europe in, for instance, Gray's 'Alliance of Government and Education', ll. 59–67. His own confidence seems to have struck a chord in Herder: 'Let savage nations burst in upon Europe, they could not withstand our tactics; and no Attila will again extend his march from the shores of the Black Sea and the Caspian to the plains of Catalonia. Let monks, sybarites, fanatics, and tyrants, arise, as they will; it is no longer in their power, to bring back the night of the Middle Ages' (*Reflections on the Philosophy of the History of Mankind*, p. 111).

[27] *Œuvres*, III.470; compare Hume, *History*, I.134 and *Encyclopédie*, VIII.ii.

disturbs faith in causal regularity, because the past no longer exhibits the sure return of causes and effects which had supported such faith. Modern European civilisation has narrowed the range of what can occur, and has rendered henceforth impossible the true, but nevertheless marvellous, events which took place in the imperial twilight. Gibbon devotes the final instalment of *The Decline and Fall* to an attempt thoroughly to understand the implications of the fact that those clouded centuries contained such gigantic and unparalleled events.

Volumes IV, V and VI – 1788

In describing the events of life, it is the business of the historian to represent them as they really happened . . .

Alison

I look back with amazement on the road which I have travelled, but which I should never have entered had I been previously apprized of its length.

. . . we advance in freedom as we advance in years.

Gibbon

13

'A dead uniformity of abject vices'

Experience soon shows us the tortuosities of imaginary rectitude, the complications of simplicity, and the asperities of smoothness.

Johnson

The final instalment of *The Decline and Fall* covers the period from the birth of Theodoric the Ostrogoth in 455 to the death of Mahomet II in 1481 (although in Chapter LXX Gibbon's perspective is sufficiently long to take in Sixtus V and the late sixteenth century). Thus, between the years 1781 and 1788 Gibbon's attention was largely occupied by the Byzantine or 'lower' empire.

It has been generally agreed that here Gibbon is at his least impressive. J. B. Bury, with a decisiveness perhaps quickened by the bruised *amour propre* of an historian whose subject is not receiving its due, deplores Gibbon's 'contemptuous attitude' to Byzantium and brands his account of the internal history of the empire after Heraclius as 'a sketch' which is 'not only superficial; it gives an entirely false impression of the facts'.[1] G. M. Young finds this second half of *The Decline and Fall* both misleading and null:

> . . . the first step towards the comprehension of Byzantine history is to forget all that Gibbon has said about it.[2]

Poor Gibbon! How could he help getting it wrong when his classical intellectual furniture, in which Young imagines he was so comfortable as hardly to realise that it *was* furniture, prevented him from ever viewing Byzantium in a true light. Even John Burrow's excellent and up-to-date introduction to Gibbon perpetuates the idea that he suffered from a 'general prejudice against Byzantium' which was 'his weakest spot'.[3]

Accuracy is always a virtue. But standards of accuracy change. Given that when Bury edited *The Decline and Fall* he was trying to reposition it on the leading edge of historical knowledge, it was both inevitable and appropriate that he should systematically correct what he saw as errors of fact.[4] How-

---

[1] J. B. Bury (ed.), *The History of the Decline and Fall of the Roman Empire*, I.liii–liv.
[2] G. M. Young, *Gibbon*, p. 151; compare also p. 153.
[3] J. W. Burrow, *Gibbon*, p. 109: note also 'the history of Byzantium, which he found uncongenial and contemptible' (p. 36).
[4] Bury's attitude as an editor is explained in the second sentence of his introduction: 'He [Gibbon] concerns us here as an historian; our business is to consider how far the view which

ever, when later commentators persist in Bury's attitude, it is hard not to feel that this is, in the strict sense, impertinent; particularly when it is acknowledged that what modern historical scholarship perceives as Gibbon's shortcomings on Byzantium can be largely attributed to the then comparatively unworked nature of the subject.[5] Now that *The Decline and Fall* has the status of a classic, rather than of an essentially sound textbook nevertheless requiring some modification, the obliquities and frustrations of Gibbon's account of the lower empire must be considered from a different angle.

Today Bury's project of refurbishing *The Decline and Fall* seems the misguided but understandable enterprise of an age of historical positivism. It is as if, with a few ingenious modifications, we could turn a quill into a typewriter. Without adopting the extreme views of E. H. Carr, one can still acknowledge that a work is informed by its age. This is not to say that it will be obliged to mouth the prejudices of its time. Different writers may write with varying degrees of opposition to the nostrums of their day and, as we have seen, Gibbon himself is not always the spokesman of eighteenth-century English attitudes. But that a book was produced at one time, and not at another, is a circumstance which can never be ignored. There is no timeless and accumulating order of facts, as Bury implicitly believed; intellectual progress is not linear. We possess a number of texts written from different standpoints and at different moments which demand to be considered as much in the light of what their authors knew, as what we now know.

However, we may feel that to sit in judgement on a book in that way is merely to protect ourselves from the scepticism we are willing to train on others, and to substitute the bringing in of a verdict for the difficult business of passing judgement. To place a tick or a cross alongside different sections of *The Decline and Fall* is an empty undertaking, since although our present judgement may arise out of a wider knowledge than Gibbon possessed, it is itself partial and liable to supersession. It, too, will be the provisional utterance of a limited perception.

It would be odd, then, for us now to think that we at last had got it right and could give the ultimate correction to *The Decline and Fall*. Our sensitivity to the moment from which a writer speaks will prevent us from trying to judge him *sub specie aeternitatis*, and will encourage us to consider him in terms both of his time and of his relation to his time. Much of the most impressive recent work on *The Decline and Fall* has been cast in this mould, and has variously set Gibbon in his period.[6]

---

he has presented of the decline and fall of the Roman Empire can be accepted as faithful to the facts, and in what respects it needs correction in the light of discoveries which have been made since he wrote' (I.xxxi).

[5] G. M. Young admits this (*Gibbon*, p. 151). It seems strange that he should then go on to crow over Gibbon's not knowing what it was apparently impossible for him to know.

[6] Guiseppe Giarrizzo, *Edward Gibbon e la Cultura Europea del Settecento*, and Michel Baridon,

However, so to contextualise *The Decline and Fall* may actually hinder an understanding of these final volumes. Unless one approaches Gibbon's account of Byzantium with an awareness of the pressures for historiographic change which have accumulated throughout Volumes II and III of *The Decline and Fall*, one may be misled into seeing Gibbon, hampered both by a lack of spadework and temperamental incompatibility, acquiescing in the widespread disparagement of Byzantium he would have encountered in his contemporaries.[7] But if we read the final instalment of *The Decline and Fall* with an awareness of the distending energies liberated by the recalcitrance of the past in Volumes II and III, we shall find that Gibbon is not complacent in the attitudes and assumptions which, as he realises, hinder him from accurately taking the measure of Byzantium. Far from being happily imprisoned in a padded cell of Enlightenment disdain for the later empire, we shall find Gibbon struggling to extend the adequacy of his historical imagination, and to emancipate himself from the convictions about the past and historiography, once accepted as natural and universally applicable, which now choke the hardly articulable, yet unignorable, ideas this difficult area of the past provokes.[8] Gibbon records that the 'conclusion of my work appears to have diffused a strong sensation'.[9] As ever, he chooses his words with care. We might expect a work which stretches and frets the habitual, quotidian consciousness of its time, as well as of its author, to make the inexpressible but unmistakable impact 'sensation' suggests.

In the *Considérations*, Montesquieu characterised Byzantine history as formless and unstructured – a mass of undifferentiated, minute and uniform particularity:

Edward Gibbon et le Mythe de Rome, are the two most notable examples. J. G. A. Pocock's articles explore a different context of *The Decline and Fall* of which his promised book on Gibbon may be expected to broaden our knowledge: 'Gibbon's *Decline and Fall* and the world view of the Late Enlightenment' (reprinted in *Virtue, Commerce and History*, pp. 143–56); 'Between Machiavelli and Hume: Gibbon as civic humanist and philosophical historian'; and 'Gibbon and the shepherds: the stages of society in the *Decline and Fall*'. John Burrow's *Gibbon* finds space in its brief compass to touch finely on the interesting connexions between *The Decline and Fall* and the *literati* of the Scottish Enlightenment.

[7] Giarrizzo has recognised that 'il medioevo tornava come problema assillante alla coscienza storiografica del Settecento' (*Edward Gibbon e la Cultura Europea del Settecento*, p. 407). Many, such as Mably (*Observations on the Romans*, pp. 233–4) viewed this period with open scorn. For others, it was a touchstone for dullness – 'the dull Annals of a drowsy eastern Monarchy' (Thomas Blackwell, *Memoirs of the Court of Augustus*, I.3) – or an unprofitable wasteland of history (e.g. Thomas Bever, *History of the Legal Polity of the Roman State*, p. 493). Walpole complained of 'the annals of the Byzantine Empire, marked only by vices and follies' (*Correspondence*, XXIII.499). Hence it is not surprising to find that historians tend to skip these centuries, marking their existence in only the most summary manner (e.g. *Abrégé de l'Histoire Romaine à l'Usage des Élèves de l'École Royale Militaire à Paris*, p. 287 and Chastellux, *De la Félicité Publique*, I.336–7).

[8] Once again Collingwood seems close to Gibbon's position; see 'The theory of historical cycles' in *Essays in the Philosophy of History*, p. 83.

[9] *Memoirs*, p. 182.

L'histoire de l'empire Grec . . . n'est plus qu'un tissu de révoltes, de séditions & de perfidies.

. . . sous les derniers empereurs, l'empire, réduit aux fauxbourgs de Constantinople, finit comme le Rhin, qui n'est plus qu'un ruisseau lorsqu'il se perd dans l'Océan.[10]

Yet, as John Burrow has observed, this shapelessness does not baffle Montesquieu's philosophic gaze, since Byzantium is for him 'the representative of a category of eighteenth-century social and political theory . . . "oriental despotism" '.[11] Gibbon naturally knew of Montesquieu's understanding of Byzantium; a phrase such as 'the form and spirit of a despotic monarchy' is plainly drawn from Montesquieu's thesaurus of political language.[12] Yet the distinction between the two men is that whereas Montesquieu, with philosophic imperturbability, can turn the sterility of despotism to intellectual account, the Byzantine empire is for Gibbon a desert from which neither profit nor pleasure can be drawn, despite his sanguine hopes in 1781 of 'a long series of instructive lessons'.[13] In the event, the 'patient reader' derives no 'adequate reward of instruction or amusement'.[14] The history of these years is repulsive and wearisome – so far Gibbon is in agreement with Montesquieu. But whereas Montesquieu's distaste for Byzantium does not impede his understanding of it, Gibbon, whose attention is not restricted to political categories, finds in the repetitions of Byzantine history the source of its unintelligibility. To be obliged to repeat is wearying for the historian:

A repetition of such capricious brutality, without connection or design, would be tedious and disgusting . . .[15]

But the lack of connexion and design is more disquieting than distasteful when considered in the light of the implications it has for the structure of events in these centuries. Narrating the history of a period containing 'events by which the fate of nations is not materially changed', Gibbon is obliged to confront 'the same hostilities, undertaken without cause, prosecuted without glory, and terminated without effect'.[16] For the philosophic historian, the investigation of causation made the past both profitable and comprehensible; the dead were similar people to ourselves from whose experience we could learn. But

---

[10] *Œuvres*, III.505 and 528. Voltaire notes that the imperial twilight was an historiographic morass which his own work would skirt (*Œuvres Complètes*, XI.164).

[11] *Gibbon*, p. 50.

[12] *The Decline and Fall*, VI.374: compare also 'in an absolute government, which levels the distinctions of noble and plebeian birth' (*The Decline and Fall*, V.483); 'in this common captivity, the ranks of society were confounded' (*The Decline and Fall*, VI.502); and his borrowing of Montesquieu's ingenious illustration of the wasteful violence of despotic government, the 'Indian who fells the tree, that he may gather the fruit' (*The Decline and Fall*, VI.523).

[13] *The Decline and Fall*, III.628.

[14] *The Decline and Fall*, V.1–2.

[15] *The Decline and Fall*, VI.526: see also 'I must often repeat' (*The Decline and Fall*, V.285). Such sighs begin to appear as early as Volume II; 'the tedious repetition' (*The Decline and Fall*, II.620); 'I am at a loss how to vary the narrative of similar crimes' (*The Decline and Fall*, II.553).

[16] *The Decline and Fall*, IV.464–5.

when history displays only the cancelled or arrested causality of inconsequential gestures (rather than of *events*), it is difficult to repress the baffled realisation that these people may have been quite different from us: 'Yet these men once commanded the respect of mankind.'[17]

This anomaly of the imperial twilight – the way that in these centuries energy which at other times might have exerted a causal, shaping force is absorbed or dissipated – first catches Gibbon's eye in Volume II, although there it tends to be annexed to the wry amusement he takes in men's religious behaviour. With a sense of comic disproportion veiling but not blunting a satiric edge turned towards Constantius, Gibbon records the ever escalating resources impotently focused upon Athanasius: 'Counts, praefects, tribunes, whole armies, were successively employed to pursue a bishop and a fugitive.'[18] It is the strength of Athanasius' religious beliefs which turns effort to inconsequence. So paradoxical is religious life that weak and shallow beliefs have the same effect:

It is indeed more than probable, that the restoration and encouragement of Paganism revealed a multitude of pretended Christians, who, from motives of temporal advantage, had acquiesced in the religion of the former reign; and who afterwards returned, with the same flexibility of conscience, to the faith which was professed by the successors of Julian.[19]

The full significance of this anomaly is masked by its proximity to the remains of Gibbon's infidel irony. When placed close to contempt, the anomalous appears more risible than intriguing. The awareness that this shrugging off of human endeavour is a crucial feature of the history of Byzantium seems first to occur to Gibbon when it is presented in the context of the distortions caducity creates in political life:

. . . it is the misfortune of those princes who laboriously sustain a declining monarchy, that, to obtain some immediate advantage, or to avert some impending danger, they are forced to countenance, and even to multiply, the most pernicious abuses.[20]

Despite its local subtlety of analysis, Montesquieu's model of political life rests on the simple, fundamental belief that all political processes are reversible. By recognising and embracing the principles which lead to prosperity, decline can be arrested and turned back.[21] Gibbon's more minute and scholarly investigation of the circumstances of decline leads him to the opposite notion; that those in the toils of decline are obliged to take short views, and that their struggles only enmesh them more tightly in the predicament from which they desire to escape. Energy intended to reform and support is insensibly redirected into channels which contribute to the stream of decline. All human effort, however enlightened its intentions, is assimilated into the indeflectible drift of the past.

---

[17] *The Decline and Fall*, V.548 n. 17. [18] *The Decline and Fall*, II.289.
[19] *The Decline and Fall*, II.381. [20] *The Decline and Fall*, III.460.
[21] See above, pp. 14–15 and 190–1.

In 1788 this idea moves into sharper focus and greater prominence. The congruity of the evanescence of men's religious convictions with the impossibility of decisively shaping the political life of these centuries is recognised:

Yet the powers of the East had been bent, not broken, by this transient hurricane. After the departure of the Greeks, the fugitive princes returned to their capitals; the subjects disclaimed their involuntary oaths of allegiance; the Moslems again purified their temples, and overturned the idols of the saints and martyrs; the Nestorians and Jacobites preferred a Saracen to an orthodox master; and the number and spirit of the Melchites were inadequate to the support of the church and state.[22]

'It is a Maxim in *Politics*, founded upon the Experience of Ages, *That it is much easier to make Conquests than keep them*'; but Gibbon is doing more than just exemplify Blackwell's maxim.[23] Nicephorus Phocas and John Zimisces leave no indelible impression on their times, despite the unimpeachable vigour and address which makes them, considered in themselves, second Trajans. But to compare the language from Volume I in which Gibbon discusses the impermanence of Trajan's conquests is to see how in 1788 he has had to modify his ideas of the nature of historical events in order to cope with these later, shaded years of the empire:

But the death of Trajan soon clouded the splendid prospect; and it was justly to be dreaded, that so many distant nations would throw off the unaccustomed yoke, when they were no longer restrained by the powerful hand which had imposed it.[24]

The earlier revolution is marked by abrupt, human violence (the imposition and rejection of the yoke), rather than the impersonal, natural violence of the hurricane which Gibbon finds closest to the texture of the past in 1788. And the fact that it is Trajan's death which precipitates the change implies the effectiveness of the great individual, 'the powerful hand' which can exert a shaping influence on history. Thus in 1776 Gibbon's language betrays his assumption that men can intervene decisively in the course of history. Compare another, similar moment from the instalment of 1788:

As soon as the arms of the Franks were withdrawn, the impression, though not the memory, was erased in the Mahometan realms of Egypt and Syria.[25]

Even in such slight details as the plural and banally literal 'the arms' (contrast the striking image of 'the powerful hand' of Volume I) or the choice of 'were withdrawn' in place of 'no longer restrained', Gibbon shows his sensitivity to the diminished scope for individual action these centuries afford. Moreover, the impermanence of the conquests made by Nicephorus Phocas and John Zimisces is caused not by their deaths, but by this inherent elasticity of their

---

[22] *The Decline and Fall*, V.463.
[23] *Memoirs of the Court of Augustus*, I.104.
[24] *The Decline and Fall*, I.6–7: I.8. See also the behaviour of the Caledonians towards Septimus Severus (*The Decline and Fall*, I.132–3: I.158).
[25] *The Decline and Fall*, VI.206–7.

times, the refusal of their age to take a durable impression. Hence, in contrast to the definiteness of the undoing of Trajan's achievements (note the energy of the verbs 'throw off' and 'restrained'), Gibbon's language in 1788 is tuned to evoke the quiet resumption of a former course: 'returned', 'disclaimed', 'preferred' (only 'overturned' might suggest vigour).

Gibbon is increasingly preoccupied with the easy eluding of definition these centuries manifest. Even the most epochal event he records in 1788 – the fall of Constantinople in 1453 – seems, to his careful eye, not the absolute watershed it was for, say, the author of the *Universal History*. There we read: 'The death of the last *Roman* emperor, the loss of *Constantinople*, and the final dissolution of the *Constantinopolitan Roman* empire, happened on the twenty-ninth of *May* in the year of the *Greeks* 6961. of the *Hegira* 857. and of the Christian aera, according to the most probable opinion, 1453.'[26] Gibbon, however, is alert to the underlying inertia which belies such sharp divisions:

From a gigantic picture of the greatness, population, &c. of Constantinople and the Ottoman empire . . . we may learn, that in the year 1586, the Moslems were less numerous in the capital than the Christians, or even the Jews.[27]

The vigour of Islam had seemed to stand out from the general enervation of these centuries, but even in its greatest triumph it falls prey to their malaise of inconsequence, their character as an age of causeless duration and tendency outside the influence of human help or hindrance. The emperor Manuel, in reproving his son, utters the truth about the straitened times through which he lived: ' "My son deems himself a great and heroic prince; but, alas! our miserable age does not afford scope for heroism or greatness. His daring spirit might have suited the happier times of our ancestors; but the present state requires not an emperor, but a cautious steward of the last relics of our fortunes." '[28] The military history of 'the present state' shares its character and comprises a 'series of bloody and indecisive conflicts', which are sometimes not even bloody:

Their spirit was intrepid; yet such is the uncertainty of courage, that the two armies were suddenly struck with a panic; they fled from each other, and the rival kings remained with their guards in the midst of an empty plain.[29]

It would be a mistake to read this as Gibbon tempting us with irony to measure the reputation of the Lombards for intrepidity of spirit against the concrete evidence of this virtue which falls within the purview of the historian: Gibbon says unequivocally that 'their spirit was intrepid'. Instead, what we are asked to accept is that, in this period of decline, there is no straightforward relationship between the qualities races or individuals may possess and their deeds. The

[26] *Universal History*, XVII.217.   [27] *The Decline and Fall*, VI.508–9 n. 80.
[28] *The Decline and Fall*, VI.395–6.   [29] *The Decline and Fall*, IV.217.

loose weave of these centuries frustrates, deflects and dissipates the energy of those who inhabit them. The historian must acknowledge both that energy and that frustration. But in order to maintain such a mental stretch, he will have to discard his supposition of proportionate and necessary causality, since that would prevent him from acknowledging genuine qualities, such as the intrepidity of spirit possessed by the Lombards, which however have no effect and thus threaten to drop below the horizon of the historian's vision. He will also have to curb his taste for irony, because the complacency from which it springs will tend to make sluggish the historical, imaginative sympathy this period so strongly demands. To narrate the decline of the empire in the East while doing justice to its dumbfounding endurance requires an historical intellect too subtly principled to adhere inflexibly to suppositions or idioms the historian may find congenial, but which blinker his perceptions.

The indistinct and muted character of the long and irregular slope of Roman decline in the East is reflected also in the fissures by which it is veined and which make it so resistant to the generalising historian. Justinian's legal reforms are a true product of their times:

Instead of a statue cast in a simple mould by the hand of an artist, the works of Justinian represent a tesselated pavement of antique and costly, but too often of incoherent fragments.[30]

Gibbon is doing more here than indicate the existence of Tribonianisms.[31] By refusing to arrange itself 'in a simple mould' and thus take on the pellucid coherence of art, the history of Byzantium itself becomes a frustrating object of study, whose own incompletion and discontinuity inhibit order, consequences and perspicuity in the work of those who study it. Gibbon cannot rise above the confusions and disjunctions of this period and transcend them in a work which discerns underlying singleness. To do so would be to describe a mirage, and not the ungrateful, but also fascinating, landscape through which he is moving.

As Gibbon becomes acclimatised to these regions of anomaly and paradox we can see him reaching towards the realisation that the friability of the past is not an insignificant opacity above which the historian, in philosophic style, should try to rise, but a central feature he should assiduously seek out as an aperture promising a more intimate apprehension of the age. Thus, he points out and traces the interrupted rhythms of Byzantine history which exist alongside its blank uniformity:

But in the intervals of the Byzantine dynasties, the succession is rapid and broken, and the name of a successful candidate is speedily erazed by a more fortunate competitor.[32]

---

[30] *The Decline and Fall*, IV.359.
[31] It was well known that Justinian's *Pandects* were inconsistent (Thomas Bever, *History of the Legal Polity of the Roman State*, pp. 475ff.).
[32] *The Decline and Fall*, V.85.

He unmasks the baffling lack of wholeness and connexion in the psychology of the denizens of this period – for instance, the severance of inner life from environment shown by their inability to recreate what they experience:

The tragic, epic, and lyric muses, were silent and inglorious: the bards of Constantinople seldom rose above a riddle or epigram, a panegyric or tale; they forgot even the rules of prosody; and with the melody of Homer yet sounding in their ears, they confound all measure of feet and syllables in the impotent strains which have received the name of *political* or city verses.[33]

It is the phrase 'yet sounding in their ears' which makes this much more than a commonplace wringing of hands over the artistic incompetence of Byzantium. That incompetence is a cause not of scorn but of stubborn astonishment for Gibbon when he recollects the immediacy of their contact with the finest products of antiquity. Once more, the persistent question 'What people were these?' tugs at Gibbon's mind.

The reluctance of these centuries to accept and retain the impress of human exertion is illustrated with paradigmatic clarity in the bizarre circumstances of the death of Amurath I. Rejecting an alternative version of events, in which 'the sultan was stabbed by a Croat in his tent', Gibbon gives us instead this account:

As the conqueror walked over the field, he observed that the greatest part of the slain consisted of beardless youths; and listened to the flattering reply of his vizir, that age and wisdom would have taught them not to oppose his irresistible arms. But the sword of his Janizaries could not defend him from the dagger of despair; a Servian soldier started from the crowd of dead bodies, and Amurath was pierced in the belly with a mortal wound.[34]

This seems simply a moral example rebuking the haughtiness of princes; but the strange detail of the assassin's springing from a crowd of dead bodies gives it an historiographic resonance also. The vacuous lesson drawn by the vizir from what seems the accomplished fact of victory displayed before them is interrupted by the fatal knowledge that the past, and those whom we carelessly relegate to it, are not always impotent. The historian perhaps feels that he possesses irresistible arms of interpretation and authority; but history need not abide their arbitrament and may inflict an incurable wound on the intellectual stiffness which does not respond to its surprising vitality. The historiographic difficulty of the dying years of the empire deals an irreparable blow to many of the assumptions and aims with which Gibbon begins *The Decline and Fall*. Yet this is a liberating as well as a destructive blow, because it frees Gibbon from the habits of mind which would have condemned him to writing off the strange essence of this period as unmeaning monstrosity.

The startling energy of Amurath's assassin is a fine example of the general

---

[33] *The Decline and Fall*, V.516.
[34] *The Decline and Fall*, VI.321 n. 55 and VI.321.

galvanising of the moribund which continually thrusts itself before Gibbon's eyes during his study of Byzantium – which is itself history's greatest example of a refusal to pass away. That mingling of weakness and endurance prompts Gibbon to fathom the difficulty of describing in language a period of transition without freezing the process of change into a small number of fixed states; of catching the strength of the declining and the feebleness of the rising. 'The Passions of the human Mind, if truly awak'd, and kept up by Objects fitted to them, dictate a Language peculiar to themselves'; the language peculiar to Gibbon's intellectual passions in 1788 is steeped in functional equivocation.[35] It is his awareness of history's complex incongruities which transforms literal descriptions of ruined sites into images of the obliquities and insistent heterogeneity of the past:

This pontiff [Leo IV] was born a Roman; the courage of the first ages of the republic glowed in his breast; and, amidst the ruins of his country, he stood erect, like one of the firm and lofty columns that rear their heads above the fragments of the Roman forum.

Among the Greek colonies and churches of Asia, Philadelphia is still erect; a column in a scene of ruins; a pleasing example, that the paths of honour and safety may sometimes be the same.[36]

Gibbon uses the double resonance of ruins, their status as tokens of both durability and decay, to register the unevenness of decline and the consequent abrasiveness of the past – the rugged outline and jagged edges with which it affronts the inquiring historian.

Gibbon's sensitivity to the paradoxes of Byzantium is also focused in a strain of architectural imagery which bears eloquent witness to the way the disorienting aspects of the past he cannot ignore are nevertheless not calmly accepted, but still trouble his abiding notions of the normal:

. . . the edifice has subsisted after the foundations have been undermined.

. . . this baseless fabric . . .[37]

We shall consider Gibbon's use of architectural imagery again when we move on to the question of the structure of *The Decline and Fall*. Here we need only remark that these images express perfectly the unwarranted duration and absence of sufficient causes to which Gibbon so often returns in these volumes. In this, they harmonise with the images of unnatural vegetation Gibbon is prompted to coin. Such images were conventionally used to suggest regular, slow and impersonal historical change:

The feudal association was to direct and to foster chivalry; and, from chivalry, it was to receive a support or lustre. There were plants which were destined to take root about

[35] Thomas Blackwell, *An Enquiry into the Life and Writings of Homer*, p. 333.
[36] *The Decline and Fall*, V.439–40 and 314.
[37] *The Decline and Fall*, V.127 and 487.

the same period, and to sympathise in their growth, and in their decline. The seeds of them had been gathered by the barbarian in his woods; and, to whatever soil or climate his fortune was to carry him, there he was to scatter them with profusion.

. . . a little kingdom of his own; which, as from an imperceptible grain, sprang up gradually into a most luxuriant tree, and covered an immense portion of the earth with the shadow of its branches.

The seeds of destruction lay in the heart of the plant; the worm gnawed its roots, and its vital juices were corrupted: the gigantic tree, therefore, must ultimately fall to the ground.[38]

Stuart, Bever and Herder use these images straightforwardly to indicate the parallelism they see between the processes of history and natural processes. These images have none of the strange life Gibbon imparts by twisting his metaphors away from the natural:

After this deed of sacrilege and cruelty, they continued to infest the confines of Irak, Syria, and Egypt; but the vital principle of enthusiasm had withered at the root.

From every province of Europe and Asia, the rivulets of gold and silver discharged into the Imperial reservoir a copious and perennial stream. The separation of the branches from the trunk encreased the relative magnitude of Constantinople.[39]

In the *General Observations on the Fall of the Roman Empire in the West* Gibbon had indicated the triteness of an inquiry into the cause of the empire's decline by suggesting a much more puzzling object of inquiry; 'Instead of inquiring *why* the Roman empire was destroyed, we should rather be surprised that it had subsisted so long.'[40] The images Gibbon uses to evoke an empire which 'subsisted one thousand and fifty-eight years, in a state of premature and perpetual decay' show that if anything, his sense of surprise has deepened and taken on more weight with study, rather than been attenuated.[41] A tree which does not die back when stripped of its branches, a plant which is out-wardly luxuriant despite the loss of its roots – these images reveal Gibbon's understanding that only by wrenching his analogies can he convey the strange reality of Byzantium, and also the unnatural energy which allows it to prolong itself.[42] Hence the image of the imperial city as 'a leafless and sapless trunk', subsisting without sustenance and production, beyond what its cause could sanction and without any effects, is a happy one; and happy, too, is the image of the state as a tree;

Far different was the fate of the Ottoman monarchy. The massy trunk was bent to the

---

[38] Gilbert Stuart, *A View of Society in Europe*, p. 37; Thomas Bever, *History of the Legal Polity of the Roman State*, p. 4; J. G. v. Herder, *Reflections on the Philosophy of the History of Mankind*, p. 244.
[39] *The Decline and Fall*, V.451 and 478.
[40] *The Decline and Fall*, III.631.
[41] *The Decline and Fall*, III.281.
[42] Compare *The Decline and Fall*, VI.566.

ground, but no sooner did the hurricane pass away, than it again rose with fresh vigour and more lively vegetation.[43]

The hurricane recalls the 'transient hurricane' which bends but does not break the powers of the East.[44] The recollection is apt because here, too, Gibbon is trying to convey the impermeability of the men and institutions of this period to energy that at other times would have been decisive and causal. The oak is traditionally destroyed by the tempest which spares the pliant reed. That the massy trunk should also be elastic demonstrates not only how history upsets inherited nostrums, but also how wayward is the causality of these centuries.[45] In the *Rambler* Johnson deplored 'incongruous combinations of images'; but in the *Idler* he equally said that it was the business of the historian to 'decorate known facts by new beauties of method or of style'.[46] Gibbon's incongruous images are just such expressive beauties. They exemplify Blair's idea of the function of metaphor: 'Its peculiar effect is to give light and strength to description; to make intellectual ideas, in some sort, visible to the eye, by giving them colour, and substance, and sensible qualities.'[47]

That twist away from the natural shows the obstinacy with which the shards of the past have lodged in Gibbon's mind. He is prepared neither to ignore them, nor to forget their strangeness. Thus history becomes importunate:

In the East, in the West, in war, in religion, in science, in their prosperity, and in their decay, the Arabians press themselves on our curiosity . . .[48]

In its refusal to be tamely accommodated to the historian's categories, the past is energetically provocative; and although Gibbon speaks of 'the calm historian of the present hour', once we replace the phrase in its setting we can see that he is far from implying that such is his situation:

When the Arabs first issued from the desert, they must have been surprised at the ease and rapidity of their own success. But when they advanced in the career of victory to the banks of the Indus and the summit of the Pyrenees; when they had repeatedly tried the edge of their scymetars and the energy of their faith, they might be equally astonished that any nation could resist their invincible arms, that any boundary should confine the dominion of the successor of the prophet. The confidence of soldiers and fanatics may indeed be excused, since the calm historian of the present hour, who strives to follow the rapid course of the Saracens, must study to explain by what means

---

[43] *The Decline and Fall*, VI.222 and 364. Gibbon may have taken the hint for these images from one of Julian the Apostate's letters, in which he figures the languishing empire as an uprooted tree (*Œuvres Complètes*, I(2).21).

[44] See above, p. 200.

[45] The depth of this image of the flexible but massy trunk is increased if Gibbon is recollecting the use made of the oak by classical poets to suggest the unshakeable strength of the state: see Horace, *Odes*, IV.iv, ll. 50–60 (echoed in the eighteenth century by Thomson, *Liberty*, III.363ff.), and also Virgil's likening of Aeneas to an oak (*Aeneid*, IV.441–9).

[46] *Works*, II.17 and IV.426.

[47] *Lectures on Rhetoric and Belles Lettres*, I.297.

[48] *The Decline and Fall*, V.541.

the church and state were saved from this impending, and, as it should seem, from this inevitable danger.[49]

It is clear that the calmness of the eighteenth-century historian is the price exacted by historical knowledge, the equilibrium he must lose in the dust of study and the heat of striving. 'The sedentary reader' will be blankly stupefied, not richly astonished, by the past unless he overcomes his supinity and allows it to goad him into intellectual movement.[50] And what goads him will not be any large formulations about the causal structure of the past, but the abrasive grit of history; the opaque, particular facts which most resolutely refuse such large formulations, and which humble the historian's intellectual and philosophic pride while enlarging his sympathy.

For increasingly Gibbon finds that he cannot, as Usbek had advised Rhédi in *Lettres Persanes*, pass beyond that stage of historical imagination in which the past is experienced with emotions of wonder and awe as a darkly significant spectacle to reach a zone of calm comprehension. As Gibbon wrestles with Byzantium, he is obliged to discover the merit of forms of historical thought which for the *philosophes* not only had no value, but were not historical thought at all. Hume wrote: 'In sympathy there is an evident conversion of an idea into an impression.'[51] If we were to apply this notion to the final instalment of *The Decline and Fall*, we might say that, under the pressure of the imaginative sympathy which is the only medium whereby Gibbon can apprehend this stubborn area of the past, the historian moves from the philosophic stance he had adopted in 1776 and maintained, with some reverses, in 1781, and reaches a position in which historical knowledge is a question of impressions, not ideas, and in which the historian undertakes to 'unfold . . . events' rather than to explicate causality.[52]

We have seen that at the root of Volume I of *The Decline and Fall* there is a conviction about the fundamental cause of Roman decline; and that responding to the growing resistance of the past to causal analysis in Volumes II and III, Gibbon tends more to suggest the magnitude of decline by juxtaposing two separated moments than to investigate its causes. But in 1788 the annihilation of intervening time does not serve its previous purpose of measuring the scale of collapse:

After a period of thirteen centuries, the institution of Romulus expired; and if the nobles of Rome still assumed the title of senators, few subsequent traces can be discovered of a public council, or constitutional order. Ascend six hundred years, and contemplate the kings of the earth soliciting an audience, as the slaves or freedmen of the Roman senate![53]

[49] *The Decline and Fall*, V.392.
[50] *The Decline and Fall*, V.137.
[51] *Treatise of Human Nature*, p. 320.
[52] *The Decline and Fall*, V.393. And this despite the contemporary idea that it was only the study of causality which could rescue a history of decline and make it profitable: see, e.g., Blackwell, *Memoirs of the Court of Augustus*, I.128.
[53] *The Decline and Fall*, IV.305.

To measure decline by putting together two disparate periods, as Gibbon did in Volumes II and III, implies a belief in the fundamental continuity of history; one can measure only like with like. But this exclamatory punctuation (so rare in *The Decline and Fall*), and the complex tone which it creates, involving indignation and wonder, registers Gibbon's incapacity to unite the awful interval between the republic and the late empire in a chain of causality. Once one has been fully impressed by the immensity of Roman decline, the possibility of explaining it recedes. Bring together the republic and the late empire, and they spring apart in strong denial of that propinquity and its implicit belief in historical continuity. Contemplate the republic, turn back to the late empire, and you will be convinced that these two periods stand on opposite sides of an historical chasm too wide to be bridged by any plausible remarks about the consequences of constitutional changes or revolutions in religious practice.

The assumptions of causal investigation thus have only dwindling pertinence in the history of the later empire. This influences the way Gibbon uses his chapter endings, which in Volume I were the forum for causal insights. The concluding section of Chapter XLVI deals with Heraclius' victories over the Persians from 622 to 628, but the chapter's ending modulates from a triumphant key:

While the emperor triumphed at Constantinople or Jerusalem, an obscure town on the confines of Syria was pillaged by the Saracens, and they cut in pieces some troops who advanced to its relief: an ordinary and trifling occurrence, had it not been the prelude of a mighty revolution. These robbers were the apostles of Mahomet; their fanatic valour had emerged from the desert; and in the last eight years of his reign, Heraclius lost to the Arabs, the same provinces which he had rescued from the Persians.[54]

The inconsequence of Heraclius' vigour reinforces our awareness of this period's reluctance to yield the expected effects to what seem sufficient causes, and casts over the very idea of historical causation a shadow deepened by the glance at Mahomet. In allowing his chapter to set on a glimpse of this rising figure Gibbon recognises the demands made by the multiplicity of the past. This is a moment of both triumph and weakness for the empire. To which of these should the historian give priority, thus making it the 'reality' the causes of which must be accounted for? The future belongs to Mahomet, but always to follow the victor is disastrously to narrow the fullness of what was. Yet, if both the strength and the weakness were simultaneously 'real', is it possible to offer a coherent causal explanation of this oxymoron? A similar challenge is issued at the end of Chapter L:

After the reign of three caliphs, the throne was transported from Medina to the valley of Damascus and the banks of the Tigris; the holy cities were violated by impious war;

[54] *The Decline and Fall*, IV.530–1.

Arabia was ruled by the rod of a subject, perhaps of a stranger; and the Bedoweens of the desert, awakening from their dream of dominion, resumed their old and solitary independence.[55]

The impermanence of the rise of Arabia is a notable instance of a phenomenon on which we have already commented; the reluctance of the history of the later empire to be moulded, its tendency to lapse back into its previous shape and course. But the concluding detail of the Bedoweens' rejection of ambition brings the subject of the narrative close to the experience of the historian. Gibbon, too, is awakening from his dream of dominion over the past with its idle promise of dominating history through a perception of causality and, in his new sensitivity to the unmanipulable particularity of the individual historical fact, is also embracing the old and solitary. The extravagant disproportion he uncovers between possible causes and possible effects seems at once a parody of causal explanation and a gasp of admiration at the strange intimacies of this time:

. . . the lance of an Arab might have changed the history of the world.

The disorders of the moral, are sometimes corrected by those of the physical, world; and an acrimonious humour falling on a single fibre of one man, may prevent or suspend the misery of nations.[56]

In these moments we can see what has been aptly called the 'dépérissement du système causal' of *The Decline and Fall*.[57]

What are the implications of this waning of confidence in causality as a means of understanding the past for Gibbon's attitude to his own past work, in which causality had occupied such a sovereign position? We know that Gibbon never repudiated the hypothesis of the causes of Roman decline he had defended in 1776 – as we have seen, he makes a point of standing by it in his *Memoirs* (although it is perhaps significant that there he says carefully that the rise of Christianity is 'connected' with the fall of the empire). However, we have also seen how the explanation of the decline of Rome in terms of Christianity is complicated and corrected in the *General Observations* at the end of Volume III. That process of implicit revision is now taken a stage further in Gibbon's account of the rise and fall of the caliphate.

The parallels between this concentrated instance of prosperity and decadence and the larger example of the same cycle in which it is simply an episode are whispered in an allusion to Tacitus:

Amrou, the conqueror of Egypt, himself an army, was the first who saluted the new

[55] *The Decline and Fall*, V.275.
[56] *The Decline and Fall*, V.225 and VI.323: compare Montesquieu's denial of such minute causes (above, p. 11). It is only when causality is both proportionate and regular that it becomes an object of rational inquiry (see, e.g., de Crousaz, *A New Treatise of the Art of Thinking*, I.437 and Hume, *Treatise of Human Nature*, p. 651).
[57] Michel Baridon, *Edward Gibbon et le Mythe de Rome*, pp. 655–66.

monarch, and divulged the dangerous secret, that the Arabian caliphs might be created elsewhere than in the city of the prophet.[58]

Compare this sentence from the *Historiae*: 'evulgato imperii arcano posse principem alibi quam Romae fieri.'[59] Gibbon's echo of a penetrating and famous judgement about an early stage in the decline of Rome brings the two régimes of empire and caliphate together; a closeness which is increased when the causes of the decay of the caliphate unmistakably hark back to his own earlier comments on the collapse of Rome.

According to Gibbon, there are three main causes of the decline of the caliphate – first, the outrages of the soldiery:

But the nations of the East had been taught to trample on the successors of the prophet; and the blessings of domestic peace were obtained by the relaxation of strength and discipline. So uniform are the mischiefs of military despotism, that I seem to repeat the story of the praetorians of Rome.[60]

Next comes the enthusiastic sect of the Carmathians, who do for the caliphate what Christianity did for Rome, and who 'may be considered as the second visible cause of the decline and fall of the empire of the caliphs': while the 'third and most obvious cause was the weight and magnitude of the empire itself' – an historical echo of Gibbon's borrowing from Montesquieu, that 'the decline of Rome was the natural and inevitable effect of immoderate greatness'.[61]

The most obvious way of reading this is to see it as Gibbon reconfirming the validity of his earlier account of Roman decline. After all, here the same causes are producing the same results, and it was just this regularity which was supposed to validate the philosophic investigation of causes. But elsewhere we have seen that Gibbon implicitly rejected such regularity by denying the continuity between past and present on which it depends. It is interesting, then, that the repetition of causes and effects during the decline of Byzantium is too perfect:

After a period of ten centuries the same revolution was renewed by a similar cause . . .

However splendid it may seem, a regular story of the crusades would exhibit the perpetual return of the same causes and effects . . .

. . . in the fifth and sixth crusades, the same causes, almost on the same ground, were productive of similar calamities.[62]

The penetrating gaze of the philosophic historian picked out the underlying causal regularity of history beneath the deceptively various carapace below which those of common intelligence could not see. But when the repetition of causes and effects floats on the surface of history, the vision of the philosophic

---

[58] *The Decline and Fall*, V.266.
[59] *Historiae*, I.4.
[60] *The Decline and Fall*, V.449.
[61] *The Decline and Fall*, V.451–2, V.452 and III.631.
[62] *The Decline and Fall*, V.336–7, VI.75 and 115.

historian becomes superficial, even banal. The cartoon-like speed with which causes and effects are repeated in the history of the crusades makes an awareness of such causal regularity not the masterful knowledge of the philosopher, but a bauble for shallow minds. If you want to find causal regularity in history, Gibbon implies, then it is not far to seek: and his own account of the fall of the caliphate is an example of how such regularity can be found. But Gibbon makes us aware that to repose in such an explanation is to be too easily satisfied when he presents the accelerated drama of the rise and decline of the caliphate against the backdrop of the lingering empire of Byzantium, and the rebuke it administers to systems of causal explanation.[63] Byzantium, in its unwieldiness, its harbouring of virulent religious sects, and its rapacious soldiery, is a prey to all the debilitating causes which despatch the caliphate so swiftly; and its massive and inexplicable presence in the background of the portrait of the caliphate effectively questions the validity of that analysis. Gibbon crossed swords with Warburton, but here he is following the bishop's advice:

But our folly has ever been, and is likely to continue, to judge of antiquity by a modern standard: when, if we would form reasonable ideas on this subject, we should compare the parts of it with one another.[64]

Gibbon deliberately casts his deduction of the demise of the empire of the caliphs in the mould of his earlier discussion of Roman decline, a discussion whose premises and procedures have already been eroded by the groundless duration of the lower empire. The result of the montage of this resurrected idiom with the incomprehensible endurance of Byzantium is to make those confident ascriptions of cause and effect seem a glib evasion of the largest problems posed by history. By the 1780s Gibbon had little in common with William Fleetwood, the apologist for miracles, but he might have agreed with his account of how causal regularity leads to intellectual sloth:

When Natural Causes still produce their Natural Effects, according to the setled and establish'd Laws of the Creation; and Men persue their Inclinations and Desires, according to their Powers and Opportunities, and every thing proceeds uninterrupted in its usual, regular, expected Course; the world of standers-by grow, in a manner, sleepy, dull, and unaffected at what passes; and either reason little, or amiss . . .[65]

Gibbon's account of the caliphate is in fact a banishment of these simple ideas of causality, and a quiet ironising of his own past practice.[66]

---

[63] The anomalousness of Byzantium must have seemed even greater, given the denial of the possibility of political stasis by eighteenth-century thinkers: see Adam Ferguson, *Essay on the History of Civil Society* (1767) and H. Home, Lord Kames, *Sketches of the History of Man* (1774).

[64] *Julian*, p. x.

[65] *An Essay upon Miracles*, p. 231.

[66] Michel Baridon makes the good point that the projects Gibbon entertained after completing *The Decline and Fall* did not entail any elaborate investigation of causality: it is plausible to explain this in terms of the unsettling of his faith in both the practicality and use of the analysis of causes (*Edward Gibbon et le Mythe de Rome*, p. 665).

This conviction that even what we congratulate ourselves on as our most profound ideas of causality do not go far towards explaining the past turns the final review of causality in *The Decline and Fall* into a series of chronological periods and epochs. The trajectory of decline is splintered:

> The various causes and progressive effects are connected with many of the events most interesting in human annals: the artful policy of the Caesars, who long maintained the name and image of a free republic; the disorder of military despotism; the rise, establishment, and sects of Christianity; the foundation of Constantinople; the division of the monarchy; the invasion and settlements of the Barbarians of Germany and Scythia; the institutions of the civil law; the character and religion of Mahomet; the temporal sovereignty of the popes; the restoration and decay of the Western empire of Charlemagne; the crusades of the Latins in the East; the conquests of the Saracens and Turks; the ruin of the Greek empire; the state and revolutions of Rome in the middle age.[67]

As, for instance, the achronological arrangement of the *Esprit des Loix* showed, to investigate historical causation was to be freed from the linear sequence of time and to be able to range at liberty over the past. Released from narrative, the philosophic historian could emphasise functional connexion and ignore the accidental succession of event by event. But Gibbon, 'conscious of his own imperfections', concludes his history on just such a note of succession. He ends by offering not a key to the understanding of Roman decline (the phenomenon is far too complex for that), but – leaving the 'various causes and progressive effects' unstated – a list of the important events on which anyone aspiring to understand the decline of Rome must reflect.

To take the measure of how thoroughly Gibbon's ideas on historical causation have been complicated and deepened, we might cite a passage from Hume's essay 'Of the Balance of Power' in which he sets out the natural history of empire:

> Enormous monarchies, such as EUROPE at present is threatened with, are, probably, destructive to human nature; in their progress, in their continuance, and even in their downfal, which never can be very distant from their establishment. The military genius which aggrandized the monarchy, soon leaves the court, the capital, and the center of such a government; while the wars are carried on at a great distance, and interest so small a part of the state. The antient nobility, whose affections attach them to their sovereign, live all at court; and never will accept of military employments, which would carry them to remote and barbarous frontiers, where they are distant both from their pleasure and their fortune. The arms of the state, must, therefore, be trusted to mercenary strangers, without zeal, without attachment, without honour; ready on every occasion to turn them against the prince, and join each desperate malcontent, who offers pay and plunder. This is the necessary progress of human affairs . . . And the melancholy fate of the ROMAN emperors, from the same cause, is renewed over and over again, till the final dissolution of the monarchy.[68]

---

[67] *The Decline and Fall*, VI.645–6.   [68] *Essays and Treatises*, II.122–3.

Gibbon owned many copies of Hume's essays, and there are undoubtedly moments in *The Decline and Fall* when he shadows Hume's Polybian ideas on the naturalness of decline's following on from prosperity, just as in Chapter XV he is influenced by Hume's *Natural History of Religion*.[69] But that closeness is not identity. Hume finds the causes of the decline of Rome, as of every empire, transparent. However, it is the phenomenon indicated by his final sentence, which he offers as a clinching illustration of his thesis, that Gibbon finds decidedly opaque; 'And the melancholy fate of the ROMAN emperors, from the same cause, is renewed over and over again, till the final dissolution of the monarchy.' It is precisely the long separation of ultimate dissolution from decay, despite the frequent recurrence of the supposed causes of the demise of empires, which renders the history of Byzantium so complex for Gibbon, and which further distances him from philosophic history.

[69] For Gibbon's copies of Hume, see G. Keynes, *Gibbon's Library*, p. 156.

14

Structure

Matter grows under our hands. – Let no man say, – 'Come – I'll write a *duodecimo*.'

Sterne

History is a *Structure*; she demands Order and Connexion as all other Buildings; and her Materials without that, would make but a tumultuous Heap of Sand without Lime.

Le Moyne

In 'Of the Rise and Progress of the Arts and Sciences' Hume points out a literary pitfall which lies in wait for the historian committed to investigating causality:

But when the event is supposed to proceed from certain and stable causes, he may then display his ingenuity, in assigning these causes; and as a man of any subtilty can never be at a loss in this particular, he has thereby an opportunity of swelling his volumes, and discovering his profound knowledge in observing what escapes the vulgar and ignorant.[1]

Gibbon's experience is the reverse of this. It is the frustration of his attempts to grasp the causation of history which swells *The Decline and Fall*, just as the perfected structure of Volume I was the fruit of the certainty Gibbon felt in 1776 about the cause of Roman decline. John Burrow has recorded Gibbon's proud insistence 'on the coherence of the entire work'.[2] But one must be careful not to press the historian's phrase 'the unity of design and composition' too far: as Gibbon uses it, it denotes little more than his resolve not to be seduced irrecoverably from his subject of the Roman empire. It certainly does not denote a perfection of structure such as we found in Volume I. As we read through the final instalment of *The Decline and Fall*, we find an enforced but fruitful lapse from coherence and the supplanting of the ideal of unity in Gibbon's mind by other historiographic values.

The Decline and Fall has been extravagantly praised for the perfection of its structure.[3] Yet only two of its admirers have provided a detailed description of what they find so admirable: Harold Bond and Michel Baridon.[4]

The keynote of Harold Bond's argument is that in 'considering the

---

[1] *Essays and Treatises*, I.187.
[2] *Gibbon*, p. 36.
[3] See above, pp. 43–4.
[4] Harold L. Bond, *The Literary Art of Edward Gibbon*, 'The structure', pp. 49–67; Michel Baridon, *Edward Gibbon et le Mythe de Rome*, 'L'architecture du Decline and Fall: volumes et structures', pp. 749–56.

structure [of *The Decline and Fall*] , we shall find that although the first volumes were published many years before the last were even written, there is a unity of form in the whole which is nothing less than astonishing'.[5] On the strength of an examination of the disposition of the history's chapters, Bond concludes that *The Decline and Fall* has the structure of an epideictic oration, as described by Aristotle in his *Rhetoric*.[6] The argument is developed with care and learning. But I believe it to be misguided for four reasons. First, I think it improbable that Gibbon would have so flouted literary propriety as to try to cast a work published over twenty years in the mould of a genre which it is clear Aristotle supposes will be delivered on a single occasion and in a single sweep. Secondly, even supposing that Gibbon would look to Aristotle for guidance about how to construct his history, he is unlikely to have chosen the epideictic oration as a model, since he explicitly says that rhetoric is inimical to historiography.[7] Thirdly, Aristotle says that an epideictic oration can admit only 'divided narration', by which he means material cited according to the demands of argument (e.g. in order to praise a man), and without respect to chronology; but we know that in fact the proportion of chronological narrative in *The Decline and Fall* rises as the history proceeds.[8] Fourthly, Bond assumes that the changes in Gibbon's ideas as he worked at his history augmented his understanding of the phenomenon of Roman decline without disrupting his previous suppositions and hypotheses; hence the serial publication of *The Decline and Fall* does not trouble Bond's belief in its unity.[9] Many English books of the eighteenth century were published either serially or initially in incomplete form.[10] But we need to distinguish those works (such as *The Dunciad* or *Tristram Shandy*) in which the subsequent instalments or revisions either elaborate and complete the original design, or are in harmony with such of the work which is extant, from those other works (of which I believe *The Decline and Fall* to be one) in which the later writing

---

[5] *The Literary Art of Edward Gibbon*, p. 49.

[6] *The Literary Art of Edward Gibbon*, p. 57.

[7] Consider 'many experiments were made before I could hit the middle tone between a dull Chronicle and a Rhetorical declamation' (*Memoirs*, p. 155). The distinctiveness of the tone of historiography was acknowledged by others (Warburton, *A Critical and Philosophical Enquiry into the Causes of Prodigies and Miracles*, p. 100 and Wotton, *The History of Rome from the Death of Antoninus Pius to the Death of Severus Alexander*, sig. A7v).

[8] *Ancient Literary Criticism*, ed. D. A. Russell and M. Winterbottom, p. 163. Michel Baridon has indicated the shifting proportions of narrative and demonstration in his valuable analysis of the changing nature of the chapters in *The Decline and Fall* (*Edward Gibbon et le Mythe de Rome*, p. 836).

[9] 'Gibbon, working on the later section of his history, gained greater perspective and a deeper understanding of the meaning of the whole. Indeed, one can assert that the structure of the work remained fluid and unset until the final paragraph was written' (*The Literary Art of Edward Gibbon*, pp. 49–50). I find it hard to reconcile the almost mystical idea of literary structure which Bond seems to have here with his basic contention that *The Decline and Fall* has a structure as definite as that of an epideictic oration.

[10] On this aspect of book publication in the eighteenth century, see Pat Rogers, *The Augustan Vision*, pp. 29–30.

both augments and quarrels with what has gone before. I have already assembled some of the evidence for thinking that the later volumes of Gibbon's history are, in their assumptions and procedures, at variance with their predecessors. Where we find such variance, it seems to me unlikely that we are reading a work in which the additions simply fulfil the design foreshadowed in the foundations.

Michel Baridon also begins by voicing his certainties: 'Il n'est pas facile de trouver dans tout le XVIII° siècle plus magistrale illustration du *lucidus ordo*.'[11] However, the discussion which follows is not the happiest section of this uneven, but immensely valuable, study. Its grip on fact is faltering; it is odd to say that 'c'est à la fin de 1779 . . . que le *Decline and Fall* reçut sa forme définitive' when Gibbon decided to write the final three volumes only in 1782.[12] But one is most disappointed by the lack of substance in the discussion. Baridon points out that Gibbon alternates 'statiques' and 'dynamiques' chapters and assembles quotations to suggest that he had a strong appreciation of structure, particularly in the realm of architecture. But why should such an alternation of chapters create a sense of structure rather than just the pleasure of variety, when (outside Volume I) it is extremely irregular and not tied to developments of the argument? And is not the citing of Gibbon's tastes beside the point? The question is not what were his preferences in the matter of structure, but what were his achievements.

My own conviction is that, once we have left behind the tight ordering of Volume I, *The Decline and Fall* becomes increasingly loose, without, however, descending into incoherence. This diminishing of formal control arises from the growing recalcitrance of Gibbon's material. Its intractability impedes his aspirations towards literary shapeliness, while also indicating that such shapeliness could be realised only at the expense of the material it was supposed to reveal.

The neo-classic idea that perfect literary structure is the fruit of successful intention is compactly expressed in 'A General View of the Epick Poem . . . Extracted from Bossu' which introduces Pope's *Odyssey*:

In every design which a man deliberately undertakes, the end he proposes is the first thing in his mind, and that by which he governs the whole work, and all its parts.[13]

Only such works could possess what Johnson calls 'that power of attracting the attention, which a well-connected plan produces' and avoid the mockery Shaftesbury is sure awaits art which neglects 'the natural Rules of proportion': 'It must have a Body and Parts proportionable: or the very Vulgar will

---

[11] *Edward Gibbon et le Mythe de Rome*, p. 749.

[12] *Edward Gibbon et le Mythe de Rome*, p. 750. For the announcement of Gibbon's determination to compose the final instalment, see J. E. Norton, *Bibliography*, p. 57.

[13] *The Twickenham Edition of the Poems of Alexander Pope*, IX.5. Compare Dryden's conviction that 'the last line is to be considered in the composition of the first' ('An Account of *Annus Mirabilis*'; also Shaftesbury, *Characteristicks*, I.143).

not fail to criticize the Work, when *it has neither Head nor Tail.*'[14] Gibbon is perhaps echoing Shaftesbury when he boasts to Sheffield of the integrity of his first volume:

Your apprehensions of a precipitate work &c, are perfectly groundless. I should be much more addicted to a contrary extreme. The *head* is now printing? true: but it was write last year and the year before. the first Chapter has been composed de nouveau *three times*, the second *twice* and all the others have undergone reviews, corrections &c. As to the tail it is perfectly formed. . .[15]

But, broadening the prospect from the first volume to the work in its entirety, we know that the head of *The Decline and Fall* had been in print for some six years before the history's tail was even definitely contemplated, let alone fully formed.[16] It is hard to avoid the conclusion that the whole of *The Decline and Fall* was not present in Gibbon's mind before he wrote its opening words.[17] I now propose to review the discernible traces of looseness in the structure of the history. Looking back on his puerile efforts in the historical line, Gibbon comments:

Such were my juvenile discoveries; at a riper age I no longer presume to connect the Greek, the Jewish, and the Egyptian antiquities which are lost in a distant cloud: nor is this the only instance, in which the belief and knowledge of the child are superseded by the more rational ignorance of the man.[18]

Gibbon's ultimate association of historiographic maturity with a tolerance of heterogeneity (its obverse being the juvenile tendency to forge connexion irrespective of its pertinence) is a reassuring thought to bear in mind as we consider, from a variety of standpoints, the steadily more open texture of *The Decline and Fall.*

There is an obvious respect in which we can see how *The Decline and Fall* grew under Gibbon's hand and exceeded his design. He feels initially that 'The execution of such an extensive plan, as I have traced out . . . might perhaps be comprehended in about four volumes.'[19] The resulting set of six volumes shows how such long perspectives foreshorten. Further evidence of how Gibbon had misjudged his subject when setting out, of how he had not mastered and foreseen the difficulties of the terrain, emerges in Chapter

---

[14] 'Life of Milton', *Works*, VII.139; *Characteristicks*, I.145–6; see also Gray, *Poems and Memoirs*, p. 142. This ideal of structure persisted through the century: compare Blair, *Lectures on Rhetoric and Belles Lettres*, I.21–2.

[15] *Letters*, II.81.

[16] Volume I was published on 17 February 1776. Gibbon's resolution to compose the last three volumes was announced in the preface (dated 1 March 1782) to the fifth edition of the first volume. This dating is confirmed by his commonplace book (*Bibliography*, pp. 37 and 57).

[17] Note the comment in his *Memoirs* that 'so flexible is the title of my history that the final aera might be fixed at my own choice: and I long hesitated whether I should be content with the three Volumes, the fall of the Western Empire, which fulfilled my first engagement with the public' (*Memoirs*, p. 164).

[18] *Memoirs*, p. 56.

[19] *The Decline and Fall*, I.viii: I.vi.

XLVIII, when he diverges from the plan he had traced out in Volume I. The period of *The Decline and Fall* had originally been divided into three sections: from Trajan to the subversion of the empire in the West; from Justinian to Charlemagne; and from the revival of the West to the fall of Constantinople. Reviewing his actual progress, Gibbon finds that the natural divisions of his subject fall differently from how he had anticipated:

I have now deduced from Trajan to Constantine, from Constantine to Heraclius, the regular series of the Roman emperors . . . but a period of more than eight hundred years still separates me from the term of my labours, the taking of Constantinople by the Turks.[20]

The periods outlined in the plan are not observed in the production. Moreover, with the hindsight of experience, Gibbon recognises that the past demands to be considered in smaller sections than he had foreseen. The original design had viewed the subject in distant prospect and had divided the large slope of decline into three smaller parts, each of which begins with the false dawn of temporary recovery and ends in deepened catastrophe. The historian of the 1780s, immersed in his material and slowed by the unexpected density of the past, does not find the divisions predicted in 1776 by his philosophic forebear. In his *Memoirs*, Gibbon records how, reckoning the space taken up by what he had accomplished and glancing ahead to what remained, he abandoned his temperate and gentlemanly habits of work:

But when I computed the remainder of my time, and my task, it was apparent, that, according to the season of publication, the delay of a month would be productive of that of a year. I was now straining for the goal; and in the last winter many evenings were borrowed from the social pleasures of Lausanne. I could now wish that a pause, an interval had been allowed for a serious revisal.[21]

This acceleration (which Gibbon ultimately regretted) involves a change of method. In order the more thoroughly to 'explore the causes and effects of the decline and fall of the Eastern Empire' Gibbon abandons the annalistic structure which would have spun 'a prolix and slender thread . . . through many a volume' and instead organises his narrative on a geographical basis, beginning with Byzantium itself, and then considering in turn the ten nations or groups of nations that contribute to its downfall.[22] Thinking back to this pressured time, Gibbon defends his expedient:

It was not till after many designs and many tryals, that I preferred, as I still prefer, the method of grouping my picture by nations; and the seeming neglect of Chronological order is surely compensated by the superior merits of interest and perspicuity.[23]

[20] *The Decline and Fall*, V.1.	[21] *Memoirs*, p. 179.
[22] *The Decline and Fall*, V.4 and V.1.	[23] *Memoirs*, p. 179.

We should carefully note, given the reputation of *The Decline and Fall* as a flawless example of literary architectonics, that Gibbon refers to 'many designs and many tryals'; this turbulence, as we shall see, is not transcended in the resulting work. Gibbon's tone here, too, is not quite calm: 'as I still prefer' and 'surely' betray a need to justify to himself and to us the correctness of the decision he took in order to bring *The Decline and Fall* to completion. For it was indeed a drastic decision; a readoption of the philosophic features of a subordination of chronology and a concentration on causes as a means of excluding seductive and wayward material, despite the gradually stiffening doubts and reservations about the restrictive effect such measures have on the historian's sympathetic imagination. Only by trying to recover his old, philosophic domination of history can Gibbon see his way clear to completing his design.

In one respect, that design is indeed completed. The promised material is fitted into the proposed two volumes. The word 'structure', however, may denote simply the order of materials in a narrative, or it may take account of the function of those materials in an argument. In this second sense, it refers to the organisation, as opposed to the mere arrangement, of a work, and it was just such a structure which Gibbon had created in Volume I.[24] However, it is only in the former, low sense of structure that *The Decline and Fall* completes Gibbon's revised plan; for the causal demonstration Gibbon's firmer grip on his material was intended to foster wilts, as we have seen, when the resistance of the past to such inquiry increases and when his subject exerts greater deforming pressure on his shaping intentions. Gibbon records 'a rough draft of the present History' composed in 1771: we are closest to the truth when we think of *The Decline and Fall* not as a flawless example of neo-classic structural expertise, but as a work which even much preparatory rough-hewing could not bring to balance and stability.[25]

Gibbon's habit of speaking about *The Decline and Fall* in his letters as an edifice shows his awareness of how the structure of the history has been loosened. In the journal Gibbon kept while on the Grand Tour he also likens a work he has in hand, the 'Nomina Gentesque Antiquae Italiae', to a building:

J'ai revû la Dissertation de Muratori avec soin. Je me [suis] donnè la peine d'extraire de la table de bronze les rentes auxquelles un si grand nombre des Citoyens de Veleia s'etoient assujetis et les fonds sur lesquels on les avoit assignées. C'est un travail sec et ingrat, mais quand on construit un Edifice il faut en creuser les fondemens. L'on est obligè de faire le role de macon aussi bien que celui d'Architecte. J'espere pouvoir tirer quelque chose de cette espèce de recensement.[26]

[24] It is in this context that the ambiguity of Pope's term 'end' ('the end which he proposes'), meaning both conclusion and intention, is so apt. For Pope, structure is intimately connected with intention, and so he tends to think of structure in its 'high' sense. Blair demands 'high' structure of historiography (*Lectures on Rhetoric and Belles Lettres*, II.261–2).

[25] *The Decline and Fall*, III.169 n. 86.

[26] *Gibbon's Journey from Geneva to Rome*, p. 129. For the 'Nomina Gentesque', see *Miscellaneous Works*, IV.153–326.

This, one might say, is the standard use of the figure. By likening his book to a building Gibbon suggests a cemented security of research and presentation. The author is a mason as well as an architect. By dressing his materials he turns their durability from an impediment into an asset his own structure will enjoy.[27] If we look at the way Gibbon uses these images in the 1770s and 1780s, we find opposite connotations:

. . . deux gros Volumes in quarto, et l'assemblage des materiaux, l'echaffaudage, les souvereins lui ont couté encore plus de tems et travail que l'edifice meme.

. . . a great book like a great house was never yet finished at the given time.

I had some hopes of compleating it [*The Decline and Fall*] this year, but let no man who builds a house, or writes a book presume to say when he will have finished.

I am building a great book, which besides the three stories already exposed to the public eye will have three stories more before we reach the roof and battlements.

My great building is, as it were, compleated . . .

After building a great house, a thousand little alterations, improvements and ornaments present themselves to the architect.[28]

How light the tone of these comments is after the youth's earnest note to himself! When Gibbon is writing *The Decline and Fall* the figurative house which his letters describe is no longer four-square and solid, but ramshackle; and he uses the image when his book is resisting his architectural aims, rather than when it proves amenable to them. In the twenty years since he quarried Muratori, his use of this image, and also perhaps his understanding of, and esteem for, 'literary structure', have changed. These images now suggest not a completed and unshakeable construction, but a recalcitrance which can never be absolutely overcome and an assembly which can be only 'as it were, compleated', immediately inviting 'a thousand little alterations, improvements and ornaments'. In the midst of composition and at the point of emerging from it, Gibbon uses the image of the house or building not to crown the success of his bids for structural perfection, but wryly to indicate their subsidence.[29]

---

[27] D. M. Oliver, in his 'Gibbon's use of architecture as symbol', draws his understanding of the significance of architectural imagery in the eighteenth century from A. R. Humphreys: 'Yet architecture becomes the ''mistress-art'' of the Augustans; in England ''its styles . . . paid homage to an ideal antiquity, to the harmony and order which humanism asserted. Its ideals of balance, lucidity, and controlled power were those that Augustan literature looked to as the standards of human nature'' ' (p. 78); and he holds that Gibbon always uses architectural imagery in this simple way. Compare Shaftesbury, *Characteristicks*, II.285.

[28] *Letters*, II.262; III.40; III.44; III.59; III.64; and III.75. Compare the opening paragraph of Dryden's 'Preface' to *Fables, Ancient and Modern* (1700).

[29] Michel Baridon has written that 'Gibbon . . . a de la littérature une conception de bâtisseur, de maçon, et . . . sait construire un livre avec un sens infaillible des structures' (*Edward Gibbon et le Mythe de Rome*, p. 806); this seems to me accurate for the young scholar, but increasingly untrue for the historian.

The weakening of Gibbon's ability to mould his material into a legible form, such as that he had achieved in 1776, springs from the heterogeneity of the centuries with which he has to deal. It arises out of the fissiparousness and the various impurity in the past which is now so prevalent that it cannot be dismissed as the mere outer rind of history which the historian must peel back to disclose its inner unity.[30] However, not only does Gibbon endure a greater diversity in his material; he also comes to admit it. This greater tolerance is expressed as a new willingness to allow the impurity of his material to be reflected in the divisions of the narrative; for instance, in his chapters and his footnotes.

In the first two instalments, the history of the Church and of religion are filtered out into separate chapters, but in 1788 we find for the first time sacred and secular material mingling promiscuously in the same chapter.[31] The diversity of Gibbon's material in these centuries and its inhibiting of any attempt to sort it out and organise it under discrete headings of 'ecclesiastical' and 'political' means that the nature of his chapters has changed. They have lost the character they had in 1776, the character of points in a systematic plotting of the past. They are now mingled entities which serve more the purposes of record than argument and which are forced to accommodate the heterogeneity of the past at the price of their own single focus. Despite Gibbon's determination to subordinate chronology in 1788, his chapters are now much more simply the verbal account of segments of time than they were in 1776. They do not so much organise the past as follow it.

Gibbon also responds to the multivalency of history in his use of footnotes. In Volume I he will create a discrepancy between the periphrasis of the text, and the simultaneous forthrightness and decent obscurity of a learned language we discover in the note, but always with a single end (often a joke) in view. Thus Gibbon ascribes to Faustina, the libidinous wife of Marcus Aurelius, a surprising acuteness in the estimation of character:

Faustina, the daughter of Pius and the wife of Marcus, has been as much celebrated for her gallantries as for her beauty. The grave simplicity of the philosopher was ill-calculated to engage her wanton levity, or to fix that unbounded passion for variety, which often discovered personal merit in the meanest of mankind.

The footnote seals the joke:

Faustina satis constat apud Cayetam, *conditiones* sibi et nauticas et gladiatorias, elegisse. *Hist. August.* p. 30. Lampridius explains the sort of merit which Faustina chose, and the *conditions* which she exacted. *Hist. August.* p. 102.[32]

---

[30] In a letter Gibbon points out the greater 'variety' in the final instalment of *The Decline and Fall* (*Letters*, III.100).

[31] Examples of such heterogeneous chapters are XLIX, LX, LXVII and LXVI. Earlier, pure chapters are XV, XVI, XX, XXI, XXVIII and XXXVII: they also recur in 1788 – e.g. XLVII and LIV.

[32] *The Decline and Fall*, I.85: I.102 and I.xiv n. 2: I.102 n. 2. First edition: '. . . philosopher, was . . .'.

Gibbon disperses a variety of tones and manners between text and notes in Volume I, but that variety always serves a fundamental unity of purpose. In 1788, however, the discrepancy between note and text is much more radical. It now reflects a diversity of viewpoints on the past which Gibbon cannot contain within a single voice:

> The Hungarian language . . . bears a close and clear affinity to the idioms of the Fennic race . . .

But, in the note, the divided historian reveals a different truth:

> The affinity is indeed striking, but the lists are short, the words are purposely chosen; and I read in the learned Bayer . . . that although the Hungarian has adopted many Fennic words (innumeras voces), it essentially differs toto genio et naturâ.[33]

Gibbon is here not tidying up his text, as he did in 1776: what we have now is a completely alternative point of view demanded by the indefeasibly equivocal nature of the past, which impairs the large shapeliness of *The Decline and Fall*, as well as this smaller aspect of its tidiness.

Gibbon's revisions of his design indicate the difficulties which hindered his attempts to realise the clean lines of form he had glimpsed before becoming immersed in his labours. His changing attitude towards his chapter (which suggests that he eventually grouped his material less by argument and more by chronology), and his revision of the function of the footnote, testify to a certain complacency concerning the distension of *The Decline and Fall*. The relaxation of the philosophic vigilance which had watched over Volume I and admitted only such material as contributed to the overall explanatory thrust of the volume is nowhere more evident than in the development of his use of anecdote.

In the *Siècle de Louis XIV* Voltaire had stipulated the criterion against which the philosophic historian would test anecdotes, lest his historiography degenerate into mere scandalmongering:

> Les anecdotes sont un champ resserré où l'on glane après la vaste moisson de l'histoire; ce sont de petits détails longtemps cachés, et de là vient le nom d'anecdotes; ils intéressent le public quand ils concernent des personnages illustres . . . Les anecdotes les plus utiles et plus précieuses sont les écrits secrets que laissent les grands princes, quand la candeur de leur âme se manifeste dans ces monuments . . .[34]

The enlightened historian does not share the undirected curiosity of 'le public', but instead brings the anecdotes he encounters to the bar of utility. In order to earn inclusion, they must be revelatory and speaking details. Gibbon frequently introduces anecdotes by flourishing their expressive force and value:

---

[33] *The Decline and Fall*, V.550 and V.550 n. 22; see also *The Decline and Fall*, VI.355 and VI.355 n. 55.

[34] *Œuvres Complètes*, XIV.421.

I should not be apprehensive of deviating from my subject, if it were in my power to delineate the private life of the conquerors of Italy, and I shall relate with pleasure the adventurous gallantry of Autharis, which breathes the true spirit of chivalry and romance.

Among the hostilities of the Arabs, the Franks, and the Greeks, in the southern Italy, I shall select two or three anecdotes expressive of their national manners.[35]

But when we look closely at the anecdotes themselves, these assertions of illustrative value seem more like camouflage. The story of Leo and Attalus, at the end of Volume III, already indicates how the substance of Gibbon's anecdotes diverges from their overt purpose. Theodoric, having subdued the Auvergne, took hostages amongst whom (so Gregory of Tours records) was the noble Attalus. His escape is contrived by the faithful slave Leo, who insinuates himself into the barbarian's household and betrays his trust. Gibbon recounts the crisis of their flight:

Their apprehensions urged them to leave their horses on the banks of the Meuse; they swam the river, wandered three days in the adjacent forest, and subsisted only by the accidental discovery of a wild plum-tree. As they lay concealed in a dark thicket, they heard the noise of horses; they were terrified by the angry countenance of their master, and they anxiously listened to his declaration, that, if he could seize the guilty fugitives, one of them he would cut in pieces with his sword, and would expose the other on a gibbet. At length, Attalus, and his faithful Leo, reached the friendly habitation of a presbyter of Rheims . . .[36]

There is a marked disjunction here between Gibbon's firmly decorous vocabulary ('the guilty fugitives' may express the *sense* of the enraged barbarian, but the diction is the historian's) and the imaginative vivacity which we can discover lying behind the words without finding expression in them. If we juxtapose the original account of the episode from Gregory of Tours, the way Gibbon is enthralled by the anecdote, and at the same time disdains it, will be clear:

venientes autem ad Mosellam fluvium, cum transirent illum, & detinerentur à quibusdam, relictis equitibus & vestimentis, enatantes super parma positi amnem, in ulteriorem egressi sunt ripam. et inter obscura noctis ingressi silvam, latuerunt. tertia enim nox advenerat, quòd nullum cibum gustantes iter terebant. tunc nutu Dei reperta arbore plena pomis, quam vulgò prunum vocant, comedunt; & parumper sustentati ingressi sunt iter Campaniae: quibus pergentibus, audiunt pedibulum equitum currentium, dixeruntque: *prosternamur terrae, ne appareamus hominibus venientibus.* et ecce ex improviso stirps rubi magnus adfuit, post quem transeuntes, projecerunt se terrae cum gladiis evaginatis, scilicet ut si adverterentur, confestim se quasi ab improbis framea defensarent: verumtamen cum venissent in locum illum coram stirpe spineo restiterunt: dixitque unus, dum equi urinam projicerent: *vae mihi, quia fugiunt hi detestabiles, nec reperiri possunt: verùm dico per salutem meam, quid si invenirentur, unum patibulo*

---

[35] *The Decline and Fall*, IV.449 and V.585. Gibbon reveals his taste for anecdotes in a letter to Sheffield (*Letters*, II.380).

[36] *The Decline and Fall*, III.601–2.

condemnari, & alium gladiorum ictibus in frustra discerpi juberem. erat enim barbarus ille qui
haec aiebat, dominus eorum, de Remensi urbe veniens, & hos inquirens: & reperisset
utique in via, si nox obstaculum non praebuisset.[37]

Gibbon has obviously pruned Gregory's version hard; he has, for instance,
no room for the urinating horses. Thus it is all the more remarkable that one
detail of the account in *The Decline and Fall* is of Gibbon's invention: 'they
were terrified by the angry countenance of their master' is not paralleled in
the source. Behind Gibbon's obvious scorn for Gregory's farmyard latinity
and inability to discard unmeaning detail, we find an imaginative enrichment, a vivifying elaboration, of the anecdote. Is it accidental that Gibbon
should choose so to invigorate this moment of precarious liberty, given that
the anecdote is for him a temporary release from the burden of sustained,
analytical narration? Certainly the abruptness with which he shoulders that
burden again on closing the anecdote is extreme. The illustrative value he
squeezes from the episode by making its crudeness a measure of decline gives
no hint of the momentary imaginative stimulus it seems Gibbon found in the
event:

Perhaps this singular adventure, which is marked with so many circumstances of truth
and nature, was related by Attalus himself, to his cousin, or nephew, the first historian
of the Franks. Gregory of Tours was born about sixty years after the death of Sidonius
Apollinaris; and their situation was almost similar, since each of them was a native
of Auvergne, a senator, and a bishop. The difference of their style and sentiments
may, therefore, express the decay of Gaul; and clearly ascertain how much, in so short
a space, the human mind had lost of its energy and refinement.[38]

It was the marks of truth and nature, and in particular of a truth equally pertinent to the historian and the fugitives, that had recommended the anecdote
to Gibbon. The comparison with Sidonius Apollinaris is a mere appendage
that smooths the historian's return to his sequential, analytic narrative by
pretending that he had never left it. It is a tail which wags the dog only if we
do not compare Gibbon's prose with its source, and notice the discreet inner
life of this passage, its hidden clue to the disposition of the composing
historian.

Gibbon's greater relaxation in 1788 about admitting anecdotal and
digressive material whose usefulness in the explanation of decline is unclear
but whose claims on grounds of 'singularity' are strong (we recall that the
escapade of Attalus and Leo is a 'singular adventure') is well illustrated by
the 'Digression on the Family of Courtenay' which concludes Chapter
LXI.[39] It is introduced by a gracious plea that is a justifiable transgression:

The purple of three emperors, who have reigned at Constantinople, will authorise

[37] Bouquet, ed., *Rerum Gallicarum et Francicarum Scriptores*, II.195.
[38] *The Decline and Fall*, III.602.
[39] *The Decline and Fall*, VI.211–20.

or excuse a digression on the origin and singular fortunes of the house of
COURTENAY . . .[40]

But this claim for the importance of the subject, for its scanted historical
magnitude, is not translated into a claim for its illustrative potency. The pithy
motto of the Courtenays ('Ubi lapsus! Quid feci?') indicates the difficulty of
discovering sufficient causes for their dramatic ruin, and so when Gibbon
undertakes to set out 'the causes of their disgrace' we have more of a tracing
of the successive stages of collapse than an analysis of why the collapse came
about.[41] Gibbon seems more concerned to explore the singularity of the past,
its vivid paradoxes and bizarre intimacies, than to explain how it arose: 'The
last emperors of Constantinople depended on the annual charity of Rome and
Naples.'[42]

Gibbon's responsiveness to the singularity of the Courtenays, to the
resistance they put up towards historical intelligence, is illustrated if we once
more examine the use he makes of his sources. He indicates that he has 'applied, but not confined' himself to Ezra Cleaveland's *A Genealogical History of
the Noble and Illustrious Family of Courtenay*, and polishes an insult:

The rector of Honiton has more gratitude than industry, and more industry than
criticism.[43]

But, as with the anecdote drawn from Gregory of Tours, contempt for the
source masks the way the events of which the source speaks touch a nerve in
the historian. Prominent in the Edessa branch of the Courtenays is Count
Joscelin:

In a holy warfare of thirty years, he was alternately a conqueror and a captive; but
he died like a soldier, in an horse-litter at the head of his troops; and his last glance
beheld the flight of the Turkish invaders who had presumed on his age and
infirmities.[44]

Ezra Cleaveland's account is far more cluttered:

Count *Josceline*, being concerned that his Son should shew himself so timorous, immediately commands all his Forces to be gathered together, and all the Strength of the
Country, and orders a Horse-Litter to be got ready, and forgetting his Weakness and
his Pains, was carried at the Head of his Army in order to fight the Enemy; and when
in this Manner he had marched on a little Way, one of his nobles came to him (his
name was *Geoffery Monk*) and told him, *That the Sultan of Iconium, hearing of his coming,
had raised the Siege with Precipitation, and made all the haste he could to get Home*: Which when
the brave Count had heard, he orders the Horse-Litter in which he was carried to be
set down, and lifting up his Eyes to Heaven, with Tears, he gave Thanks to GOD,

---

[40] *The Decline and Fall*, VI.211.   [41] *The Decline and Fall*, VI.214.
[42] *The Decline and Fall*, VI.215.   [43] *The Decline and Fall*, VI.211 n. 70.
[44] *The Decline and Fall*, VI.212.

who in the very last Moments of his Life had been so gracious and favourable to him, as that half-dead, and just expiring, he should be such a Terror to the Enemies of the Christian Faith; and as he was returning Thanks to GOD, he gives up the Ghost.[45]

Gibbon, mindful that Cleaveland's own source here is William, Archbishop of Tyre, quietly sponges away the Christian wash with which the event has been overlaid; but the very quietness with which he does this shows by how much his indignation at the Christianising of history has diminished since Chapter XVI. Much more intriguing is his fundamental reshaping of the event. In *The Decline and Fall* the dying Joscelin *sees* the fleeing Turks his reputation has routed; their flight is not reported to him. The episode is thus transformed from an instant of improbable impiety to a moment of simultaneous debility and strength which resonates to the heart of the paradoxes of decay and endurance Gibbon is frequently called upon to meditate in 1788.

Gibbon's taste for the complex, opaque particular is thus so strongly developed in the final instalment of *The Decline and Fall* that we find him embellishing his sources in order to draw out more fully this quality in his subject; this is a matter to which we shall return when we consider the character of the new historiography Gibbon forges in 1788. As we have seen, the opaque particular is the enemy of translucent, philosophic historiography because it is uninterpretable, and thus cannot be assimilated to a discussion of causes and effects. Consequently, the philosophic historian is obliged to regard such material as an excrescence, for the order and perspicuity of his work is ensured by the firm focus on causality which organises all his material into pertinence. Gibbon still murmurs at the vagaries of his sources, but he is increasingly complacent about his own departures from the strict line of narrative (which nevertheless continue to be justified in terms of illustrative value): 'I have expatiated with pleasure on the first steps of the crusaders, as they paint the manners and character of Europe.'[46] It is interesting that Gibbon should have chosen the word 'expatiated'; his new openness to the lure of the anecdotal and singular does indeed give him more room in which to wander.

But in allowing himself to roam, his history extends beyond its planned dimensions. After completing *The Decline and Fall* he reveals how he was surprised by the mass of what he had undertaken: 'I look back with amazement on the road which I have travelled, but which I should never have entered had I been previously apprized of its length.'[47] A fascinating echo between the *Memoirs* and *The Decline and Fall* offers a further hint that Gibbon was aware of the swelling of his work, and the fracturing of its unity which

---

[45] *A Genealogical History of the Noble and Illustrious Family of Courtenay*, pp. 16–17.
[46] *The Decline and Fall*, VI.40; see also 'the Extracts of Menander . . . in which we often regret the want of order and connection' (*The Decline and Fall*, IV.233 n. 37). Other writers resist the temptation to wander which Gibbon finds it increasingly hard to resist (e.g. Saint-Evremond, *Œuvres*, I.199 and 201).
[47] *Letters*, III.107.

resulted. In draft 'C' of the *Memoirs*, completed early in 1790, Gibbon described the moment when *The Decline and Fall* was conceived in these words:

Yet the historian of the decline and fall must not regret his time or expence, since it was the view of Italy and Rome which determined the choice of the subject. In my Journal the place and moment of conception are recorded; the fifteenth of October 1764, in the close of evening, as I sat musing in the Church of the Zoccolanti or Franciscan fryars, while they were singing Vespers in the Temple of Jupiter on the ruins of the Capitol.[48]

But in draft 'E', completed in March 1791, the account has been revised:

It was at Rome on the fifteenth of October *1764*, as I sat musing amidst the ruins of the Capitol while the barefooted fryars were singing Vespers in the temple of Jupiter, that the idea of writing the decline and fall of the City first started to my mind.[49]

Why does Gibbon rephrase his account of this decisive moment in his life in precisely this way? Exactly the same sentence structure of an impersonal verb, followed by two adverbial clauses and a complex noun clause, had been used in the last volume of *The Decline and Fall*:

It was on the twenty-seventh of July, in the year twelve hundred and ninety-nine of the Christian aera, that Othman first invaded the territory of Nicomedia . . .

– and the sentence continues:

. . . and the singular accuracy of the date seems to disclose some foresight of the rapid and destructive growth of the monster.[50]

The singular accuracy of the date in the case of the conception of *The Decline and Fall* may also disclose if not foresight, at least retrospective knowledge of the history's rapid and destructive, but also enriching and emancipating, growth.

[48] *Memoirs*, p. 136. [49] *Memoirs*, p. 136.
[50] *The Decline and Fall*, VI.311.

15

'Not a system, but a series'

... the toil with which performance struggles after idea.   Johnson

The antipathy of philosophic historiography to the mere sequence of past events is clear in its devotion to the systematic, not the serial; in its aspiration to transcend the superficies of historical knowledge and comprehend the causes which informed the past, and the study of which gives purpose and value to history.[1] Voltaire is explicit:

> Si vous n'avez autre chose à nous dire, sinon qu'un Barbare a succédé à un autre Barbare sur les bords de l'Oxus & de l'Iaxarte, en quoi êtes-vous utile au public?[2]

This was in part a reaction against the more automatic kinds of annalistic historiography (of which large tracts of the *Universal History* could be cited as examples), in which the primary ambition of the historian was simply to record and in which there was consequently no attempt made to bring out, by means of narrative emphasis, the essential or significant. But, beneath that jousting engagement with previous historians, we can also see that the fact of historical sequence runs counter not only to the ambitions of a philosophic historian, but also to his assumptions. It challenges his premise that history is essentially homogeneous. Thus, as we saw in the case of Hume, the philosophic depreciation of sequence has an embarrassing obverse. If one accepts the philosophic postulate that history is at bottom uniform, then sequence is simply the deceptive surface of the past. If, however, one acknowledges that sequence and change are fundamental, running much deeper than Voltaire's facile example of the succession of monarchs, and irreducible to uniformity, then the philosophic assumption of evenness is a grave impediment to historical understanding.

The history of Byzantium flaunts sequence and succession in just the form – a sequence of monarchs – at which Voltaire had scoffed in the *Encyclopédie*. Montesquieu recognises this, and also that it imperils his ideas of historical causation:

---

[1] One must here touch on the common distinction frequently made in the eighteenth century between 'esprit de système' (the intellectual vice of favouring your own ideas in the teeth of evidence) and 'esprit systématique' (the intellectual virtue of approaching your subject in an organised way). The *philosophes* claimed to embrace the latter and shun the former; but Gibbon's analysis of philosophic historiography in 'Sur la Monarchie des Mèdes' shows how easily the one can slide into the other (see above, pp. 136–8).

[2] *Encyclopédie*, 'Histoire', VIII.225. This attitude was not confined to France: see Thomas Blackwell, *Memoirs of the Court of Augustus*, I.3.

Les révolutions même firent les révolutions, & l'effet devint lui-même la cause. Comme les Grecs avoient vu passer successivement tant de diverses familles sur le trône, ils n'étoient attachés à aucune; & la fortune ayant pris des empereurs dans toutes les conditions, il n'y avoit pas de naissance assez basse, ni de mérite si mince, qui pût ôter l'espérance.[3]

Causality is short-circuited when 'l'effet devint lui-même la cause'; and the difficulty Montesquieu has in adequately accounting for this phenomenon is suggested also by his invocation of 'Fortune', since the cornerstone of his whole intellectual endeavour is that 'ce n'est pas la fortune qui domine le Monde'.[4]

Gibbon is aware of the tendency of the philosophic historian to diminish the importance of historical change when he is himself immersed in narrating the period – the history of Byzantium – which is least susceptible to such intellectual *brio*:

Voltaire, who casts a keen and lively glance over the surface of history, has been struck with the resemblance of the first Moslems and the heroes of the Iliad; the siege of Troy and that of Damascus . . .[5]

The slap at Voltaire's superficiality has a disguised weight which makes its impact only when one realises that it was precisely through such virtuoso perceptions that the *philosophe* claimed to strip away the deceptive integument of history. The philosophic historian is justified, in his own eyes at least, in drawing together these widely separated areas of the past because of his conviction that history shows no essential development, no rising of the genuinely new and passing away of the unique. For him, the appearance of change is created by adjustments of emphasis amongst constant and universal elements which always and everywhere comprise the core of human affairs. In 1776, when Gibbon's allegiance to philosophic historiography was firm, we saw (for instance in his account of the Roman legion) that he shared this belief that historical change was accidental, not substantial.[6] But when, in Volume V, Gibbon castigates the *Tactics* of Leo and Constantine for doing what he himself did in Volume I, for confounding 'the most distant and discordant institutions . . . the legions of Cato and Trajan, of Augustus and Theodosius', it is clear that his idea of historical change has been revised in just the way his criticism of Voltaire suggests.[7] Indeed, so sensitised is Gibbon to the

---

[3] *Œuvres*, III.507.

[4] *Œuvres*, III.482.

[5] *The Decline and Fall*, V.301 n. 55.

[6] See above, pp. 93–4. Such indifference to periods was not uncommon: Kennett, in describing the Roman 'Art of War', pays no attention to historical change (*Romae Antiquae Notitia*, pp. 183–246).

[7] *The Decline and Fall*, V.467. In one of the revisions to the first volume of *The Decline and Fall*, penned in the margin of Gibbon's copy but never realised, he chastises himself for an insensitivity to different periods. In Chapter I we read of the Dacians conquered by Trajan that 'to the strength and fierceness of barbarians, they added a contempt for life, which was derived

indissoluble reality of sequence and change that now even single characters differ so markedly in their stages of life that summary description could be only caricature:

> At the conclusion of the life of Mahomet, it might perhaps be expected, that I should balance his faults and virtues, that I should decide whether the title of enthusiast or impostor more properly belongs to that extraordinary man . . . at the distance of twelve centuries, I darkly contemplate his shade through a cloud of religious incense; and could I truly delineate the portrait of an hour, the fleeting resemblance would not equally apply to the solitary of mount Hera, to the preacher of Mecca, and to the conqueror of Arabia.[8]

Nor is this an isolated instance. Gibbon confesses his inability to find or construct a perspective in which Heraclius' character seems coherent:

> Of the characters conspicuous in history, that of Heraclius is one of the most extraordinary and inconsistent. In the first and last years of a long reign, the emperor appears to be the slave of sloth, of pleasure, or of superstition, the careless and impotent spectator of the public calamities. But the languid mists of the morning and evening are separated by the brightness of the meridian sun: the Arcadius of the palace, arose the Caesar of the camp; and the honour of Rome and Heraclius was gloriously retrieved by the exploits and trophies of six adventurous campaigns.[9]

As he did with Julian, when faced with Heraclius Gibbon calls on past emperors in order to circumscribe the range of possibilities posed by this contradictory figure. However, Gibbon now acquiesces more in the disjunctions he uncovers; there is none of the restiveness, the reflexive search for a single organising point of view, which stamped his portrait of the Apostate. The plain statement 'the Arcadius of the palace, arose the Caesar of the camp' admits the fissure in Heraclius' character without trying to overcome it. The meteorological image merely describes, and does not explain, Heraclius' character.[10] It is in such respectful handling of the divergent and unfocused that Gibbon's wrestling with the character of Julian – which was also a wrestling with different ideas of identity – issues. Once again it is Voltaire who in *Tancrède* displays the complementary, philosophic unscrupulousness: 'I must gently reproach the poet, for infusing into the Greek subjects the spirit of modern knights and ancient republicans.'[11] 'An ignorant age transfers its own language and manners to the most distant times', and although the

from a warm persuasion of the immortality and transmigration of the soul' (*The Decline and Fall*, I.5: I.6. first edition: 'Barbarians'). But the wiser Gibbon doubts whether the 'Religion of Zamolxis subsisted in the time of Trajan' (*The English Essays of Edward Gibbon*, pp. 338–9).

[8] *The Decline and Fall*, V.249.

[9] *The Decline and Fall*, IV.509.

[10] Compare also Justinian, the fragments of whose character can be reflected but not resolved in narrative ('Justinian has been already seen in the various lights of a prince, a conqueror, and a lawgiver: the theologian still remains . . .': *The Decline and Fall*, IV.577).

[11] *The Decline and Fall*, V.437 n. 83.

philosophes were saved from crass errors by their gestures towards historical relativism – Voltaire insists that 'On exige que l'*histoire* d'un pays étranger ne soit point jettée dans le même moule que celle de votre patrie', and Montesquieu notes that 'Il ne faut pas prendre, de la ville de Rome . . . l'idée que nous donnent les villes que nous voyons aujourd'hui' – nevertheless the inflexibility of their fundamental position ensures that these can never be more than gestures.[12]

Gibbon's most striking evocation of sequence, and the surest indication of the importance it now has in his ideas, is 'the long and tedious' Chapter XLVIII, in which he reviews the succession of Byzantine princes from Constantine III to the Latin conquest.[13] The greatest merits of this chapter have been impugned: 'a single chapter which is little more than a catalogue of rulers'.[14] But to object to its rapid sequence of princes is to ignore the attention paid to the idea of sequence in Gibbon's educated ideas of history and historiography.

With a tentativeness which reveals his strengthening circumspection about causality, Gibbon says that his purpose in Volumes V and VI will be to '*explore* the causes and effects of the decline and fall of the Eastern empire'.[15] To this end, and conforming to the traditional wisdom that circumstantial narratives ought to be prefaced with general views, Chapter XLVIII will be 'a rapid abstract, which may be supported by a *general* appeal to the order and text of the original historians'.[16] The purpose of beginning the study of a period with a general epitome was traditionally so that the cogency of the later, more detailed work would be strengthened by a previous knowledge of outline. But Chapter XLVIII does not fulfil this function, despite being avowedly a preface. The chapter is ostensibly a series of reigns, a march past of the Byzantine emperors, and the velocity with which Gibbon moves from monarch to monarch generates a powerful impression of sequence enhanced by this being the only chapter of *The Decline and Fall* free of footnotes. Nothing interrupts the onward flow of narrative.

But as well as with a parade of princes the reader is faced also with a series of opaque, unconnected episodes and gestures; for example, Theophilus' extraordinary method of choosing a bride, the ceremony of the golden apple, and

---

[12] *The Decline and Fall*, VI.253 n. 53; *Encyclopédie*, VIII.225; *Oeuvres*, III.351.

[13] The judgement is Patricia Craddock's (*Young Edward Gibbon*, p. 293).

[14] C. Dawson, in 'Edward Gibbon', p. 168.

[15] *The Decline and Fall*, V.4; the emphasis is mine.

[16] *The Decline and Fall*, V.5. The practice of giving an initial, general view is advocated and in part realised by Bossuet, in his *Discours sur l'Histoire Universelle* (1681); by Bodin, in his *Methodus ad Facilem Historiarum Cognitionem* ('primum igitur communem velut omnium temporum tabulam, nudam illam ac simplicem nobis ad intuendum propanamus': p. 15); and by Thomas Hearne, in his *Ductor Historicus* ('Students in History ought first to Read over some Epitomies': I.127).

the 'unseasonable wit' of Icasia.[17] Such events form no part of an organised explanation of the past. They are 'singular', a word Gibbon uses often in this chapter: and, as he notes in connexion with the character of Manuel, singularity is akin to contradiction and paradox. It gives birth to the resistance to comprehension which constitutes opacity:

> But the most singular feature in the character of Manuel, is the contrast and vicissitude of labour and sloth, of hardiness and effeminacy.[18]

Chapter XLVIII abounds in figures such as John Zimisces, whose 'gentle and generous behaviour delighted all who approached his person', but who also 'enjoyed the inhuman spectacle of revenge'.[19] It is the domain of the 'inconstant principle', where the rational satisfactions of apodeixis must yield to the importunate claim of romance to be admitted to history:

> The story of his [Manuel's] exploits, which appear as a model or a copy of the romances of chivalry, may induce a reasonable suspicion of the veracity of the Greeks: I will not, to vindicate their credit, endanger my own; yet I may observe, that in the long series of their annals, Manuel is the only prince who has been the subject of similar exaggeration.[20]

Philosophic scepticism, supposedly a universal historiographic tool, may be 'reasonable', but here it is also shallow and misleading. These centuries demand from the historian a generous responsiveness to the marvellous but also actual elements which give them their patina of romance.

Philosophic historiography had implied that the only alternative to its sceptical, explanatory attitude to the past was the antiquarianism which could see nothing more in history than a dusty pile of individual facts. But in Chapter XLVIII we can see Gibbon moving towards an historiography which is certainly not philosophic, yet which is equally not antiquarian. He transcends the 'copious barrenness' of the Byzantine annals inasmuch as he transforms barrenness into fertility, but without removing its particularity. The unmeaning particular is placed in a setting which reveals its rich and elusive

---

[17] *The Decline and Fall*, V.34–5. We saw that in 1776 the paucity of 'unconnected' elements in the narrative was a token of Gibbon's successful exertion of shaping influence over *The Decline and Fall*. But, as he moves into an area of the past whose intrinsic character seems to be stamped with a lack of connexion, then too great an organisation and internal coherence in its historiography would be suspicious. It is on these grounds of a wholeness its material will not countenance that Gibbon pauses over Procopius' *Anecdota*: 'Ambiguous actions are imputed to the worst motives: error is confounded with guilt, accident with design, and laws with abuses: the partial injustice of a moment is dextrously applied as the general maxim of a reign of thirty-two years' (*The Decline and Fall*, IV.81).

[18] *The Decline and Fall*, V.71.

[19] *The Decline and Fall*, V.52 and 51.

[20] *The Decline and Fall*, V.71. The episode of Alboin and Rosamund contains all the elements of romance (horror, abrupt vengeance, the *outré*) to which Gibbon responds with most relish (*The Decline and Fall*, IV.430–1), and his exclamation when writing of Richard I ('Am I writing the history of Orlando or Amadis?' *The Decline and Fall*, VI.106) shows how in the history of Byzantium romance legitimately and inescapably intersects with historiography.

suggestiveness. Gibbon is becoming less like Usbek, and more like Rhédi; but a Rhédi who wonders at the past not because he is ignorant of the philosophic attitude to history, but because he has experienced, tested and passed beyond it.

Chapter XLVIII is thus a cardinal chapter in *The Decline and Fall*, in which we can see gathered together many of the rising elements in Gibbon's historical understanding which combine to urge him towards a new historiography; the increased sensitivity to the sequence of events, the recognition of the substantial difference of periods, the relish for the arresting and singular prompted not by sentimental antiquarianism but by an understanding that such moments are a valuable corrective to the ahistorical tendency of philosophic historiography. It is appropriate that at the end of a chapter in which the grounds of Gibbon's changing ideas are so plain, he should have a reformed sense of what gives history its impact, and of the fruit we can reasonably hope to gather from it:

A being of the nature of man, endowed with the same faculties, but with a longer measure of existence, would cast down a smile of pity and contempt on the crimes and follies of human ambition, so eager, in a narrow span, to grasp at a precarious and short-lived enjoyment. It is thus that the experience of history exalts and enlarges the horizon of our intellectual view. In a composition of some days, in a perusal of some hours, six hundred years have rolled away, and the duration of a life or reign is contracted to a fleeting moment: the grave is ever beside the throne; the success of a criminal is almost instantly followed by the loss of his prize; and our immortal reason survives and disdains the sixty phantoms of kings who have passed before our eyes, and faintly dwell on our remembrance. The observation, that, in every age and climate, ambition has prevailed with the same commanding energy, may abate the surprise of a philosopher; but while he condemns the vanity, he may search the motive, of this universal desire to obtain and hold the sceptre of dominion.[21]

The philosopher may make reflections to diminish the surprise he so disdains, but this does not remove the real source of wonder. It does not 'explain' the past, merely restate it in different terms. The philosopher must still 'search the motive' for human ambition, because despite our knowledge of history 'there are few among us who would obstinately refuse a trial of the comforts and the cares of royalty'.[22] The motive for this rush to the throne remains occluded; and Gibbon's sharpened sense of the enigma of human nature (on a clear understanding of which the critical method of philosophic historiography depended) transforms his idea of history from a tableau transparent to the penetrating vision of the philosopher to a chiaroscuro procession in which the flashes of illumination measure the profundity and magnitude of the surrounding shadows. Coleridge loathed Gibbon, but that did not prevent him from responding faithfully to the nature of the last three volumes:

[21] *The Decline and Fall*, V.85–6.   [22] *The Decline and Fall*, V.421.

When I read a chapter in Gibbon, I seem to be looking through a luminous haze or fog: figures come and go, I know not how or why, all larger than life, or distorted or discoloured; nothing is real, vivid, true; all is scenical, and, as it were, exhibited by candlelight.[23]

Because the past is clouded and equivocal, it is not docile to the pragmatic aims of philosophic historians. It cannot be made to yield maxims helpful in the practical conduct of life, or guidance for politicians about how to avoid decline. It eludes the myths of uniformitarianism through which the philosophic historian tries to strain it, and which may move, but never dispose of, the challenges it poses to our understanding. In the place of practical guidance, Gibbon suggests that the profit of history lies in the forcible expression it can give to those inescapable, massive facts of our moral life which are too immense for the intellect: 'The grave is ever beside the throne.' And the origins of that forcible expression are to be found in the distortions of time peculiar to historiography, but registered only by those who are alert to the sequence and duration philosophic historiography tries to surmount: 'In a composition of some days, in a perusal of some hours, six hundred years . . .'[24]

This setting to one side of the assumptions and ambitions of philosophic historiography influences the style of *The Decline and Fall*. In particular, as we have seen, it inflects its tone. The prose of Volume I had been marked by subtle vindications of authority which led smoothly into the irony of Chapters XV and XVI. In 1788 when the smile which Gibbon had earlier endorsed as an equable and temperate response to the follies of history now suggests the vitiating distance between us and the past that the historian must try to close, the irony which had accompanied that smile gives way to a studied concentration on the obliquities of history. The rhythms of the prose, which in Volume I were the faithful auxiliaries of Gibbon's irony, now seem the direct transcription of a firm meditativeness and a supple, articulated historical awareness. The remainder of *The Decline and Fall* explores the consequences of this renovation; but before moving on, it would be as well to show how the developments in Gibbon's historical understanding which Chapter XLVIII shows in an emphatic form are duplicated in his handling of historical characters and problems.

The figure of Belisarius dominates the middle of the fourth volume of *The Decline and Fall*. He is introduced in the language of romance and adventure: 'one of those heroic names which are familiar to every age and to every

---

[23] Coleridge, *Table Talk and Omniana*, p. 293. For Coleridge's other, extremely acute and jaundiced comments on Gibbon, see his *Notebooks*, notes 3823 and 4334.

[24] The unphilosophic nature of historical narration emerges if we juxtapose a passage from Hume's *Treatise of Human Nature*: 'On the contrary, time or succession, tho' it consists likewise [i.e. likewise to space] of parts, never presents to us more than one at once' (p. 429). According to Gibbon, an historical narrative does just this by putting different and widely separated periods of time in parallel.

nation'.[25] Montesquieu, unresponsive to the traditional admiration for Belisarius, had found in him a transparent exemplification of the thesis of the *Considérations*, that Rome fell because of its abandonment of the ancient principles which had produced its success:

On peut trouver, dans les qualités de ce grand homme, les principales causes de ses succès. Avec un général qui avait toutes les maximes des premiers Romains, il se forma une armée telle que les anciennes armées Romaines.[26]

But Gibbon, who takes a closer and much more circumstantial view of Belisarius than does Montesquieu, finds that some of the hero's actions conflict with the idea he had formed of his character. He is reduced to conjecture:

They both [Belisarius and Antonina] performed the customary adoration; and falling prostrate on the ground, respectfully touched the footstool of a prince who had not unsheathed his sword, and of a prostitute, who had danced on the theatre . . . however trained to servitude, the genius of Belisarius must have secretly rebelled.[27]

Gibbon tries, with this supposed secret rebellion, to approximate Belisarius to the model psychology and to the standard idea of the heroic which his career and character flout. We find the same fundamental puzzlement when Gibbon considers what Belisarius' inner feelings might have been when faced with the striking military success of the eunuch Narses:

I desire to believe, but I dare not affirm, that Belisarius sincerely rejoiced in the triumph of Narses. Yet the consciousness of his own exploits might teach him to esteem without jealousy the merit of a rival . . .[28]

Belisarius was probably envious of Narses' success, yet was sufficiently exceptional, in his achievements and his character, not to be so. This final, qualifying admission shows up more clearly the tendency of the preceding conjecture. Faced with the remarkable Belisarius, the historian tries to bring him within ascertained patterns of behaviour; but with every crux the likelihood that Belisarius in fact conformed to that pattern is diminished.

   That likelihood is further trimmed by the fact that Belisarius himself perceives and exploits the general truths to which the mass of ordinary men conform:

Belisarius saw and pitied their sufferings; but he had foreseen, and he watched the decay of their loyalty, and the progress of their discontent.

Belisarius praised the spirit of his troops, condemned their presumption, yielded to their clamours, and prepared the remedies of a defeat, the possibility of which he alone had courage to suspect.

His foresight was justified by the encrease of the public distress, as soon as the Goths had occupied two important posts in the neighbourhood of Rome.

[25] *The Decline and Fall*, IV.127. In the *Reason of Church Government* (Keynes, p. 198) Gibbon would have read of Tasso's project of a poem on the subject of Belisarius' struggle with the Goths.
[26] *Œuvres*, III.498.
[27] *The Decline and Fall*, IV.153.
[28] *The Decline and Fall*, IV.314.

. . . while ten thousand voices demanded the battle, Belisarius dissembled his knowledge, that in the hour of trial he must depend on the firmness of three hundred veterans.[29]

In his shrewd application of the constant and universal principles of human nature, Belisarius is here almost a philosophic historian embedded in the past.[30] But in the adroit use he makes of uniformitarian beliefs, he demonstrates their uselessness to the historian. Like the laws of probability, those beliefs are 'so true in general, so fallacious in particular'.[31] The mass of men may conform to a general image of human nature, but those who distinguish themselves, and to whom the historian must therefore pay his finest attention, do not. Like Belisarius, whose profiting from the general image of human nature is a token of his being outside it, the major figures of history disrupt the hunches which comprise the uniformitarian creed. The phrases Gibbon uses of Belisarius accentuate that disruption:

. . . the conqueror of Italy renounced, without a murmur, perhaps without a sigh, the well-earned honours of a second triumph.

. . . the husband of Antonina [a notorious adulteress] was never suspected of violating the laws of conjugal fidelity.

. . . the unconquerable patience and loyalty of Belisarius appear either *below* or *above* the character of a MAN.[32]

Reconciling apparent contradictions ('the genius to command, and the virtue to obey, resided only in the mind of Belisarius'), he baffles comprehension and elicits admiration. Possessed of a disproportionate causal influence ('the genius of one man repressed the passions of a victorious army'), opaque where others are transparent, he absorbs the historian's fascinated and frustrated scrutiny.[33] Moreover, he is a cynosure of history, as well as the cynosure of the historian:

The fate of Italy depended on his life; and the deserters pointed to the conspicuous horse, a bay, with a white face, which he rode on that memorable day. 'Aim at the bay horse,' was the universal cry. Every bow was bent, every javelin was directed against that fatal object . . .[34]

The historian's efforts to pierce this figure are ultimately as unavailing as those of the Goths.

---

[29] *The Decline and Fall*, IV.186; IV.183–4; IV.185 and IV.316.

[30] He certainly has the philosophic historian's ability to see past distracting minutiae and grasp the essential: 'Amidst tumult and dismay, the whole plan of the attack and defence was distinctly present to his mind; he observed the changes of each instant, weighed every possible advantage, transported his person to the scenes of danger, and communicated his spirit in calm and decisive orders' (*The Decline and Fall*, IV.182).

[31] *Memoirs*, p. 188.

[32] *The Decline and Fall*, IV.202; IV.203 and IV.211.

[33] *The Decline and Fall*, IV.168 and IV.141.

[34] *The Decline and Fall*, IV.177.

How does Gibbon's handling of Belisarius compare with his handling of Julian? In both men Gibbon encounters resistance to his attempts to understand the past. In Julian this produces a struggle between praiseworthy and blameworthy aspects which carries through to the last word of the portrait.[35] But with Belisarius, the ambivalence, from the grasp of which Gibbon cannot escape in the case of Julian, is willingly embraced. The ease with which Belisarius baffles expectation and fractures what we take to be universal truths does not pose a problem of judgement, but is evidence to be accepted and on which judgements are to be made. At every turn the career of Justinian's lieutenant exposes to Gibbon the stiffness of philosophic historiography; and the historian reveals his education in a reflection which undermines the constant values on which philosophic historiography relies, and to which his eyes are opened by Belisarius:

Our estimate of personal merit is relative to the common faculties of mankind. The aspiring efforts of genius, or virtue, either in active or speculative life, are measured, not so much by their real elevation, as by the height to which they ascend above the level of their age or country . . . In this view, the character of Belisarius may be deservedly placed above the heroes of the ancient republics.[36]

This greater care and superior discrimination contrasts strongly with the summariness of Montesquieu.

That care and discrimination are also called into play by Andronicus Comnenus, a protean figure from the Byzantine history who in *The Decline and Fall* usurps twelve pages of narrative. Like the Saracens, Andronicus lures Gibbon away from his 'strict and original line'; indeed, almost away from historiography altogether: 'His genuine adventures might form the subject of a very singular romance.'[37] In the propinquity of 'genuine' and 'romance' we see once more what a philosophic historian might dismiss as mere contradiction, but which in *The Decline and Fall* evokes the atmosphere of substantial paradox which in 1788 is Gibbon's element. Once again it is the fragmentariness of the character, its composition out of vivid and jarring pieces, which catches his attention:

He pressed, with active ardour, the siege of Mopsuestia: the day was employed in the boldest attacks; but the night was wasted in song and dance; and a band of Greek comedians formed the choicest part of his retinue.[38]

The succession of wassail and campaign is compressed powerfully to suggest Andronicus' various capacity.

---

[35] See above, pp. 156–168.

[36] *The Decline and Fall*, IV.212–13. Gibbon is perhaps echoing Johnson: 'Every man's performances, to be rightly estimated, must be compared with the state of the age in which he lived, and with his own particular opportunities' (*Preface to Shakespeare* (1765), *Works*, V.124).

[37] *The Decline and Fall*, V.541 and V.72–3.

[38] *The Decline and Fall*, V.73; see also 'His government exhibited a singular contrast . . .' (*The Decline and Fall*, V.81).

An episode in one of his exploits might stand as an emblem of his character. Being escorted back to captivity in Constantinople

his presence of mind again extricated him from this danger. Under the pretence of sickness, he dismounted in the night, and was allowed to step aside from the troop: he planted in the ground his long staff; clothed it with his cap and upper garment; and, stealing into the wood, left a phantom to amuse, for some time, the eyes of the Walachians.[39]

Historians, as well as guards, may be given the slip. A man whose 'persuasive eloquence could bend to every situation and character of life' and who 'could assume the manners of every climate' is not easily pinned down.[40] Such perfect camouflage makes the attempt to penetrate to firm knowledge impossibly difficult, yet also most rewarding. It is to these recalcitrant areas of the past that the historian should pay greatest attention.

However, there is a price for such attentiveness. After Andronicus has been put to death, Gibbon comments on the narrative consequences of his account of the prince:

I have been tempted to expatiate on the extraordinary character and adventures of Andronicus; but I shall here terminate the series of the Greek emperors since the time of Heraclius.[41]

'Extraordinary' has a felicitous degree of literal truth.[42] As we have seen, anecdotes and adventures resist Gibbon's attempts to construe them and seduce his attention to the detriment of literary structure. Andronicus breaks ranks because of the space he peremptorily demands and receives. One need only consult the summary accounts Gibbon gives in Volume II of deaths similar to that suffered by Andronicus to see how the historian now sees more substance in the lures of the past:

They rudely seized the praefect and the quaestor, and tying their legs together with ropes, they dragged them through the streets of the city, inflicted a thousand insults and a thousands wounds on these unhappy victims, and at last precipitated their mangled and lifeless bodies into the Orontes.

The Catholics rose in the defence of their bishop; the palace of Hermogenes was consumed; the first military officer of the empire was dragged by the heels through the

---

[39] *The Decline and Fall*, V.75.

[40] *The Decline and Fall*, V.73 and V.76.

[41] *The Decline and Fall*, V.84. J. B. Bury held that Gibbon 'never lost himself in his labour' (*Autobiography*, p. vii); but we know that such self-loss was a part of Gibbon's historical temperament. The most famous example is preserved in the *Memoirs*, when 'the summons of the dinner-bell reluctantly dragged me from my intellectual feast' off what one would have thought was the lenten fare of 'the continuation of Echard's Roman history' (p. 42). Nor was this a merely juvenile phenomenon. On 25 July 1780 he wrote to Sheffield: 'I am alive, but as I am immersed in the decline and fall, I shall only make the sign. – It is made. – ' (*Letters*, II.246–7).

[42] Gibbon often uses words with an eye to their etymology; see also his use of 'literal' in his comment on the Foulis Homer (*The English Essays of Edward Gibbon*, p. 547).

streets of Constantinople, and, after he expired, his lifeless corpse was exposed to their wanton insults.[43]

The detailed account of Andronicus' death is too long to quote, but it has an intentness which forms the strongest contrast with the baldness of these earlier, parallel instances. Its concluding sentences will perhaps give some sense of the way in which Gibbon's perplexity at Andronicus' character is not calmed: 'In this long and painful agony, "Lord have mercy upon me! and why will you bruise a broken reed?" were the only words that escaped from his mouth. Our hatred for the tyrant is lost in pity for the man.'[44] Even in death Andronicus provokes a divided response in Gibbon. The historian's final response may be unalloyed pity: but this is so different from the hatred which preceded it that the hatred is recalled in an abrupt oscillation of emotion. The sentence ends on a note of scorn: 'Nor can we blame his pusillanimous resignation, since a Greek Christian was no longer master of his life.' Such thwarted twistings of response are inevitable when 'we think, and even feel, that *one will*, a sole principle of action, is essential to a rational and conscious being', but when history confronts us with such violently opposed examples.[45]

It is not simply in respect of character that Gibbon finds the history of Byzantium stretching and embarrassing his ideas. Chapter XLIV is Gibbon's 'brief and brilliant exposition of the principles of Roman law', and here, if anywhere in the final instalment of *The Decline and Fall*, we might expect to find vestiges of philosophic historiography.[46] Not only does the study of laws harmonise perfectly with the philosophic historians' effort to make historiography more sociological and to draw the scope of its concentration away from courts and battles; it had been singled out as a subject almost uniquely fitted to philosophic study both by Montesquieu in his *Esprit des Loix* and by Hume, who wrote that 'Nothing can better show the genius of the age than . . . a review of the laws.'[47]

Gibbon almost repeats Hume's opinion ('The laws of a nation form the most instructive portion of its history') and reinforces the philosophic character of the chapter with a scepticism which might have come straight from 'On the Populousness of Ancient Nations':

. . . nor do I see any reason to reject these consequences, which moderate our ideas of the poverty of the first Romans.[48]

However, his allegiance is not confined to Hume. His characterising of the Romans as wise borrowers from other races comes most immediately from

[43] *The Decline and Fall*, II.133 and II.297.
[44] *The Decline and Fall*, V.84. Compare 2 Kings, 8.21, Isaiah, 36.6 and 42.3.
[45] *The Decline and Fall*, IV.586.
[46] Bury, *The Decline and Fall*, I.lii.
[47] *History*, IV.300: see also Gray, *Poems and Memoirs*, p. 100.
[48] *The Decline and Fall*, IV.333–4 and IV.339 n. 27.

Montesquieu.[49] We might also see the influence of Montesquieu in the intellectual *sprezzatura* which can trace legislative procedure from vigour to decline in a single, connected sweep:

> Yet as long as the tribes successively passed over narrow *bridges*, and gave their voices aloud, the conduct of each citizen was exposed to the eyes and ears of his friends and countrymen. The insolvent debtor consulted the wishes of his creditor; the client would have blushed to oppose the views of his patron: the general was followed by his veterans, and the aspect of a grave magistrate was a living lesson to the multitude. A new method of secret ballot abolished the influence of fear and shame, of honour and interest, and the abuse of freedom accelerated the progress of anarchy and despotism. The Romans had aspired to be equal; they were levelled by the equality of servitude; and the dictates of Augustus were patiently ratified by the formal consent of the tribes or centuries.[50]

Moreover, like Ferguson, who five years earlier had published his *Progress and Termination of the Roman Republic* (1783) and remained politely unconvinced of the sincerity of the Romans' ferocious punishments for insolvent debtors, Gibbon too thinks that here the application of a touch of philosophic *vraisemblance* would not be amiss:

> The advocates for this savage law have insisted, that it must strongly operate in deterring idleness and fraud from contracting debts which they were unable to discharge; but experience would dissipate this salutary terror, by proving, that no creditor could be found to exact this unprofitable penalty of life or limb.[51]

But as the chapter progresses, these philosophic foundations are unsettled by evidence Gibbon cannot avoid. The effects of sequence, which the philosophic historians had tried especially to control and from which Chapter XLIV, as something of a dissertation embedded within narrative but untouched by its onward press of chronology, might have been expected to be free, intrude with reminders of the undecided character of the past:

> In the progress from primitive equity to final injustice, the steps are silent, the shades are almost imperceptible, and the absolute monopoly is guarded by positive laws and artificial reason.[52]

Close to the end of the chapter, philosophic clarities are again blurred when Gibbon contradicts Montesquieu on the subject of paederasty:

> A French philosopher has dared to remark, that whatever is secret must be doubtful, and that our natural horror of vice may be abused as an engine of tyranny. But the favourable persuasion of the same writer, that a legislator may confide in the taste and

---

[49] '. . . the Romans had emerged from barbarism, since they were capable of studying and embracing the institutions of their more enlightened neighbours' (*The Decline and Fall*, IV.336); compare Montesquieu, *Œuvres*, III.352 and Saint-Evremond, *Œuvres*, I.200. This commonplace can be traced back to Polybius (VI.xxv.11).

[50] *The Decline and Fall*, IV.340.

[51] *The Decline and Fall*, IV.402. Ferguson is confident that 'Their ideas in either [the penalties for debtors and the wide powers of the father over his household], it is probable, were never realized' (*Progress and Termination of the Roman Republic*, I.38 n. 29).

[52] *The Decline and Fall*, IV.385.

reason of mankind, is impeached by the unwelcome discovery of the antiquity and extent of the disease.[53]

Mankind is more various in inclination than Montesquieu would allow; and it is for the Montesquieuan blemish of an insufficiently scrupulous attention to variety and difference that Gibbon finally criticises Justinian's scheme to systematise the whole body of Roman law:

> Justinian, the Greek emperor of Constantinople and the East, was the legal successor of the Latian shepherd who had planted a colony on the banks of the Tyber. In a period of thirteen hundred years, the laws had reluctantly followed the changes of government and manners; and the laudable desire of conciliating ancient names with recent institutions, destroyed the harmony, and swelled the magnitude of the obscure and irregular system.[54]

Justinian's legal reforms are a rash attempt to synthesise a single and coherent body of laws from the successive accretions and revisions of thirteen centuries. They bear the same relation to Roman law that philosophic historiography bears to the centuries Gibbon is studying in 1788. In both cases the intrinsic and ingrained roughness of the material, its insistence on its serial character, prohibits the proposed systematic smoothness of finish. But what kind of historiography *will* it tolerate? It is to Gibbon's attempts actively to encompass this refractory period, rather than to his responses to its uncompliant nature, that we must now turn: to his revisions of his critical method, to the consequent changes in stance and tone, and to his imaginative revivifications of the past.

[53] *The Decline and Fall*, IV.409–10.   [54] *The Decline and Fall*, IV.415.

16

'A keener glance'

Boldness means ignorance and reflection brings hesitation.   Thucydides

Every man . . . has conviction forced upon him . . .   Johnson

Throughout the final instalment of *The Decline and Fall*, then, Gibbon is repeatedly and variously made aware that philosophic historiography, for all its apparent critical acuity and sharpness of tone, is in fact a blunt instrument with which to dissect these centuries. It does not cut and display, but obscures by merely bruising and mangling.

It is the tenet of uniformitarianism which irreparably mars the edge of philosophic historical understanding. Uniformitarianism was not, of course, a belief confined to the *philosophes*. Chesterfield thought that a conviction of the uniformity of human nature was the sober knowledge which came with maturity; while Addison, writing of *Chevy-Chase*, commented incidentally and as if stating an indubitable truth that 'Human nature is the same in all reasonable creatures.'[1] But there is the rub; what if you are dealing with people who in your terms are not 'reasonable'? Would it be possible, after Hume's demystification of the idea of reason, to dismiss such people as irrational barbarians, thus reposing in the idea of a timeless and unchanging standard of reason of which your age was a perfect possession? Mrs Radcliffe, writing almost contemporarily with Gibbon, is sure not:

. . . human reason cannot establish her laws on subjects, lost in the obscurity of imagination, any more than the eye can ascertain the form of objects, that only glimmer through the dimness of night.[2]

It would be hard to think of words better suited to describe Gibbon's situation when writing the history of Byzantium – indeed, these are almost the words Coleridge *did* use. *The Mysteries of Udolpho* was published in 1794, the year of Gibbon's death. But if he had thought back to his reading during his banishment to Lausanne in the 1750s, he might have recalled a comment of de

---

[1] *Letters*, II.137 and *Spectator*, no. 70; *Works*, II.509. See also J. W. Johnson, *The Formation of English Neo-Classical Thought*, pp. 33, 235 and 237. I shall argue that uniformitarianism is a background against which we must view *The Decline and Fall*, but which we should not expect to be duplicated within it.

[2] *Mysteries of Udolpho*, p. 330. Gibbon also touches on the feebleness of reason: *Letters*, III.328; *The English Essays of Edward Gibbon*, p. 542; and *Memoirs*, pp. 4 and 124.

Crousaz's, who when writing about 'the limits of the Understanding' exposes the narrow basis of uniformitarian convictions:

There are some People ridiculous enough to look upon themselves as the Measure and Rule of all Things. Whatsoever is above their Ideas, passes with them for an Impossibility and a Chimera.[3]

It is precisely to this embarrassing restrictedness that philosophic historiography, with its aim of cleansing the Augean stables of historical writing through a liberal application of scepticism, commits its practitioners; we saw the consequences of such commitment in the work of Hume. Gibbon's subject prevents him from ignoring this embarrassment, and in this section I wish to examine how generously he rises to this challenge, neither seeing it as simply an affront, nor diminishing its true depth.

We have seen that the uniformitarian tenets of the philosophic historian were primarily invoked in the context of critical method; they offered a yardstick whereby he could decide what he should or should not believe. What effect does Gibbon's expanded idea of the possible, with its consequent abrasion of his faith in uniformitarianism, have on his critical practice? In the journal he kept while in Lausanne during his European tour of the mid-1760s, Gibbon ponders a problem raised by the Circus Maximus:

Tout peut nous convaincre que le Cirque etoit capable de contenir un peuple nombreux; mais Denys d'Halicarnasse le fixe à 150,000 personnes, Pline, à 260,000, Victor à 380,000, le Victor moderne à 385,000, et la Notice de l'Empire à 405,000. Au milieu de ces differences énormes quel parti faut il prendre? Celui de consulter les faits, les lieux et l'experience.[4]

But not all historical cruces lend themselves so easily to calculation as that of determining how many could sit in the Circus Maximus at one time. Nor is the way of 'les faits, les lieux et l'experience' always a smooth or even a single path. It is Gibbon's experience as he writes *The Decline and Fall* that geography, testimony and conjecture often diverge. To trace Gibbon's ideas about the historian's critical method is a question of following the course of decay and erosion and of noting the replacement of early confidence by an informed reticence, a 'rational ignorance', which might have both sighed and smiled over the bluff assault on the past which the phrasing of the youth's question – 'quel parti faut-il prendre?' – implies constitutes historical inquiry.

Hume's congratulatory letter to Gibbon, on the occasion of the publication of Volume I of *The Decline and Fall*, comments on Gibbon's discussion of Ossian and betrays his own, extreme position on historical criticism:

---

[3] De Crousaz's *Logique ou Système de Réflexions* was first published in 1712, and Gibbon records that the mastery of this 'universal instrument' was one of the crucial events in his intellectual life during his first, enforced residence in Lausanne (from June 1753 to April 1758). There is no copy recorded in Gibbon's library. The quotation is taken from the English translation, *A New Treatise of the Art of Thinking*, I.28.

[4] *Le Journal de Gibbon à Lausanne*, pp. 66–7.

I see you entertain a great Doubt with regard to the Authenticity of the Poems of Ossian. You are certainly right in so doing. It is, indeed, strange, that any man of Sense could have imagin'd it possible, that above twenty thousand Verses, along with numberless historical Facts, could have been preservd by oral Tradition during fifty Generations, by the rudest, perhaps, of all European Nations; the most necessitous, the most turbulent, and the most unsettled. Where a Supposition is so contrary to common Sense, any positive Evidence of it ought never to be regarded. Men run with great Avidity to give their Evidence in favour of what flatters their Passions, and their national Prejudices. You are, therefore, over and above indulgent to us in speaking of the Matter with Hesitation.[5]

It is odd that Hume should spend a quarter of his letter discussing what is the most minor of details in *The Decline and Fall*. Macpherson had published the disputed poems well over a decade previously, Blair had brought out his *Critical Dissertation on the Poems of Ossian* in 1763, and the squabble between Macpherson and Johnson had been at its height over a year before, in the early months of 1775. The authenticity of Ossian's poems is thus hardly the debate of the moment. Hume raises the question of Ossian, however, not as a matter of lively dispute, but as a touchstone for sound principles of historical criticism. For Hume, the value of the debate over Ossian is that the whole vexed issue teaches us a sharp lesson about the spirit in which we should approach the records of the past; it adumbrates a central critical truth which alone could furnish historians with a clue to the mazy deceptions of historical evidence. The 'great avidity' to tell and applaud flattering untruths present in all men, and so recently exemplified, places an immediate question mark alongside all historical testimony.[6] In the midst of this uncertainty our surest resource, as Hume had made clear in 'Of Miracles', is mathematical calculation. We should accept only that testimony in which the probability of what is asserted is greater than the probability that the witness is lying. It is the mathematical character of Hume's theorising on critical method which explains why he dwells so much on figures in his letter to Gibbon: 'fifty Generations', 'numberless historical Facts', 'twenty thousand Verses'. He depicts the full enormity of what we must accept if we maintain the genuineness of Ossian, and then considers the easy truth of the vanity of human nature. No reasonable man could hesitate, especially since the principle on which the decision is to be made is firmer than evidence itself: 'Where a Supposition is so contrary to common Sense, any positive Evidence of it ought never to be regarded.'[7] We have seen that Hume's historiographic practice is far from this ferocity, and in this letter, at the extremity of his life, he is being

---

[5] Hume, *Letters*, II.310–11: also reprinted in *Memoirs*, p. 168.
[6] Compare Shaftesbury, *Characteristicks*, II.325–6 for a similar wringing of hands over the vulgar taste for prodigies.
[7] For the delicacy of Hume's behaviour in the Ossian controversy *vis à vis* Blair, see Richard Sher, *Church and University in the Scottish Enlightenment*, pp. 252–8.

deliberately extreme.[8] Assuming a position familiar to historical pyrrhonists since Bayle, Hume asserts that historiography can be preserved from error and credulity only by a surgical application of this principle of probability and the normative idea of human nature on which it relies.[9] Gibbon's touching on Ossian allows Hume, with an appearance of decent pertinence, to instil this sovereign principle into the most recent member of the triumvirate of eighteenth-century British historians. It is the legacy he would press into the hands of his successor. In the volumes that follow, Gibbon moves steadily away from the philosopher; but this strong and argued scepticism, found also in men such as Bayle, Beaufort and Pouilly, was an influential and inescapable component in Gibbon's intellectual milieu.

Yet strong measures are ever the resource of weak men, and we may plausibly read the intemperance of Hume's comments on historical criticism as evidence that even 'le bon David' could be goaded into exasperation. He tries to introduce an impertinent clarity into an area of thought which Gibbon eventually realises is only distorted by the formulation of absolute principles, and which requires in each instance a supple negotiation between the frequently competing, rather than collaborating, claims of evidence and experience. Whenever we find Gibbon employing Hume's downright prescriptiveness, he is betrayed either by his youth, here arguing for a hierarchy of probabilities –

Je conviens que ce ne sont là que des probabilités, mais dans la Science de la Critique, il paroit que les probabilités doivent faire disparoitre les possibilités et ceder à leur tour aux preuves.[10]

– or by annoyance at the egregious soft-mindedness of one of his sources, such as Chalcocondyles, whose

. . . credulity and injustice may teach an important lesson; to distrust the accounts of foreign and remote nations, and to suspend our belief of every tale that deviates from the laws of nature and the character of man.[11]

Gibbon's critical thought is not normally stamped with this severity (although we may note in passing that to suspend belief is not the same as to disbelieve).

---

[8] Hume died five months after writing to Gibbon, on 25 August 1776, and refers in the letter to his impending dissolution.

[9] As an example of this, consider Louis de Beaufort's celebrated *Dissertation sur l'Incertitude des Cinq Premiers Siecles de l'Histoire Romaine*. The ferocity of his criticism is plain: 'La Conséquence est facile à tirer. Une Histoire, qui ne donne point d'autres Garants des Faits qu'elle rapporte, que ceux mêmes qui sont convaincus d'en avoir altéré la Vérité, ou de les avoir supposés, ne peut être que fabuleuse & incertaine' (I.144). This may seem to liberate the historian from falsehood, yet it also imprisons him, as the volume's final flourish suggests: 'Cependant, si j'avois poussé trop loin mes Doutes, je ne refuserai jamais de me rendre aux Preuves qu'on pourra me donner de la Certitude de cette Histoire: & je serai le prémier à abbandonner l'Opinion que j'ai défendue, dés que je la trouverai réfutée par des Raisons solides' (II.436). When Beaufort has defined his idea of proof so narrowly and stringently, how promptly would he recognise counter-arguments? It is from this sclerosis of thought that Gibbon frees himself.

[10] *Letters*, I. 98.

[11] *The Decline and Fall*, VI.393.

But before I go on to consider the nuanced criticism of sources in *The Decline and Fall*, I want first to discuss another influence on the young Gibbon, which counters historical pyrrhonism with conservatism.

The precocious exile in Lausanne

> maintained a Latin correspondence, at first anonymous and afterwards in my own name with Professor Breitinger of Zurich, the learned Editor of a Septuagint Bible: in our frequent letters we discussed many questions of antiquity, many passages of the Latin Classics. I proposed my interpretations and amendments: his censures, for he did not spare my boldness of conjecture, were sharp and strong; and I was encouraged by the consciousness of my strength, when I could stand in free debate against a Critic of such eminence and erudition.[12]

Gibbon's memory is not deceived. Breitinger's letter of 17 November 1756 begins with a reproof of the young man's 'boldness of conjecture':

> Sint criticae disciplinae studiosi in sollicitandis veterum auctorum locis cautiores, et in legendis ipsis auctoribus diligentiores, atque ita intelligant, quantae diligentiae sit haec critica ars, et quam temere faciant, qui, ut aliquid concoquere non possunt, aut non satis vel analogiae respondens vel dialecticis praeceptiunculis suis conveniens putant, ita mutare sustinent . . .[13]

The restraint which flows naturally from a clear understanding of the limitations of our present perspective advocated by Breitinger took root in his young correspondent. Sixteen months later, in his essay 'Sur la Succession de l'Empire Romain', Gibbon robes that restraint in historiographical, not philological, dress, and introduces it as an irrefragable guide:

> J'aurai cependant la hardiesse d'en proposer quelques autres [objections], après avoir posé un principe qui me paroît incontestable: c'est que la témoignage d'un historien contemporain est d'une toute autre autorité dans ces matières que les inductions que nous autres François pouvons tirer des faits qui se rencontrent dans leurs écrits. La raison en est claire. C'est que nous ne voyons l'histoire de ces tems qu'en gros, au lieu qu'ils la voyoient en détail: et c'est de ce détail que tout dépend dans des discussions aussi délicates que celles-ci.[14]

Gibbon's own best historical criticism consists of exclusive adherence to neither Hume's aggressive excisions nor Breitinger's conservatism, but of imaginative manoeuvres between these two boundaries of 'haec critica ars', and careful contemplation of 'ce détail [dont] tout dépend dans des discussions aussi délicates que celles-ci'. In a note made in his Lausanne journal while reading Voltaire's *Traité sur la tolérance à l'occasion de la mort de Jean Calas*, Gibbon shows his understanding that any true historical criticism would have to find its place between austere scepticism and windy credulity:

> J'aime beaucoup ses conclusions fausses et contradictoires sur l'histoire ancienne.

[12] *Memoirs*, p. 81.
[13] *Miscellaneous Works*, I.466.
[14] Dated 20.iii.1758; *Miscellaneous Works*, III.172.

L'histoire ancienne (dit-il) est remplie de prodiges: Ils ne sauroient etre vrais. Donc tout y est fable et conjecture . . . L'histoire ancienne est remplie de prodiges: on ne peut que les adopter. Donc les hommes et la nature meme n'avoit dans ces tems reculés rien de comun avec nous . . .[15]

Bonnard locates the passages in question and comments that Gibbon may not have recognised 'le ton ironique' in which Voltaire advanced the second alternative.[16] It would indeed be a prodigy were Gibbon deaf to irony. But his judgement that both alternatives are 'fausses' would not preclude his understanding (as he certainly understood by the time he wrote *The Decline and Fall*) that Voltaire, like Hume and Beaufort, in fact believed that much ancient history was 'fable et conjecture'; while also showing his awareness that one need not be trapped in Voltaire's dilemma. Ancient history is neither pure fable nor absolutely alien, although it may partake of both the alien and the fabulous. It demands to be weighed by the historian, who will employ by turns both testingness and receptiveness and supplement them both with an imaginative entry into the past. Gibbon's praise of Bayle is fascinating in its grasp of how the imagination could be set free by an immersion in scepticism:

Dans tous ses raisonnemens sur l'Infaillibilité, les droits d'une conscience erronée je vois un Dialecticien precis, clair, mais un peu diffus. Jamais homme n'a sû comme Bayle se mettre à la place de son adversaire, revetir son systeme et prevoir tous les avantages qu'il en pouvoit tirer. C'est la un des effets les plus precieux de la Philosophie Sceptique.[17]

In his own career Gibbon, too, moves through scepticism to sympathy. Intellectually aware before he began *The Decline and Fall* that 'l'incredulité de ce siecle est souvent aussi aveugle que la foi de leurs ancetres' and that 'l'ignorance a deux filles, l'incrédulité et la foi aveugle', over the course of its publication we can see Gibbon coming to possess, and not merely ascertain, that knowledge.[18]

As I have pointed out, the governing ironies of Chapters XV and XVI, and thus the whole carefully chosen stance of Volume I, depend on a probabilistic critical method such as that sketched by Hume in 'Of Miracles' and in his congratulatory letter to Gibbon. Not only does Gibbon's irony rely on his reader's believing that men have in all times and places been essentially the same (after all, if the reader does not hold that belief, but thinks that the early Christians and Grotius may have been quite different in kind, then the conclusion of Chapter XVI will not entrap him, just as the dilemmas of Chapter

---

[15] *Le Journal de Gibbon à Lausanne*, pp. 239–40.

[16] *Le Journal de Gibbon à Lausanne*, p. 240 n. 3.

[17] *Le Journal de Gibbon à Lausanne*, pp. 256–7. This propinquity could be viewed with a less appreciative eye: 'however scepticism and credulity may seem to be at the greatest distance from each other; yet the latter will appear to be akin to the former in a very near degree of descent' (James Tunstall, *Lectures on Natural and Revealed Religion*, p. 74).

[18] *Le Journal de Gibbon à Lausanne*, p. 254 and *Miscellaneous Works*, IV.55.

XV will not have embarrassed him). It also enhances the probability of his explanation of Roman decline if he can suggest that the problems posed by ancient history are hardly different in kind or magnitude from the problems posed by more recent history. That essential similarity will seem to guarantee at least the possibility of a more than superficial knowledge of the past.

However, once the thesis of Volume I has reached its consummation in Chapters XV and XVI, Gibbon simultaneously advances into more featureless historical terrain which does not show to good effect in such a perspective. Thus, just at the moment when the completion of his explanation of Roman decline releases Gibbon from that intentness of demonstration, he also ventures into a region of history much less hospitable to such intentness. In examining the changing emphases and values of *The Decline and Fall*, I have tried to connect those changes to alterations in the way Gibbon perceived the past, and to that end have looked at aspects of the practice of historiography which mediate between the narrative and its subject – for instance, causality, which is both a tissue of relations informing the past and a consideration which shapes narrative. Critical method is another such mediator. It is a means of deciding what is to be included in narrative which is also full of implicit judgements about the past; and the evolution of critical method in *The Decline and Fall* may be expressed as Gibbon's appreciation of the consequences which flow from the interdependence of what philosophers now call critical and speculative philosophy of history. Gibbon comes to understand that critical method cannot be a timeless arithmetical manipulation. If it is not to misrepresent the past, it must move and flex with history on its course through time. In 1776, Gibbon views critical method as a sieve through which the written legacies of history may be winnowed. In 1788, he sees it as an imaginative process whereby a sense of the spaciousness of the past may be communicated.

In the second instalment of 1781 we still find the confident, probabilistic inference of Volume I – most often in connexion with the statistical cruces to which it lends itself. Reducing the barbarian casualties in the skirmishes before the battle of Châlons to fifteen thousand, Gibbon reveals his thinking in a footnote:

The common editions read XCM; but there is some authority of manuscripts (and almost any authority is sufficient) for the more reasonable number of XVM.[19]

This is already a noticeable softening of Hume's position that positive evidence in favour of the extraordinary ought not to be regarded. Gibbon will not reject positive evidence in favour of unsupported inference, although the slightest evidence is sufficient to support a probable conjecture. Elsewhere in this instalment we find no underminings of popular but fallacious belief on the scale or with the thoroughness of Chapter IX. But Gibbon, convinced that

---

[19] *The Decline and Fall*, III.411 n. 40.

the maxim 'many things which have stood the test of time cannot endure that of reason' was true of nothing so much as of historiography, still clips away at the extravagances of his sources:

The stern policy of Genseric justified his frequent examples of military execution: he was not always the master of his own passions, or of those of his followers; and the calamities of war were aggravated by the licentiousness of the Moors, and the fanaticism of the Donatists. Yet I shall not easily be persuaded, that it was the common practice of the Vandals to extirpate the olives, and other fruit-trees, of a country where they intended to settle: nor can I believe that it was a usual stratagem to slaughter great numbers of their prisoners before the walls of a besieged city, for the sole purpose of infecting the air, and producing a pestilence, of which they themselves must have been the first victims.[20]

To be sure, the Vandals were unpleasant people; but even *their* ferocity must have been subservient to the universal motive of self-interest. Thus in an historic doubt such as this we can see that Gibbon, if faced with an egregious but isolated crux, will still invoke the normative idea of human nature espoused by Hume.

However, at the same time, Gibbon is also faced in this instalment with large historical problems, such as the character of Julian the Apostate, which are not susceptible of such swift arbitration, and which, as we have seen, permanently stretch his idea of what is, in the technical sense, probable. Moreover, an awareness of the constancy of human nature, with which the philosophic historian had pared away the extraordinary and thus given history a familiar appearance, in these centuries may deepen the respect with which Gibbon contemplates the past:

As long as the same passions and interests subsist among mankind, the questions of war and peace, of justice and policy, which were debated in the councils of antiquity, will frequently present themselves as the subject of modern deliberation. But the most experienced statesman of Europe, has never been summoned to consider the propriety, or the danger, of admitting, or rejecting, an innumerable multitude of Barbarians, who are driven by despair and hunger to solicit a settlement on the territories of a civilized nation.[21]

The conditionally expressed, uniformitarian conjecture of the first sentence is, with deliberate abruptness, brought up against the intransigent uniqueness of the historical fact; and in that collision the potential misleadingness of a faith in the constancy of human nature, and the dulling of historical sensibility it may induce, becomes clear.

The effect this has on Gibbon's critical method can be judged if, remembering that he has discounted the reported atrocities of the Vandals, we consider this parallel detail from the instalment of 1788:

[20] *The Decline and Fall*, III.341–2.   [21] *The Decline and Fall*, II.592–3.

. . . many flourishing cities were reduced to ashes, and the agriculture of Thrace was almost extirpated by the wanton cruelty of the Goths, who deprived their captive peasants of the right hand that guided the plough.[22]

It is the small word 'their' which is so important here, because it shows Gibbon's acceptance of just the kind of irrationality in the atrocities of the Goths – that is to say, that they rebound on the perpetrators – which he would not accept in the case of the Vandals. As Addison said, human nature is the same in all reasonable creatures; but in 1788 Gibbon understands that what he, positioned in the late eighteenth century, now perceives as the unreasonable and the extraordinary are woven into his period with a firmness that critical method cannot ignore. Indeed, reason is now often not the key to historical understanding, but the touchstone which reveals the full magnitude of what Gibbon must struggle to understand:

The Koran inculcates, in the most absolute sense, the tenets of fate and predestination, which would extinguish both industry and virtue, if the actions of man were governed by his speculative belief. Yet their influence in every age has exalted the courage of the Saracens and Turks.[23]

Hume had accounted for the limited influence of 'speculative belief' on our quotidian lives by invoking our habitual carelessness and inattention, thereby assuming that whenever we thought seriously, we thought rigorously and rationally.[24] But the unpredictable courage of the Saracens and Turks opens up another possibility: that men in different times and places thought in serious ways nevertheless quite distinct from those we now dub 'reasonable'. And the more richly intersected is the past with fissures dividing periods in which different ideas of reason seem to have prevailed, the more will a rationalist, uniformitarian critical method indicate to us merely the edges of the fragment of time on which we happen to find ourselves.[25]

Gibbon's account of the discovery of the holy lance at Antioch shows his thoughtful attitude to what, for example, Voltaire would be content simply to mock as religious imposture. The language in which the episode is introduced suggests amusement stemming from the confirmation of a worldly view of government:

. . . their confidence was revived by a visible sign, the seasonable and splendid discovery of the HOLY LANCE. The policy of their chiefs has on this occasion been admired, and might surely be excused; but a pious fraud is seldom produced by the cool conspiracy of many persons; and a voluntary impostor might depend on the support of the wise and the credulity of the people.[26]

---

[22] *The Decline and Fall*, IV.6.
[23] *The Decline and Fall*, V.231. Compare J. W. Johnson, *The Formation of English Neo-Classical Thought*, p. 218.
[24] *Treatise of Human Nature*, pp. 263–74.
[25] Compare Collingwood, *The Idea of History*, pp. 218–19.
[26] *The Decline and Fall*, VI.52.

Bartholemy the monk duly discovers the lance, which inspires the besieged Christians to rout their enemies. But jealousy provokes murmurs, and Bartholemy is forced 'to submit his life and veracity to the judgement of God', dying the next day of his burns. Gibbon closes the matter:

. . . he expired the next day; and the logic of believing minds will pay some regard to his dying protestations of innocence and truth. Some efforts were made by the Provincials to substitute a cross, a ring, or a tabernacle, in the place of the holy lance, which soon vanished in contempt and oblivion. Yet the revelation of Antioch is gravely asserted by succeeding historians; and such is the progress of credulity, that miracles, most doubtful on the spot and at the moment, will be received with implicit faith at a convenient distance of time and space.[27]

The achievement of this passage is its conveying, through its studiously impartial though regretful tone, of how bluntly to reject the story of the holy lance is just as misguided as blithely to accept it. Contempt and oblivion are as inappropriate as that paradox, the logic of believing minds. In the division of opinion into those who support and those who deny, the essence of the event is in danger of being lost. Philosophic critical method tells us what we hardly needed to know, that the lance was a fake; but in the resultant babble of squabbling voices, the really strange is overlooked.[28] That a 'voluntary impostor' should be found is as remarkable as that the holy lance should be discovered.[29]

One particularly notices Gibbon's new patience with the anomalous when it touches religion because of his whole-hearted adoption of the opposed view in 1776; but his patience is not confined to the religious. Discussing the traditional accounts of the engineering feats of Justinian's reign, Gibbon distinguishes his critical attitude from that of the philosophers whose unwillingness to accept the partialness of their own perspective impoverishes their view of history:

Both the theory and practice of the arts which depend on mathematical science and mechanical power were cultivated under the patronage of the emperors; the fame of Archimedes was rivalled by Proclus and Anthemius; and if their *miracles* had been related by intelligent spectators, they might now enlarge the speculations, instead of exciting the distrust, of philosophers.[30]

Gibbon shows that his own distrust is not dominant when he goes on to redeem the story of the incinerating mirrors with which Proclus burnt the

---

[27] *The Decline and Fall*, VI.54–5.

[28] Kames states the philosophic attitude to the anomalous: 'The improbability I talk of, is that of an irregular fact, contrary to the order and course of nature, and therefore unaccountable . . . an irregular fact always puzzles the judgement. Doubtful of its reality we immediately enter upon reflection, and discovering the cheat, lose all relish and concern' (H. Home, Lord Kames, *Elements of Criticism*, I.124).

[29] A good comparison, which shows the growing suppleness of Gibbon's criticism, is with the passage in which he discusses the relics discovered by the clergy of Jerusalem (*The Decline and Fall*, II.384).

[30] *The Decline and Fall*, IV.89.

Gothic ships in the harbour of Constantinople, and when he reinstates, through an amalgam of scholarship and imagination, traditions abolished with 'too liberal and indiscriminate disdain' by philosophers such as Hume and Voltaire.[31] The uniformity of human nature, such as it is, is not the end of an historian's critical inquiries, but the beginning:

> . . . both sexes were accused as equally inaccessible to pity, and their appetite for raw flesh might countenance the popular tale, that they drank the blood and feasted on the hearts of the slain. Yet the Hungarians were not devoid of those principles of justice and humanity, which nature has implanted in every bosom. The licence of public and private injuries was restrained by laws and punishments . . .[32]

Gibbon does not acquiesce in the 'popular tale', but nor does he dismiss it as mere fabrication. Together with the fact which 'might countenance' it, it is positioned alongside the more regular elements in the humanity of the Hungarians to produce just that sense of displacement and incongruity, of a finer shade of fact, which in 1788 prevents Gibbon from reposing in uniformitarianism, and which turns it from the rock which had served as the foundation of Volume I to a stone over which the historian stumbles in his efforts clearly to assess the magnitude of the past. This is why he refuses to be precipitate when approaching the edges of certainty:

> [Boniface VIII] was succeeded by Benedict the eleventh, the mildest of mankind. Yet he excommunicated the impious emissaries of Philip, and devoted the city and people of Anagni by a tremendous curse, whose effects are still visible to the eyes of superstition.

The footnote runs:

> It is difficult to know whether Labat (tom. iv. p. 53–57.) be in jest or in earnest, when he supposes that Anagni still feels the weight of this curse, and that the corn-fields, or vineyards, or olive-trees, are annually blasted by nature, the obsequious handmaid of the popes.[33]

In Volume I, the reader would have had little doubt that this was ironic; and indeed, an ironic smile still plays over the phrase 'the obsequious handmaid of the popes'. But there is also a genuine doubt in the words 'It is difficult to know . . .'. In 1788 Gibbon does find the anomalous problematic; and the reason for this is to be found in the striking expression, 'the

---

[31] *The Decline and Fall*, VI.83. Examples of such reinstatements are the iron cage in which Tamerlane kept Bajazet (*The Decline and Fall*, VI.352–6) and the massive cannon Mahomet II directed against Constantinople (*The Decline and Fall*, VI.475–7). Gibbon rebukes Hume in *The Decline and Fall*, I.xxi n. 18: I.161 n. 18, and Voltaire in *The Decline and Fall*, II.135 n. 23 and VI.58 n. 106.

[32] *The Decline and Fall*, V.553.

[33] *The Decline and Fall*, VI.555 and n. 78.

eyes of superstition'. Gibbon recognises that the historian is called upon to understand these alien casts of mind, not to vilify them.[34]

It is for this reason that Gibbon tends to redirect attention away from physical anomalies, and towards what we might call moral prodigies. Nature and nature's laws have probably remained constant (though even here we should hesitate before assuming we have taken their measure). But one cannot say the same for human nature:

Avarice was the only defect that tarnished the illustrious character of Mahmud; and never has that passion been more richly satiated. The Orientals exceed the measure of credibility in the account of millions of gold and silver, such as the avidity of man has never accumulated; in the magnitude of pearls, diamonds, and rubies, such as have never been produced by the workmanship of nature. Yet the soil of Hindostan is impregnated with precious minerals; her trade, in every age, has attracted the gold and silver of the world; and her virgin spoils were rifled by the first of the Mahometan conquerors.[35]

It is appropriate to recall the hold that the fabulous East had over the imagination of young Edward Gibbon, since here we can see that the historian, at the end of his career, is adopting a position in which the fabulous is not dismissed as juvenile extravagance and banished from history, as the *philosophes* had demanded.[36] Hume-like scepticism, in the intellectual style of 'On the Populousness of Ancient Nations', is given its due, but it is immediately checked by an acknowledgement of the extraordinary profusion of gems in India. And the life of the language here is so important: 'impregnated' and 'virgin' in such close proximity savour of the paradox and prodigy which is so often Gibbon's lot in these centuries, while underlining the anomaly of Indian wealth, which disables philosophic scepticism, by suggesting a fecundity more animal than mineral. Thus the effect of this passage is to leave us dwelling on the past in a state of enlightened ignorance. Mahmud's avarice was slaked, but we can know neither how great it was, nor the measure of the riches which satisfied it. The natural prodigy is justified and brought within the bounds of the regular; however, we are then immediately confronted with the moral prodigy, the extension of our idea of human nature, posed by Mahmud's enormous appetite for wealth. Gibbon does not pass judgement,

---

[34] If we examine Labat's *Voyages du P. Labat . . . en Espagne et en Italie*, we can further appreciate why Gibbon was genuinely bemused. He begins by affirming the disastrous effects of the curse: 'La malediction de ce S. Pape a eu son effet tout entier, & l'avoit encore dans le tems que j'ai vu cette ville desolée' (p. 83). But later his piety, to an uninnocent ear, comes close to irony: 'L'espérance de quelque chose de meilleur a toujours soutenu les étrangers qui s'y sont venus établir à la place de cette race maudite qui est presque entièrement éteinte; il n'en restoit plus en 1709 qu'une fille qui avoit pres de soixante ans, & par conséquent hors d'état de faire revivre cette malheureuse génération. Je me suis étonné bien des fois comment on ne l'avoit point aidée à aller promptement joindre ses ancêtres; Dieu ne le permet pas, il faut que le vase de sa colère ne soit pas encore vuide' (p. 85).

[35] *The Decline and Fall*, V.650.

[36] Compare *Memoirs*, p. 36.

but leaves the matter implicit in prose which, instead of pronouncing, leads the reader to a point of contemplation. If we recollect Gibbon's portrait of Augustus from Volume I, which was also marked with reserve, the significance of his refusal to allow his critical thinking to emulsify history will be clear. The portrait of Augustus had a legible imperfection which Gibbon eventually resolved, and both the imperfection and its resolution were moves in his large, shaping strategy in that volume. But the incompleteness, the suspension of judgement, we discover in 1788 grows out of the obstinacy of the past in the face of the historian's scrutiny which put paid to such ambitions.

Gibbon's enlarged apprehension of the past in 1788 calls into being a critical method which to a strictly philosophic eye might seem neither critical nor methodical. It aims not to pass a verdict, but, by viewing evidence from a variety of standpoints – sceptical, scholarly, imaginative, sympathetic – to open a question up, not close it down. Gibbon's review of the number of Crusaders, a topic on which a surgical, probabilistic critical method would have cut deep, is a good example of his new practice:

The conquest of Asia was undertaken and atchieved by Alexander, with thirty-five thousand Macedonians and Greeks; and his best hope was in the strength and discipline of his phalanx of infantry. The principal force of the crusaders consisted in their cavalry; and when that force was mustered in the plains of Bithynia, the knights and their martial attendants on horseback amounted to one hundred thousand fighting men, completely armed with the helmet and coat of mail. The value of these soldiers deserved a strict and authentic account; and the flower of European chivalry might furnish, in a first effort, this formidable body of heavy horse. A part of the infantry might be enrolled for the service of scouts, pioneers, and archers; but the promiscuous crowd were lost in their own disorder; and we depend not on the eyes or knowledge, but on the belief and fancy, of a chaplain of count Baldwin, in the estimate of six hundred thousand pilgrims able to bear arms, besides the priests and monks, the women and children, of the Latin camp. The reader starts; and before he is recovered from his surprise, I shall add, on the same testimony, that if all who took the cross had accomplished their vow, above SIX MILLIONS would have migrated from Europe to Asia. Under this oppression of faith, I derive some relief from a more sagacious and thinking writer, who, after the same review of the cavalry, accuses the credulity of the priest of Chartres, and even doubts whether the *Cisalpine* regions (in the geography of a Frenchman) were sufficient to produce and pour forth such incredible multitudes. The coolest scepticism will remember, that of these religious volunteers great numbers never beheld Constantinople and Nice. Of enthusiasm the influence is irregular and transient: many were detained at home by reason or cowardice, by poverty or weakness; and many were repulsed by the obstacles of the way, the more insuperable as they were unforeseen to these ignorant fanatics. The savage countries of Hungary and Bulgaria were whitened with their bones: their vanguard was cut in pieces by the Turkish sultan; and the loss of the first adventure by the sword, or climate, or fatigue, has already been stated at three hundred thousand men. Yet the myriads that survived, that marched, that pressed forwards on the holy pilgrimage, were a subject of astonishment to themselves and to the Greeks. The copious energy of her language sinks under the efforts of the princess Anne: the image of locusts, of leaves and flowers, of the sands of the sea, or the stars of heaven, imperfectly represent what she had seen and heard; and the daughter of Alexius exclaims, that Europe was loosened from its foundations, and hurled against Asia. The ancient hosts of Darius and Xerxes labour under the same doubt of a vague and indefinite magnitude; but I am inclined to believe, that a larger number has never been contained within the lines of a single camp than at the siege of Nice, the first operation of the Latin princes.[37]

De Crousaz instructed the youthful Gibbon that histories were 'Books that require the least Attention of any'.[38] This passage shows by how far Gibbon has exceeded his intellectual matrix, for what is remarkable about the quotation is the very great attention it demands from its reader. Gibbon does not announce his conclusion and then argue for it (he has nothing so definite as a conclusion). Instead, we find that it is only at the end of a series of sentences rich in diverse testimony and reflection that Gibbon pauses on his inclination – which is not a litotes for 'conviction', but a direct expression of the provisional and hesitant notions in which historical study now culminates. We begin with the historical parallel. There follows a stream of evidence and inference which Gibbon is careful to prevent from settling down into simple and direct exposition. Thus we have repeated changes of tack, the unveilings of new perspectives or additional and transforming information, usually introduced with an adversative conjunction ('but the promiscuous crowd', 'yet the myriads that survived', 'but I am inclined to believe'); the nod towards 'the coolest scepticism', but also the determination to inquire into, and not merely dismiss, this startling matter; and finally the introduction of contrasting contemporary opinions – that of Fulcherius Cartonensis, 'a chaplain of Count Baldwin', that of 'the more sagacious and thinking' Guibert, and that of 'the princess Anne'.

The collocation of this mass of evidence and opinion, which Gibbon presents, rather than judges, conveys to the reader a more spacious intimation of the possibilities of history. To read this prose gives one the sense of being in contact with a fine historical intelligence, but caught while in the process of itself contemplating the past. The diversity of the evidence Gibbon collects marks out the ground on which the past may be imaginatively apprehended, and gaping, startled astonishment transformed into a deep, measured admiration shared by both the historian and his reader, now initiated into that process of alert and mobile thought which constitutes historical knowledge.[39]

---

[37] *The Decline and Fall*, VI.38–9. In fact, Hume does not strain at the multitudes of Crusaders he encounters in his sources, and transcribes from Matthew Paris without a murmur the total of '700,000 combatants' (*History*, I.327); a good example of the gap between Hume's historiographic practice and his theorising.

[38] *A New Treatise of the Art of Thinking*, I.269.

[39] I imagine it is to this aspect of Gibbon's style that Coleridge is referring when he deplores what he sees as 'an odd sort of narration in the form of *argument* which reminds one of Lucian's Historian who related every event in a multitude of separate Syllogisms' (*Notebooks*, note 3823). If one compares Gibbon's account of the supposed revolt of the mint suppressed by Aurelian

Addison, articulating the common sense of the early years of the eighteenth century, thought that a wise man, faced with conflicting evidence, stayed neutral. But Gibbon finds that it is just such conflict which engages and piques the historian, who in following its coils traces the boundaries of the historical.[40] At the end of Volume I Gibbon had said, with the air of one invoking an irrefragable critical principle, 'I cannot determine what I ought to transcribe, till I am satisfied how much I ought to believe.'[41] In 1776 it had seemed obvious that composition could only follow criticism, whose handmaid it was and whose findings it becomingly expressed. Like so much of Volume I, that firm position is undermined by the passage of time. The inquisitive flexibility of Gibbon's critical thought in 1788 suggests a fresh conviction that the fullest understanding of the past does not precede composition, but comes only when phrasing at length and casting history into words. Composition and criticism are coeval and interpenetrating elements in the complex, unformulable process which, for Gibbon in 1788, is historiography. No wonder he thought historians were born, not made.[42]

Gibbon arrives, then, at a critical method which is far from an immobile and magisterial process of either acceptance or denial carried out in a single and unchanging voice. Instead of the decisiveness and sense of closure which marked Volume I, we find in Gibbon the complex succession of accents proper to an historian willing to examine history from a number of different angles without unreservedly committing himself to any one of them.[43] In 1776 Gibbon's allusions to more recent history had proclaimed his modernity and the independent point of vantage on the past which had preserved his independence while guaranteeing his perceptiveness.[44] In 1788 he talks more of the sacrifice of settled composure the past demands of him:

(*The Decline and Fall*, I.317–19: I.378–80) with this discusssion of the number of Crusaders, the difference is plain. In Volume I, we find none of the play between conflicting material that Gibbon sets up in 1788; instead, we have what is in effect a short essay, in which Gibbon argues single-mindedly for this not being a sedition fomented by the mint-workers, but a conspiracy against the new emperor by the senate, the equestrian order and the praetorian guard. As is usual in Volume I, Gibbon wishes to impress us with his authority, not share with us his uncertainty. Other examples of Gibbon's ultimate, flexible critical thought are the calculations on p. 77 of Volume VI of *The Decline and Fall*, or his remarks on Athens (*The Decline and Fall*, VI.255).

[40] *Spectator* no. 117; *Works*, III.43.
[41] *The Decline and Fall*, I.582: I.699.
[42] 'After his oracle Dr Johnson, my friend Sir Joshua Reynolds denies all original Genius, any natural propensity of the mind to one art or science rather than another. Without engaging in a metaphysical or rather verbal dispute, I *know* by experience that from my early youth, I aspired to the character of an historian' (*Memoirs*, p. 119). Compare Shaftesbury's ideas on 'conatural aptitude' in his *Philosophical Regimen*.
[43] For a contrasting example from Volume I, consider Gibbon's discussion of Alexander Severus' Persian campaign (*The Decline and Fall*, I.213–15: I.253–6).
[44] See above, p. 97.

After pursuing above six hundred years the fleeting Caesars of Constantinople and Germany, I now descend, in the reign of Heraclius, on the eastern borders of the Greek monarchy.[45]

It would be a mistake to ignore the elements of playfulness in this. But it would equally be a mistake to write it off as mere playfulness, because its image of the historian as a phantom traveller, observing but unobserved, voyaging imaginatively through the past, is but a slight exaggeration of what we have seen is actually the case.

The growing suppleness and mobility of Gibbon as an historian affects more than the critical method of *The Decline and Fall*. Now that critical method for Gibbon is not a process of thought which comes before the writing of narrative (which is its product), but invades the domain of narrative with its intricate considerations, the mobility of Gibbon's critical thought also influences the narrative procedures of *The Decline and Fall*.

Gibbon frequently introduces general figures into his narrative: the philosopher, the philosophic historian, the sceptic, the historian of the Roman empire. Some critics – for example, David Jordan in his *Gibbon and his Roman Empire* – have assumed that these are all periphrases for 'I', and thus versions of Gibbon himself. This is sometimes so:

He [Caecilius] affirms with the most perfect confidence, that in the night which preceded the last battle against Maxentius, Constantine was admonished in a dream to inscribe the shields of his soldiers with the *celestial sign of God*, the sacred monogram of the name of Christ; that he executed the commands of heaven, and that his valour and obedience were rewarded by the decisive victory of the Milvian bridge. Some considerations might perhaps incline a sceptical mind to suspect the judgment or the veracity of the rhetorician, whose pen, either from zeal or interest, was devoted to the cause of the prevailing faction.[46]

Whose is the 'sceptical mind'? A footnote suggests that it might belong to Lardner, or to Le Clerc, who had questioned Caecilius' reliability in the *Bibliothèque Ancienne et Moderne*.[47] But the critical principle of evaluating evidence in the light of the witness' allegiances was a commonplace, and so when we find Gibbon later incorporating the inclinations of the sceptical mind into his own arguments, it seems clear that the 'sceptical mind' is an urbane circumlocution which allows him to question Caecilius' honesty without bumptiously giving him the lie direct.[48]

---

[45] *The Decline and Fall*, V.170.

[46] *The Decline and Fall*, II.196.

[47] *The Decline and Fall*, II.196 n. 40.

[48] On this principle for evaluating evidence, see Locke, *Essay Concerning Human Understanding*, IV.15.4–16.10. It is for the same reason that Gibbon seems to be 'the historian' in the following quotation. He himself subsequently does what he notes is permitted to the historian: 'The historian may therefore be permitted respectfully to withdraw the veil of the sanctuary; and to deduce the progress of reason and faith, of error and passion, from the school of Plato to the decline and fall of the empire' (*The Decline and Fall*, II.237).

But we may remember that Gibbon's contemporaries were fond of literary forms which, without being in the fullest sense dramatic, nevertheless produced their meaning out of the collision of a number of points of view, none of which had full authority; one might think of *Rasselas*, or *Pamela* and *Clarissa*. Gibbon, too, often uses these shadowy, generalised figures to create such an effect – for instance, when discussing the religious suicides of the Donatists:

When they were disappointed of every other resource, they announced the day on which, in the presence of their friends and brethren, they should cast themselves headlong from some lofty rock; and many precipices were shewn, which had acquired fame by the number of religious suicides. In the actions of these desperate enthusiasts, who were admired by one party as the martyrs of God, and abhorred by the other, as the victims of Satan, an impartial philosopher may discover the influence and the last abuse of that inflexible spirit, which was originally derived from the character and principles of the Jewish nation.[49]

Since Gibbon himself has earlier written of the inflexible spirit of the Jews, one might plausibly take him to be this impartial philosopher.[50] But the passage deals so much with the different perspectives on these suicides – that of the friends and brethren who watch the spectacle, those of the opposed parties of admirers and abhorrers, and finally that of the impartial philosopher – that, despite the change of tense in 'may discover', which announces the modernity of the philosopher, Gibbon's point of view is more ample than that of this distant observer. The impartial philosopher, standing on the ground Gibbon had occupied in 1776, is now simply one of a number of points of view contained in the passage, which comes at the end of a paragraph, and whose conflict of perspectives is not decided by Gibbon's finally speaking in unmistakably his own voice. He leaves us to form our own judgements of the varying degrees of credibility appropriate to impartiality flawed by distance, and propinquity stained with passion.

Thus we often find, in and after the second instalment of 1781, that when Gibbon uses one of these general figures he takes care to prevent their submerging or replacing his own independent vision. Indeed, he appears sometimes to be correcting possible misconceptions about the range and flexibility of his mind:

A philosopher may deplore the eternal discord of the human race, but he will confess, that the desire of spoil is a more rational provocation than the vanity of conquest.

Their [the monks'] natural descent, from such painful and dangerous virtue, to the common vices of humanity, will not, perhaps, excite much grief or indignation in the mind of a philosopher.[51]

In the first example, Gibbon indicates that his thoughts go beyond the philosopher's blame of man's discord (although a philosopher nevertheless

---

[49] *The Decline and Fall*, II.303–4.   [50] See *The Decline and Fall*, I.451–4: I.537–41.
[51] *The Decline and Fall*, II.530 and III.521.

can be brought to acknowledge the justice of Gibbon's more extensive view); while in the second, his awareness of the narrowness of the philosopher's sympathies implies his own wider and more blended feelings.

Gibbon's comments about the tone proper to historiography are pertinent here. Quintilian had maintained that the true historical voice could be described in terms of other, purer voices.[52] In his *Memoirs*, Gibbon echoes the Roman by ascribing to historiography an accent suspended between conflicting, vicious alternatives into which it might lapse: 'Many experiments were made before I could hit the middle tone between a dull Chronicle and a Rhetorical declamation.'[53] The difficult poise of the best historiographical idiom, its ability to touch on many accents and its need to be confined to none, is most germane to the great enrichment of tone we find in 1788, and which we shall consider in a moment. But it also bears on these personifications. The true historical perspective can be described in terms only of what it is not. Its range can be plotted, but not its essence defined. As we proceed through *The Decline and Fall* these generalised figures cease to be momentary disguises for Gibbon's voice and become instead ideal positions he places within his narrative, each of which helps to define, but none of which comprises, the authorial point of view. At times he firmly separates himself from them:

The Protestant and philosophic readers of the present age will incline to believe, that, in the account of his own conversion, Constantine attested a wilful falsehood by a solemn and deliberate perjury . . . A conclusion so harsh and so absolute is not, however, warranted by our knowledge of human nature, of Constantine, or of Christianity.[54]

In 1788 Gibbon may remove himself still further by replacing these figures with abstract qualities:

Humanity may drop a tear on the fate of Nestorius: yet justice must observe, that he suffered the persecution which he had approved and inflicted.[55]

Gibbon partakes of both humanity and justice, but he is neither. Nor is he charity, still less an inquisitive polytheist:

. . . charity will hope that many of his [Mahomet's] proselytes entertained a serious conviction of the truth and sanctity of his revelation. In the eyes of an inquisitive polytheist, it must appear worthy of the human and the divine nature.[56]

[52] 'historia est . . . proxime poetis et quodam modo carmen solutum' (*Institutio Oratoria*, X.i.31).
[53] *Memoirs*, p. 155. His projected 'History of the Swiss' came to grief through not being able to maintain this fine balance: 'I was conscious myself, that my style, above prose and below poetry, degenerated into a verbose and turgid declamation' (*Memoirs*, p. 142).
[54] *The Decline and Fall*, II.201. This is not an uncommon feature of prose at the end of the eighteenth century; see, for instance, Mrs Radcliffe's *The Italian*, p. 173.
[55] *The Decline and Fall*, IV.563.
[56] *The Decline and Fall*, V.382–3. One should also note those moments when an apparently anonymous figure disguises an actual person, identified in a footnote: see *The Decline and Fall*, IV.98 (Montesquieu), IV.178 (d'Anville) and V.537 (Halley).

In life, Gibbon (who considered that he himself possessed 'the flexible temper which can assimilate itself to every tone of society from the court to the cottage') was fascinated by those whose personality could assume other guises, and who thus might be said almost to have no personality of their own:

I can't help mentioning here the surprising versatility of Mrs. Pritchard's talents, who rehearsed, almost at the same time, the part of a furious Queen in the Greenroom, and that of a Coquette on the stage; and passed several times from one to the other with the utmost ease and happiness.[57]

Gibbon's practice as an historian is close to these models of mercurial virtuosity. While never unreservedly and exclusively becoming one of the ideal figures who people the narrative of *The Decline and Fall*, he moves ceaselessly between them, now closer to one, now closer to another.

Gibbon gives what seems to be the conventional explanation of the appeal and utility of history:

Nature has implanted in our breasts a lively impulse to extend the narrow span of our existence, by the knowledge, of the events that have happened on the soil which we inhabit . . .

Our imagination is always active to enlarge the narrow circle in which Nature has confined us.[58]

It was the traditional belief of pragmatic historians that history enlarged those who contemplated it by extending their basis of analogy through the knowledge it provided of other times and other places. But *The Decline and Fall* instructs us that there is a further sense in which the practice of history may extend the historian. Because Gibbon's narrative position is situated in the midst of a number of ideal, pure positions and braced by the tensions they engender, he is always aware of the numerous and divergent claims on his allegiance these positions exert. In partially resisting some, he necessarily and simultaneously yields in part to others. Thus the kind of independence Gibbon ultimately achieves in *The Decline and Fall* is badly figured by Hume's inviolable rock: his independence consists of endless diplomacy between competing, strident and simplifying voices into which the unwary, insufficiently reflective and sympathetic historian might lapse. That unceasing negotiation, demanding both a truly impartial critical method and an imaginative penetration of the past, is manifested in a scrupulous nuance of tone which on the surface is indistinguishable from the determined philosophic accents of 1776, but which in intent, in its sympathetic openness to the past, is quite its opposite. And in that movement, Gibbon has himself been extended: both the number and the quality of his ideas have increased.[59]

---

[57] *Memoirs*, p. 136; *Gibbon's Journal to January 28th, 1763*, p. 186. Note also his admiration for Texier who, like Henry Crawford, could take all the parts in a play: 'At last I have heard Texier; wonderful!' (*Letters*, II.97).

[58] *The English Essays of Edward Gibbon*, p. 534; *Memoirs*, p. 3.

[59] There is thus great felicity in Walpole's praising *The Decline and Fall* to Mason in a way which

The suspension of Gibbon's narrative voice I have just described gives it in 1788 the suppleness and mobility required by the historian's imaginative travelling through the past. That voyaging is registered in another resource of style Gibbon's command of language offers him. Considering a crisis when Constantius' self-confidence wavered, Gibbon quotes from Ammianus Marcellinus in a footnote, and adds: 'He then expresses, in their own words, the flattering assurances of the courtiers.'[60] Gibbon can be sure that the words Ammianus uses are intended to belong to the courtiers, because he uses *oratio obliqua*: 'infatuabant hominem, nihil esse ita asperum dictitantes.'[61] The grammatical inflexion marks off the language of Ammianus from that of the persons in his narrative. But, in English, indirect speech is not so un-equivocally marked, and Gibbon is adept at exploiting our shock when we realise that words and opinions to which we had granted an authorial status are in fact not the author's at all. In the unpublished essay 'Sur la Succession de l'Empire Romain', Gibbon comments straightforwardly on the grounds of the praetorians' belief that their electoral role was sovereign under the principate:

Autrefois toute la nation étoit soldats, et toute la nation élisoit ses chefs; sous les empereurs la partie la plus choisie l'étoit, et cette partie sembloit avoir succédé aux droits du tout, et devoir concourir avec le sénat dans l'élection de ses princes. Par cette raison, les prétoriens habitans de Rome croyoient y avoir plus de droit que les légion-naires, qui n'étoient que citoyens Romains . . .[62]

When Gibbon came to work this up in *The Decline and Fall*, the simple tracing of facts which had contented the youth of twenty is replaced by a studied prose which first entices, and then abandons, the reader:

But where was the Roman people to be found? Not surely amongst the mixed multitude of slaves and strangers that filled the streets of Rome; a servile populace, as devoid of spirit as destitute of property. The defenders of the state, selected from the flower of the Italian youth, and trained in the exercise of arms and virtue, were the genuine representatives of the people, and the best entitled to elect the military chief of the republic. These assertions, however defective in reason, became unanswerable, when the fierce Praetorians increased their weight . . .[63]

It is only when we are told that these arguments are 'defective in reason' that

---

suggests not only a vigorous newcomer bursting through the ruck of extant historians, but also the particularity rising out of the narrative's suspension between different positions: 'Lo, there is just appeared a truly classic work: a history, not majestic like Livy, nor compressed like Tacitus; not stamped with character like Clarendon; perhaps not so deep as Robertson's *Scotland*, but a thousand degrees above his *Charles*; not pointed like Voltaire, but as accurate as he is inexact; modest as he is *tranchant* and sly as Montesquieu without being so *recherché*' (*Correspondence*, XXVIII.243).

60 *The Decline and Fall*, II.139 n. 30
61 *Res Gestae*, XV.viii.2.
62 *Miscellaneous Works*, III.176–7.
63 *The Decline and Fall*, I.108: I.129–30.

we know for certain that the sentences from 'Not surely . . .' to '. . . the republic' are not authorial comments, but the sentiments, given indirectly, of the praetorians themselves. And in our consequent reassessment of what we have just read, we find that Gibbon has adroitly enlisted our scorn and our support; that he has mobilised our admiration for his superior discrimination and our dismay at the events he narrates.

However, in 1788 such graces of style serve to add not distinction to the historian, but distinctness to the past. They become means whereby Gibbon can momentarily occupy the positions of the actors in history:

The Greeks affected to despise the poverty and ignorance of the Franks and Saxons; and in their last decline, refused to prostitute to the kings of Germany the title of Roman emperors.[64]

Gibbon has exposed the vices of the Byzantine court sufficiently for us to know that Otho, for all his flaws, would have added lustre to the title of Roman emperor, rather than the reverse. 'Prostitute' is not Gibbon's but Byzantium's word, and in it is displayed, but also created and realised, the groundless pride of the Eastern empire. It is as if the narrative were momentarily taken over by the past and revived for an instant in Gibbon's imagination. The same is true of a telling indeterminacy in Gibbon's account of the deposition of Alexius and his father by Mourzoufle:

The emperor Isaac Angelus soon followed his son to the grave, and Mourzoufle, perhaps, might spare the superfluous crime of hastening the extinction of impotence and blindness.[65]

'Might spare' is a critical conjecture on Gibbon's part; but in the way 'might' captures Mourzoufle's haughtiness and disdain, it is also indirect speech conveying the vivid pride of new majesty.

A passage from Volume I, which seems in its approximation of narrative and past to be similar, but which in fact is not, will focus the point. Gibbon is discussing the emigration of the Goths from Scandinavia into Prussia:

To cross the Baltic was an easy and natural attempt. The inhabitants of Sweden were masters of a sufficient number of large vessels, with oars, and the distance is little more than one hundred miles from Carlscroon to the nearest ports of Pomerania and Prussia. Here, at length, we land on firm and historic ground.[66]

For Gibbon to speak of his narrative landing on firm and historic ground when his subject is navigation may seem a notable approximation of history and historiography similar to the closeness which arises from the use of disguised indirect speech. But in their effects they differ in a way which illustrates the change from 1776 to 1788 in Gibbon's aims as an historian and

---

[64] *The Decline and Fall*, V.151.   [65] *The Decline and Fall*, VI.162.
[66] *The Decline and Fall*, I.247: I.294–5.

in his historic sensibility. In using the expression 'we land on firm and historic ground', Gibbon is exemplifying his competence to avoid inappropriate imagery and his wit in finding pertinent expressions.[67] As so often in 1776, Gibbon is seeking yet further accreditation as a supremely competent historian able in one breath to be scholarly and stylish. In its ultimate tendency this passage from Volume I is thus the reverse of those later moments from the final three volumes when the authorial voice is for a time extinguished. In Volume I Gibbon's authorial personality is a distinctive and constant part of the narrative. In the later volumes, he is less concerned to define and buttress his own perspective – the difficulty of the past has in any case so complicated his thoughts that he no longer possesses anything so well defined as a perspective. Instead, we find that he is more willing to turn his narrative open and allow the past to enter it through the medium of his imagination.

This seems close to what Collingwood has said about history being what the historian thinks, and thus re-experiences mentally.[68] But this is too cerebral a notion for Gibbon. In *The Decline and Fall* history is eventually a vision and the past an object of perception:

Before I lose sight of the field of Warna . . .

Puoi se saceva stare denante a se, mentre sedeva, li baroni tutti in piedi ritti co le vraccia piecate, e co li capucci tratti. Deh como stavano paurosi! . . . He saw them, and we see them.[69]

It is the imagination, dubbed by Michel Baridon 'l'auxiliare précieux de l'historien', which presents the past to the historian in this way. In so doing it furnishes, to those who trust it, knowledge more full and discriminating than we can derive from our physical vision: 'In a twenty years residence at Cairo, the consul Maillet had contemplated that varying scene, the Nile . . . From a college at Cambridge, the poetic eye of Gray had *seen* the same objects with a keener glance.'[70]

---

[67] The *desideratum* of metaphorical propriety is well stated in the later eighteenth century by Goldsmith, who in his essay 'Metaphor' censures the 'young author [who] is apt to run into a confusion of mixed metaphors, which leave the sense disjointed, and distract the imagination' (*The Miscellaneous Works of Oliver Goldsmith*, p. 332). Its most notorious invocation is by Johnson when criticising Addison.

[68] For instance, 'all history, is the re-enactment of past thought in the historian's own mind' (*The Idea of History*, p. 215). Compare Popper: 'In fact, if we know anything about different attitudes in different historical periods, then it is from experiments, carried out in our imagination' (*The Poverty of Historicism*, p. 95).

[69] *The Decline and Fall*, VI.451 and VI.585 n. 41.

[70] *Edward Gibbon et le Mythe de Rome*, p. 804; *The Decline and Fall*, V.347 n. 129. By contrast, the *philosophe* and pyrrhonist Louis de Beaufort scorns imagination as the source of only error: 'Cet Auteur a orné ses Narrations de quantité d'Episodes, qui ne sont que le Fruit de son Imagination' (*Dissertation sur l'Incertitude des Cinq Premiers Siecles de L'Histoire Romaine*, I.183). Gibbon, however, might have agreed with Collingwood that 'the historical imagination . . . is properly not ornamental but structural' (*The Idea of History*, p. 241; compare *Essays in the Philosophy of History*, p. 48), for he frequently indicates in 1788 that the imagination is the faculty through which we experience and appreciate history (*The Decline and Fall*, VI.50 and 358). Gibbon's

Gibbon's greater humility before the past, and his realisation that its resistance to his intelligence is grounds for careful inquiry, not impatient dismissal, goes together with his understanding that the extraordinary and wonderful are not merely the offal of history. However unprofitable they may seem to the historian's reason, they may nevertheless be appreciated by his imagination. The primacy of the imagination, and the rehabilitation of the wonderful, conspire in 1788 to change the nature of Gibbon's irony. We saw that in 1776 irony for Gibbon was not just a question of style, even though the demands of his irony governed every detail of his style. That whole first volume has a structure and a strategy which, in its sustained dissimulation, is properly called ironic. In the last volumes of *The Decline and Fall*, however, the scale of Gibbon's irony is reduced from chapters to sentences. It now provides mere flashes of amusement and has decayed to the level of witticism:

The unreasonable request of an empress, who wished to deprive the Romans of their sacred treasure, the head of St. Paul, was rejected with the deepest abhorrence; and the pope asserted, most probably with truth, that a linen which had been sanctified in the neighbourhood of his body, or the filings of his chain, which it was sometimes easy and sometimes impossible to obtain, possessed an equal degree of miraculous virtue.[71]

The play of meanings in 'unreasonable', the possible, malicious literalness of 'treasure' (the rumoured possession of relics being a certain source of income), the urbanity of 'most probably with truth', the polished delaying of 'equal degree of miraculous virtue' which freshens an old ploy – these are all attractive notes which recall, but cannot equal, the much richer orchestration of irony in Chapter XV.[72] We have here the shallow irony of mere style, with Gibbon no longer the heir of the grave and temperate Pascal, but simply the dandy of disingenuousness. We are far from the concentration, even urgency, with which, despite its polished manner, irony is employed in the service of thought in Volume I.

use of the word 'imagination' in 1788, and its implications for the kind of thought he felt historiography demanded, suggest that he was moving away from the commonsensical position derived from Locke and restated for a wider audience by Addison in *Spectator* no. 411, that our imagination can never picture anything which has not previously been registered by our sight, but by compounding ideas derived from sensations can produce images which do not correspond to things already seen. By the time he comes to write the final instalment of *The Decline and Fall*, Gibbon is moving away from a narrow reasonableness in both critical method and the larger field of epistemology.

[71] *The Decline and Fall*, IV.455–6.

[72] Compare also 'His spirit . . .' (*The Decline and Fall*, IV.42) and 'In this dangerous estimate . . .' (*The Decline and Fall*, VI.11–12). Often the phrasing of this simpler irony is shaped by irresistible wit: '. . . the most scandalous charges were suppressed; the vicar of Christ was only accused of piracy, murder, rape, sodomy, and incest' (*The Decline and Fall*, VI.605). My point is not that Gibbon suddenly becomes an inept ironist, but that irony is no longer of much use to him in the effort to express his deepest experience as an historian, since it is almost the exact opposite of the receptiveness to the wonderful, to everything which exceeds, eludes or baffles the understanding, which in 1788 Gibbon is obliged to develop.

These moments of irony in the last instalment of *The Decline and Fall* are, from a literary point of view, much less complex than the elaborate irony of Volume I. But emotionally they are far more alloyed. The artifice and indirectness of Gibbon's strategy in Volume I is, paradoxically, a sign of the simplicity of his intentions. Indignant at the foreman's role played by the Church in the demolition of classical culture, Gibbon is obliged by his circumstances to couch his downright emotions in a veiled and oblique form. The less concerted disparagements of the Church we find in 1788 required no such careful handling – their very fragmentariness ought to have secured them against any charge of malice.[73] The literary effects they aim at are much simpler than those Gibbon has in view in Volume I. He is still concerned to point out the discrepancy between Christian professions and Christian practice which had been so prominent in Chapter XV, but he now lets the discrepancy appear much more readily, and with none of the elaborate deference which he had earlier used so successfully to expose his unwitting victim to the imminent wound.

That literary simplification is the outward token of Gibbon's more complicated ideas about the past, and about the role of the historian in conveying it. In 1776, Gibbon was sure of what he thought about Rome and concentrated on impressing the substance of that certainty on his reader. In 1788, Gibbon finds the past far less easy to grasp; and because of its ability more thoroughly to absorb his attention, we have seen that his narrative is less the becoming expression of thoughts already cut and dried, than a forum in which the past can be further explored. Hence his prose often has a new tentativeness, which is not absent even from these instances of apparently simple mockery. For Gibbon finds a melancholy interest in the gap between the maxims and behaviour of the Church. It moves him both to puzzled sadness and to satire. As a man, he finds it ridiculous and disgusting, but as an historian, teasing and too prominent a feature of these centuries simply to be scoffed at. And the fact that these moments of irony are no longer marshalled into large schemes, as they were in 1776, testifies, in its comparative trivialising of the irony, to the diminishing importance of their satiric charge for Gibbon, while simultaneously allowing their other qualities to emerge more clearly.[74] When they stand in isolation, rather than in concert, they become an accumulation of fragments, an ever-greater and more unignorable pile of sobering, inexplicable and yet also undeniable fact.[75]

[73] But apparently the 'religious clamour was revived' in 1788 (*Memoirs*, p. 182).
[74] Gibbon's loss of interest in the kind of irony he had employed in Volume I is evident in, for instance, the detachment with which he reviews Boulainvilliers' similar attempts to subvert Christianity, and his 'wicked intentions' (the very overstatement carries with it traces of condescension and amusement) in the *Vie de Mahomed*. Gibbon is now directing his own energies elsewhere.
[75] For the powerfully anomalous operation of religion as a cause in history, see Hume, *History*, I.61.

This contamination of irony by sentiments and notions which corrode the 'sottile soddisfazione intellettuale' on which it depends is shown by Gibbon's account of the death of Tiberius, the son of Justinian:

> His son Tiberius had taken refuge in a church; his aged grandmother guarded the door; and the innocent youth, suspending round his neck the most formidable relics, embraced with one hand the altar, with the other the wood of the true cross. But the popular fury that dares to trample on superstition, is deaf to the cries of humanity . . .[76]

In Volume I, the impotence of relics would have dominated the account. Now, in 1788, 'formidable' is still a word that attracts our attention; but not because it engages our scorn. It is the presence of the aged grandmother guarding the door which so decisively deflects the tone of this passage away from irony. She, like the relics, is a negligible defence popular fury will trample. The passage invites us not to smile over misplaced confidence, or even to censure religious imposture, but to cast a sad and sympathetic eye on hapless innocence, both young and old. Porson's remark that Gibbon's humanity never slumbered except when women were ravished and monks killed probably owes its celebrity to our delight in Gibbon's antipathy to the Church and curiosity about his unsatisfactory relationships with women. But we should not forget, in attending to the exceptions, that Porson pays tribute to the overall humanity in Gibbon which we see exercised in this passage.[77] It is, however, not the easy sympathy of like for like, because underlying this arresting tableau of violent oppositions – of youth and age, innocence and guilt, and the few and the many – we can see in Gibbon the perplexed fascination of a man murmuring to himself 'What people *are* these?' It is the insistence of that question which unsettles the poise the ironist requires.

The tones that replace irony are pondered and sober, darkened with the incomprehension and awe that come from repeated exposure to the shocking. The expostulation 'I know not how to believe' no longer veils disingenuity but springs immediately from exasperation and astonishment.[78] In one sense, of course, Rome – the Rome of the dazzlingly victorious republic, the Rome of stupendous architecture – had always been a touchstone for wonder.[79] But the wonder Gibbon feels for Rome in 1788 is not admiration for surpassing prowess. Both the object and the nature of the emotion are different.

---

[76] The phrase is Giuseppe Giarrizzo's (*Edward Gibbon e la Cultura Europea del Settecento*, p. 310); *The Decline and Fall*, V.18.

[77] This in itself is a sufficient reproof of Leslie Stephen's opinion that Gibbon 'has given an admirable summary of the bare facts of history, but he is deficient in that sympathetic power which enables an imaginative writer to breathe life into the dead bones of the past' (*A History of English Thought in the Eighteenth Century*, I.447).

[78] *The Decline and Fall*, IV.210.

[79] It is in this vein that the young Gibbon admires Rome: 'les Romains ce peuple genereux qui nous a laissé tant de choses à admirer et à imiter' (*Letters*, I.83). Compare Kennett, *Romae Antiquae Notitia*, p. 1; Louis de Beaufort, *La Republique Romaine*, I.i; and Thomas Bever, *The History of the Legal Polity of the Roman State*, p. i.

Coolness of mind has been held a virtue at least since Horace.[80] But for the *philosophes*, committed as they were to the penetrating investigation of causality, to be amazed was not simply a failure of deportment; the disposition to marvel was the intellectual vice which threatened to obscure what they had laboured to expose. So, in 'Le Philosophe', we read that 'C'est toujours le merveilleux qui corrompt le raisonnable'; and in the *Esprit des Loix* Montesquieu, believing that the wonderful was but a shameful, yet plausible, form of ignorance, suggested that its incomprehending gaze could be loosened by reasonable inquiry: 'Après des questions & des réponses très-sensées, le merveilleux s'est évanoui.'[81] In Volume I of *The Decline and Fall* Gibbon shares this disdain of the marvellous: by 1788, however, we can discern that he is frequently in the grip of a tougher and more elastic astonishment which is not to be dissolved by the application of reason, but is rather the residue which remains behind when reason has done its work.[82] The reported prodigies at the battle of Ceramio provoke what seems to be the old irony, a masking of stubborn disbelief with docile acceptance:

In the field of Ceramio, fifty thousand horse and foot were overthrown by one hundred and thirty-six Christian soldiers, without reckoning St. George, who fought on horseback in the foremost ranks.[83]

To the practical critic, this must seem unambiguously ironic. But the tone of this passage is decisively coloured by the fact that it comes as the last in a whole series of previous, similar events of which the practical critic is unaware:

. . . the generous enthusiasm of the Aquileians was exalted into a confidence of success, by the opinion, that Belenus, their tutelar deity, combated in person in the defence of his distressed worshippers.

. . . and if, in the decisive battle of Fano, the Allemanni fancied they saw an army of spectres combating on the side of Aurelian, he received a real and effectual aid from this imaginary reinforcement.

[St. James] charged at the head of the Spanish cavalry in their battles against the Moors.

. . . the glory of the day was ascribed to a phantom or a stranger, who fought in the foremost ranks under the character of St. Andrew the apostle.

In a hard-fought day, as the two armies alternately yielded and advanced, a phantom was seen, a voice was heard, and Ravenna was victorious by the assurance of victory.

---

[80] 'nil admirari prope res est una, Numici, / solaque quae possit facere et servare beatum' (*Epistles*, I.vi. 1–2).

[81] *Le Philosophe*, p. 62; *Œuvres*, I.169.

[82] Hence his blame of 'stupid wonder' (*The Decline and Fall*, I.350: I.416) and the implication in a phrase such as 'nor will it any longer excite our surprise' (*The Decline and Fall*, I.431: I.513) that to be amazed is an immature state of mind.

[83] *The Decline and Fall*, V.607.

On a sudden, the charge was sounded; the Arabian camp poured forth a swarm of fresh and intrepid warriors; and the long line of the Greeks and Africans was surprised, assaulted, overturned, by new squadrons of the faithful, who, to the eye of fanaticism, might appear as a band of angels descending from the sky.[84]

A dry understanding that opinion is a sovereign mistress of effects was part of the worldly wisdom of 'le monde' in the eighteenth century; it is certainly something to which Chesterfield wished to open Philip Stanhope's eyes.[85] But Gibbon's deadpan recounting of these traditional prodigies is different from Chesterfield's disenchantment. Indeed, paradoxically it is the very consistency of their literary treatment, the repeated and careful blankness of tone, which betrays Gibbon's changing attitude to these traditions. We may assume that, in keeping with the philosophic character of Volume I, Gibbon's unruffled way with these episodes in 1776 is the sign of polite and ironic disbelief. But as the number of these episodes increases, the real question they pose for the historian is not that of whether or not the apparitions actually occurred, but that of why history is so prolific of them. Gibbon ceases to be interested in their *content*, but is intrigued by the fact of their existence. Thus the blankness of tone is transformed from the mask of irony to the natural expression of the historian's recognition that it is as remarkable that men should so consistently have deluded themselves as that they should receive supernatural aid. This reading is supported by the change in Gibbon's attitude towards miracles over the period of the publication of *The Decline and Fall*. In Volume II, he wrote that 'the frequent repetition of miracles seems to provoke, where it does not subdue, the reason of mankind'.[86] In the late 1770s Gibbon conceives only of our submitting ourselves to miracles or of our rational rejection of them: reason is either provoked or subdued. But in 1783, when he was at work on the final instalment of *The Decline and Fall*, Gibbon wrote to Priestley stigmatising the question of miracles as 'a trite and antient topic of controversy'.[87] It is a change which illustrates the increasing limberness of Gibbon's mind. His lack of interest in miracles as a 'topic of controversy' means that his reason is no longer called upon either to support or deny, but is released from that dilemma to play more freely and fruitfully over the larger matter of the historical significance of these common traditions. So released, Gibbon finds in these episodes not yet more evidence of man's foolishness (as did Chesterfield), but another aspect of the strange essence of the imperial twilight.

[84] *The Decline and Fall*, I.188: I.224; I.303: I.362 (first edition: 'he received a very powerful aid'); I.511: I.611; V.473; V.110; and V.353.

[85] 'And that silly, sanguine notion, which is firmly entertained here, that one Englishman can beat three Frenchmen, encourages, and has sometimes enabled, one Englishman, in reality, to beat two' (*Letters* II.140). Gibbon frequently indicates the power of opinion: 'The power of opinion is irresistible' (*The Decline and Fall*, I.347: I.412); 'An imaginary cause is capable of producing the most serious and mischievous effects' (*The Decline and Fall*, II.496; see also *Miscellaneous Works*, III.316). The *locus classicus* is to be found in the *Aeneid*, V.231.

[86] *The Decline and Fall*, II.197. It is interesting to note that when Gibbon recounts the story of his own brush with miracles during his temporary conversion to Catholicism he echoes this phrasing (*Memoirs*, p. 68).

[87] *Letters*, II.321.

Gibbon's irony, then, is supplemented and transformed by awe, astonishment, wonder – it matters little which of the near-synonyms we choose from the *congeries* of terms which denote the suspension, arrest or surpassing of comprehension. That change is also discernible in the intimate register of thought which, for Gibbon, is style. If we examine the use Gibbon makes of insect imagery, we can see how his growing appreciation of the positive aspects of wonder is inscribed in his use of language.

Paul Fussell has proposed that two distinct groups of writers in the eighteenth century used images of insects for their separate, divergent purposes. The Augustan humanists (amongst whom he includes Gibbon) used such images satirically to diminish and demean their enemies. Writers of a more scientific inclination, however, used insects to express their sense of the marvels of nature.[88] Harold Bond, noticing that Gibbon occasionally uses insect imagery and recollecting the 'Sporus' passage from Pope's *Epistle to Dr. Arbuthnot*, suggests that whenever insects occur in *The Decline and Fall* they are used to apportion blame: 'From Alexander Pope he may have learned the value of reducing his enemies to the size and form of insects and then displaying his own virtuosity in destroying them.'[89] The passage from the *Epistle* is, of course, memorable for the whole-heartedness of its violent execration:

> Yet let me flap this bug with gilded wings,
> This painted child of dirt, that stinks and stings;
> Whose buzz the witty and the fair annoys,
> Yet wit ne'er tastes, and beauty ne'er enjoys . . .[90]

This is the apotheosis of the vituperative use of insects, a literary convention already widespread and current before Pope began publishing.[91]

Yet this famous passage from the *Epistle to Dr. Arbuthnot* does not express the totality of connotation Pope could draw from insects. He also responds to the positive appreciation of them which originates probably in Virgil's *Georgics*, and to which he lends his voice in the *Essay on Man*:

> See him from Nature rising slow to Art!
> To copy Instinct then was Reason's part;
> Thus then to Man the voice of Nature spake –
> 'Go, from the Creatures thy instructions take:
> Learn from the birds what food the thickets yield;

---

[88] *The Rhetorical World of Augustan Humanism*, Chapter 10: 'The image most accessible for this purpose [the portrayal of depravity], it proves, is that of the nasty or showy or unstable insect', but 'to the Moderns . . . the world of insects suggests an optimistic, often Deistic conviction of divine benignity' (pp. 233 and 241). Gibbon is in the former, humanist, camp: 'Gibbon's use of the humanist insect figure is less profound, more like the practice of the Pope of the anti-Grub Street satires' (p. 249).

[89] *The Literary Art of Edward Gibbon*, pp. 128–9.

[90] ll. 309–12 – compare *Epistle to Burlington*, ll. 107–8 (*Works*, IV.24 and III.191).

[91] Milton compares the ineffectual blandishments of Satan to 'a swarm of flies' (*Paradise Regained*, IV.15–20). In *Religio Laici*, Dryden gives the image a greater edge of contempt and makes its implications more explicit (ll. 417–22). See also Edward Meredith, *Some Remarques Upon a Late Popular Piece of Nonsense Call'd Julian the Apostate &c*, sig. Dv; Thomson, *Liberty*, IV.785–90 and V.593–6; and Chesterfield, *Letters*, III.311.

> Learn from the beasts the physic of the field;
> Thy arts of building from the bee receive . . .
> Learn each small People's genius, policies,
> The Ant's republic, and the realm of Bees . . .[92]

Thus it is misleading of Fussell to imply that eighteenth-century writers can be divided into two exclusive camps in respect of how they use insect images; certain writers, such as Pope, may at different times explore different areas of the spectrum of connotation possessed by such images.

It is also, however, a simplification to assume that each individual image will be either a means of merely blaming or merely admiring, because some writers – for instance, Hume in 'Of Suicide' – are adroit enough to allow the complex, double resonance of these images to make itself felt in a single instance:

A hair, a fly, an insect, is able to destroy this mighty being whose life is of such importance. Is it an absurdity to suppose that human prudence may lawfully dispose of what depends on such insignificant causes?[93]

Hume finds the ambiguity of insects, their double status as images of both the contemptuous and the wonderful, apt to his purpose of lowering human life in our scale of value – or, rather, awakening us to its true, small value. The sequence 'A hair, a fly, an insect' is on the one hand a diminuendo, in which the ultimate triviality of 'insect' is a token of the vulnerability from which Hume argues for our insignificance. Yet it is also a subtle crescendo, in which our steadily lowered estimate of man's value and capacity is accompanied by a corresponding enlargement of our esteem for everything which is not human. That we can be killed by an insect is a reflection proper to cast dust over our vanity, but also proper to cast a new lustre over insects.[94] Thus Hume adroitly makes his writing include two different perspectives. The first, anthropocentric perspective finds bitter knowledge in our liability to a creature as insignificant as an insect. But as soon as we swallow that bitter knowledge and acquiesce in our inconsequence, another perspective opens in which the fact that so large an animal can be dispatched by one so small is more elating than depressing. An overpowering sense of one's own momentousness is, after all, a burden from which one might reasonably wish to be free, and from which Hume does free us by making us scorn a point of view

---

[92] *Georgics*, IV.1–5; IV.149–57; IV.219–21 – compare Shaftesbury, *Characteristicks*, II.96. *Essay on Man*, III.169–75 and 183–4. A. D. Nuttall and Reuben Brower have noticed the complexity of Pope's attitude to insects (A. D. Nuttall, *Pope's Essay on Man*, pp. 6–7: R. A. Brower, *Alexander Pope and the Poetry of Allusion*, p. 253). A positive note could be found also in Goldsmith's essay, 'The Sagacity of some Insects' (*The Bee*, 27 October 1759). In the *Age of Reason* (1794) Paine held that 'The most beautiful parts of the creation to our eye are the winged insects' (*Writings*, IV.179).

[93] *Essays Moral, Political and Literary*, II.410 (this essay was suppressed in the 1760 edition of *Essays and Treatises*); compare also the complexity attaching to insects in Gray's 'Ode on the Spring'.

[94] Hume pivots on the doubleness of insects, profiting first from our contempt for them, and then from our astonishment at them, at the end of Book I, Part II, Section 1 of his *Treatise of Human Nature*, p. 28.

in which we see every object in relation to our own humanity. The passage thus vibrates between the polar emotions of scorn and wonder.

Armed with this richer knowledge of context, we can better understand the use Gibbon makes of insect imagery in *The Decline and Fall*. Throughout his life, he was adept at the polemical use of these images. In *A Vindication* and in his *Memoirs*, his critics swarm round the nourishment of his life's work:

Under the hands of a malicious surgeon, the sting of a wasp [Davis] may continue to fester and inflame, long after the vexatious little insect has left its venom and its life in the wound.

The freedom of my writings has indeed provoked an implacable tribe: but as I was safe from the stings, I was soon accustomed to the buzzing of the hornets . . .[95]

That strain recurs in *The Decline and Fall* and runs evenly throughout:

Under the warm influence of a feeble reign, they [agents] multiplied to the incredible number of ten thousand . . .

. . . the swarms of monks, who arose from the Nile, overspread and darkened the face of the Christian world.

. . . the number of eunuchs could be compared only with the insects of a summer's day.

. . . the torrent was loud and irresistible, and the insects who had basked in the sunshine of royal favour disappeared at the blast of the storm.[96]

But in the final instalment of 1788 this satiric tone is attenuated and complicated. On close inspection, even apparently straightforward examples reveal equivocation:

Origen he detested; but the writings of Clemens and Dionysius, of Athanasius and Basil, were continually in his hands: by the theory and practice of dispute, his faith was confirmed and his wit was sharpened: he extended round his cell the cobwebs of scholastic theology, and meditated the works of allegory and metaphysics, whose remains, in seven verbose folios, now peaceably slumber by the side of their rivals.[97]

One recalls initially Pope's couplet from *An Essay on Criticism*:

> Scotists and Thomists, now, in Peace remain,
> Amidst their kindred cobwebs in Duck-Lane.[98]

Then the *Battle of the Books*, and Swift's use of the spider to denote those scribblers who spin the slight, self-pleasing thread to manufacture books from their own bowels; perhaps also Bacon's *Advancement of Learning*, where we read that the Schoolmen 'did out of no great quantity of matter, and infinite agitation of wit, spin out unto us those laborious webs of learning, which are extant in

---

[95] *The English Essays of Edward Gibbon*, p. 234; *Memoirs*, p. 188.
[96] *The Decline and Fall*, II.58; II.218; II.341; V.79.
[97] *The Decline and Fall*, IV.546: compare also Gray, *Poems and Memoirs*, p. 141; 'I am a sort of spider . . .'
[98] ll. 444–5: *Works*, I.111.

their books'.[99] But these analogues do not match the fullness of what we find in *The Decline and Fall*. St Cyril eventually extends the cobwebs of scholastic theology, but the webs in which he is initially ensnared are not of his own making, even though his own 'seven verbose folios' ultimately thicken them. Consequently, Gibbon's satire is blended with tones of elegy absent from Swift and Bacon: Cyril had sharp wit, but that virtue was smothered in the hostile atmosphere of scholasticism. This softening of satire, and the attenuation of scorn by the recognition of positive value (even if frustrated) where only the worthless might have been supposed to exist, is a small example of the change in Gibbon's attitudes, and the surprising extension of his sympathies, we find throughout Volumes IV, V and VI.[100]

At other moments, Gibbon explicitly draws on the ability of insects to mobilise wonder and admiration to which Hume had been so fruitfully alert:

A magnificent temple is a laudable monument of national taste and religion, and the enthusiast who entered the dome of St. Sophia, might be tempted to suppose that it was the residence, or even the workmanship of the Deity. Yet how dull is the artifice, how insignificant is the labour, if it be compared with the formation of the vilest insect that crawls upon the surface of the temple![101]

Gibbon, as well as Hume, makes a central switch of perspective balance around the introduction of an insect into our field of vision. Once more a point of view intoxicated with man and his works is replaced by a larger, truer perspective in the vertiginous shift we seem to make as we move from gazing up at the monument to gazing down, from the fabric and in the position of the insect, to realise our lowness.

That Gibbon is here adjusting our easy but erroneous assumptions is confirmed by the way this passage refers back to, and also corrects, two popular eighteenth-century works, both of which were in his library: *Guardian*, no. 70 and an intermediate rewriting of it from Thomson's *Seasons*.[102] For Berkeley, the spectator of the temple has the larger and more elevated view, while the insect which crawls upon it is an emblem of smallness of mind:

As I was, the other Day, taking a solitary Walk in St. *Paul*'s, I indulged my Thoughts in the Pursuit of a certain Analogy between the Fabrick and the *Christian Church* in the largest Sense. The Divine Order and Oeconomy of the one seemed to be emblematically

---

[99] *Advancement of Learning*, I.iv.5: *Works*, I.16.

[100] Cowper, in *The Task* (1785), uses the topos in a very similar way (IV, 'The Winter Evening', ll. 723–6): 'Ingenious Cowley! and, though now reclaim'd / By modern lights from an erroneous taste, / I cannot but lament thy splendid wit / Entangled in the cobwebs of the schools.' It is possible that Gibbon is alluding to Cowper, but the balance of probability is against it. He had retired to Lausanne by this time, and although he had new books sent out to Switzerland punctually, Cowper does not appear in the catalogue of his library. Moreover, he records that he completed Volume IV, from which the passage on St Cyril is taken, in June 1784.

[101] *The Decline and Fall*, IV.96; compare Sherlock, *The Doctrine of the Blessed Trinity Stated and Defended*, p. 17.

[102] Keynes, pp. 257 and 266.

set forth by the just, plain, and majestick Architecture of the other. And as the one consists of a great Variety of Parts united in the same regular Design, according to the truest Art, and most exact Proportion; so the other contains a decent Subordination of Members, various sacred Institutions, sublime Doctrines, and Solid Precepts of Morality digested into the same Design, and with an admirable Concurrence tending to one View, the Happiness and Exaltation of Human Nature.

In the midst of my Contemplation I beheld a Fly upon one of the Pillars; and it straightway came into my Head, that this same Fly was a *Free-Thinker*. For it required some Comprehension in the eye of the Spectator, to take in at one view the various Parts of the Building, in order to observe their Symmetry and Design. But to the Fly, whose Prospect was confined to a little part of one of the Stones of a single Pillar, the joint Beauty of the whole, or the distinct Use of its Parts, were inconspicuous, and nothing coud appear but small inequalities in the Surface of the hewn Stone, which in the view of that Insect seemed so many deformed Rocks and Precipices.[103]

Thomson's versification of this passage faithfully preserves its emphases:

> Let no presuming impious railer tax
> CREATIVE WISDOM, as if aught was form'd
> In vain, or not for admirable ends.
> Shall little haughty ignorance pronounce
> His works unwise, of which the smallest part
> Exceeds the narrow vision of her mind?
> As if upon a full proportion'd dome,
> On swelling columns heav'd, the pride of art!
> A critic fly, whose feeble ray scarce spreads
> An inch around, with blind presumption bold,
> Should dare to tax the structure of the whole.[104]

The essence of Gibbon's revision is that he, unlike Berkeley and Thomson, does not contrast the breadth of the human observer's vision with the smallness of the insect's, thereby suggesting the difference in competence between a true perspective and one which is merely captious. Instead, he transforms Berkeley and Thomson's banal critic or free-thinking fly into an example of the natural wonders to which the little haughty ignorance of man tends to be blind, particularly when preening itself on the comprehensiveness of its view.

This development in the figurative language of *The Decline and Fall* connects directly with the more fundamental changes in Gibbon's conception of the past and his idea of the purpose of the historian in 1788. In the final instalment of *The Decline and Fall* Gibbon finds obliquity worthy of his attention where previously it had seemed likely he would find only the contemptible; and he also finds that the insects which had figured his contempt may now also express his new sense of awe at the past because they are vivid examples

---

[103] *The Guardian*, I. 297-8.
[104] *The Seasons*, 'Summer', ll. 318-28, pp. 63-4. The dome was a touchstone of classicism: compare Pope, *An Essay on Criticism*, ll. 247-52 and Addison, *Spectator* no. 415 (*Works*, III.467).

of the extraordinary, but nonetheless actual, to which he is alerted.[105] Sir Ronald Syme imagines Gibbon would have been displeased by Byron's description of him 'hiving wisdom with each studious year': 'Had Gibbon survived to read those words, he would have been moved to irony, if not expostulation; he would have deprecated this entomological metaphor.'[106] Byron knew better: and as each studious year passed, Gibbon would have found more of a compliment in the image, more to admire in Byron's faithful response to the changing values of *The Decline and Fall*.

[105] Gibbon notes that the angles of the cells in a beehive are within a shade of the geometric ideal, although 'the bees are not masters of transcendant geometry' (*The Decline and Fall*, V.424 n. 52).

[106] *Childe Harold's Pilgrimage*, III.cvii; in Ducrey et al., eds., *Gibbon et Rome*, p. 48.

17

Realising the past

What thin partitions Sense from Thought divide   Pope

In *An Essay on Criticism* (1711) Pope humorously attends to some common errors of poetic taste and poetic composition:

> But most by *Numbers* judge a Poet's Song,
> And *smooth* or *rough*, with them, is *right* or *wrong*;
> In the bright *Muse* tho' thousand *Charms* conspire,
> Her *Voice* is all these tuneful Fools admire,
> Who haunt *Parnassus* but to please their Ear,
> Not mend their Minds; as some to *Church* repair,
> Not for the *Doctrine*, but the *Musick* there.
> These *Equal Syllables* alone require,
> Tho' oft the Ear the *open Vowels* tire,
> While *Expletives* their feeble Aid *do* join,
> And ten low Words oft creep in one dull Line,
> While they ring round the same *unvary'd Chimes*,
> With sure *Returns* of still *expected Rhymes*.
> Where-e'er you find *the cooling Western Breeze*,
> In the next Line, it *whispers thro' the Trees*;
> If *Chrystal Streams with pleasing Murmurs creep*,
> The Reader's threaten'd (not in vain) with *Sleep*.
> Then, at the *last*, and *only* Couplet fraught
> With some *unmeaning* Thing they call a *Thought*,
> A *needless Alexandrine* ends the Song,
> That like a wounded Snake, drags its slow length along.[1]

The repetition of the rhyme in the first and last couplets (song/wrong, song/along) seals off these lines from their surroundings and presents them as a distinct section of Pope's total argument in the *Essay*. Within its boundaries, the passage is unified by his interest in a specific kind of poetic blemish, at which the keynote of 'song', beginning and ending the passage, hints. Taking for his subject those who relish poetry only for its 'voice' and in order 'but to please their ear', Pope explores that devalued poetry in which sound is not the echo to sense, but the quality whose attainment has banished sense. His method is to display the banality of such verse by making his own lines mimic

---

[1] ll. 337–57: *Works*, I.106–7. Since I am not concerned here with any possible response of Gibbon's to this passage, I quote it as it appears in the Twickenham edition of Pope.

the faults of which they speak.[2] After the triplet (ear/repair/there) and the identical rhymes of the couplets on either side (conspire/admire, require/tire), the reader is indeed fatigued by open vowels. As required, Pope writes a sluggish alexandrine and a pentameter of monosyllables, enlists the feeble aid of an expletive, and allows two of his own couplets to be taken over by the 'still *expected Rhymes*'.

This is more than cleverness. Pope's imitations, whether formal or incidental, are never simulacra, and his imitations here, though 'perfect', are also quite distinct from their models. The easy mastery of language and of verse which allows Pope to weave these poetic failures into his own successful poetry is itself an implicit comment on the unmeaning yielding to the 'poetic' which he is attacking. In order to duplicate these failings he must mobilise his own contrary virtues of control and concentration. With unfaltering pertinence Pope attacks verse whose own pertinence falters, and which thus ceases to be about its subject. Even at the end of his life, Pope was still reflecting on the different ways poetry can be 'about' things:

> For thee explain a thing till all men doubt it,
> And write about it, Goddess, and about it[3]

It is the touch of Dullness which transforms 'about', when repeated, from a word which suggests focused attention to one which suggests the loss of such attention. In *An Essay on Criticism* Pope is already vexed by writing which, instead of proceeding directly, ambles round its subject. Such writing is, he suggests, about only itself. If offers nothing to mend the mind, but only an assortment of tropes which comprise, in a depleted sense, the 'poetic'.

In deploring the poverty of such writing, Pope was voicing, and also deepening, a central Augustan literary principle. Waller, whose importance in shaping the literary awareness of those who came after him is indicated by Dryden's saying that if Waller had not written, 'none of us could', was praised by Atterbury for his 'fine ear' and for knowing 'how quickly that sense was cloyed by the same round of chiming words still returning upon it'.[4] Such jingles are even more calamitous in prose. Chesterfield, instructing Philip Stanhope in 'euphonia', illustrates how his choice of word should be determined by the need to avoid distracting harmonies of sound.[5] Blair, at the end of the century, insists that the 'public ear is become refined. It will not easily bear what is slovenly and incorrect.'[6]

Gibbon, too, corrected his prose in the light of this principle. Thus in draft 'F' of his *Memoirs*, he originally wrote 'their *swords*, though less frequently

---

[2] This grace of Pope's was recognised at the time. See Paul Hammond, 'An Early Response to Pope's *Essay on Criticism*'.

[3] *Dunciad*, IV.251–2 (1742).

[4] Waller, *Poems*, I.xxii.

[5] *Letters*, III.235.

[6] *Lectures on Rhetoric and Belles Lettres*, I.7.

than of old, are sometimes stained with each other's brothers blood', but then removed the chime by crossing out 'brothers'.[7] In the first edition of Volume I of *The Decline and Fall* he writes 'and while they concealed from others, and perhaps from themselves, the secret motive of their actions, they too frequently relapsed into all the turbulent passions of active life'; but in the third edition he corrects it to 'the secret motives of their conduct', thereby removing the echo of 'actions' in 'active'.[8] Moreover, Gibbon broadens the principle until it embraces not only parallelisms of sound, but of structure. In *A Vindication* he writes: 'Our two Universities most undoubtedly contain the same mixture, and most probably the same proportions, of zeal and moderation, of reason and superstition.'[9] Even in a sentence which is about duplication, Gibbon watchfully restrains the elements of reflection in his order of words: 'reason and superstition' inverts the order of the first pair of vices and virtues, 'zeal and moderation'.

The prose of *The Decline and Fall* is penned in the light of this principle. When Josephus writes of the Romans' military efficiency, he does so chiastically:

καὶ οὐκ ἂν ἁμάρτοι τις εἰπὼν τὰς μὲν μελέτας αὐτῶν χωρὶς αἵματος παρατάξεις, τὰς παρατάξεις δὲ μεθ' αἵματος μελέτας.[10]

Gibbon acknowledges, but also suppresses, much of the prettiness of the aphorism in his own version:

. . . and it is prettily remarked by an ancient historian who had fought against them, that the effusion of blood was the only circumstance which distinguished a field of battle from a field of exercise.[11]

Or consider the following:

The savage who hollows a tree, inserts a sharp stone into a wooden handle, or applies a string to an elastic branch, becomes in a state of nature the just proprietor of the canoe, the bow, or the hatchet.[12]

The fundamental structure of the sentence is one of antithesis: the processes come before their products. But within that large antithesis, the sense of

---

[7] *Memoirs*, p. 46. He was not always sufficiently vigilant. Horace Walpole's sharper ear caught echoes to which Gibbon was deaf, and which he underlined in his copy of *The Decline and Fall*. For instance, he disdains this phrasing at which the historian had nodded: 'the *meanest* of the Romans in those *menial* offices'. Walpole's presentation copy of *The Decline and Fall*, which is rich in marginalia, is housed in the Rothschild collection in the Wren Library, Trinity College, Cambridge. The quoted fragment is to be found in Volume I, p. 70, and the emphasis is Walpole's.

[8] *The Decline and Fall*, I.488: I.582.

[9] *The English Essays of Edward Gibbon*, p. 285. In his distaste for the mindless symmetries of Timon's estate, Pope also extends the principle beyond the realm of sound (*To Burlington*, ll. 117ff.).

[10] *Jewish War*, III.75.

[11] *The Decline and Fall*, I.11: I.14.

[12] *The Decline and Fall*, IV.384.

parallelism, of structural chime, has been carefully weakened; where we might expect 'the hatchet or the bow', we read 'the bow, or the hatchet'. At times, it is difficult to tell how far there is a parallel structure in the writing. This sentence is particularly elusive:

The historian may therefore be permitted respectfully to withdraw the veil of the sanctuary; and to deduce the progress of reason and faith, of error and passion, from the school of Plato to the decline and fall of the empire.[13]

The doubt arises when one tries to understand the relation between reason, faith, error and passion. Are the two pairs of nouns sorted on the basis of first the two virtues, and then their vicious opposites (error standing against reason, passion against faith)? That surely is part of it. But Gibbon was fully aware of the tension between reason and faith; and thus the four nouns seem to be arranged sequentially, as well as in parallel, so as to describe the gradually steepening declension of men departing further from reason. The manifold possibilities of sense keep the structure of the sentence flexible, and thus prevent it from lapsing into triteness.

In all these passages, Gibbon's intention seems to be to make his prose as far as possible a transparent medium through the eradication of gratuitous duplications of sound or phrasing. In such irritating chimes, writing draws attention to itself, rather than letting that attention pass through to its subject.

Gibbon's ideas about how writing could take the decline and fall of Rome for its subject changed; and, as they changed, we find that the transparency of his writing allows different objects to appear. In Volume I, his prose seems the natural and immediate register of a judging mind, expert in the analysis of causes; in consequence, it is freed from what Michel Baridon has called 'les impuretés du concret', because it appears to have passed through the mire of mere particularity to reach the commanding heights of true historical knowledge.[14] When Gibbon's faith in the validity of those large, unified perspectives wanes, however, then the concrete is the grit around which he makes his pearls:

They dispersed the first line, consisting of the troops of Asia; forced a rampart of stakes, which had been planted against the cavalry; broke, after a bloody conflict, the Janizaries themselves; and were at length overwhelmed by the numerous squadrons that issued from the woods, and charged on all sides this handful of intrepid warriors.[15]

It is the placing of 'after a bloody conflict' which organises the sentence. The breaking of the Janizaries exhausts the strength of the French charge at Nicopolis, and the pause as the reader takes in the parenthetic 'after a bloody conflict' suggests well the resistance and effort of which it speaks. In addition,

---

[13] *The Decline and Fall*, II.237.   [14] In Ducrey et al., eds., *Gibbon et Rome*, p. 89.
[15] *The Decline and Fall*, VI.325.

it invites us to look afresh at the placing of the commas in the first and final limbs of the sentence, where their slight check is sufficient to evoke the successful violence first of the French and then of Bajazet's troops, who accord a slight slowing of their onward career as the only monument of what they overcome.

This is far from any crude mimesis. The sound must seem an echo to the sense, but it cannot actually *become* the sense. Gibbon indicates the scope and nature of what he is undertaking when he writes that 'the historian may imitate the speed with which he [John Zimisces] overran the once-famous cities of Samosata, Edessa, Martyropolis, Amida, and Nisibis'.[16] The past cannot be fully represented in prose, but the historian, commanding language and held by imagination, can catch the speed of John Zimisces and suggest the rhythm of the battle of Nicopolis. Successful historical writing seems to touch history, but admits that the past cannot be possessed.

A careful sentence from Volume I shows by contrast how the resources of Gibbon's style were originally devoted not to expressing the texture of the past, but to conveying the firm distinctions of an analytical historical intelligence:

The name of the senate was mentioned with honour till the last period of the empire; the vanity of its members was still flattered with honorary distinctions . . .[17]

The inflexion of 'honour' into 'honorary' (which according to Johnson denoted then as now a merely apparent advantage) communicates the decline of the senate with great economy, but it does so not by evoking the past itself (how could an event as vast as the decline of the senate be caught in words?) but by suggesting the thoughts of the historian, whose sharp discrimination is given definition in the substitution of the adjective for the noun, the shadow for the substance. Gibbon's description of the battle of Nicopolis, on the other hand, does not display the mind of the historian, but elides it in order to make the past itself, the particular event, fleetingly palpable to the readers of the present.

Gibbon does not always mould his prose around the particularity of history as directly as he does when writing of Nicopolis. But that instance may fairly stand for the tendency of the instalment of 1788, which is to replace the illustrative with the opaque, and dissertation with narration. Volumes IV, V and VI are studded with irreducible facts presented in their original state and without any setting of reflection or analysis. As *The Decline and Fall* progresses Gibbon becomes steadily more determined not to impoverish facts by discounting or softening their awkwardness:

At this dangerous moment, seven notorious assassins of both factions, who had been condemned by the praefect, were carried round the city, and afterwards transported

---

16 *The Decline and Fall*, V.462.
17 *The Decline and Fall*, I.386: I.460. First edition: '. . . distinction . . .'.

to the place of execution in the suburb of Pera. Four were immediately beheaded; a fifth was hanged: but when the same punishment was inflicted on the remaining two, the rope broke, they fell alive to the ground, the populace applauded their escape, and the monks of St. Conon, issuing from the neighbouring convent, conveyed them in a boat to the sanctuary of the church.

. . . the fleet of Belisarius was guided in their course by his master-galley, conspicuous in the day by the redness of the sails, and in the night by the torches blazing from the masthead.[18]

In their different ways, both these examples embody what is new and distinctive in Gibbon's historical intelligence by the time he completes *The Decline and Fall*. Chastised by the baffling obliquities of history into the knowledge that he cannot penetrate below the surface of the past and know its efficient structure, as he had believed in 1776, and yet convinced by those same obliquities of the awkward and tangled reality of the past, he now gazes upon history, rather than scrutinising it. His regard traverses the long sequence of years and catches on whatever is salient or extraordinary, be it the undeserved good fortune of the Blues' and Greens' assassins, or a detail of the disposition of Belisarius' fleet. Blair cites 'a great variety of unconnected facts' as a prime historiographic blemish; in 1788 Gibbon might deny that the historian has any alternative to such a promiscuous throng.[19] Once more, a passage from Volume I will reveal the magnitude of the change:

The masters of the fairest and most wealthy climates of the globe, turned with contempt from gloomy hills assailed by the winter tempest, from lakes concealed in a blue mist, and from cold and lonely heaths, over which the deer of the forest were chased by a troop of naked barbarians.[20]

This language is *grammatically* particular, but it differs from the examples I have quoted from the instalment of 1788 because it refers to no specific event. It is an example of what we might call synthetic synecdoche. Gibbon has not taken a single past event and made it stand for many such events, but has instead painted one of what he later calls 'those general pictures which compose the use and ornament of a remote history', but whose light and effect are destroyed by the 'faint and broken rays' of the Byzantine annals.[21] It is in this construable form that particularity is admitted into the first volume of *The Decline and Fall*.

We have seen how the refractory nature of Byzantine history obliges Gibbon to stay more at the level of the particular; but we must also recognise that he kisses the rod and actively enhances the particularity of *The Decline and Fall*. We encounter not simply details which Gibbon adopts from his sources, but instances of his striving to uncover a particularity denied or obscured in the accounts from which he is working:

[18] *The Decline and Fall*, IV.65 and IV.133.
[19] *Lectures on Rhetoric and Belles Lettres*, II.266.
[20] *The Decline and Fall*, I.5: I.6: compare Thomson's description of Scythia (*Liberty*, III.516ff.).
[21] *The Decline and Fall*, V.2 and V.3.

Whatever might be the grounds of his security, Alboin neither expected nor encountered a Roman army in the field. He ascended the Julian Alps, and looked down with contempt and desire on the fruitful plains to which his victory communicated the perpetual appellation of LOMBARDY.[22]

No footnote is appended, giving references: there is nothing to show whether Gibbon is describing an actual event or depicting in another 'general picture' what he surmised were Alboin's motives and emotions. The reality is both more complicated and more interesting than those alternatives. Muratori records the occurrence in a passage Gibbon must have read:

Giunto Alboino con quel gran seguito a i confini dell'Italia, sali sopra un alto Monte de que' luoghi per vagheggiare fui dove potea il bel paese, ch'egli già contava per suo. Era fama a' tempi di Paolo Diacono, che da li innanzi quel Monte prendesse il nome di *Monte del Re*, o sia *Monreale*.[23]

Going back further to Paulus Diaconus, we find another account of the event:

Igitur cum Rex Alboin cum omni exercitu suo, vulgique promiscui multitudine, ad extremos Italiae fines pervenisset, montem qui in eisdem locis prominet, ascendit, indeque, prout conspicere potuit, partem Italiae contemplatus est. Qui mons propter hanc, ut fertur, causam ex eo tempore Mons regis appellatus est.[24]

If we look at the progression of the event through the accounts of Paulus Diaconus and Muratori to its appearance in *The Decline and Fall*, we can see how it gradually becomes more vivid. Paulus Diaconus describes neither Alboin's emotions nor the landscape he could see. In Muratori, we learn for the first time of 'il bel paese' and are given a hint about Alboin's inner feelings with 'vagheggiare'. But in *The Decline and Fall* these banal embellishments (what could be more predictable than to be pleased by the beautiful?) are adopted and adulterated: 'and looked down with contempt and desire on the fruitful plains'. 'Fruitful' offers a straightfoward gain in specificity over Muratori's bland 'bel'; but it is the implications of Gibbon's elaboration of 'vagheggiare' into 'contempt and desire' which are most striking. 'Desire' is the most intense word which could translate 'vagheggiare', but there is nothing in either Paulus Diaconus or Muratori to sanction Gibbon's 'contempt'. It is a small, yet transfiguring addition. His sketch of Alboin's contradictory feelings is a vivid dramatisation of barbarian psychology, and the fruit of an imaginative entry into an event which his sources transmit passively. Gibbon rescues the event from the featurelessness within which it had lain disguised and casts it in a vividly particular mould; yet at the same time, he makes it the reverse of illustrative. Gripped by the great contradiction of the barbarians' attitude towards the empire, their craving for its products and

---

[22] *The Decline and Fall*, IV.428.
[23] *Annali d'Italia*, III.415. Gibbon drew from Muratori when composing his 'Nomina Gentesque Antiquae Italiae' (1763–4) (*Miscellaneous Works*, IV.153–326: see *Memoirs*, p. 147 and *Gibbon's Journey from Geneva to Rome*, p. 129).
[24] *De Gestis Langobardorum*, II.viii, p. 54.

scorn for the way of life which created them, Gibbon reifies the paradox in an incident. We cannot, of course, know whether it happened like this, but it is worth drawing out how unusual 'contempt' is as an authorial interjection. Bacon had proposed it as a critical principle that 'the most corrected copies are commonly the least correct', presumably on the grounds that writers tend to correct in accordance with their own predilections, thus making things easy for themselves.[25] But Gibbon's 'correction' of Muratori does not smooth the event down and make it more digestible, as Muratori's amplification of Paulus Diaconus seems to do. Rather, Gibbon makes the event more anomalous, and turns it into the intense realisation of a paradox. C. S. Lewis thought that Gibbon lacked 'the roughness and density of life'; but in 1788, he directs *The Decline and Fall* away from generalisation and towards 'roughness and density'.[26]

Once more, a comparison with a parallel instance from Volume I may better define the transformation in Gibbon's convictions about historical narrative over the intervening twelve years. Discussing the deaths of the two Decii while fighting against the Goths, Gibbon prefers the account of Jornandes to that of Aurelius Victor:

Aurelius Victor allows two distinct actions for the deaths of the two Decii; but I have preferred the account of Jornandes.[27]

Why does Gibbon prefer Jornandes? He wrote later than Aurelius Victor, may have been indebted to him, and is likely to have been less impartial.[28] Some light is shed on the matter if we compare the two accounts; first Jornandes, then Aurelius Victor:

venientesque ad conflictum, ilicò Decii filium sagitta saucium crudeli vulnere confodiunt. quod pater animadvertens, licet ad confortandos animos militum dixisse fertur; nemo tristetur, perditio unius militis non est reipublicae diminutio: tamen paternum affectum non ferens hostes invadit, aut mortem aut ultionem filii exposcens; veniensque abrupto Moesiae civitatem, circumseptus à Gothis & ipse extinguitur, imperii finem vitaéque terminum faciens. qui locus hodiéque Decii ara dicitur, eò quòd ibi ante pugnam miserabiliter idolis immolaret.

Decii, barbaros trans Danubium persectantes, Abryti fraude cecidere, exacto regni biennio. sed Deciorum mortem plerique illustrem ferunt: namque filium audacius congredientem cecidisse in acie; patrem autem, cum perculsi milites ad solandum

---

[25] *Advancement of Learning*, II.xix.1; *Works*, I.89.

[26] *Surprised by Joy*, p. 202. Giarrizzo notices 'l'indulgere ai particolari esotici e pittoreschi' in the final volumes, although he does not connect it with intellectual changes and seems to view it simply as a shift in taste (*Edward Gibbon e la Cultura Europea del Settecento*, p. 425). See also Collingwood, *Essays on the Philosophy of History*, p. 31.

[27] *The Decline and Fall*, I.xxxviii n. 45: I.303 n. 45.

[28] Jornandes' *floruit* was A.D. 550, and his *De Rebus Geticis* has been dated to A.D. 551. H. W. Bird estimates that Aurelius Victor's *De Caesaribus* was composed between A.D. 358 and 360 (*Sextus Aurelius Victor*, p. 10).

imperatorem multa praefarentur, strenue dixisse detrimentum unius militis parum videri sibi. ita refecto bello, cum impigre decertaret, interisse pari modo.[29]

It is clear that Aurelius Victor offers a less dramatic version of the incident, and the detail on which Gibbon comments, his allocation of the deaths of father and son to separate engagements, is a token of his more dissipated, less vivid account. Jornandes, on the other hand, gives the episode a lurid concentration by having the son expire in front of his father, and, by the words he puts into the mouth of the elder Decius, 'perditio unius militis non est *reipublicae* diminutio' (my emphasis), makes the moment almost generalise itself. Thus the vividness of his account is not at the expense of legibility, but enhances it. Jornandes gives us a tableau full of implicit comment on the demise of the empire; the death of the son before the father suggests the wastage of the empire's strength, while the father's ineffective invocation of the vocabulary of pristine virtue shows how impotent are such gestures to arrest the process of decline. It seems that Gibbon's preference for Jornandes over Aurelius Victor, although apparently a critical decision, has not been made on genuinely critical grounds, but rather on the basis of what best suits his authorial purposes. This becomes still more likely when we note that Gibbon takes his leave of the imperial Decii by saying that they 'deserved to be compared, both in life and death, with the brightest examples of ancient virtue'.[30] The two examples which come immediately to mind are the two republican Decii, again father and son, who (so Livy records) on different occasions devoted themselves to death in order that Rome might be victorious against her enemies.[31] The contrast with the later Decii is complete. In place of the willed heroism recounted by Livy, which averts disaster and ensures victory, Gibbon is obliged to give us an act of despair which seals disaster. Instead of the son's being strengthened by the father's example, the father is distracted by the son's misfortune. Instead of the triumph of Rome, we are given its collapse. The more concentrated version of Jornandes is better able to evoke, by contrast, the Livyan original of which it seems the decayed and imperial counterpart. It recommends itself to Gibbon because of the precision with which it suits his book, whereas his (equally groundless, from a strict point of view) elaboration of Alboin's prospect over Italy is not made in order to support his interpretation of decline, but rather to distil something of the extraordinary and paradoxical essence of the later years of the empire's decline on which that interpretation had come to grief.

When we look into how Gibbon has managed his sources in his account of Julian's investiture with the purple, we can appreciate that this process of making the past more, rather than less, particular, was already under way in 1781:

---

[29] *De Rebus Geticis*, XVIII and *De Caesaribus*, XXIX.4–5.

[30] *The Decline and Fall*, I.254–5: I.304.

[31] The first Publius Decius devoted himself against the Latins in AUC 414 (*Ab Urbe Condita*, VIII.ix.6–8), his son, also Publius Decius, against the Gauls in AUC 459 (X.xxviii.6–18).

The approbation of the soldiers was testified by a respectful murmur: they gazed on the manly countenance of Julian, and observed with pleasure, that the fire which sparkled in his eyes was tempered by a modest blush, on being thus exposed, for the first time, to the public view of mankind.[32]

What is Gibbon's authority for the fire in Julian's eyes? His modern sources, de la Bleterie and Fleury, note that Julian had flashing eyes; but they, of course, have no independent authority.[33] Gregory of Nazianzus reports that Julian had a 'wild gaze', Mamertinus notes that his eyes glittered with astral fires ('sidereis ignibus'), and Ammianus Marcellinus describes his eyes as flashing ('venustate oculorum micantium flagrans'). But none of these writers attach this detail to Julian's investiture.[34] Nor do any of the five sources for the investiture Gibbon cites – Zosimus, Ammianus Marcellinus, Aurelius Victor, Victor Junior and Eutropius – mention Julian's eyes sparkling on this occasion.[35] Once again, as with Alboin's both acquisitive and scornful gaze over Italy, we can see Gibbon retouching his sources to produce a picture at once more vividly imagined and less straightforward. Instead of the tension between desire and contempt in Alboin, in Julian we find the conflict of bashfulness and vivacity.

It is when the past approaches the character of oxymoron that Gibbon finds his imagination engaged, and we find his prose take on a heightened, rather than diminished, particularity. Belisarius' discovery of Antonina with her lover Theodosius is another case in point:

During their residence at Carthage, he surprised the two lovers in a subterraneous chamber, solitary, warm, and almost naked. Anger flashed from his eyes. 'With the

32 *The Decline and Fall*, II.141.
33 De la Bleterie says without hesitation that 'ce qu'il y a de certain, c'est que Maxime lui prédit l'empire; qu'il fit bruler à ses yeux le projet singulier de détruire la religion dominante, pour rétablir celle de ses ancêtres',and that Julian had 'le regard d'un feu surprenant' (*Vie de l'Empereur Julien*, pp. 48 and 59). Fleury is also unequivocal: 'Ses yeux étoient vifs' (*Histoire Ecclésiastique*, III.434).
34 Gregory of Nazianzus, *Orat.* 5.23; Mamertinus, *Panegyr.* 6.4; Ammianus Marcellinus, *Res Gestae* XXV.iv.22.
35 *The Decline and Fall*, II.141 n. 35. Zosimus, in Book III, records Julian's investiture, but says nothing of its circumstances. Eutropius remarks baldly 'mox Julianum Caesarem ad Gallias misit [Constantius]' (*Epitome*, Book X). Aurelius Victor is hardly more informative: 'qua caussa ne quid apud Gallos natura praecipites movaretur, praesertim Germanes pleraque earum partium populantibus, Julianum Caesarem, cognatione acceptum sibi, Transalpinis praefecit' (*De Caesaribus*, XLII.17). Victor Junior is similarly brief: 'Constantius Claudium Julianum, Fratrem Galli, honore Caesaris adsumit, annos natum fere tres atque viginti' (*Epitome de Caesaribus*, XLII.12). It is only in Ammianus that we find an account as circumstantial as Gibbon's. There we find some sanction for the 'modest blush' in words given to Constantius: 'Julianum hunc fratrem meum patruelem (ut nostis), verecundia qua nobis ita ut necessitudine carus est, recte spectatum, iamque elucentis industriae iuvenem, in Caesaris adhibere potestatem exopto' (XV.viii.8). The soldiers respond to Julian's eyes, but on account of their gracefulness – the glitter comes from the silken purple: 'immane quo quantoque gaudio praeter paucos Augusti probavere iudicium, Caesaremque admiratione digna suscipiebant, imperatorii muricis fulgore flagrantem. cuius oculos cum venustate terribilis, vultumque excitatius gratum, diu multumque contuentes, qui futurus sit colligebant velut scrutatis veteribus libris, quorum lectio per corporum signa pandit animorum interna' (XV.viii.15–16).

help of this young man,' said the unblushing Antonina, 'I was secreting our most precious effects from the knowledge of Justinian.' The youth resumed his garments, and the pious husband consented to disbelieve the evidence of his own senses.[36]

The only source for this encounter is Procopius, who elsewhere supplies Gibbon with some of his most curious and apparently redundant details; but he does not mention Belisarius' flashing eyes, saying only that the general was enraged.[37] However, by inserting the detail, Gibbon has imparted to the moment a sharpness it would otherwise have lacked. It is a much more powerful expression of the teasing fragmentariness and discontinuities of Belisarius' character to say that he 'disbelieved the evidence of his own senses' when we have just seen the organ of one of those senses responding with such liveliness. When the senses react so vigorously, for Belisarius to subdue them elevates his foolishness to an almost sublime level; just as Antonina's corresponding self-mastery in being both warm and unblushing gives an extra polish to her brazenness. Gibbon has again imbued a comparatively banal moment with singularity. Once we have excavated a little way beneath the surface of *The Decline and Fall*, it appears that Gibbon's occasionally free way with his sources, although a constant feature of his history, changes in nature between 1776 and 1788 in a way which supports the view that he leaves behind the philosophic aim of overleaping the particular and responds creatively to the check the recalcitrance of the past administered to the explanation of decline he advanced in Volume I.

This reversal of his attitude towards the particular has consequences for Gibbon's idea of the purpose and methods of historical writing. In Volume I, he is cool and quizzical in the face of barbarian historiography; 'The immortality so vainly promised by the priests, was, in some degree, conferred by the bards.'[38] The claim of language to preserve is viewed with polite irony by the historian who holds that it is the function of history not to embalm the past, but to lay bare through dissection its causal skeleton; the parenthetic 'in some degree' deftly uncovers the gap between the literal immortality which the priests promised with such audacious fraud, and the depleted, figurative immortality which is all the bards can furnish. Both priests and bards are charlatans by whose deceptions the historian is, as yet, neither beguiled nor troubled. But in 1781 and 1788, Gibbon looks on these images of apparently naive historiography with a more neutral eye:

. . . the attention of the guests was captivated by the vocal harmony, which revived and perpetuated the memory of their own exploits: a martial ardour flashed from the

---

[36] *The Decline and Fall*, IV.205.

[37] *Anecdota*, I.xix–xx. It is from Procopius' *History of the Wars* (V.x.14–20), for instance, that Gibbon learns exactly how Belisarius insinuated his troops into Naples (*The Decline and Fall*, IV.172).

[38] *The Decline and Fall*, I.235: I.281.

eyes of the warriors, who were impatient for battle; and the tears of the old men expressed their generous despair, that they could no longer partake the danger and glory of the field.

. . . the recital, in prose or verse, of an obsolete feud was sufficient to rekindle the same passions among the descendents of the hostile tribes.[39]

We have here not a mere modish relishing of the primitive and barbarous (already as well established in 1776 as 1788), but the interest of an historian in traditions of relating the past quite foreign to his own, and towards which his subject, through its refusal of his original, philosophic allegiances, was inclining him.[40] In the process of devoting less energy to criticism (narrowly conceived), he concentrates more on the expressive and affecting evocation of the findings of the imagination.

That new idea of the function of historiography, and thus of the role of the historian, influences Gibbon's choice of word when expressing the hope that the enormity of his subject will break any philosophic prejudices among his readers concerning the profit of history:

I have long since asserted my claim to introduce the nations, the immediate or remote authors of the fall of the Roman empire; nor can I refuse myself to those events, which, from their uncommon magnitude, will interest a philosophic mind in the history of blood.[41]

The image of sexual surrender ('nor can I refuse myself') is drawn from the vocabulary of conception and childbirth Gibbon uses to describe the historian's work at important moments in *The Decline and Fall*, the *Memoirs* and the *Letters*.[42] To speak of a book as a child, or even of a child as a book, was not unusual in the eighteenth century.[43] However, in Gibbon's case the image speaks not only of his care for his work, but of the kind of work it is. The past – independent energy and life – is born through the historian, whose activity of creative collaboration with the records of history may be figured

---

[39] *The Decline and Fall*, III.385 and V.185.

[40] Gibbon is amused, but not convinced, by the 'pleasing romance' of the cult of the Gothic (*The Decline and Fall*, VI.626).

[41] *The Decline and Fall*, VI.288.

[42] The most famous example comes in the *Memoirs*, when Gibbon describes the 'moment of conception' of *The Decline and Fall* (p. 136). This is not a figure of speech on which Gibbon alighted in retrospect. In his letters of the 1770s and 80s, the image of the book as a child is common: the copies of the first edition of Volume I are 'mes enfans' (*Letters*, II.105), while the second edition is referred to as 'my new birth' (*Letters*, II.111). He enjoins care on Septchênes, his French translator, by whimsically enlarging the image: *The Decline and Fall* is 'un enfant cheri, egarè sans guide au milieu de Paris et exposè au danger de deshonorer par des liaisons honteuses le nom qu'il portoit' (*Letters*, II.131). The metaphor is revived for the two later instalments: 'I believe that in twelve or fourteen months I shall be brought to bed – perhaps of twins; May they live, and prove as healthy as their eldest brother' (*Letters*, II.225); 'the impression of three quarto volumes which will require nine months (a regular parturition)' (*Letters*, III.65). Gray, too, speaks of 'a parent's fond foolishness' (*Poems and Memoirs*, p. 108).

[43] Chesterfield compares Philip Stanhope to a text which needs careful editing (*Letters*, I.261–2).

sexually as surrender and response. The force which seduced Gibbon may win the philosophic mind from its famous scorn of the history of blood, and make it appreciate that we are the poorer for so segregating the past. What dead men have done is a whole which demands to be embraced and admitted. The distinctions and principles whereby the philosophic historians purported to purge the past of error and imposture in fact emasculated it, protecting them from the disruptive energy which Gibbon feels and for which he develops a taste, but at the price of sterilising the resulting works. Yet it would be an overstatement to maintain that Gibbon forsakes philosophic historiography absolutely. It would be better to say that in the later volumes of *The Decline and Fall* he tries to renovate and redefine the philosophic ideal – to temper its laudable acuteness and seriousness of interest in the past with sensitivity and openness, and thereby to attain a true impartiality free from the coldness of neutrality.

The kind of historiography which results is exemplified in Chapter LXXI, the account of the ruins of Rome and Gibbon's last word as a practising historian. Its lineaments are, however, well represented in Wordsworth's 'The Pillar of Trajan'. The pillar's setting embodies a deep truth:

> Where towers are crushed, and unforbidden weeds
> O'er mutilated arches shed their seeds;
> And temples, doomed to milder change, unfold
> A new magnificence that vies with old;
> Firm in its pristine majesty hath stood
> A votive Column, spared by fire and flood: – [44]

Despite being surrounded with mutability and decay, the column remains erect and unshaken. Its independence is more than an architectural strength, since the column is a special kind of monument, recording 'Things that recoil from language', and thus an independent source of knowledge about the past complementing 'Trajan as by Pliny seen'.[45]

Wordsworth then goes on to deplore the imperialism which could 'enslave whole nations on their native soil', but nationalism, however sincere, is not at the heart of the poem. He is fascinated by the question of how we apprehend the past, and sees in Trajan's column not just a tribute to 'him who thus survives by classic art', but also an object extending to us the possibility of an intimate, imaginative knowledge of history through the rapt attention it provokes:

> Still are we present with the imperial Chief,
> Nor cease to gaze upon the bold Relief
> Till Rome, to silent marble unconfined,
> Becomes with all her years a vision of the Mind.[46]

[44] *Poetical Works*, III.229–30, ll. 1–6.   [45] ll. 39 and 28.
[46] ll. 26 and 70–3.

So much of this is congruent with Gibbon's mature thoughts on historiography. The power of the past to elude the net of language; the power of art, nevertheless, to allow survival to the past; the gaze which frees history, 'unconfined', from its relics – all these aspects of the struggle to imagine the past and preserve that imagination in language had impinged, forty years before, on another Englishman whose distinction was to give birth to his 'vision of the Mind' in language.

18

'The wide and various prospect of desolation'

. . . how much more our minds can conceive, than our bodies can perform . . .

Nothing is ended with honour, which does not conclude better than it begun.

Johnson

We know that Gibbon's 'original plan was circumscribed to the decay of the City, rather than of the Empire'; it is thus especially interesting that he should finally attach a chapter discussing the spoliation of the city to *The Decline and Fall*.[1] In the last chapter of the history, we see the tried historian visiting the site of his youthful intentions. When he began 'to methodize the form, and to collect the substance' of his work, he 'almost grasped the ruins of Rome in the fourteenth Century, without suspecting that this final chapter must be attained by the labour of six quartos and twenty years'.[2] We can understand the force of that '*must* be attained' only when we have seen how, in the richly modulated prose of Chapter LXXI, the full range of Gibbon's extension as an historian is in play, and the laboriously acquired suppleness of his historical imagination applied to the project he had contemplated, then set aside, two decades before.

In Chapter LXXI Gibbon considers the various causes of the decay of Rome. At the beginning of the century, Pope had pinned the blame squarely on the barbarians and the Church:

> See the wild Waste of all-devouring years!
> How Rome her own sad Sepulchre appears,
> With nodding arches, broken temples spread!
> The very Tombs now vanish'd like their dead! . . .
> Some felt the silent stroke of mould'ring age,
> Some hostile fury, some religious rage;
> Barbarian blindness, Christian zeal conspire,
> And Papal piety, and Gothic fire.[3]

But when Gibbon considers what he revealingly calls the 'wide and various prospect of desolation', he finds these two causes insufficient for the breadth

---

[1] *Memoirs*, p. 136.
[2] *Memoirs*, pp. 146 and 147.
[3] 'To Mr. Addison, Occasioned by his Dialogues on Medals', ll. 1–4 and 11–14; *Works*, III.200–2.

and multifariousness of the phenomenon. He thus adds three further causes: the 'injuries of time and nature', the 'use and abuse of the materials', and the 'domestic quarrels of the Romans'.[4] Moreover, he partially absolves the barbarians and the Church, noting that the former were neither inclined nor able to inflict calamitous damage on Rome, while the latter in fact preserved as much as they destroyed. Gibbon is too scrupulous to overlook the consecration of the Coliseum by Benedict XIV, and 'the meritorious act of saving and converting the majestic structure of the Pantheon'.[5]

The chapter thus has a clear revisionary thrust; but to remark its tendency is not to take its full measure, since so much of the quality of Gibbon's thought is apparent not in its findings but in the richly hybrid prose through which it is expressed. As Gibbon undertakes to write about those 'scattered fragments' which 'so far surpass the most eloquent descriptions', he registers the amplitude and disparity of his subject in an array of styles, each the medium of a separate kind of thought.[6]

Even where we might expect the writing to be most narrow in its range, most intent on simply arguing for and vindicating a particular point of view, Gibbon surprises us with his flexibility. In his diminishing of the consequence of the hostile attacks of the barbarians and Christians, we find not a mere attack on exaggeration and misrepresentation, but the indication of a more intricate truth. Gibbon begins by pointing out the carelessness of previous writers:

The crowd of writers of every nation, who impute the destruction of the Roman monuments to the Goths and the Christians, have neglected to enquire how far they were animated by an hostile principle, and how far they possessed the means and the leisure to satiate their enmity.[7]

Then, with a certain formality, he produces his own credentials:

In the preceding volumes of this History, I have described the triumph of barbarism and religion; and I can only resume, in a few words, their real or imaginary connection with the ruin of ancient Rome.[8]

At this point, the tone changes and a broader note of amusement is introduced as he sets out the crude history written by those who view the past through the nostalgic, and thus arrogant, lens of the romanticised cult of the Gothic:

Our fancy may create, or adopt, a pleasing romance, that the Goths and Vandals sallied from Scandinavia, ardent to avenge the flight of Odin, to break the chains, and to chastise the oppressors, of mankind; that they wished to burn the records of classic literature, and to found their national architecture on the broken members of the Tuscan and Corinthian orders.[9]

---

[4] *The Decline and Fall*, VI.623.   [5] *The Decline and Fall*, VI.628.
[6] *The Decline and Fall*, VI.640.   [7] *The Decline and Fall*, VI.626.
[8] *The Decline and Fall*, VI.626.   [9] *The Decline and Fall*, VI.626–7.

This baseless structure is made to totter at the merest touch of 'simple truth', adduced with an economy reminiscent of Montesquieu or the philosophic Gibbon of Volume I (the change in sentence length is particularly effective here):

But in simple truth, the northern conquerors were neither sufficiently savage, nor sufficiently refined, to entertain such aspiring ideas of destruction and revenge.[10]

This is philosophic in manner without, however, being thoroughly philosophic. Montesquieu, and Gibbon himself in 1776, had used such telling brevity to overturn the muddle of received notions and replace them with a clearer and more regular idea of the past. Although the truth Gibbon introduces here is 'simple', its consequences are not, since it replaces the clear but misconceived image of vengeful barbarians with a much less conclusive and defined picture of these races. Conjecturing from his by now vast knowledge of fact, Gibbon paints the features of barbarism less boldly but more carefully:

The shepherds of Scythia and Germany had been educated in the armies of the empire, whose discipline they acquired, and whose weakness they invaded: with the familiar use of the Latin tongue, they had learned to reverence the name and titles of Rome; and, though incapable of emulating, they were more inclined to admire, than to abolish, the arts and studies of a brighter period.[11]

That general reflection is then applied to the matter in hand:

In the transient possession of a rich and unresisting capital, the soldiers of Alaric and Genseric were stimulated by the passions of a victorious army; amidst the wanton indulgence of lust or cruelty, portable wealth was the object of their search; nor could they derive either pride or pleasure from the unprofitable reflection, that they had battered to the ground the works of the consuls and Caesars.[12]

This conjecture is immediately seconded by precise knowledge, both of dates and of ancient architecture:

Their moments were indeed precious; the Goths evacuated Rome on the sixth, the Vandals on the fifteenth, day; and, though it be far more difficult to build than to destroy, their hasty assault would have made a slight impression on the solid piles of antiquity.[13]

And the demolition is complete when from the rubble Gibbon produces evidence which the old, crude image of ravaging barbarians could not accommodate and thus ignored, but which now makes its impact:

We may remember, that both Alaric and Genseric affected to spare the buildings of the city; that they subsisted in strength and beauty under the auspicious government

---

[10] *The Decline and Fall*, VI.627. [11] *The Decline and Fall*, VI.627.
[12] *The Decline and Fall*, VI.627. [13] *The Decline and Fall*, VI.627.

of Theodoric; and that the momentary resentment of Totila was disarmed by his own temper and the advice of his friends and enemies.[14]

Before Gibbon has cleared the site, however, he must still dispatch the companion *canard* to the barbarians, the Catholic Church; for from 'these innocent Barbarians, the reproach may be transferred to the Catholics of Rome'.[15] He begins by seeming to admit the substance of the reproach:

> The statues, altars, and houses, of the daemons were an abomination in their eyes; and in the absolute command of the city, they might labour with zeal and perseverance to eraze the idolatry of their ancestors.[16]

Their similar and authenticated behaviour elsewhere appears to put the matter beyond doubt:

> The demolition of the temples in the East affords to *them* an example of conduct, and to *us* an argument of belief; and it is probable, that a portion of guilt or merit may be imputed with justice to the Roman proselytes.[17]

But then, weaving pregnant facts with imaginative inferences, and throwing out hints which in their pithiness suggest an apprehension of antiquity replete to the point of ineffability (note the transition from precision to dreaminess in 'the change of religion was accomplished, not by a popular tumult, but by the decrees of the emperors, of the senate, and of time'), he reveals how small that portion may have been:

> Yet their abhorrence was confined to the monuments of heathen superstition; and the civil structures that were dedicated to the business or pleasure of society might be preserved without injury or scandal. The change of religion was accomplished, not by a popular tumult, but by the decrees of the emperors, of the senate, and of time. Of the Christian hierarchy, the bishops of Rome were commonly the most prudent and least fanatic: nor can any positive charge be opposed to the meritorious act of saving and converting the majestic structure of the Pantheon.[18]

And there the matter is left, on the resonance of that commonly overlooked, yet incontrovertible, deed. Nothing could better express Gibbon's eventual understanding that the true historical mind, amply stored with precise knowledge, is more frequently called upon to suspend judgement than to pass it; an understanding to which the evasions, reservations, silences and understatements of his prose are as apt as they were to the irony of 1776.[19] Yet the style has been stretched, as well as the mind of which it is the image. The decorum of Volume I would not have permitted the discontinuities of vocabulary we find here:

[14] *The Decline and Fall*, VI.627.
[15] *The Decline and Fall*, VI.627.
[16] *The Decline and Fall*, VI.627–8.
[17] *The Decline and Fall*, VI.628.
[18] *The Decline and Fall*, VI.628.
[19] Jeffrey Smitten's stimulating article, 'Impartiality in Robertson's *History of America*', deals with these issues in the work of Gibbon's contemporary; see especially p. 62.

The art of man is able to construct monuments far more permanent than the narrow span of his own existence: yet these monuments, like himself, are perishable and frail; and in the boundless annals of time, his life and his labours must equally be measured as a fleeting moment. Of a simple and solid edifice, it is not easy however to circumscribe the duration. As the wonders of ancient days, the pyramids attracted the curiosity of the ancients: an hundred generations, the leaves of autumn, have dropt into the grave; and after the fall of the Pharaohs and Ptolemies, the Caesars and caliphs, the same pyramids stand erect and unshaken above the floods of the Nile. A complex figure of various and minute parts is more accessible to injury and decay; and the silent lapse of time is often accelerated by hurricanes and earthquakes, by fires and inundations.[20]

From the loftiness of the tombstone reflection on the 'boundless annals of time' and a perspective in which all earthly things are invisible, we pass to the almost technical vocabulary of 'a complex figure of various and minute parts' via an allusion to Homer.

The heterogeneity of this writing is not, however, that of an anthologist. Single words can vibrate with multiple possibilities as a result of our acquaintance with the extreme mobility of the historian's intellect generated by those abrupt alternations:

Fire is the most powerful agent of life and death: the rapid mischief may be kindled and propagated by the industry or negligence of mankind; and every period of the Roman annals is marked by the repetition of similar calamities. A memorable conflagration, the guilt or misfortune of Nero's reign, continued, though with unequal fury, either six, or nine days. Innumerable buildings, crowded in close and crooked streets, supplied perpetual fewel for the flames; and when they ceased, four only of the fourteen regions were left entire; three were totally destroyed, and seven were deformed by the relics of smoking and lacerated edifices. In the full meridian of empire, the metropolis arose with fresh beauty from her ashes; yet the memory of the old deplored their irreparable losses, the arts of Greece, the trophies of victory, the monuments of primitive or fabulous antiquity. In the days of distress and anarchy, every wound is mortal, every fall irretrievable; nor can the damage be restored either by the public care of government or the activity of private interest.[21]

The initial generalisation narrows swiftly to the details of the burning of Rome during the reign of Nero; the allusion to the phoenix inflects the writing away from record; while the list of the irreparable losses of art, of the fruits of victory and of a lively sense of the past, because it seems almost a catalogue of the symptoms of the larger phenomenon of decline, broadens the final sentence into a comment on that larger phenomenon, as well as on civil architecture. The impression, as the writing moves with so little gradation from the most minute to the most immense, finally drawing the clear and the cloudy together, is of a mind both nimble and loaded with information striving to encompass history in its fullest extent, and ready to find in every particle of the

---

[20] *The Decline and Fall*, VI.623. [21] *The Decline and Fall*, VI.624.

past a prompting to a larger thought and the prospect of a more extensive view.

That sense of the possibility of a more inclusive knowledge which can be indicated but, because lying out of reach, not grasped, is even more powerful here:

Soon after the triumph of the first Punic war, the Tyber was encreased by unusual rains; and the inundation, surpassing all former measure of time and place, destroyed all the buildings that were situate below the hills of Rome. According to the variety of ground, the same mischief was produced by different means, and the edifices were either swept away by the sudden impulse, or dissolved and undermined by the long continuance, of the flood. Under the reign of Augustus, the same calamity was renewed: the lawless river overturned the palaces and temples on its banks; and, after the labours of the emperor in cleansing and widening the bed that was incumbered with ruins, the vigilance of his successors was exercised by similar dangers and designs. The project of diverting into new channels the Tyber itself, or some of the dependent streams, was long opposed by superstition and local interests; nor did the use compensate the toil and cost of the tardy and imperfect execution. The servitude of rivers is the noblest and most important victory which man has obtained over the licentiousness of nature; and if such were the ravages of the Tyber under a firm and active government, what could oppose, or who can enumerate, the injuries of the city after the fall of the Western empire?[22]

The personification of geography which runs through this passage ('the lawless river', 'the servitude of rivers', 'the ravages of the Tyber under a firm and active government') may seem fanciful or capricious.[23] But at the end of the *Epistle To Burlington*, Pope had cited just such a taming of the environment, 'those great and public works which become a Prince', as a central part of the Augustan ideal:

> Bid Harbours Open, public Ways extend,
> Bid Temples, worthier of the God, ascend;
> Bid the broad Arch the dang'rous Flood contain,
> The Mole projected break the roaring Main;
> Back to his bounds their subject Sea command,
> And roll obedient Rivers thro' the Land:
> These Honours, Peace to happy Britain brings,
> These are Imperial Works, and worthy Kings.[24]

The 'richness, energy and imperious strength' of these lines have recently received their due.[25] Juxtaposed with the passage from *The Decline and Fall*,

---

[22] *The Decline and Fall*, VI.625–6.

[23] We may, however, recollect the phrases from the end of Chapter LXX which prepare for it: 'In Rome the voice of freedom and discord is no longer heard; and, instead of the foaming torrent, a smooth and stagnant lake reflects the image of idleness and servitude' (*The Decline and Fall*, VI.615; compare *Tatler*, no. 161).

[24] Ll. 197–204; *Works*, III.198–9. Compare also the conclusion of *Liberty*, V.701–20.

[25] Howard Erskine-Hill, *The Augustan Idea in English Literature*, p. 290; see also the same author's longer discussion of this passage in his earlier *The Social Milieu of Alexander Pope*, pp. 321–6.

we can see that they have not only the energy proper to exhortation, but also the simplicity. Indeed, one might say that Gibbon is entirely occupied with the practical problems which Pope, reposing for a moment in the ideal after the discomforts of Timon's villa, disguises in the repeated word of easy command, 'bid'. Pope makes the way lie plain for Burlington; but as Gibbon traces the more twisting path of actuality, the connexion between masterful government and a subjugated terrain cannot be affirmed (even under Augustus 'the same calamity was renewed'), but is kept as a metaphor which may momentarily illuminate a fragment of the past. The final question, which is not entirely rhetorical (there were undoubtedly many injuries: but who can take their measure?) appropriately suggests the reserve and the curiosity of an historian fully awake to the way the manifold and imperfectly recorded past both inhibits and stimulates those who contemplate it.

That same blend of reserve and enthusiasm is found in the chapter's last sentence:

The fame of Julius the second, Leo the tenth, and Sixtus the fifth, is accompanied by the superior merit of Bramante and Fontana, of Raphael and Michael-Angelo: and the same munificence which had been displayed in palaces and temples, was directed with equal zeal to revive and emulate the labours of antiquity. Prostrate obelisks were raised from the ground, and erected in the most conspicuous places; of the eleven aqueducts of the Caesars and consuls, three were restored; the artificial rivers were conducted over a long series of old, or of new, arches, to discharge into marble basins a flood of salubrious and refreshing waters: and the spectator, impatient to ascend the steps of St. Peter's, is detained by a column of Egyptian granite, which rises between two lofty and perpetual fountains, to the height of one hundred and twenty feet. The map, the description, the monuments of ancient Rome, have been elucidated by the diligence of the antiquarian and the student: and the footsteps of heroes, the relics, not of superstitition, but of empire, are devoutly visited by a new race of pilgrims from the remote, and once savage, countries of the North.[26]

Gibbon moves easily from the generosity of the Renaissance restoration of Rome to that different sort of restoration which is historical study, and deposits us at the point of historical awareness. Some things, such as the column, are to be measured; others, which elude determination (such as the 'lofty and perpetual fountains'), appreciated: and from such alternating devotion and observation comes the historical betterment which has turned the abode of savages into the hive of sympathetic minds dedicated to the study of the classical past – a past by which they are educated ('once savage'), but from which they will always be, in some measure, 'remote'. The intellectual counterparts to that remoteness – doubt, hesitation, reserve, scruple, silence – these are now not tokens of a failure in historical imagination. They attend the frame of mind in which historical apprehension is alone possible.

In January 1787, when on the point of completing *The Decline and Fall*,

[26] *The Decline and Fall*, VI.644–5. I have benefited from Ian White's discussion of this passage in his 'The subject of Gibbon's History'.

Gibbon wrote to Sheffield and made no bones about the impediments and tantalising deferrals under which he laboured:

A long while ago when I contemplated the distant prospect of my work I gave you and myself some hopes of landing in England last Autumn but alas when autumn drew near, hills began to rise on hills, Alps on Alps, and I found my journey far more tedious and toilsome than I had imagined.[27]

This is most obviously an allusion to Pope:

> But *those attain'd*, we tremble to survey
> The growing Labours of the lengthen'd Way,
> Th' *increasing* Prospect *tires* our wandring Eyes,
> Hills peep o'er Hills, and *Alps* on *Alps* arise![28]

That Pope, too, has annexed this image to literary frustration obviously makes Gibbon's use of the same image an allusion to more than Pope's words. A closeness of experience accompanies the striking closeness of phrasing. Yet Pope's lines are also an allusion. In the *Punica*, Silius Italicus describes Hannibal's magnificent journey thus:

> quoque magis subiere iugo atque, evadere nisi,
> erexere gradum, crescit labor. ardua supra
> sese aperit fessis et nascitur altera moles,
> unde nec edomitos exsudatosque labores
> respexisse libet; tanta formidine plana
> exterrent repetita oculis; atque una pruinae
> canentis, quacumque datur promittere visus,
> ingeritur facies.[29]

Silius Italicus was as close to Gibbon's hand as was Pope, and the *Punica* is as germane to Gibbon's experience in the closing stages of *The Decline and Fall* as is *An Essay on Criticism*.[30] Hannibal stirringly failed to conquer Rome. The city was approached, but never entered. The confidence of philosophic historiography sprang from the faith that the past would become transparent before the correctly equipped and placed philosophic observer. Gibbon's enforced meditation on the profound obscurities and fine reticulations of history awakens him from the vanity of that happy dream; and by making *The Decline and Fall* not conclude with a triumphant résumé of the causal analysis through which a *philosophe* like Montesquieu would have claimed to have penetrated and possessed Rome, but rather cease on an account of the ruined site testifying in equal measure to the elusiveness and fascination of the Eternal City, as well as through the amalgam of laborious heroism and ultimate failure

---

[27] *Letters*, III.59: see also III.44 and 29.
[28] *An Essay on Criticism*, ll. 229–32; *Works*, I.101.
[29] III.528–35.
[30] Gray, crossing the Alps in a bier carried by eight mountaineers, reads this passage of Silius Italicus (*Poems and Memoirs*, p. 68). Gibbon crossed the Alps in the same fashion in 1764 (*Gibbon's Journey from Geneva to Rome*, pp. 5–6).

on which he touches in his oblique glance at Silius Italicus, Gibbon reticently expresses to both his readers and his friend the realisation that historical certainty is endlessly deferred – always about to come within one's grasp but always out of reach. We should neither overlook nor dismiss as unmeaning modesty Gibbon's final comment on *The Decline and Fall* when he deposited it before the curiosity and candour of his public, that as an account of the immensity and wonder of 'the greatest, perhaps, and most awful scene, in the history of mankind' it is 'inadequate to my own wishes'.[31]

[31] *The Decline and Fall*, VI.645–6.

Appendix

Gibbon's 'translation' of Ammianus' characterisation of the Roman nobles, the original passages of the *Res Gestae*, and an analysis of the detailed reliance of the English on the Latin.

(a) *The Decline and Fall* III.202–11. The greatness of Rome (such is the language of the historian) was founded on the rare, and almost incredible, alliance of virtue and of fortune. The long period of her infancy was employed in a laborious struggle against the tribes of Italy, the neighbours and enemies of the rising city. In the strength and ardour of youth, she sustained the storms of war; carried her victorious arms beyond the seas and the mountains; and brought home triumphal laurels from every country of the globe. At length, verging towards old age, and sometimes conquering by the terror only of her name, she sought the blessings of ease and tranquillity. The VENERABLE CITY, which had trampled on the necks of the fiercest nations; and established a system of laws, the perpetual guardians of justice and freedom; was content, like a wise and wealthy parent, to devolve on the Caesars, her favourite sons, the care of governing her ample patrimony. A secure and profound peace, such as had been once enjoyed in the reign of Numa, succeeded to the tumults of a republic: while Rome was still adored as the queen of the earth; and the subject nations still reverenced the name of the people, and the majesty of the senate. But this native splendour (continues Ammianus) is degraded, and sullied, by the conduct of some nobles; who, unmindful of their own dignity, and that of their country, assume an unbounded license of vice and folly. (1) They contend with each other in the empty vanity of titles and surnames; and curiously select, or invent, the most lofty and sonorous appellations, Reburrus, or Fabunius, Pagonius, or Tarrasius, which may impress the ears of the vulgar with astonishment and respect. (2) From a vain ambition of perpetuating their memory, they affect to multiply their likeness, in statues of bronze and marble; nor are they satisfied, unless those statues are covered with plates of gold: an honourable distinction, first granted to Acilius the consul, after he had subdued, by his arms and counsels, the power of king Antiochus. (3) The ostentation of displaying, of magnifying perhaps, the rent-roll of the estates which they possess in all the provinces, from the rising to the setting sun, provokes the just resentment of every man, who recollects, that their poor and invincible ancestors were not distinguished from the meanest of the soldiers, by the delicacy of their food, or the splendour of their apparel. (4) But the modern nobles measure their rank and consequence according to the loftiness of their chariots, and the weighty magnificence of their dress. Their long robes of silk and purple float in the wind; and as they are agitated, by art or accident, they occasionally discover the under garments, the rich tunics, embroidered with the figures of various animals. (5) Followed by a train of fifty servants, and tearing up the pavement, they move along the streets with the same impetuous speed as if they travelled with post-horses; and the example of the senators is boldly imitated by the matrons and ladies, whose covered carriages are continually driving round the immense space of the city and suburbs. Whenever these persons of high distinction condescend to visit the public baths, they assume, on their entrance, a tone of loud and insolent command, and appropriate to their own use the conveniences which were designed for the Roman people. If, in these places of mixed and general resort, they meet any of the infamous ministers of their pleasures, they express their affection by a tender embrace; while they proudly decline the salutations of their fellow-citizens, who are not permitted to aspire above the honour of kissing their hands, or their knees. (6) As soon as they have indulged themselves in the refreshment of the bath, they resume their rings, and the other ensigns of their dignity; select from their private wardrobe of the finest linen, such as might suffice for a dozen persons, the garments the most agreeable to their fancy, and maintain till their departure the same haughty demeanour; which perhaps might have been excused in the great Marcellus, after the conquest of Syracuse. (7) Sometimes, indeed, these heroes undertake more arduous atchievements; they visit their estates in Italy, and procure themselves, by the toil of servile hands, the amusements of the chase. If at any time, but more especially on a hot day, they have courage to sail, in their painted gallies, from the Lucrine lake, to their elegant villas on the sea-coast of Puteoli and Cayeta, they compare their own expeditions to the marches of Caesar and Alexander. Yet should a fly presume to settle on the silken folds of their gilded umbrellas; should a sunbeam penetrate through some unguarded and imperceptible chink, they deplore their intolerable hardships, and lament, in affected language, that they were not born in the land of the Cimmerians, the regions of eternal darkness. (8) In these journeys into the country, the whole body of the household marches with their master. In the same manner as the cavalry and infantry, the heavy and the light armed troops, the advanced guard and the rear, are marshalled by the skill of their military leaders; so the domestic officers, who bear a rod, as an ensign of authority, distribute and arrange the numerous train of slaves and attendants. The baggage and wardrobe move in the front, and are immediately followed by a multitude of cooks, and inferior ministers, employed in the service of the kitchens, and of the table. The main body is composed of a promiscuous crowd of slaves, increased by the accidental concourse of idle or dependent plebeians. The rear is closed by the favourite band of eunuchs, distributed from age to youth, according to the order of seniority. Their numbers, and their deformity, excite the horror of the indignant spectators, who are ready to execrate the memory of Semiramis, for the cruel art which she invented, of frustrating the purposes of nature, and of blasting in the bud the hopes of future generations. (9) In the exercise of domestic jurisdiction, the nobles of Rome express an exquisite sensibility for any personal injury, and a contemptuous indifference for the rest of the human species. When they have called for warm water, if a slave has been tardy in his obedience, he is instantly chastised with three hundred lashes: but should the same slave commit a wilful murder, the master will mildly observe, that he is a worthless fellow; but that, if he repeats the offence, he shall not escape punishment. (10) Hospitality was formerly the virtue of the Romans; and every stranger, who could plead either merit or misfortune, was relieved, or rewarded, by their generosity. At present, if a foreigner, perhaps of no contemptible rank, is introduced to one of the proud and wealthy senators, he is welcomed indeed in the first audience, with such warm professions, and such kind inquiries, that he retires, enchanted with the affability of his illustrious friend, and full of regret that he had so long delayed his journey to Rome, the native seat of manners, as well as of empire. Secure of a favourable reception, he repeats his visit the ensuing day, and is mortified by the discovery, that his person, his name, and his country, are already forgotten. If he still has resolution to persevere, he is gradually numbered in the train of dependents, and obtains the permission to pay his assiduous and unprofitable court to a haughty patron, incapable of gratitude or friendship; who scarcely deigns to remark his presence, his departure, or his return. (11) Whenever the rich prepare a solemn and popular entertainment, whenever they celebrate, with profuse and pernicious luxury, their private banquets, the choice of the guests is the subject of anxious deliberation. The modest, the sober, and the learned, are seldom preferred; and the nomenclators, who are commonly swayed by interested motives, have the address to insert in the list of invitations, the obscure names of the most worthless of mankind. (12) But the frequent and familiar companions of the great, are those parasites, who practise the most useful of all arts, the art of flattery; who eagerly applaud each word, and every action of their immortal patron; gaze with rapture on his marble columns, and variegated pavements; and strenuously praise the pomp and elegance, which he is taught to consider as a part of his personal merit. At the Roman tables, the birds, the *squirrels*, or the fish, which appear of an uncommon size, are contemplated with curious attention; a pair of scales is accurately applied, to ascertain their real weight; and, while the more rational guests are disgusted by the vain and tedious repetition, notaries are summoned to attest, by an authentic record, the truth of such a marvellous event. (13) Another method of introduction into the houses and society of the great, is derived from the profession of gaming, or, as it is more politely styled, of play. The confederates are united by a strict and indissoluble bond of friendship, or rather of conspiracy: a superior degree of skill in the *Tesserarian* art (which may be interpreted the game of dice and tables) is a sure road to wealth and reputation. A master of that sublime science, who in a supper, or assembly, is placed below a magistrate, displays in his countenance the surprise and indignation, which Cato might be supposed to feel, when he was refused the praetorship by the votes of a capricious people. (14) The acquisition of knowledge seldom engages the curiosity of the nobles, who abhor the fatigue, and disdain the advantages, of study; and the only books which they peruse are the satires of Juvenal, and the verbose and fabulous histories of Marius Maximus. (15) The libraries, which they have inherited from their fathers, are secluded, like dreary sepulchres, from the light of day. But the costly instruments of the theatre, flutes, and enormous lyres, and hydraulic organs, are constructed for their use; and the harmony of vocal and instrumental music is incessantly repeated in the palaces of Rome. (16) In those palaces, sound is preferred to sense, and the care of the body to that of the mind. It is allowed as a salutary maxim, that the light and frivolous suspicion of a contagious malady, is of sufficient weight to excuse the visits of the most intimate friends; and even the servants, who are dispatched to make the decent inquiries, are not suffered to return home, till they have undergone the ceremony of a previous ablution. (17) Yet this selfish and unmanly delicacy occasionally yields to the more imperious passion of avarice. The prospect of gain will urge a rich and gouty senator as far as Spoleto; every sentiment of arrogance and dignity is subdued by the hopes of an inheritance, or even of a legacy; and a wealthy, childless, citizen is the most powerful of the Romans. (18) The art of obtaining the signature of a favourable testament, and sometimes of hastening the moment of its execution, is perfectly understood; and it has happened, that in the same house, though in different apartments, a husband and a wife, with the laudable design of over-reaching each other, have summoned their respective lawyers, to declare, at the same time, their mutual, but contradictory, intentions. (19) The distress which follows and chastises extravagant luxury, often reduces the great to the use of the most humiliating expedients. When they desire to borrow, they employ the base and supplicating style of the slave in the comedy; but when they are called upon to pay, they assume the royal and tragic declamation of the grandsons of Hercules. If the demand is repeated, they readily procure some trusty sycophant, instructed to maintain a charge of poison, or magic, against the insolent creditor; who is seldom released from prison, till he has signed a discharge of the whole debt. (20) These vices, which degrade the moral character of the Romans, are mixed with a puerile superstition, that disgraces their understanding. They listen with confidence to the predictions of haruspices, who pretend to read, in the entrails of victims, the signs of future greatness and prosperity; and there are many who do not presume either to bathe, or to dine, or to appear in public, till they have diligently consulted, according to the rules of astrology, the situation of Mercury, and the aspect of the moon. It is singular enough, that this vain credulity may often be discovered among the profane sceptics, who impiously doubt, or deny, the existence of a celestial power.

(b) Ammianus, *Res Gestae*, XIV.vi 1. inter haec Orfitus praefecti potestate regebat urbem aeternam, ultra modum delatae dignitatis sese offerens insolenter, vir quidem prudens, et forensium negotiorum oppido gnarus, sed splendore liberalium doctrinarum minus quam nobilem decuerat institutus. quo administrante seditiones sunt concitatae graves ob inopiam vini, cuius avidis usibus vulgus intentum, ad motus asperos excitatur et crebros.

2. et quoniam mirari posse quosdam peregrinos existimo, haec lecturos forsitan (si contigerit), quam ob rem cum oratio ad ea monstranda deflexerit quae Romae geruntur, nihil praeter seditiones narratur et tabernas et vilitates harum similis alias, summatim causas perstringam, nusquam a veritate sponte propria digressurus.

3. tempore quo primis auspiciis in mundanum fulgorem surgeret victura dum erunt homines Roma, ut augeretur sublimibus incrementis, foedere pacis aeternae Virtus convenit atque Fortuna, plerumque dissidentes, quarum si altera defuisset, ad perfectam non venerat summitatem. 4. eius populus ab incunabulis primis ad usque pueritiae tempus extremum, quod annis circumcluditur fere trecentis, circummurana pertulit bella; deinde aetatem ingressus adultam, post multiplices bellorum aerumnas, Alpes transcendit et fretum; in iuvenem erectus et virum, ex omni plaga quam orbis ambit immensus, reportavit laureas et triumphos; iamque vergens in senium, et nomine solo aliquotiens vincens, ad tranquilliora vitae discessit. 5. ideo urbs venerabilis, post superbas efferatarum gentium cervices oppressas, latasque leges, fundamenta libertatis et retinacula sempiterna, velut frugi parens et prudens et dives, Caesaribus tamquam liberis suis regenda patrimonii iura permisit. 6. et olim licet otiosae sint tribus, pacataeque centuriae, et nulla suffragiorum certamina, sed Pompiliani redierit securitas temporis, per omnes tamen quot orae sunt partesque terrarum, ut domina suscipitur et regina, et ubique patrum reverenda cum auctoritate canities, populique Romani nomen circumspectum et verecundum.

7. sed laeditur hic coetuum magnificus splendor, levitate paucorum incondita, ubi nati sunt non reputantium, sed tamquam indulta licentia vitiis, ad errores lapsorum atque lasciviam. ut enim Simonides lyricus docet, beate perfecta ratione victuro, ante alia patriam esse convenit gloriosam. 8. ex his quidam aeternitati se commendari posse per statuas aestimantes, eas ardenter affectant, quasi plus praemii de figmentis aereis sensu carentibus adepturi, quam ex conscientia honeste recteque factorum, easque

auro curant imbratteari, quod Acilio Galbrioni delatum est primo, cum consiliis ar-
misque regem superasset Antiochum. quam autem sit pulchrum, exigua haec
spernentem et minima, ad ascensus verae gloriae tendere longos et arduous, ut
memorat vates Ascraeus, Censorius Cato monstravit. qui interrogatus quam ob rem
inter multos ipse statuam non haberet, 'malo' inquit 'ambigere bonos, quam ob rem
id non meruerim, quam (quod est gravius) cur impetraverim mussitare.'

9. alii summum decus in carruchis solito altioribus, et ambitioso vestium cultu ponentes,
sudant sub ponderibus lacernarum, quas in collis insertas iugulis ipsis annectunt, nimia
subtegminum tenuitate perflabilis, exceptantes eas manu utraque et vexantes crebris
agitationibus, maximeque sinistra, ut longiores fimbriae tunicaeque perspicue luceant,
varietate liciorum effigiatae in species animalium multiformes. 10. alii nullo quaerente,
vultus severitate assimulata, patrimonia sua in immensum extollunt, cultorum (ut putant)
feracium multiplicantes annuos fructus, quae a primo ad ultimum solem se abunde
iactitant possidere, ignorantes profecto maiores suos per quos ita magnitudo Romana por-
rigitur, non divitiis eluxisse, sed per bella saevissima, nec opibus nec victu nec indumen-
torum vilitate gregariis militibus discrepantes, opposita cuncta superasse virtute. 11. hac
ex causa collaticia stipe Valerius humatur ille Publicola, et subsidiis amicorum mariti, inops
cum liberis uxor alitur Reguli, et dotatur ex aerario filia Scipionis, cum nobilitas florem
adultae virginis diuturnum absentia pauperis erubesceret patris.

12. at nunc si ad aliquem bene nummatum tumentemque ideo, honestus advena
salutatum introieris primitus, tamquam exoptatus suscipieris, et interrogatus multa
coactusque mentiri, miraberis numquam antea visus, summatem virum tenuem te sic
enixius observantem, ut paeniteat ob haec bona tamquam praecipua non vidisse ante
decennium Romam. 13. hacque affabilitate confisus, cum eadem postridie feceris, ut
incognitus haerebis et repentinus, hortatore illo hesterno suos enumerando, qui sis vel
unde venias diutius ambigente. agnitus vero tandem et asscitus in amicitiam, si te
salutandi assiduitati dederis triennio indiscretus, et per totidem dierum defueris tempus, reverteris ad paria perferenda, nec ubi esses interrogatus, et ni inde miser
discesseris, aetatem omnem frustra in stipite conteres summittendo. 14. cum autem
commodis intervallata temporibus, convivia longa et noxia coeperint apparari, vel
distributio sollemnium sportularum, anxia deliberatione tractatur, an exceptis his
quibus vicissitudo debetur, peregrinum invitari conveniet, et si digesto plene consilio,
id placuerit fieri, is adhibetur qui pro domibus excubat aurigarum, aut artem
tesserariam profitetur, aut secretiora quaedam se nosse confingit. 15. homines enim
eruditos et sobrios, ut infaustos et inutiles vitant, eo quoque accedente, quod et
nomenclatores, assueti haec et talia venditare, mercede accepta, lucris quosdam et
prandiis inserunt subditicios ignobiles et obscuros.

16. mensarum enim voragines et varias voluptatum illecebras, ne longius pro-
grediar, praetermitto, illuc transiturus, quod quidam per ampla spatia urbis, subver-
sasque silices, sine periculi metu properantes equos velut publicos, ignitis quod dicitur
calcibus agitant, familiarium agmina tamquam praedatorios globos post terga
trahentes, ne Sannione quidem (ut ait comicus) domi relicto. quos imitatae matronae
complures, opertis capitibus et basternis, per latera civitatis cuncta discurrunt. 17. ut-
que proeliorum periti rectores primo catervas densas opponunt et fortes, deinde leves
armaturas, post iaculatores ultimasque subsidiales acies (si fors adegerit) iuvaturas,
ita praepositis urbanae familiae suspense digerentibus atque sollicite, quos insignes fa-
ciunt virgae dexteris aptatae, velut tessera data castrensi, iuxta vehiculi frontem omne
textrinum incedit: huic atratum coquinae iungitur ministerium, dein totum promisce
servitium, cum otiosis plebeis de vicinitate coniunctis; postrema multitudo spadonum

a senibus in pueros desinens, obluridi distortaque lineamentorum compage deformes, ut quaqua incesserit quisquam, cernens mutilorum hominum agmina, detestetur memoriam Samiramidis reginae illius veteris, quae teneros mares castravit omnium prima, velut vim iniectans naturae, eandemque ab instituto cursu retorquens, quae inter ipsa oriundi crepundia, per primigenios seminis fontes, tacita quodam modo lege vias propagandae posteritatis ostendit.

18. quod cum ita sit, paucae domus studiorum seriis cultibus antea celebratae, nunc ludibriis ignaviae torpentis exundant, vocabili sonu, perflabili tinnitu fidium resultantes. denique pro philosopho cantor, et in locum oratoris doctor artium ludicrarum accitur, et bybliothecis sepulcrorum ritu in perpetuum clausis, organa fabricantur hydraulica, et lyrae ad speciem carpentorum ingentes, tibiaeque et histrionici gestus instrumenta non levia.

19. postremo ad id indignitatis est ventum, ut cum peregrini ob formidatam haud ita dudum alimentorum inopiam pellerentur ab urbe praecipites, sectatoribus disciplinarum liberalium, impendio paucis, sine respiratione ulla extrusis tenerentur mimarum asseculae veri, quique id simularunt ad tempus, et tria milia saltatricum, ne interpellata quidem, cum choris totidemque remanerent magistris. 20. et licet, quocumque oculos flexeris, feminas affatim multas spectare cirratas, quibus, (si nupsissent) per aetatem ter iam nixus poterat suppetere liberorum, ad usque taedium pedibus pavimenta tergentis, iactari volucriter gyris, dum exprimunt innumera simulacra, quae finxere fabulae theatrales.

21. illud autem non dubitatur, quod cum esset aliquando virtutum omnium domicilium Roma, ingenuous advenas plerique nobilium, ut Homerici bacarum suavitate Lotophagi, humanitatis multiformibus officiis retentabant. 22. nunc vero inanes flatus quorundam, vile esse quicquid extra urbis pomerium nascitur aestimant praeter orbos et caelibes, nec credi potest qua obsequiorum diversitate coluntur homines sine liberis Romae. 23. et quoniam apud eos, ut in capite mundi, morborum acerbitates celsius dominantur, ad quos vel sedandos omnis professio medendi torpescit, excogitatum est adminiculum sospitale, nequi amicum perferentem similia videat, additumque est cautioribus paucis remedium aliud satis validum, ut famulos percontatum missos quem ad modum valeant noti hac aegritudine colligati, non ante recipiant domum, quam lavacro purgaverint corpus. Ita etiam alienis oculis visa metuitur labes. 24. sed tamen haec cum ita tutius observentur, quidam vigore artuum imminuto, rogati ad nuptias, ubi aurum dextris manibus cavatis offertur, impigre vel usque Spoletium pergunt. haec nobilium sunt instituta.

(c) Ammianus, *Res Gestae*, XXVIII.iv 6. et primo nobilitatis, ut aliquotiens pro locorum copia fecimus, dein plebis digeremus errata, incidentia veloci constringentes excessu. 7. prae nominum claritudine conspicui quidam (ut putant) in immensum semet extollunt, cum Reburri et Flavonii et Pagonii Gereonesque appellentur, ac Dalii cum Tarraciis et Ferasiis, aliisque ita decens sonantibus originum insignibus multis. 8. non nullos fulgentes sericis indumentis, ut ducendos ad mortem, vel ut sine diritate ominis loquamur, praegresso exercitu, arma cogentes, manipulatim concitato fragore sequitur multitudo servorum. 9. tales ubi comitantibus singulos quinquaginta ministris, tholos introierint balnearum, 'ubi ubi sunt nostri?' minaciter clamant: si apparuisse subito ignotam compererint meretricem, aut oppidanae quondam prostibulum plebis, vel meritorii corporis veterem lupam, certatim concurrunt, palpantesque advenam, deformitate magna blanditiarum ita extollunt, ut Samiramim Parthi vel Cleopatras Aegyptus aut Artemisiam Cares vel Zenobiam Palmyreni. et haec admittunt hi quorum apud maiores censoria nota senator afflictus est, ausus dum adhuc non deceret, praesente communi filia coniugem osculari.

10. ex his quidam cum salutari pectoribus oppositis coeperint, osculanda capita in modum taurorum minacium obliquantes, adulatoribus offerunt genua savianda, vel manus, id illis sufficere ad beate vivendum existimantes, et abundare omni cultu humanitatis peregrinum putantes, cuius forte etiam gratia sunt obligati, interrogatum, quibus thermis utatur aut aquis, aut ad quam successerit domum.

11. et cum ita graves sint et cultores virtutum, (ut putant) si venturos undelibet equos aut aurigas quendam didicerint nuntiasse, ita sollerter imminent eidem et percunctantur, ut Tyndaridas fratres eorum suspexere maiores, cum priscis illis victoriis indicatis gaudio cuncta complessent.

12. horum domus otiosi quidam garruli frequentant, variis assentandi figmentis, ad singula ulterioris fortunae verba plaudentes, parasitorum in comoediis facetias affectando. ut enim illi sufflant milites gloriosos, obsidiones et pugnas contra milia hostium, eisdem ut heroicis aemulis assignantes, ita hi quoque columnarum constructiones, alta fronte suspensas mirando, atque parietes lapidum circumspectis coloribus nitidos, ultra mortalitatem nobiles viros extollunt. 13. poscuntur etiam in conviviis aliquotiens trutinae, ut appositi pisces et volucres ponderentur, et glires, quorum magnitudo saepius replicata, non sine taedio praesentium, ut antehac inusitata, laudatur assidue, maxime cum haec eadem numerantes, notarii, triginta prope assistant, cum thecis et pugillaribus tabulis, ut deesse solus magister ludi litterarii videretur.

14. quidam detestantes ut venena doctrinas, Iuvenalem et Marium Maximum curatiore studio legunt, nulla volumina praeter haec in profundo otio contrectantes, quam ob causam non iudicioli est nostri. 15. cum multa et varia pro amplitudine gloriarum et generum lectitare deberent, audientes destinatum poenae Socratem, coniectumque in carcerem, rogasse quendam scite lyrici carmen Stesichori modulantem, ut doceretur id agere, dum liceret: interroganteque musico, quid ei poterit hoc prodesse, morituro postridie, respondisse, 'ut aliquid sciens amplius e vita discedam.'

16. ita autem pauci sunt inter eos severi vindices delictorum ut, si aquam calidam tardius attulerit servus, trecentis affligi verberibus iubeatur: si hominem sponte occiderit propria, instantibus plurimis, ut damnetur ut reus, dominus hactenus exclamabit: 'Quid faciat male factis famosus et nequam? et siquid aliud eius modi deinceps ausus fuerit, corrigetur.'

17. civilitatis autem hoc apud eos est nunc summum, quod expedit peregrino fratrem interficere cuiuslibet, quam cum rogatus sit ad convivium excusare: defectum enim patrimonii se opimi perpeti senator existimat, si is defuerit quem aliquotiens libratis sententiis, invitaverit semel.

18. pars eorum si agros visuri processerunt longius, aut alienis laboribus venaturi, Alexandri Magni itinera se putant aequiperasse, vel Caesaris: aut si a lacu Averni lembis invecti sunt pictis Puteolos, velleris certamen, maxime cum id vaporato audeant tempore. ubi si inter aurata flabella laciniis sericis insederint muscae, vel per foramen umbraculi pensilis radiolus irruperit solis, queruntur quod non sunt apud Cimmerios nati. 19. dein cum a Silvani lavacro vel Mamaeae aquis ventitant sospitalibus, ut quisquam eorum egressus, tenuissimis se terserit linteis, solutis pressoriis, vestes luce nitentes ambigua diligenter explorat, quae una portantur sufficientes ad induendos homines undecim: tandemque electis aliquot involutus, receptis anulis quos (ne violentur humoribus) famulo tradidit, digitis ut metatis abit.

20. enim vero siqui vetus in commilitio principis recens digressus fuerit in otium ut

aevi provecti, ille tali praesente coetu . . . mirionum . . . cantilenae praesul existimatur: ceteri taciturni audiunt dicta . . . solus pater familias textui narrans aliena, et placentia referens, et erudite pleraque fallendo.

21. quidam ex his (licet rari) aleatorum vocabulum declinantes, ideoque se cupientes appellari potius tesserarios: inter quos tantum differt, quantum inter fures atque latrones. hoc tamen fatendum est, quod cum omnes amicitiae Romae tepescant, aleariae solae, quasi gloriosis quaesitae sudoribus, sociales sunt et affectus nimii firmitate plena conexae: unde quidam ex his gregibus inveniuntur ita concordes, ut Quintilios esse existimes fratres. ideoque videre licet ignobilem artis tessarariae callentem arcana, ut Catonem Porcium ob repulsam praeturae, nec suspectam antea nec speratam, incedere gravitate composita maestiorem, quod ei in maiore convivio vel consessu proconsularis quidam est antelatus.

22. subsident aliqui copiosos homines senes aut iuvenes, orbos vel caelibes, aut etiam uxores habentes seu liberos (nec enim hoc tutulo discrimen aliquod observatur), ad voluntates condendas allicientes eos praestrigiis miris: qui cum, supremis iudiciis ordinatis, quaedam reliquerint his quibus morem gerendo testati sunt, ilico pereunt, ut id impleri sorte fatorum operante nec putes, nec facile possit aegritudo testari nec funus comitatur his quisquam.

23. alius cum dignitate (licet mediocri), cervice tumida gradiens, notos antea obliquato contuetur aspectu, ut post captas Syracusas existimes reverti Marcellum.

24. multi apud eos negantes esse superas potestates in caelo, nec in publicum prodeunt nec prandent nec lavari arbitrantur se cautius posse, antequam ephemeride scrupulose sciscitata didicerint, ubi sit verbi gratia signum Mercurii, vel quotam Cancri sideris partem polum discurrens obtineat luna.

25. alius si creditorem suum flagitare molestius adverterit debitum, ad aurigam confugit, audentem omnia praelicenter, eumque ut veneficum curat urgeri: unde non nisi reddita cautione, dispendioque afflictus gravi discedit. et additur huic, debitorem voluntarium includit ut proprium, nec ante eius professionem absolvit.

26. parte alia uxor, ut proverbium loquitur vetus, eamdem incudem diu noctuque tundendo, maritum testari compellit, hocque idem ut faciat uxor, urget maritus instanter: et periti iuris altrinsecus assciscuntur, unus in cubiculo alter eius aemulus in triclinio, repugnantia tractaturi: eisdemque subseruntur genitalium fatorum interpretes controversi, hinc praefecturas profusius largientes, et sepulturas divitum matronarum; inde ad exsequias virorum iam adventantes necessaria parari oportere iubentes: et testatur ancilla suapte natura pallidior, spiritu pridie consumpto defuncta . . . um Roma atque, ut Tullius ait: 'nec in rebus humanis quicquam bonum norunt nisi quod fructuosum sit: amicos tamquem pecudes eos potissimum diligunt, ex quibus se sperant maximum fructum esse capturos.'

27. cumque mutuum illi quid petunt, soccatos ut Miconas videbis et Lachetas: cum adiguntur ut reddant, ita coturnatos et turgidos, ut Heraclidas illos Cresphontem et Temenum putes. hactenus de senatu.

(d) Analysis of the various sections of Gibbon's rendering of Ammianus' character of the Roman nobles in respect of the Latin on which they rely.

Gibbon, Section 1 ARG XIV.vi.3–7
                2 ARG XXVIII.iv.7
                3 ARG XIV.vi.8
                4 ARG XIV.vi.10
                5 ARG XIV.vi.9, XXVIII.iv.8
                6 ARG XXVIII.iv.8–10, XIV.vi.16

7 ARG XXVIII.iv.19, XXVIII.iv.23
8 ARG XXVIII.iv.18
9 ARG XIV.vi.17
10 ARG XXVIII.iv.16
11 ARG XIV.vi.12
12 ARG XIV.vi.14–15
13 ARG XXVIII.iv.12–13
14 ARG XXVIII.iv.21
15 ARG XXVIII.iv.14
16 ARG XIV.vi.18
17 ARG XIV.vi.23
18 ARG XIV.vi.22 and 24
19 ARG XXVIII.iv.26
20 ARG XXVIII.iv.27 and 25
21 ARG XXVIII.iv.24

Bibliography of works cited

(The place of publication is London unless stated otherwise.)

Abrégé de l'Histoire Romaine à l'Usage des Élèves de l'École Royale Militaire à Paris ('Londres', 1795)

Adams, J., *The Flowers of Modern History* (1796)

Adams, W., *An Essay on Mr. Hume's Essay on Miracles* (1752)

Addison, J., *The Evidences of the Christian Religion* (1730)
   Works, 4 vols (Birmingham, 1761)

Alembert, J. le R. d', *Œuvres Complètes*, 5 vols. (Paris, 1821–2)

Bacon, Sir Francis, *Works*, 5 vols. (1765)

Baridon, M., *Edward Gibbon et le Mythe de Rome* (Paris, 1977)

Barrell, J., *English Literature in History 1730–80: an Equal, Wide Survey* (1983)

Bayle, P., *Critique Generale* ('Ville Franche' (Amsterdam), 1683)
   Dictionaire Historique et Critique, 4 vols. (Amsterdam, 1740)

Beaufort, L. de, *Dissertation sur l'Incertitude des Cinq Premiers Siecles de l'Histoire Romaine*, 2 vols. (The Hague, 1750)
   La Republique Romaine, 2 vols. (The Hague, 1766)

Bever, T., *A Discourse on the Study of Jurisprudence and the Civil Law* (Oxford, 1766)
   History of the Legal Polity of the Roman State (1781)

Bird, H. W., *Sextus Aurelius Victor: A Historiographical Study* (Liverpool, 1984)

Black, J. B., *The Art of History* (1926)

Blackstone, Sir William, *Commentaries on the Laws of England*, 4 vols. (Oxford, 1773)

Blackwell, T., *An Enquiry into the Life and Writings of Homer* (1735)
   The Memoirs of the Court of Augustus, 3 vols. (Edinburgh and London, 1753–63)

Blair, H., *Lectures on Rhetoric and Belles Lettres*, 2 vols. (1783)

Bleterie, J. P. R. de la, *Vie de l'Empereur Julien* (Paris, 1775)

Bodin, J., *Methodus ad Facilem Historiarum Cognitionem* (Lyons, 1583)

Bolingbroke, H. St John, Viscount, *Works*, 5 vols. (1754)

Bond, H. L., *The Literary Art of Edward Gibbon* (Oxford, 1960)

Bossuet, J. B., *Discours sur l'Histoire Universelle* (Paris, 1681)

Boswell, J., *Life of Johnson*, ed. G. B. Hill, rev. L. F. Powell, 6 vols. (Oxford, 1934–50)

Boulainvilliers, H. de, *La Vie de Mahomed* ('London', 1730)

Bouquet, Dom. M. et al., eds., *Rerum Gallicarum et Francicarum Scriptores*, 24 vols. (Paris, 1738–1904)

Bowersock, G. W., *Julian the Apostate* (1978)

Bowersock, G. W. et al., eds., *Edward Gibbon and the Decline and Fall of the Roman Empire* (Harvard, 1977)

Braudy, L., *Narrative Form in History and Fiction* (Princeton, 1970)
Brower, R., *Alexander Pope and the Poetry of Allusion* (Oxford, 1959)
Burrow, J. W., *Evolution and Society* (Cambridge, 1966)
  Gibbon (Oxford, 1985)
Campbell, G., *A Dissertation on Miracles* (Edinburgh, 1776)
Cave, W., *Primitive Christianity* (1675)
Chastellux, F. J. de, *De la Félicité Publique*, 2 vols. (Bouillon, 1776)
Chesterfield, P. D. Stanhope, Earl of, *Letters*, 4 vols. (1774)
Church, T., *A Vindication of the Miraculous Powers* (1750)
Clark, J. C. D., *English Society 1688–1832* (Cambridge, 1985)
Cleaveland, E., *A Genealogical History of the Noble and Illustrious Family of Courtenay* (Exeter, 1735)
Coleridge, S. T., *Table Talk and Omniana* (Oxford, 1917)
  Notebooks, ed. K. Coburn (1957–)
Collingwood, R. G., *The Idea of History* (Oxford, 1961)
  Essays in the Philosophy of History, ed. W. Debbins (New York, 1985)
Collins, A., *Discourse Concerning Ridicule and Irony* (1729)
Cowley, A., *Works*, 3 vols. (1700)
Cowper, W., *The Task* (1785)
Craddock, P. B., 'Gibbon's revision of The Decline and Fall', *Studies in Bibliography*, 21 (1968), pp. 191–204
  Young Edward Gibbon (Baltimore, 1982)
Crousaz, J.-P. de, *A New Treatise of the Art of Thinking*, 2 vols. (1724)
Dawson, C., 'Edward Gibbon', *Proceedings of the British Academy*, 20 (1934), pp. 159–80
Dedieu, J., *Montesquieu et la Tradition Politique Anglaise en France* (Paris, 1909)
Defence of Natural and Revealed Religion, A, (the Boyle lectures), 3 vols. (1739)
Defoe, D., *General History of Discoveries and Improvements* (1725–7)
Dickinson, H. T., *Politics and Literature in the Eighteenth Century* (1974)
Dobel, D., *Primitive Christianity* (1755)
Dodwell, H., *Dissertationes Cyprianicae* (1684)
Dryden, J., *Miscellaneous Works*, 4 vols, (1760)
Ducrey, P. et al., eds., *Gibbon et Rome à la Lumière de l'Historiographie Moderne* (Geneva, 1977)
Dyer, J., *Ruins of Rome* (1740)
Dyson, A. E., 'A note on dismissive irony', *English*, 2 (1957), pp. 222–5
Empson, W., *Seven Types of Ambiguity* (Harmondsworth, 1961)
Encyclopédie, ou Dictionaire Raisonné des Arts, des Sciences et des Lettres, 31 vols. (Paris, 1751–80)
Erskine-Hill, H. H., *The Social Milieu of Alexander Pope* (Yale, 1975)
  The Augustan Idea in English Literature (1983)
Ferguson, A., *The Progress and Termination of the Roman Republic*, 3 vols. (1783)
Filmer, Sir Robert, *Patriarcha* (1680)
Fleetwood, W., *An Essay upon Miracles* (1701)
Fleury, C., *Discours sur l'Histoire Ecclésiastique*, 2 vols. (Paris, 1716)
  Histoire Ecclésiastique, 36 vols. (Paris, 1719–58)
Fontenelle, B. le Bovier de, *Oeuvres*, 5 vols. (Paris, 1818)
Forbes, D., *Hume's Philosophical Politics* (Cambridge, 1975)
Forster, E. M., *Selected Letters*, eds. M. Lago and P. N. Furbank (1983)
Fussell, P., *The Rhetorical World of Augustan Humanism* (Oxford, 1965)

Gay, P., *Style in History* (1975)

Ghosh, P., 'Gibbon's Dark Ages: some remarks on the genesis of *The Decline and Fall*', *Journal of Roman Studies*, 73 (1983), pp. 1–23

Giarrizzo, G., *Edward Gibbon e la Cultura Europea del Settecento* (Naples, 1954)

Gibbon, E., *The History of the Decline and Fall of the Roman Empire*, 6 vols. (1776–88)

    Miscellaneous Works, ed. Lord Sheffield, 5 vols. (1814)

    The History of the Decline and Fall of the Roman Empire, ed. J. B. Bury, 7 vols. (1897–1900)

    Autobiography, ed. J. B. Bury (1907)

    Gibbon's Journal to January 28th, 1763, ed. D. M. Low (1929)

    Le Journal de Gibbon à Lausanne, ed. G. A. Bonnard (Lausanne, 1945)

    Miscellanea Gibboniana, ed. G. R. de Beer et al. (Lausanne, 1952)

    Letters, ed. J. E. Norton, 3 vols. (1956)

    Gibbon's Journey from Geneva to Rome, ed. G. A. Bonnard (1961)

    Memoirs of my Life, ed. G. A. Bonnard (1966)

    The English Essays of Edward Gibbon, ed. P. B. Craddock (Oxford, 1972)

Godley, A. D., ed. and tr., *Herodotus*, 4 vols. (1946)

Goldsmith, O., *Roman History*, 2 vols. (1769)

    Miscellaneous Works (1925)

Gossman, L., *The Empire Unpossess'd: An Essay on Gibbon's Decline and Fall* (Cambridge, 1981)

Gray, T., *Poems and Memoirs* (York, 1775)

Greene, E., *Critical Essays* (1770)

Greig, J. Y. T., *David Hume* (1931)

Guthrie, W., *A General History of the World*, 13 vols. (1764)

Hammond, P., 'An early response to Pope's *Essay on Criticism*', *Notes and Queries*, 230 (1985), pp. 198–9

Harris, J., *Hermes* (1751)

Hearne, T., *Ductor Historicus*, 2 vols. (1723–4)

Herder, J. G. v., *Outlines of a Philosophy of the History of Man*, tr. T. Churchill (1800)

    Reflections on the Philosophy of the History of Mankind (Chicago, 1968)

Hobbes, T., *Leviathan* (1651)

Home, H., Lord Kames, *Elements of Criticism*, 3 vols. (Edinburgh, 1762)

Hopkins, W., *Animadversions on Mr. Johnson's Answer to Jovian* (1691)

Houtteville, A. C. F., *La Religion Chrétienne Prouvée par les Faits* (Paris, 1722)

Hume, D., *Essays and Treatises on Several Subjects*, 4 vols. (1760)

    The History of England, 8 vols. (1770)

    Dialogues Concerning Natural Religion (1779)

    Essays Moral, Political and Literary, ed. T. H. Green and T. H. Grose, 2 vols. (1875)

    The Letters of David Hume, ed. J. Y. T. Greig, 2 vols. (Oxford, 1932)

    A Treatise of Human Nature, ed. L. A. Selby-Bigge, rev. P. H. Nidditch (Oxford, 1978)

Jenyns, S., *A View of the Internal Evidence of the Christian Religion* (1776)

Johnson, J. W., *The Formation of English Neo-Classical Thought* (Princeton, 1967)

Johnson, S., *Julian's Arts to Extirpate and Undermine Christianity* (1689)

Johnson, S., *Works*, 9 vols (Oxford, 1825)

Jordan, D., *Gibbon and his Roman Empire* (Illinois, 1971)

Joyce, M., *Edward Gibbon* (1953)

Julian the Apostate, *Juliani Opera*, ed. E. Spanheim, 3 vols. (Leipzig, 1696)

    Œuvres Complètes, ed. J. Bidez et al., 2 vols. in 4 (Paris, 1924–64)

Kennett, B., *Romae Antiquae Notitia* (1713)

Keynes, G., *Gibbon's Library* (1940)

Kliger, S. J., *The Goths in England* (Harvard, 1952)

Kramnick, I., 'Augustan politics and English historiography', *History and Theory*, 6 (1967), pp. 33–65

 Bolingbroke and his Circle: The Politics of Nostalgia in the Age of Walpole (Harvard, 1968)

Labat, J. B., *Voyages* (Paris, 1730)

Leavis, F. R., *The Common Pursuit* (Harmondsworth, 1962)

Leibnitz, G. W. v., *Opera*, ed. L. Dutens, 6 vols. (Geneva, 1768)

Leigh, R. A., 'The loss of Gibbon's literary maidenhead', *Voltaire and his World: Studies Presented to W. H. Barber*, ed. R. J. Howells et al. (Oxford, 1985), pp. 323–34

Lewis, C. S., *Surprised by Joy* (1955)

Locke, J., *An Essay Concerning Human Understanding* (1690)

Lonsdale, R., ed., *The Poems of Gray, Collins and Goldsmith* (1969)

Lyttelton, George, Baron, *Works* (1774)

Mably, G. Bonnot de, *Observations on the Romans*, tr. 'D.Y.' (Lynn, 1770)

Machiavelli, N., *Tutte le Opere*, 2 vols. ('Londra', 1747)

Manuel, F. E., *Shapes of Philosophical History* (1965)

Meehan, M., *Liberty and Poetics in Eighteenth Century England* (1986)

Meinecke, F., *Die Entstehung des Historismus* (Munich, 1936): tr. J. E. Anderson, *Historism: the Rise of a New Historical Outlook* (1972)

Meredith, E., *Some Remarques Upon a Late Popular Piece of Nonsense Call'd Julian the Apostate* &c (1682)

Meyer, P. H., 'Voltaire and Hume as historians', *Publications of the Modern Language Association*, 73 (1958), pp. 51–68.

Milton, J., *The Works of John Milton, Historical, Political and Miscellaneous*, 2 vols. (1753)

Momigliano, A., *Studies in Historiography* (1966)

Montesquieu, C. de Secondat, Baron de, *Œuvres*, 3 vols. ('Londres', 1767)

 Œuvres Complètes, ed. A. Masson, 3 vols. (Paris, 1950)

Mossner, E. C., 'Was Hume a Tory historian?', *Journal of the History of Ideas*, 2 (1941), pp. 225–36

 The Life of David Hume (Edinburgh, 1954)

Moyle, W., *Works*, 3 vols. (1726–7)

Muratori, L. A., *Annali d'Italia*, 14 vols. (Lucca, 1762–70)

Nisbet, R. A., *Social Change and History* (New York, 1969)

Nokes, D., *Jonathan Swift: A Hypocrite Reversed* (Oxford, 1985)

Norton, J. E., *A Bibliography of the Works of Edward Gibbon* (Oxford, 1940)

Nuttall, A. D., *Pope's Essay on Man* (1984)

O'Brien, G. D., 'Does Hegel have a philosophy of history?', *Hegel*, ed. M. Inwood (Oxford, 1985), pp. 174–98

Oliver, D. M., 'Gibbon's use of architecture as symbol', *Texas Studies in Literature and Language*, 14 (1972), pp.77–92

Paine, T., *The Writings of Thomas Paine*, ed. M. Conway, 4 vols (New York, 1894–6)

Parkinson, R. N., *Edward Gibbon* (New York, 1973)

Pascal, B., *Pensées* (Paris, 1962)

Patey, D. L., *Probability and Literary Form* (Cambridge, 1984)

Paulus Diaconus, *De Gestis Langobardorum* (Leiden, 1595)

Pocock, J. G. A., *The Ancient Constitution and the Feudal Law* (Cambridge, 1957)

 The Machiavellian Moment (Princeton, 1975)

'Gibbon's *Decline and Fall* and the world view of the Late Enlightenment', *Eighteenth-Century Studies*, 10 (1977), pp. 287–303

'Gibbon and the shepherds: the stages of society in the *Decline and Fall*', *History of European Ideas*, 2 (1981), pp. 193–202

Virtue, Commerce and History (Cambridge, 1985)

Pope, A., *Works*, ed. W. Warburton, 9 vols. (1751)

The Correspondence of Alexander Pope, ed. G. Sherburn, 5 vols. (Oxford, 1956)

The Twickenham Edition of the Poems of Alexander Pope, ed. J. Butt et al., 10 vols. (1961–7)

Popper, K., *The Poverty of Historicism* (1960)

Price, M., ' "The Dark and Implacable Genius of Superstition": an aspect of Gibbon's irony', *Augustan Worlds*, ed. J. C. Hilson et al. (Leicester, 1978), pp. 241–59

Radcliffe, A., *The Mysteries of Udolpho*, ed. B. Dobrée (Oxford, 1966)

The Italian, ed. F. Garber (Oxford, 1968)

Radzinowicz, Sir Leon, *A History of English Criminal Law*, 5 vols. (1948–86)

Robertson, J. M., *Pioneer Humanists* (1907)

Robertson, W., *The History of Charles V*, 3 vols. (1769)

Works, 12 vols. (1820)

Rogers, P., *The Augustan Vision* (1978)

Rousseau, J. J., *Lettre à d'Alembert* (Amsterdam, 1758)

Russell, D. A. and M. Winterbottom, eds., *Ancient Literary Criticism* (Oxford, 1972)

Sainte-Beuve, C. A., *Causeries du Lundi*, 14 vols. (Paris, 1853)

Saint-Evremond, C. de, *Œuvres*, 7 vols. ('Londres', 1711)

Scott, P. H., *John Galt* (Edinburgh, 1986)

Shackleton, R., *Montesquieu, a Critical Biography* (Oxford, 1961)

Shaftesbury, A. A. Cooper, Earl of, *Characteristicks*, 3 vols. (1727)

Some Reflections on the Characters of Augustus, Maecenas and Horace (1740)

Sher, R., *Church and University in the Scottish Enlightenment* (Edinburgh, 1985)

Sherlock, W., *The Doctrine of the Blessed Trinity Stated and Defended* (1719)

Skinner, Q., 'The principles and practice of opposition; the case of Bolingbroke versus Walpole', *Historical Perspectives: Studies in English Thought and Society in Honour of J. H. Plumb*, ed. N. Mackendrick (1974)

Smitten, J., 'Impartiality in Robertson's *History of America*', *Eighteenth-Century Studies*, 19 (1985–6), pp. 56–77

Steele, Sir Richard, *The Tatler*, 4 vols. (1774)

Stephen, Sir Leslie, *A History of English Thought in the Eighteenth Century*, 2 vols. (1876)

Sterling, J., *Poems* (Dublin, 1782)

Strachey, L., *Portraits in Miniature* (1931)

Stuart, G., *A View of Society in Europe* (Edinburgh, 1778)

Swift, J., *Prose Works*, ed. H. Davis et al., 14 vols. (Oxford, 1939–59)

Sydney, A., *Works* (1772)

Syme, Sir Ronald, *The Roman Revolution* (Oxford, 1939)

Tacitus, *The Works of Cornelius Tacitus*, tr. A. Murphy, 4 vols. (Dublin, 1794)

Teggart, F. J., *Theory and Processes of History* (California, 1941)

Temple, Sir William, *Works*, 4 vols. (1770)

Thomson, D., 'Edward Gibbon the master builder', *Contemporary Review*, 151 (1937), pp. 583–91

Thomson, J. *The Seasons*, ed. J. Sambrook (Oxford, 1981)

Liberty, The Castle of Indolence and other Poems, ed. J. Sambrook (Oxford, 1986)

Tillemont, L. S. le Nain de, *Histoire des Empereurs*, 6 vols. (Paris, 1700–38)

Tillotson, J., *The Rule of Faith* (1727)

Trevor-Roper, H. R., Lord Dacre, 'The historical philosophy of the Enlightenment',
    Studies on Voltaire and the Eighteenth Century, 27 (1963), pp. 1667–87

Tunstall, J., *Lectures on Natural and Revealed Religion* (1765)

Turner, T., *The Diary of Thomas Turner*, ed. D. Vaisey (Oxford, 1984)

Tytler, W., *An Historical and Critical Enquiry* (Edinburgh, 1760)

Universal History, 21 vols. (1747–54)

Vertot d'Auberf, R. A. de, *Histoire des Revolutions Arivées Dans le Gouvernement de la
    République Romaine*, 3 vols. (The Hague, 1737)

Voltaire, F. M. A. de, *Œuvres Complètes*, 52 vols (Paris, 1877–85)

Waller, E., *Poems*, ed. G. Thorn Drury, 2 vols (1905)

Walpole, H., *Correspondence*, ed. W. S. Lewis et al., 48 vols. (1937–83)

Warburton, W., *A Critical and Philosophical Enquiry into the Causes of Prodigies and Miracles*
    (1727)
    The Divine Legation of Moses Demonstrated (1738–40)
    Julian (1751)

Warburton, W. and R. Hurd, *Remarks on Mr. David Hume's Essay* (1757)

Weinbrot, H., *Augustus Caesar in 'Augustan' England* (Princeton, 1978)

White, H., and F. E. Manuel, *Theories of History* (Los Angeles, 1978)

White, I., 'The subject of Gibbon's History', *The Cambridge Quarterly*, 3 (1968), pp.
    299–309

Wind, E., 'Julian the Apostate at Hampton Court', *England and the Mediterranean Tradi-
    tion* (Oxford, 1945), pp. 131–8

Woolf, V., *Collected Essays*, 4 vols, (1966–7)

Wordsworth, W., *Poetical Works*, ed. E. de Selincourt and H. Darbishire, 5 vols.
    (Oxford, 1940–9)

Wortley Montagu, Lady Mary, *The Complete Letters of Lady Mary Wortley Montagu*, ed.
    R. Halsband, 3 vols. (Oxford, 1965)

Wotton, W., *Reflections upon Ancient and Modern Learning* (1694)
    The History of Rome from the Death of Antoninus Pius to the Death of Severus Alexander (1701)

Young, G. M., *Gibbon* (1932)

Ziegler, R. J., 'Edward Gibbon and Julian the Apostate', *Papers on Language and
    Literature*, 10 (1974), pp. 131–8

Index

Entries have been made for proper names in text and footnotes, but names of works have been listed only under names of authors. Subject entries have been added where they seemed important to the book's argument.